T5-DHH-568

Essentials of Risk Financing

Volume I

Essentials of Risk Financing

Volume I

GEORGE L. HEAD, Ph.D., CPCU, ARM, CSP, CLU
Vice President
Insurance Institute of America

MICHAEL W. ELLIOTT, CPCU, MBA
Director of Curriculum
Insurance Institute of America

JAMES D. BLINN
Vice President
Reliance National Insurance Company

Second Edition • 1993

INSURANCE INSTITUTE OF AMERICA
720 Providence Road, Malvern, Pennsylvania 19355-0770

Second Edition • July 1993

Library of Congress Catalog Number 93-77520
International Standard Book Number 0-89462-076-2

Printed in the United States of America

Foreword

The American Institute for Chartered Property Casualty Underwriters and the Insurance Institute of America are independent, nonprofit, educational organizations serving the needs of the property and liability insurance business. The Institutes develop a wide range of programs—curricula, study materials, and examinations—in response to the educational requirements of various elements of the business.

The American Institute confers the Chartered Property Casualty Underwriter (CPCU®) professional designation on those who meet the Institute's experience, ethics, and examination requirements.

The Insurance Institute of America offers associate designations and certificate programs in the following technical and managerial disciplines:

Accredited Adviser in Insurance (AAI®)
Associate in Claims (AIC)
Associate in Underwriting (AU)
Associate in Risk Management (ARM)
Associate in Loss Control Management (ALCM®)
Associate in Premium Auditing (APA®)
Associate in Management (AIM)
Associate in Research and Planning (ARP®)
Associate in Insurance Accounting and Finance (AIAF)
Associate in Automation Management (AAM®)
Associate in Marine Insurance Management (AMIM®)
Associate in Reinsurance (ARe)
Associate in Fidelity and Surety Bonding (AFSB)
Certificate in General Insurance
Certificate in Supervisory Management
Certificate in Introduction to Claims
Certificate in Introduction to Property and Liability Insurance

The Institutes began publishing textbooks in 1976 to help students meet the national examination standards. Since that time, we have produced more than seventy-five individual textbook volumes. Despite the vast differences in the subjects and purposes of these volumes, they all have much in common. First, each book is specifically designed to increase knowledge and develop skills that can improve job performance and help students achieve the educational objectives of the course for which it is assigned. Second, all of the manuscripts of our texts are widely reviewed prior to publication, by both insurance business practitioners and members of the academic community. In addition, all of our texts and course guides reflect the work of Institute staff members. These writing or editing duties are seen as an integral part of their professional responsibilities, and no one earns a royalty based on the sale of our texts. We have proceeded in this way to avoid even the appearance of any conflict of interests. Finally, the revisions of our texts often incorporate improvements suggested by students and course leaders.

We welcome criticisms of and suggestions for improving our publications. It is only with such constructive comments that we can hope to improve the quality of our study materials. Please direct any comments you may have on this text to the Curriculum Department of the Institutes.

Norman A. Baglini, Ph.D., CPCU, CLU
President and Chief Executive Officer

Preface

This second edition of *Essentials of Risk Financing* is a two-volume text developed primarily for the Insurance Institute of America's ARM 56 course of the same name. It is one of the three Institute texts for the three courses and examinations leading to the Associate in Risk Management (ARM) designation awarded by the Insurance Institute of America. The other texts are *Essentials of Risk Management* (for ARM 54) and *Essentials of Risk Control* (for ARM 55). If possible, ARM students should study ARM 54 before undertaking either ARM 55 or ARM 56; the latter two courses, which presume knowledge of ARM 54, may be taken in either order.

Although tailored to the educational objectives of the ARM program, all three of these risk management texts should prove useful to persons who perform, or are responsible for, the risk management function within an organization—whether as its risk manager or a member of its risk management staff, as its insurance agent or broker, as an underwriter of its property-liability insurance, or as its risk management or safety consultant.

This text on risk financing—the planning, organizing, directing, and controlling of an organization's sources and uses of funds for financing recovery from accidental losses that strike the organization or for which it is legally or ethically responsible—is fundamental to the risk management decision/administrative process that is set forth in ARM 54. Having identified any given possibility of accidental loss (that is, any loss exposure) and having analyzed how frequent, severe, and unpredictable the losses from this exposure are likely to be, an organization's management has only two basic options: (1) reduce the likelihood of these losses happening or make them less severe or more predictable through sound risk control or (2) pay to restore the resulting property, net income, liability, or personnel losses by using risk financing techniques that draw on the organization's own funds (risk retention), techniques that rely on others' funds (risk transfer), or hybrid techniques that combine elements of retention and transfer.

Where feasible, risk control is usually more economically efficient than risk financing, both for a single organization and for society as a whole. This greater efficiency stems from the fact that risk control preserves rather than replaces an organization's or an economy's productive resources. Alone, however, risk control is never sufficient. Any safety device or program for risk control is certain to fail eventually, making some planned form of risk financing essential to restoring the resulting loss. No person or organization can cost-effectively stop all accidental losses; hence, all persons and organizations need cost-effective risk financing.

This second edition of *Essentials of Risk Financing* strives to help students by improving the first edition in at least three significant ways. First, the discussions of forecasting an organization's losses and resulting risk financing needs have been strengthened. Students should also find it more meaningful to study these complex subjects in Chapters 9 and 10 of the second edition than they did in much earlier chapters of the first edition. Second, the treatment of risk financing alternatives has been reorganized. Instead of following the first edition's pattern of separate chapters focused on financing different *types of losses* (with, say, one chapter on property losses and another on liability losses), Chapters 3 through 7 of the second edition each treat one or more *types of risk financing techniques* as they may be used to finance recovery from any accidental losses. Students should find this technique-centered sequencing of their ARM 56 studies more logical and efficient than the previous loss-centered sequence. Finally, the authors and the Institute's staff have made a concerted effort to improve the writing style, clarity, and general readability of this new edition. Risk financing is a very challenging subject; the way this text is written should ease, not intensify, this challenge.

A fundamental objective of all these improvements in the second edition has been to make the text more educationally beneficial, thereby eliminating unnecessary stress for students and course leaders. For special assistance in pursuing this objective, George L. Head, the Institute staff member most directly responsible for this text, owes particular gratitude to his wife, Alice Ann R. Head, who holds the Certified Healthcare Risk Manager designation and is a registered nurse.

Essentials of Risk Financing presents the shared output of the authors. Because most of the work has been done collegially, no single chapter or portion of any chapter can be meaningfully ascribed to any one author. In particular, it would be improper to hold any one of the authors accountable in any judicial, legislative, or regulatory proceeding for any statement in this book. Although each author contributed meaningful material to this text, the Institute—rather than any of the individual authors—determined the final content of this book.

In addition to the authors named on the front cover, many experts have contributed ideas or written brief passages for, or have given detailed written critiques of, one or more chapters and have thus enhanced the accuracy, clarity, and relevance of this text. These experts include:

Annese Ashton, M.A., ARM, Risk Manager, Genesee County, Michigan

Anita Benedetti, ARM, Director of Research and Education, Risk and Insurance Management Society, Inc.

Andy Bradbury, Senior Risk Analyst, Alumax Inc.

Louis J. Drapeau, ARM, Manager, Insurance and Risk Management, The Budd Company

Donald E. Dresback, CPCU, ARM, CIC, The Beacon Group, Inc.

David A. Ellis, Ph.D., Vice President for Business and Financial Affairs, Pine Manor College, Brookline, Massachusetts

Charles W. Fix, ARM, Risk Manager, City of Pompano Beach, Florida

Karen Fleming, ARM, Manager, Risk Management, Bell Atlantic Corp.

Edward W. Frye, Jr., CPCU, ARe, President and Principal, Underwriting Consultant Service of Connecticut

James P. Garrison, ARM, Risk Management Administrator, City of Phoenix, Arizona

Paul Goularte, CPCU, Managing Director, Marsh & McLennan

Alice Ann R. Head, RN, CHRM

Bob A. Hedges, Ph.D., CPCU, CLU, Professor Emeritus of Risk Management and Insurance, Temple University

J. Jay Hill, CPCU, ARM, CIC, Senior Account Executive, Johnson & Higgins of Utah

Dennis M. Kirschbaum, ARM, Executive Director, Public Risk Management Association

Donald D. Malecki, CPCU, President, Donald S. Malecki & Associates, Inc.

Elizabeth D. Puddington, CPCU, ARM, Executive Director, New Hampshire School Boards Insurance Trust, Inc.

Kevin M. Quinley, CPCU, ARM, Vice President, Risk Services, MEDMARC Insurance Co. and Hamilton Resources Corp.

Ronald W. Stasch, CPCU, ARM, Manager, Risk Management Services, Federal-Mogul Corp.

Steven B. Steinberg, CPCU, President, Entrust Risk Management Services

Glen Trutner, Vice President, Marsh & McLennan

Richard T. Zatorsky, Princeton Insurance Company

Beyond the individual contributions acknowledged above, the authors received the invaluable assistance of the Institute's Publications Department and other staff members in integrating, editing, and proofreading the entire text. Therefore, any errors of fact or opinion should be ascribed to the authors—and primarily to George Head—rather than to any other person. Still, like the accidents that even the best risk management cannot stop completely, errors are bound to have occurred. Please tell the Institute about all errors and omissions. The insights of students, course leaders, and other readers will help in correcting these shortcomings when preparing the next edition.

George L. Head
Michael W. Elliott
James D. Blinn

Table of Contents

CHAPTER 1

Setting Risk Financing Objectives

Risk financing is the management of the sources and uses of funds with which an organization finances its recovery from accidental property, net income, liability, and personnel losses. Risk financing involves, first, planning and arranging for the sources of these funds *before* any such losses occur and, second, directing and controlling the funds drawn from these sources as needed *after* losses occur. This responsibility requires the coordination of all an organization's sources of funds for paying for accidental losses—both sources within the organization and its economic family and external sources. Such coordination is necessary for (1) making cost-effective risk financing choices, (2) balancing overall expenditures for risk financing with those for risk control, and (3) allocating funds appropriately between an organization's risk management objectives (for both risk financing and risk control) and its general operating objectives.

Risk financing is thus an integral part of managing any organization. Risk financing is essential to the following:

- An organization's general financial management, which plans, organizes, directs, and controls the sources and uses of all the funds an organization needs for all its business purposes, one of which is recovery from accidental losses
- The risk management decision/administrative process (examined in ARM 54), which plans, organizes, directs, and controls all the financial and other resources and activities of an organization to prevent or pay for accidental losses
- The overall strategic management of an organization, which helps to ensure its survival and the achievement of its mission through sound financial management

This chapter describes risk financing within the context of overall financial and general management. Specifically, it examines the following:

1. Why the core of risk financing, as of all management, is a process for deciding among alternative uses of resources that typically are not sufficient to fulfill all the objectives to which these resources might be applied
2. How the overall mission or objectives of an organization determine its financial management objectives and how these financial objectives lead, in turn, to its risk financing objectives
3. Why achieving any organizational objective requires efficient use of an organization's cash and other resources

Thus, risk management is a specialty within the general field of management. It is the process of making and carrying out decisions that minimize the adverse effects of accidental losses on an organization. *Management* may be defined as the process of planning, organizing, directing, and controlling the resources and activities of an organization in order to fulfill cost-effectively that organization's objectives.

Risk management and general management should be unified for the better practice of each. This unity can be achieved through the principles of financial management as they apply to any profit-seeking or nonprofit, private or public, organization. Although these principles are familiar to readers of the ARM 54 text, they are summarized in this chapter. Financial management principles provide (1) a common process for reaching decisions, including risk financing decisions; (2) a method for stating and measuring the interrelated objectives of the organization as a whole, including its risk financing activities; and (3) procedures for making optimum use of funds for risk financing, as well as for other activities.

THE RISK FINANCING DECISION PROCESS

Because risk management is a specialty within the general field of management, it—like all management—requires the making and implementing of decisions that are directed toward the goals of the organization. Whether these goals are for profit or not, whether they are achieved through a private enterprise or a public one, or whether they are for the future or a specific, short-term project, risk management contributes to an organization's success by minimizing the adverse effects that accidental losses might otherwise have on its ability to meet these goals within scheduled time frames. Sound, cost-effective risk management provides this protection through risk control and risk financing without unnecessarily depriving the organization of financial or other resources that can better be devoted to the organization's positive, productive "mission."

Stated somewhat differently, *risk financing* is a decision process for making and implementing choices that serve the objectives of an organization by reliably and cost-effectively providing funds to restore an organization's accidental losses. In the context of risk financing, the decision process consists of the following five steps:

1. Identifying and analyzing exposures—For example, a manufacturer or a municipality should recognize that it will need to pay for any damage to its vehicles or for any liability claims that may be brought against it.
2. Examining alternative risk financing techniques—The manufacturer or municipality should evaluate the likely costs and benefits of each of the retention and transfer techniques through which it may obtain funds to pay any such losses.
3. Selecting the most promising technique(s)—The manufacturer or municipality—in light of its profit-seeking, public service, growth, or other goals, and with regard to statutory requirements and organizational financial structure and capabilities—should develop a "decision rule" for selecting the best risk financing technique (or combination of techniques) for paying for any vehicle damage or liability claims that its risk control program does not prevent.
4. Implementing the chosen technique(s)—The manufacturer or municipality should purchase insurance, enter into noninsurance contractual transfers, or establish funded or unfunded retention mechanisms before any losses occur; after a loss, the manufacturer or municipality can look to such source(s) for the needed funds as planned.
5. Monitoring the results—The manufacturer or municipality should review its risk financing experience to correct any situations where funds needed to pay losses have been unavailable, too costly, or too uncertain to be reliable.

As shown in Exhibit 1-1, each of these five steps in the risk financing decision process involves several sets of concepts, which are discussed in the following paragraphs.

Identifying and Analyzing Loss Exposures

For both risk financing and risk control, identifying and analyzing exposures to loss is the most crucial first step. Regardless of which group of risk management techniques is to be used, the risk management professional must cooperate with others in and outside the organization

Exhibit 1-1
Steps in Risk Financing Decision Making

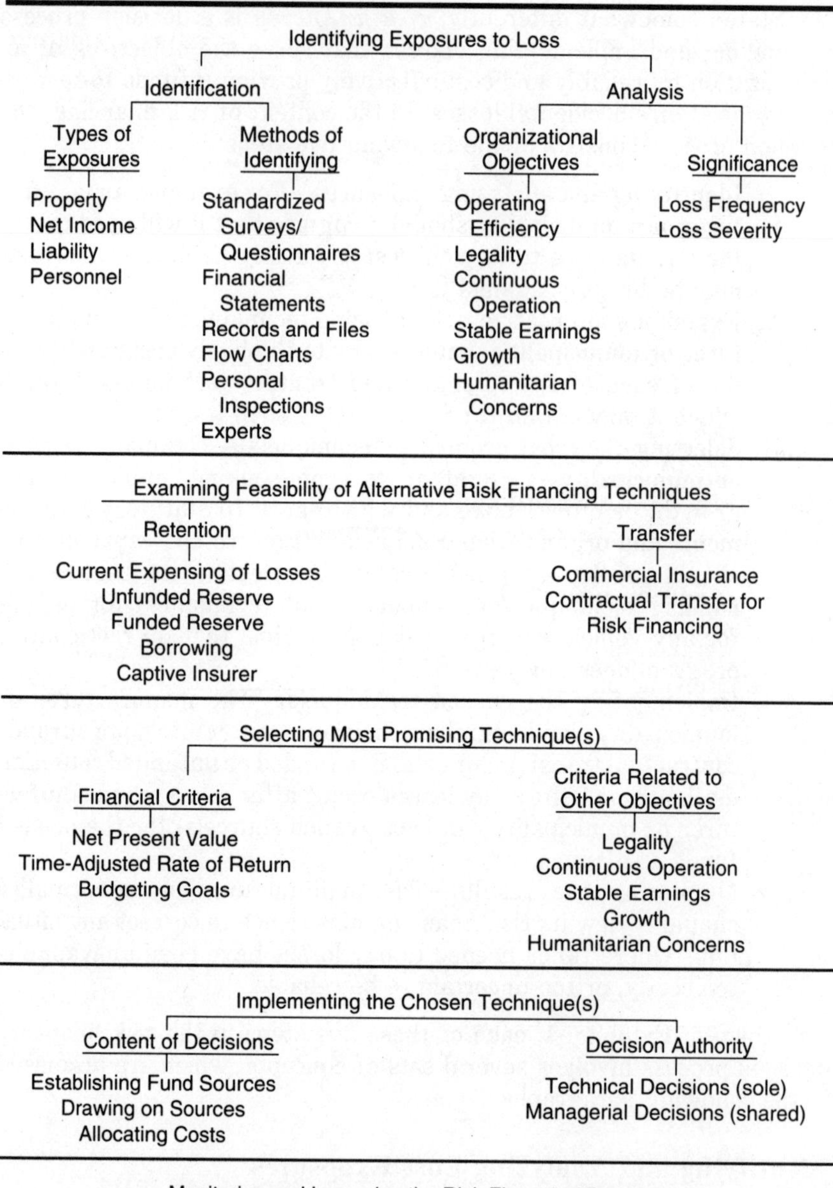
Identifying Exposures to Loss
Identification
Analysis
Types of Exposures
Property
Net Income
Liability
Personnel
Methods of Identifying
Standardized Surveys/ Questionnaires
Financial Statements
Records and Files
Flow Charts
Personal Inspections
Experts
Organizational Objectives
Operating Efficiency
Legality
Continuous Operation
Stable Earnings
Growth
Humanitarian Concerns
Significance
Loss Frequency
Loss Severity
Examining Feasibility of Alternative Risk Financing Techniques
Retention
Current Expensing of Losses
Unfunded Reserve
Funded Reserve
Borrowing
Captive Insurer
Transfer
Commercial Insurance
Contractual Transfer for Risk Financing
Selecting Most Promising Technique(s)
Financial Criteria
Net Present Value
Time-Adjusted Rate of Return
Budgeting Goals
Criteria Related to Other Objectives
Legality
Continuous Operation
Stable Earnings
Growth
Humanitarian Concerns
Implementing the Chosen Technique(s)
Content of Decisions
Establishing Fund Sources
Drawing on Sources
Allocating Costs
Decision Authority
Technical Decisions (sole)
Managerial Decisions (shared)
Monitoring and Improving the Risk Financing Program
Purposes
To Ensure Proper Implementation
To Detect, and Adapt to, Changes
Control Program
Results Standards
Activities Standards

to identify property, net income, liability, and personnel losses by the methods shown in the second column of the upper portion of Exhibit 1-1.

Analyzing the significance of these exposures requires evaluating both the extent to which a loss from a particular exposure would interfere with the organization's objectives and the expected and the maximum potential frequency and severity of losses from each exposure. Losses that might interfere most directly with the organization's objectives are usually more deserving of both risk control and risk financing attention than are losses that could affect these objectives only indirectly. An exposure characterized by either high loss frequency or high loss severity needs more attention than does an exposure characterized by both low frequency and low severity of losses. Neither high frequency nor high severity alone is always the more important consideration. The accumulation of highly frequent losses and the relatively rare occurrence of highly severe losses can be equally detrimental to an organization.

Examining the Feasibility of Alternative Risk Management Techniques

Risk financing focuses only on ways of paying for recovery from losses that cannot be totally controlled. In practice, risk financing and risk control techniques usually need to be combined to be most cost-effective. Relying on risk control without adequate risk financing is dangerous because some major loss will *eventually* occur. Relying solely on risk financing without risk control is unnecessarily expensive because it sacrifices the savings that good safety practices could achieve. Nevertheless, this text focuses primarily on risk financing, usually assuming that a reasonable level of risk control is being practiced.

As shown in Exhibit 1-1, the two basic risk financing techniques are retention (using an organization's own funds or those from within its economic family to finance recovery from its losses) and transfer (using others' funds originally coming from outside sources). Retention options include current expensing of losses, using unfunded reserves, using funded reserves, borrowing, and relying on an affiliated "captive" insurer. Transfer options are insurance and contractual transfers for risk financing (such as hold-harmless provisions and other indemnity agreements that are distinct from such contractual transfers for risk control as subcontracts, leases, and exculpatory agreements). These techniques are elaborated in subsequent chapters of this text.

Selecting the Most Promising Risk Financing Technique(s)

The third step in the risk management decision process, choosing among risk financing alternatives, requires developing a selection procedure (technically, a "decision rule") for making choices that can be defended if challenged by senior management, stockholders, or others. One such decision rule focuses on how risk financing techniques affect the organization's net cash flows (cash inflows minus cash outflows during a given time period). Cash flows are a better measure than accounting profits of the efficiency with which an organization uses its funds. Cash, rather than profits, is the resource through which an organization obtains all its other productive resources. Therefore, available net cash flows are the best measure of an organization's ability to command resources to fulfill its goals, including the goal of cost-effectively financing recovery from accidental losses. Thus, the best general decision rule is the following: *Subject to other constraints,* an organization should choose that combination of risk financing techniques that maximizes either the present value of its differential expected annual net cash flows or, equivalently, the time-adjusted rate of return on the organization's resources.

Almost every decision process is subject to constraints. Constraints on risk financing decisions include the following:

- A desire for financial security (also expressed as an aversion to uncertainty), which may motivate an organization's managers or owners to choose insurance rather than retention, even though retention would generate a higher expected present value of future net cash flows
- Legal requirements, such as (1) statutes requiring the organization to purchase insurance rather than retain its workers compensation and other liability exposures; (2) routine business contracts of purchase or supply obligating one party to provide surety bonds as a condition to the other parties' becoming bound to the contract; and (3) collectively bargained labor agreements specifying that employee benefits will be provided through insurance rather than through the employer's internal funds
- Budget constraints, which limit the total financial resources available to an organization in any given period, may restrict its ability to retain certain loss exposures, thus requiring it to buy insurance to smooth expenditures over time
- Humanitarian or public interest concerns, which may motivate an organization's senior or other managers to take actions they cannot justify financially—for example, operating a free public skating rink or subsidizing van transport for the elderly—and for which the related insurance and other risk financing measures are not intended to enhance the organization's net cash flows

These constraints limit the contribution that risk financing can make to achieving an organization's goals, either because of lack of resources or because the goals conflict with one another.

Implementing the Chosen Technique(s)

For any given exposure, implementing a risk financing program entails (1) establishing the selected risk financing mechanisms (such as retention programs, insurance policies, and indemnity agreements) as sources of funds for future losses; (2) drawing upon these sources to finance recovery from a loss; and (3) allocating risk financing (and other risk management) costs among an organization's departments in ways that promote equity, encourage managers to practice sound risk management, and accurately measure the true costs of risk in the various parts of an organization. Implementation is a continuous process of establishing, drawing upon, and evaluating and adjusting the sources of risk financing funds.

As in all risk management, implementing chosen risk financing techniques requires both technical decisions made by the risk management professional alone and managerial decisions made by risk management professionals in cooperation with other organization personnel. Most of the technical decisions are clearly within the direct, personal authority of the risk management professional upon whom the organization relies for this expertise. Insurance coverages and markets, appropriate risk retention levels and mechanisms, and the best ways to allocate risk management costs should be part of the expertise and responsibility of a risk management professional. This expertise should be used to carry out the decisions made jointly in the third step of selecting the most promising risk financing techniques. Reaching these decisions may have required the risk management professional to seek guidance from senior management. Implementing these decisions is usually the sole responsibility of the risk management professional working out the technical details of the earlier fundamental decisions. Similarly, after a loss has occurred, the task of raising funds to pay for it—collecting from insurers, drawing on the organization's internal funds, or seeking indemnity from an outside party—typically calls for the technical knowledge of risk management professionals.

In contrast to the purely technical aspect of implementation, a risk management cost-allocation system needs the support of managers throughout an organization. All must cooperate in gathering the necessary information, in reinforcing among their subordinates the safety and other motivational aspects of the system, and in accepting the risk management costs the system charges against their respective departments. Here, therefore, the risk management professional must seek the understanding, agreement, and often participation of other managers in shared, managerial decisions about the design and operation of this cost allocation system. Implementing many other aspects of a risk financing program also requires such joint, collegial decision making among an organization's executives.

Monitoring the Results

Controlling and assessing a risk financing program involves applying standards that measure activities and results in order to determine whether the program is meeting its objectives. It also involves adapting the program to changing conditions. Activity standards pertain to the processes by which any activity, such as risk financing, is performed. Examples of activity standards include whether the organization follows proper procedures in seeking bids for its insurance, in settling insured or retained property losses or liability claims, in filing reports as required by law or by the organization's risk management procedures manual, and, in general, "how things are done." Results standards focus on goal achievement, including, for example, whether administrative costs for the risk management department are within tolerable bounds, whether anticipated insurance has in fact provided indemnity for losses as expected, or whether the organization's risk retention plans have functioned as smoothly as anticipated. In short, results standards ask the question, "Regardless of how we achieved them, have our results been satisfactory?" Most organizations generally expect their risk financing activities to meet a combination of activity and results standards.

The most widely recognized results standard for an organization's risk management activities has become known as the "cost of risk." As Exhibit 1-2 shows, an organization's cost of risk for a particular year is the total of its expenditures for (1) retained losses, (2) insurance premiums (including those paid to affiliated, or captive, insurers), (3) risk control costs, and (4) administrative expenses of the risk management department.[1] Cost of risk often is used to assess the performance of a risk management department in terms of year-by-year changes in the organization's cost of risk or comparisons of the cost of risk among comparable organizations in the same industry. Because the cost of risk concept is relatively new and subject to some challenge, however, it is not a universally recognized measure of risk management performance.

Senior executives who are alert to risk management concerns expect a risk financing program to adapt to changing conditions. Therefore, a risk management professional should regularly review an organization's current risk financing measures and general financial condition to make sure that these measures remain suited to any recent changes in (1) the type or magnitude of the organization's loss exposures, (2) the organiza-

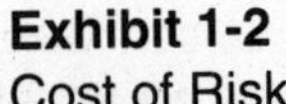

Exhibit 1-2
Cost of Risk

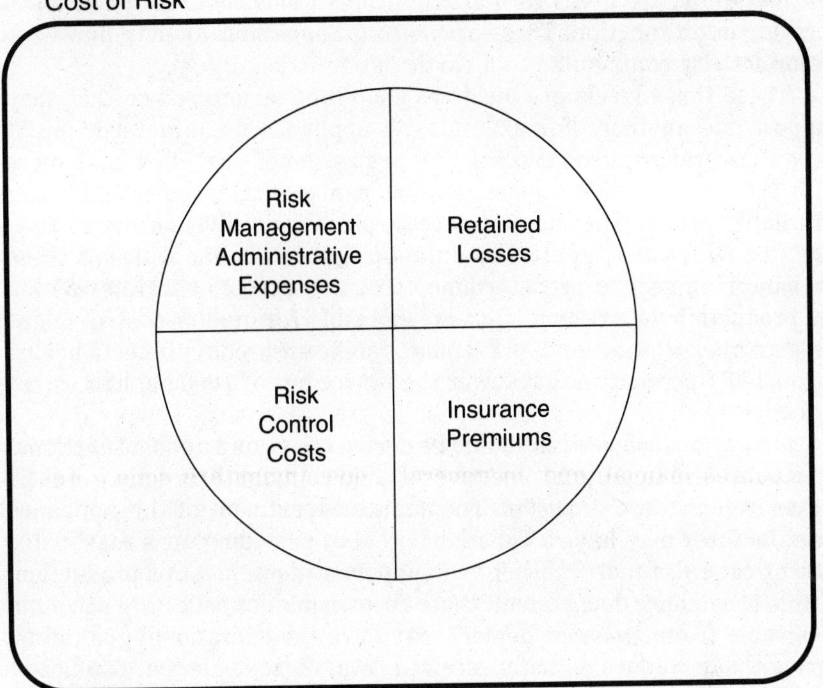

tion's objectives and the priorities among them, (3) the relative costs and availabilities of alternative risk management techniques (including both the balance between risk control and risk financing and the balance between retention and transfer among risk financing techniques), and (4) any legal requirements expressing how society expects the organization to finance the losses that it suffers or that its activities impose on others.

INTEGRATING ORGANIZATIONAL, FINANCIAL, AND RISK FINANCING OBJECTIVES

Every organization has objectives that can be arranged according to a three-tiered hierarchy. First, at the top, are one or a few very broad, fundamental, long-term goals for the entire organization. These define its "mission" or *organizational objectives.* Second, in the middle, are goals for particular functions within the organization such as production, marketing, financial, or human resources. These *functional objectives* describe how each functional division in the organization should contribute to the organization's overall mission. Third, at the base of this hierarchy, are goals for particular operations that are essential to carrying out a function. These *operational objectives* specify how each major activity contributes to a particular functional goal.

These three levels of objectives should be structured so that they support one another. For example, an appliance manufacturer might have an overall *organizational* goal or mission of providing customers with the best possible appliances that can profitably be marketed at affordable prices. The manufacturer's production division might then have the *functional* goal of manufacturing certain quantities of these appliances subject to predetermined cost and time constraints. Within the production department, those responsible for quality control might have an *operational* goal of keeping significant product defects below, say, 0.3 of 1 percent so that fewer than three out of 1000 appliances are defective.

Operational objectives should be derived from and uphold functional objectives, and functional objectives should contribute directly to fulfilling an organization's mission. The finance department of this appliance manufacturer may have a functional goal of providing, at a reasonable cost of capital, funds sufficient to support a given level of production. Within the finance department, those responsible for collecting accounts receivable from appliance dealers may have the operational goal of assuring that revenues actually received from these dealers are sufficient to pay manufacturing costs. Consequently, the organizational goal of meeting consumers' needs for appliances that meet given cost and quality standards implies a financial department functional goal of generating specific regular cash inflows to pay production costs, and a major part of this inflow is generated by diligent collections of receivables. In short, a mission statement of organizational goals yields functional (or departmental) goals which, in turn, imply goals for each operation within each department.

This hierarchy of organizational, functional, and operational objectives applies to all activities within an organization, including its risk financing activities. For any organization to fulfill its mission, it must make effective use of its resources, including cash and other sources of funds. Managing sources and uses of funds is the core of the finance function in any organization, one of the three functions—along with production and marketing—traditionally recognized as indispensable in every organization.

One significant use of any organization's funds is to finance recovery from any accidental losses that may occur. Thus, arranging before an accidental loss for internal or external sources of these recovery funds, as well as drawing on these sources when needed after a loss and monitoring the effectiveness of the uses of these risk financing funds, are important activities within the general finance function of any organization. It follows that the operational goals of risk financing activities should support the functional goals of the organization's finance department and that these functional goals should support the organization's more comprehensive mission. Conversely, the organizational goals of any enterprise do much to determine the objectives of its finance function, and the functional objectives for financing greatly influence the operational goals of its risk financing activities.

The following discussion describes and illustrates these interrelationships among organizational, functional, and operational objectives in a risk financing context.

Organizational Objectives

The senior managers of various organizations have different concepts of, and different ways of expressing, their fundamental objectives. These varied conceptions of underlying purpose affect any organization's functional objectives for its financial activities and, within these, various operational objectives for risk financing arrangements.

Types of "Mission" Statements. Every organization has one or more fundamental objectives, its reason(s) for being, that may be explicit or implicit in its statements of policies and procedures. Private business firms strive to maximize profits. For nonprofit organizations and governmental bodies, organizational objectives or mission statements usually focus on providing some good or service to a particular group or for a particular purpose. Examples include governing the residents of a particular jurisdiction, providing medical care and research to benefit those suffering from a specified disease, granting scholarships or other awards to outstanding students or artists, or pursuing any other public purpose. Rather than seek profits, public and nonprofit organizations usually strive to maximize their output of the specified good or service within a limited budget.

While reflecting these maximizing goals, mission statements may also incorporate nonfinancial objectives. Some mission statements also introduce diverse constituencies (often called "stakeholders") whose interests the organization is committed to serving. For example, a mission statement may read as follows:

> The fundamental objective of our organization is to earn profits for stockholders in ways that are consistent with the health, safety, and welfare of employees, customers, and the general public.

To reverse the foregoing emphasis, a profit-seeking organization might also express its mission this way:

> Our fundamental goal is to produce goods and services that meet the needs of customers, employees, and the general community, consistent with a reasonable level of profit for stockholders.

Similarly, the charter of a nonprofit organization dedicated to the interest of those afflicted with a particular disease might contain these dual objectives:

> Our organization allocates its funds and other resources to provide care to those suffering from [a specified disease] who cannot adequately finance their own care and to support research to find more effective treatments and ideally a cure for [that disease], recognizing that paying competitive wages and salaries to our employees is essential to this care and research.

All organizations—private and public—meet a variety of needs for diverse groups beyond their owners, beneficiaries, or citizens. Among these groups are an organization's customers (to whom it provides goods and services), employees (who earn their livelihoods working for the organization), creditors (who receive income that the organization pays as interest on its debts), and the public at large (toward whose well-being the organization pays taxes). An organization's management should make decisions that serve the interests of all these constituencies. Therefore, the interests of all major groups should be reflected in an organization's mission statement, structure, policies, and procedures. This broadened approach to organizational objectives is evident in the composition of the boards of directors in public and private organizations, on which sit representatives of labor, consumers, creditors, government, and perhaps other interests.

Implications for Financial Management and Risk Financing. All well-managed risk management (and, therefore, risk financing) programs are generally recognized as having several pre-loss and post-loss objectives. The post-loss objectives, which define the desired condition of an organization after any foreseeable accidental loss, include survival of the organization, continuity of its operations, efficiency/profitability, stability of earnings, growth, good "citizenship," and humanitarian conduct. Pre-loss objectives, defining the desired position of the organization if it has no losses, include efficiency/profitability, a level of uncertainty that is tolerable to managers regarding exposures to accidental loss, legality of operations, good "citizenship," and humanitarian conduct.

Most discussions of these pre-loss and post-loss objectives make no mention of an organization's overall strategic mission. These risk management goals are assumed to be the same regardless of that mission. Therefore, each of these general goals of risk management should have some implicit or explicit place in the risk financing objective of every organization. However, the relative importance of these post-loss and pre-loss goals is likely to vary between profit and nonprofit organizations, between private and public organizations, and between those organizations whose mission statements focus on the well-being of a single group and those organizations whose missions encompass the interests of diverse constituencies. For all organizations, the rudimentary objectives of survival, efficiency, and tolerable uncertainty are likely to rank high among any array of risk financing objectives. Survival of an organization is a necessary precondition to achieving any other objective. Efficiency in risk financing, by lowering the cost of financing or recovery of accidental losses, leaves any organization more funds to devote to its fundamental purpose, whatever that may be. Similarly, the managers of an organization normally desire that the level of uncertainty regarding potential accidental losses be kept at a level that they can tolerate.

Nonprofit organizations are less likely than profit-oriented ones to emphasize low risk financing costs, stability of revenues, or growth. Nonprofit organizations probably would favor risk financing plans that assure continuity of operations, good citizenship, and humanitarian conduct. Consequently, this nonprofit orientation could incline these organizations more toward insurance than to retention because insurance usually provides greater certainty that funds will be available to pay for recovery from accidental losses. Furthermore, the fact that the insurance proceeds come from an outside source usually forestalls debate about whether the organization should divert funds from its public-service activities to pay for recovery from an accidental loss.

Similarly, an organization that expresses its mission in terms of service to several diverse constituencies is more likely to purchase insurance (rather than to retain losses) than is an organization for which maximum profits for its owners is the fundamental mission. Purchasing insurance tends to make the availability of funds for any given loss somewhat "automatic" in the wake of the loss. The decision to buy insurance before any losses occur usually can be justified as a way of protecting the interests of all the groups the organization serves.

These generalizations about how an organization's mission statement affects its risk financing program do not apply universally. In some cases, a statute, ordinance, or the terms under which a nonprofit organization has borrowed funds or issued bonds will require it to purchase insurance, leaving no option for retention. In other cases, insurance will not be available or will be too costly for an organization, either profit or nonprofit, to purchase. Nonetheless, an organization's mission can often give direction to, or establish priorities among, its risk financing options as part of its overall financial management objectives.

Functional Objectives for Finance

Regardless of which department performs them, an organization's risk financing activities—arranging for sources of funds to restore losses that may occur, calling upon those sources for funds when needed, and monitoring the cost and reliability of these sources—are part of the organization's financial management function.

Elements of the Financial Function. The fundamental responsibilities of financial management are: (1) to forecast the organization's needs for funds (the amounts that will be needed, the times these amounts will be required, and the sources from which they may be derived) for all purposes, including risk financing; (2) to obtain these funds (from customers, creditors, owners, insurers, and other sources); (3) to manage the effective use of the funds obtained; and (4) to meet special financial needs, such as those that may arise to finance a merger, because of some catastrophic happening, or because of any other extraordinary, unpredictable event.

Relationships to Risk Financing. Financing recovery of accidental losses—paying for an organization's own losses and defending or settling claims against the organization—is one significant use of an organization's funds. The process of making pre-loss arrangements for these funds and then drawing upon and using funds from within the organization or from insurers (or other external sources) relates directly to all four of these basic functions of financial management:

1. Risk financing requires forecasting an organization's needs for funds to restore losses—particularly the amounts and the timing of these needs—that may extend well beyond the time a particular accident causes damage or injury.
2. Risk financing also requires obtaining funds by filing and documenting claims with insurers or other outside transferees, as well as drawing funds from sources within the organization to pay for retained losses.
3. These funds, once obtained, must be managed, that is, directed to the providers of goods and services or claimants to pay for recovery from incurred losses.
4. Most accidental losses create special, nonroutine needs for funds (even though recurring losses may be more "routine" than "special" for well-managed risk financing programs).

Thus, even though most financial texts ignore risk financing and other aspects of risk management, risk financing activities directly involve all fundamental aspects of the financial management function for any organization.

Specific Functional Objectives for Financial Management. Financial management contributes to an organization's fundamental mission by providing reliable, low-cost funds, at the times and in the amounts needed, to pursue this mission. The specific functional objectives of the finance function are as follows:

- *Low cost of funds* in required amounts and in time to meet the organization's financial needs
- *Liquidity,* so that the organization can generate predictable funds whenever needed by holding, or converting its other assets into, predeterminable amounts of cash
- *Solvency,* so that the organization's liabilities never exceed its assets, which would render the organization bankrupt
- *Legality,* so that the ways an organization raises funds and employs them—the organization's sources and uses of funds—comply with all legal requirements imposed by statutes, agreements with its bondholders and other creditors, and any other legal limitations on the organization's financing activities

Low Cost of Funds. An organization's financial activities should be efficient, enabling it to raise needed amounts of funds at low cost. The dividends, interest rates, bond premiums, and other payments to its owners, creditors, or other providers of funds should be relatively low, giving the organization a low "cost of capital." The lower the cost of capital to an organization, the greater the proportion of its total financial resources that organization can devote to its mission. For a profit-seeking organization, lower cost of capital means greater profitability. For any organization, reducing its cost of capital lowers the cost at which it can produce goods or services or, conversely, increases the output it can achieve given its commitment of financial and other resources.

In a risk financing context, increasing efficiency by lowering the cost of capital means reducing the cost of the funds an organization uses to finance recovery from accidental losses. Funds for risk financing come from a variety of sources, each of which has a cost of capital associated with it. Funds provided by an organization's owners, either directly or as appropriations of the organization's retained earnings (or accumulated past profits or surpluses), have a cost of capital equal to the percentage dividend rate the organization pays to its stockholders or other owners on the equity capital they provide. Risk financing funds generated from bondholders or other creditors carry a cost of capital equal to the effective rate of interest paid on these debts. The cost of funds received as indemnity payments from insurers is the premium paid for that insurance. The cost of funds received from other indemnitors (such as under "hold harmless" or other contractual arrangements) is the value bargained in exchange with these indemnitors. A well-managed risk financing program seeks to control—ideally, to minimize—the aggregate cost of risk financing funds generated from all of these sources by finding the appropriate balance of various risk retention and risk transfer measures.

A properly designed risk financing program also enhances the value of an organization to its owners, as well as to other constituencies whose interests that organization may serve, by reducing fluctuations in net revenues (that is, income minus expenses) from one period to the next. Proper risk financing provides funds promptly to pay for losses. This availability of funds reduces disruptions in an organization's operations that accidental losses may cause when they randomly reduce the organization's normal revenues or increase its normal expenses. The value of an organization to its owners or to others benefited by the organization's operations depends upon the amount, timing, and variability of the organization's future net cash flows. The greater these net cash flows, the sooner they are realized, and the less the fluctuations in these net cash flows from one accounting period to the next, the greater the value of the organization to its owners and to its other constituencies. By facilitating recovery from any accidental losses, effective risk financing both lowers an organization's cost of risk and decreases the fluctuations in its net cash flows.

Liquidity. Every asset has some degree of liquidity. The *liquidity* of an asset is a measure of the speed with which that asset can be converted into a predictable amount of cash at any time. An asset is highly liquid if it can be converted quickly and easily into a known amount of cash at any time. It is highly illiquid if such conversion is not possible. Thus, bank deposits and money market funds are highly liquid. Stocks and bonds are also liquid, but their value at a particular time is less. The finished goods and the merchandise inventories of a manufacturer or retailer are usually less liquid than most financial assets. Fixed assets, such as machinery or real estate, tend to be quite illiquid.

Highly liquid assets often are called "short-term" assets because an organization's normal operations convert them into cash quite promptly and predictably. Less liquid assets are generally described as fixed or long-term assets because they are not quickly and routinely converted into cash as part of the organization's normal operations. For example, a manufacturer's or retailer's inventories are normally sold and converted into cash revenues within a few days, weeks, or perhaps months. In contrast, such a retailer's or manufacturer's buildings and land remain illiquid, noncash assets because they are hardly ever sold or otherwise converted into cash.

For several reasons, some liquidity is essential to every organization's operations. First, every organization needs cash to carry out its normal business transactions. Some organizations (such as those in retail trade) need more cash relative to their total assets than do others (such as utilities). Second, some reserves of cash (or highly liquid assets) are needed as cushions against fluctuations in an organization's normal cash revenues and expenses. If revenues fall more rapidly than expenses, or expenses rise more rapidly than revenues, cash reserves must be available to support normal productive activities. Third, the management of many organizations seeks to maintain reserves of cash or highly liquid assets in order to exploit opportunities that may arise for profit or public service. The liquidity of an organization's overall asset structure (that is, the ratio of an organization's highly liquid assets to its total assets) greatly affects its ability to respond to these situations promptly. Many creditors accept this liquidity ratio as an indicator of an organization's ability to pay its bills as they fall due. Should this liquidity ratio fall below an accepted minimum (often 2:1, but with variations among industries), the credit standing of an organization may decline and make it less attractive to potential lenders and investors.

Insufficient liquidity lowers the value of an organization to its owners and to others whose interests it serves. Excessive liquidity—too high a portion of an organization's overall assets in cash or near-cash holdings, too little in longer-term capital investment in productive assets—also reduces the value of an organization. Holding cash and other highly liquid assets is relatively risk-free. Therefore, they earn a relatively low rate of return when compared with other long-term investments in more tangible, physically productive assets like factories and machinery. Hence, being too liquid reduces the rate of return of any organization's overall assets, making them less valuable to their owners, employees, customers, creditors, and others whose interests they serve.

On balance, therefore, an organization must maintain a suitable degree of liquidity, neither inadequate nor excessive. In fact, as discussed later in this chapter, liquidity conflicts with cost as a financial management objective. Accidental losses can disrupt an organization's liquidity, either (1) by creating unexpected demands for cash to finance recovery or (2) by forcing the organization to shut down or partially curtail its normal operations, thus lowering its normal inflows of cash. In order to maintain acceptable liquidity in the wake of a significant accidental loss or series of losses, an organization needs a special plan for making these funds available through either its own resources (retention) or transfer of the financial consequences of these losses to an insurer or other contractually bound transferees. Safeguarding liquidity requires the organization's risk management professional and other managers to anticipate when and how much cash the organization will need to recover from a particular type of accidental loss and to make arrangements to have this cash on hand when needed. Without such advance planning, a serious accidental loss or an unusual series of smaller losses can drain the organization's liquidity and threaten its survival.

Solvency. In order to continue its activities, every organization must remain solvent—that is, it must always have more assets than liabilities. The opposite condition, *insolvency,* exists when an organization's total liabilities exceed its total assets. *Bankruptcy,* in contrast to insolvency, exists when an organization cannot meet its current debt obligations on a current basis even though its total assets may exceed its total liabilities. An organization that is technically solvent may still be bankrupt, unable to pay its current bills.

Because significant judgment is often involved in the valuation of both an organization's assets and its liabilities, experts may disagree on whether an organization is solvent at a given time. Nonetheless, whenever an organization is deemed by its managers or declared by the courts to be insolvent, it may undergo voluntary or involuntary bankruptcy. Its operations may then be overseen by a bankruptcy referee—for the primary benefit of its creditors, not its owners, customers, employees, or others. Its assets may be sold to generate funds with which to pay the organization's debts. Bankruptcy supervision or piecemeal sale of an organization's assets lowers its value substantially and makes fulfilling its mission impossible.

Consequently, maintaining solvency is imperative for proper financial management of any organization. Prudent risk financing helps preserve solvency by generating funds to pay for accidental losses that might otherwise bankrupt an organization by (1) depriving it of assets or disrupting the operations that produce revenue to pay its obligations or (2) creating liability claims against the organization that it cannot afford to defend or settle. If an organization's normal activities already are quite "risky," many possible adverse events quite unrelated to accidental losses—such as a fall in the demand for its products during a recession, a decline in the market price of bonds or other financial investments, or an increase in property taxes or other levies assessed against the organization—may make its solvency quite precarious. In such situations, prudent risk financing does not rely heavily upon retention, using the organization's own funds, but instead emphasizes insurance or other external sources of funds that will not drain away the cash or other assets the organization needs to remain solvent. Even though insurance or other transfer is usually more costly than retention, insurance is preferable to any attempts at retention at levels that may bankrupt the organization. In contrast, when an organization's solvency is beyond question, retained earnings or other internal sources of funds may be an inexpensive, reliable source of cash with which to finance recovery from many accidental losses.

Legality. A final functional objective of managerial finance in the organization, often overlooked but still important, is legality—compliance with all legal requirements that in any way limit how an organization obtains or uses its funds.

Federal and state securities laws, for example, prescribe or proscribe many actions an organization might take in selling its stock or bonds to the public. Holders of an organization's preferred stock or bonds are guaranteed by statute, or by the agreements under which these securities are sold, certain forms of protection not generally available to holders of common stock. Most state and municipal governmental agencies must comply with the provisions of state constitutions, and local ordinances specify the procedures they must follow in levying taxes or selling bonds or notes and in selecting providers of goods or services (including insurance protection or risk management consulting services). Many nonprofit organizations are governed by the terms of their founding charters and bylaws, as well as by various federal and state statutes that define the procedures these organizations must follow to maintain their tax-exempt status. The risk management professional of any private or public entity must be generally aware of these restrictions and must recognize and comply with those that apply to risk financing activities. Any violation of these restrictions may subject the violating organization to various civil or criminal liabilities and may also nullify the actions that violate these legal requirements.

In a risk financing context, the following situations exemplify possible legal limitations on the risk financing options available to a particular organization:

- An organization that has mortgaged or pledged its real or other property as security for a loan is often required by that agreement to insure the property, for the benefit of the lender, against many types of physical damage.
- To protect the security of an organization's bondholders, the agreement under which those bonds are sold (the bond indenture) may forbid the debtor organization from retaining more than specified amounts of particular types of losses or may mandate that the debtor purchase insurance.
- A municipal ordinance detailing the procedure a municipality must follow in requesting bids for its property or liability insurance may preclude using a less formal procedure.
- Many states have statutes or regulations defining the characteristics of organizations that can qualify as workers compensation "self-insurers" and that, therefore, may choose not to buy work-

ers compensation insurance. Any organization that does not meet these requirements must purchase workers compensation insurance—no other risk financing option is legal.

Collectively, such administrative, statutory, and common law mandates that apply to risk financing restrict the risk management professional's options in designing risk financing programs.

Operational Objectives for Risk Financing

As described earlier, a risk management program also has objectives that are usually divided into two categories: pre-loss and post-loss. Pre-loss objectives define how the risk management function should be performed regardless of accidental losses. Post-loss objectives of risk management describe the condition of an organization that its senior management or owners consider minimally acceptable in the face of the most severe foreseeable loss. The more optimistic an organization's post-loss objectives for its risk management program are, the more difficult and expensive they are to achieve, and the greater the commitment of resources to risk management they require.

Links Between Organizational Objectives and Risk Financing. The objectives for the entire organization and for its financing activities need to be coordinated to serve shared purposes. The objectives of financial management provide the link for this coordination.

Scholars and practitioners generally agree that the fundamental objective of financial management for business firms is to maximize the wealth of the owners of an organization, the value for which they could sell their ownership (or "equity") interest in a fair, rational stock market or elsewhere, such as in the private sale of the business. These scholars and practitioners also agree that to maximize the owners' wealth in an orderly market for equities requires that the present value of an organization's expected future net cash flows also is maximized. These net cash flows are important because it is cash, more than profit, that determines an organization's ability to command productive resources for any purpose.[2]

The same wealth-maximizing reasoning that guides private, profit-seeking organizations is also valid for private, nonprofit organizations (such as charities and foundations), public, profit-seeking firms (such as municipally owned public utilities), and public, nonprofit organizations (such as cities and fire or police departments). Regardless of their orientation, all organizations need to be able to command productive resources to continue activities.[3] Therefore, all organizations must at least maintain and often increase the present value of their net cash flows. Maximizing the expected present value of net cash flows thus becomes the one universally valid objective for all organizations. Similarly, all organizations need risk management for protection against the accidental losses that can disrupt and, therefore, lower the expected present value of their expected net cash flows.

Specific Risk Financing Objectives. An organization's risk financing activities, like all its operations and resources, should serve the organization's objectives that are shown in Exhibit 1-1. However, because these organization objectives often conflict, a risk financing program may, at any given time, promote one objective more than it does others.

Survival. The most fundamental organization objective is survival. An organization that does not at least survive cannot fulfill any other objectives. Consequently, a risk financing program must provide at least the funds for minimum quantities of machinery and raw materials, managerial and support personnel, and enough operating capital to maintain the "critical mass" of the organization as a structured, ongoing system. More specifically, the essentials for survival can be defined, in a managerial setting, as (1) the ability to meet financial and other legal obligations, (2) sufficient physical and financial assets to resume operations, (3) a management structure, and (4) public acceptance of the organization's viability, integrity, and products or services.[4] In a more production-oriented context, these requirements for survival can be defined as (1) organizational structure, (2) adequate support personnel, (3) production facilities, (4) operating funds, and (5) markets for the resources required by the organization and for its output of goods or services.[5]

As any living creature requires a virtually continuous supply of water to survive, so an organization requires that these essentials not be absent for any appreciable length of time. Maintaining these essentials requires money. Therefore, every sound risk financing program must provide funds to purchase the essentials for the survival of the organization. It must also provide these funds virtually immediately following even the most severe foreseeable loss. Without adequate funds for these essentials, an organization cannot be expected to survive much longer than an animal could without water.

The immediacy of the need for survival funds typically requires that the organization obtain this financing through some form of retention. Relying on retention ensures that the organization can secure these funds with virtually none of the delay that often accompanies a request for outside funds. These immediate survival needs can be met within minutes through available cash, highly liquid financial assets, or established lines of credit.

Cost of Funds. No organization wants to waste money by spending unnecessarily on the costs of production, including the cost of funds for financing recovery from accidental losses. Unnecessary expenditures only reduce the profitability of a profit-seeking organization and make it more difficult for a nonprofit organization to meet its budget goals. Thus, every organization should have the pre-loss objective of spending no more than necessary before any accidental losses occur to ensure the availability of post-loss funds. Stated somewhat differently, an important objective of risk financing is that the greatest possible percentage of an organization's risk financing expenditures actually are devoted to restoring losses as they occur, with the smallest percentage being "drained away" as an administrative cost of providing post-loss funds.

A transferee, particularly an insurer, typically charges a fee or receives something else of value in exchange for the transfer to cover its operating expenses and to generate some expected profit. An organization that retains its loss exposures saves paying a transferee's expense and profit "loadings." Retention can often reduce an organization's risk financing costs, lower its overall cost of risk, and enhance its operating efficiency.

Retention is not always most efficient, however, because retention also imposes costs on the transferring organization, known as the transferor. Some of these costs are (1) increased uncertainty (discussed under the following heading), (2) the costs of operating a retention program, and (3) the costs of replacing (providing for itself or purchasing from a vendor) those record-keeping, loss control, and other services that an insurer or other transferee would have provided as part of a risk transfer. Thus, retention is more expensive than transfer—and will actually decrease operating efficiency—if the added uncertainty and other costs of retention are greater than would be the loading the insurer or other transferee would charge or require in exchange for accepting the transfer.

Tolerable Uncertainty. The senior executives of every organization should recognize that no risk financing plan can absolutely guarantee the survival of the organization under all circumstances. For example, in the event of war, financial security may not be possible. The possibility of such a catastrophe is a source of uncertainty that must be tolerated because providing funds for restoring such devastating losses is impossible, and certainly beyond the scope of risk management.

Short of such disasters, a sound risk financing program should include reliable plans to provide financing for all losses. These plans, essentially contingency plans, must provide for the various types and sizes of losses that may strike the organization and must give reasonable assurance to managers and owners that funds from one or more sources will be available to finance restoration. These plans almost certainly will include a wide range of risk financing techniques. For example, minor fire or vehicle damage losses may be charged as current expenses, and larger losses may be insured to the face amount of the applicable insurance. Recovery from even larger losses (if any are possible) may be financed through long-term borrowing or restored over a period of years through retained earnings.

The risk management professional should be able to assure an organization's owners and senior management that its risk financing program is adequate. This assurance implies a high probability that funds will be available as planned and when needed to restore the accidental losses for which the funds were intended. Although this assurance does not guarantee survival, it should relieve senior executives of the chilling effects of intolerable uncertainty. It should reduce their reluctance to undertake promising projects that at first appear too "risky" or to invest new equity capital in the organization.

The risk financing objectives of operating efficiency/profitability and tolerable uncertainty tend to conflict with one another. Insurance, for example, can keep uncertainty within tolerable limits (providing that the insurers are themselves financially secure and willing to pay legitimate claims); but insurance tends to be more costly than other, less certain risk financing techniques such as current expensing of losses or reliance on a funded or unfunded reserve. In practice, this conflict often is resolved by relying on a variety of risk financing techniques, often arranged in "layers." Small losses whose individual frequency and severity are reasonably certain are often retained to promote operating efficiency. Higher levels of loss or losses whose frequency is quite unpredictable are often insured, thus providing security against truly severe accidental losses. Insuring against rather than retaining these more serious losses costs more in dollars, but paying the insurer's loading for such coverage usually reduces uncertainty to more tolerable levels. Therefore, minimizing the total (financial and psychological) costs of financing losses from a given exposure typically calls for a mixture in which small losses are retained and larger ones are transferred in order to strike a balance between savings and uncertainty.

Legality. An organization's risk financing program, like all its other activities, should comply with legal requirements. These requirements are defined by statutes and regulations as well as the contracts to which the organization is a party. These legal requirements place some limits on how an organization may finance losses from particular exposures.

For example, a state statute may require an organization to purchase specified minimum limits of automobile liability insurance. Another statute may require it to purchase workers compensation insurance or to meet detailed requirements to qualify as a workers compensation "self-insurer." Apart from these general laws, the organization's contracts with its customers or suppliers may demand that certificates of insurance be supplied by or to various parties to these contracts. Failure to meet the insurance requirements in these contracts may make them unenforceable. Furthermore, some insurance contracts themselves may mandate certain risk financing arrangements. For example, in order to give an insured a financial interest in minimizing losses, an insurance policy that contains a substantial deductible may provide that the insured cannot separately insure losses within this deductible. To protect its rights to coverage above the deductible, the insured must, consequently, agree to retain lesser losses.

Continuous Operation. An organization that adopts continuous operation as a post-loss risk management objective wants more than survival and seeks more than to be able to reopen after a temporary shutdown. The goal is to "never close" because of any accidental loss. Public organizations such as police and fire departments or military defense units, continuous-process industries such as steel mills or distilleries, organizations that serve the public on a twenty-four-hour basis such as hospitals and many welfare-oriented facilities, and enterprises whose management believes they would lose their standing in highly competitive markets if they were to disappear even temporarily from public view such as newspapers and other mass media need to devote more resources to risk management than do organizations willing to shut down temporarily. This greater commitment to risk management resources makes continuous operation more expensive—operationally less efficient in a short-term profit-seeking or budgetary sense—than mere survival. For instance, continuous operation may mean a greater use of risk control measures such as establishing and using alternative facilities, maintaining excess capacity or spare parts, or summoning emergency personnel or equipment. So, although the less demanding goal of survival may only require that funds eventually be available to finance reopening, continuous operation requires that funds be available immediately to secure such support to forestall closing.

The greater need for immediate cash is likely to be met through retention rather than transfer because an organization typically can raise anticipated amounts of cash more quickly from internal sources than from insurers or other transferees. Thus, the short-term crisis management plan of an organization that seeks to maintain continuous operation probably relies more on its own funds. (These funds may even be deposited in several financial institutions in case a disaster that strikes the organization also closes its primary local depository.) Beyond immediate crisis needs, maintaining continuous operation is likely to call for extra risk financing to continue ordinary payroll expenses, utilities, and "normal" operations that an organization with less demanding risk management objectives would not need to finance during a temporary shutdown.

Stable Earnings. Beyond the physical effects of accidents on organization operations, management should also be concerned about how such events impact the organization's profitability (or a nonprofit organization's ability to operate within its budget). An organization often has a minimum target level of profits (or budget surpluses for nonprofit organizations), a level no accidental loss should be allowed to reduce. So that an organization's actual or reported financial results fall within the bounds set by the profit or budget standards, sound risk financing often emphasizes insurance and other risk transferring mechanisms to shift the financial consequences of severe losses. An organization seeking stable earnings tends to spend more on risk financing, particularly on insurance, than does one willing to tolerate an occasional accounting loss. The greater expenditures required to meet this post-loss goal tend to compromise the pre-loss goal of operating efficiency; but owners and senior managers are often willing to sacrifice some potential earnings by spending more on insurance and other risk financing measures in order to enjoy greater earnings stability at a somewhat lower level of net earnings (or budgetary surplus). To the extent that such an organization retains rather than transfers the financial burden of substantial losses, it is likely to stress loss reserves over current expensing of losses in order to spread the accounting recognition of retained losses over several accounting periods.

Growth. Organization growth in sales, production, market share, or facilities and personnel is a yet more demanding post-loss risk management objective. In order to grow, the aim of an organization must be to protect itself against the occurrence and the financial consequences of severe losses. This can be very difficult and costly in both risk control and risk financing commitments—even impossible if truly catastrophic accidental losses strike. Therefore, the risk financing program for a growth-oriented organization needs to be tailored to the rather precise wishes of its owners and senior managers, wishes they should be asked to make explicit after they have been informed of the organization's loss exposures and the consequences that adverse loss experience may have on their growth goals. In one setting, profit-seeking owners and managers may emphasize retention because they are willing to accept greater risk financing uncertainties in exchange for minimizing their risk financing costs. In effect, they accept retention in order to have more money to spend on expansion. In a different setting, cautious owners and managers of a growing organization may wish to protect its expanding resources so that its growth is not disrupted or reversed by one major accidental loss or a series of minor ones. For such a cautiously managed organization, a risk finance manager is likely to stress insurance.

The results of these two types of strategies can be determined or projected only in light of actual or forecast accidental losses. It is clear, however, that the risk management professional for a growth-oriented organization must explain to owners and managers the consequences of various risk financing alternatives and be sure that senior management accepts these consequences.

Humanitarian Conduct. An accident striking an organization seldom affects only its owners and managers. The health, income, and property of its employees, customers, suppliers, taxpayers, and members of the general public also are likely to be affected, especially if the organization is a public entity. Owners' and managers' social conscience or sense of moral responsibility may dictate that they protect these other groups either by initially preventing the losses or by minimizing the adverse effects of these losses on them. An organization's humanitarian actions typically are not justified by financial benefits to the organization. Humanitarian conduct that promotes goodwill among the public can, however, build an organization's future earnings by fostering a higher public opinion of the organization and thus greater acceptance of its products and by protecting the organization from liability suits brought by those who feel they have been callously treated by an organization. Humanitarian conduct is typically stimulated by an organization's senior managers and owners who want to provide for others' needs in the wake of some loss, although the organization is not legally obligated to do so. For example, senior executives may wish to rebuild damaged properties, to restore the lost income of the disabled, or to absorb their medical expenses even though these losses are not legally the "fault" of the organization. Provided that owners or senior managers have the authority to devote organization funds to these purposes without exposing themselves to directors' and officers' liability, and provided these executives understand the financial consequences of their humanitarian acts, their conduct is of little risk management concern.

From a risk financing perspective, it is important to remember that humanitarian expenditures not required by law often must be financed through retention rather than transfer. Many liability insurance policies permit the insured to use the insurer's funds to pay relatively small amounts for damage to others' property, which the insured voluntarily restores. Nevertheless, voluntary payments usually cannot be covered through insurance or financed through other transfers and must be borne through risk retention.

MAKING OPTIMUM USE OF FUNDS

Sound risk financing, like all good management, makes the best use of funds. There are three corollaries of this principle:

1. Cash flows are important.
2. Sources of cash should be matched in amount and time to cash needs for risk financing and for other organization purposes.
3. One source of cash may serve several cash needs; conversely, one need for cash may be met through several sources.

Each of these corollaries, examined in the following sections, implies that risk financing should be coordinated with financial and general management.

Risk financing through insurance or other sources of funds to finance recovery from accidental losses, or for meeting obligations to others growing out of such accidents, is only one of many uses for an organization's cash. Risk financing is a somewhat special use of funds in that money spent on risk financing safeguards or restores the organization, enabling it to strive toward its objectives. In this context, sound risk financing, like the very survival of the organization, is a prerequisite to an organization's reaching its other goals. Although proper risk financing is necessary for success, it alone is not sufficient for such success. Therefore, risk financing must compete with other potential uses of an organization's funds that often appear to be more directly mission-oriented than is the restoration of or recovery from losses.

Importance of Cash Flows

Cash enables an organization to obtain resources to fulfill its objectives. Cash—or more precisely, purchasing power, including credit—is a *necessary* means to *all* other ends. The net cash flow during any period measures an organization's ability to function effectively during that period and in the future. Therefore, in selecting uses for an organization's resources, senior management should give priority to commitments that promise the greatest net cash flow.

After-tax, not before-tax, net cash flows determine an organization's command over productive resources. Because an organization cannot use for its own purpose the cash it must pay in taxes, taxes reduce usable cash inflows. Therefore, for organizations subject to taxes, cash outflows to pay taxes reduce net cash flows available to purchase productive resources for the present and the future.

One of the reasons risk financing decisions for public entities may differ from those of private, profit-seeking organizations is that public entities generally are not subject to federal or state income or excise taxes. Therefore, computations of expected after-tax net cash flows tend to be simpler for these public organizations than for profit-seeking private enterprises. Furthermore, public organizations do not distinguish between before-tax and after-tax net cash flows, making depreciation an irrelevant expense for any tax purposes. For a public organization that does not pay taxes, the after-tax net cash flow is equal to the before-tax (and the before-depreciation) net cash flow.

In order to enhance its operating efficiency, every profit-seeking and nonprofit public or private organization needs to make the best possible use of its cash, the resource through which it purchases all of its other productive resources. Using cash most effectively requires maximizing the *expected present value of the organization's future annual after-tax net cash flows.* The choice by an organization of a particular risk control or risk financing alternative affects its current and future net cash flows. Therefore, to the extent feasible, an organization should select those risk management, particularly risk financing, alternatives that contribute most to the expected present value of its annual after-tax net cash flows. However, organizations often have other objectives besides maximizing operating efficiency. Moreover, legal requirements, owners' and senior management's tolerance for uncertainty, and simple shortages of resources may keep an organization from achieving an ideal level of operating efficiency. Nonetheless, the accurate evaluation of expected present values of future net cash flows tends to move an organization to higher levels of operating efficiency, thus improving its means of achieving its fundamental mission.

Matching Risk Management Cash Availabilities With Cash Needs

Making optimum use of funds requires more than maximizing the expected present value of an organization's future net cash flows. It requires the organization to always have enough available cash to meet current cash needs. One of these needs is the cost of financing recovery from accidental losses. The principles of managerial finance that guide an organization in matching cash sources with cash needs for any purpose also should lead to the matching of cash sources with the cash needed for risk financing.

Balancing Efficiency With Liquidity. An organization cannot commit all of its resources to long-term investments, no matter how profitable or productive they may be. An organization that does not pay enough attention to its cash requirements may have highly productive investments but may be unable to meet its current payroll or to pay for current supplies. Some resources need to be available in cash or in near-cash assets to finance short-term activities and to adjust to unexpected changes in conditions that may result from accidental losses.

In order to maintain the proper balance of cash—to meet current needs without unnecessarily sacrificing long-term profits—many organizations prepare a cash budget for each accounting period. Cash budgets typically forecast beginning cash balances, cash inflows during the period, cash outflows projected for the period, and an ending cash balance for the period. To the extent that cash needs can be closely predicted, the optimum level of cash can be quite precisely determined. However, unpredictable changes in cash inflows or outflows, such as those created by accidental losses that either reduce revenues or increase expenses, may call for a higher degree of liquidity. Thus, as one corporate finance authority has observed:

> If conditions of absolute certainty prevailed, this minimum required cash inventory would also be the actual liquid asset position that should be maintained by a firm. However, assuming there is some uncertainty with respect to the cash receipt and disbursement forecasts, it is reasonable to maintain a "cushion" of liquid assets over and above the amount implied by the transactions [cash] forecasts. It also seems reasonable to plan such a cushion in relation to the forecast of cash or liquid asset requirements. Thus a planned cushion might be measured as one that allows a company to meet its liquid asset requirements for X days or weeks independent of any cash receipts. The number of days or weeks clearly would depend on the probability of variation in the cash forecast, and on the opportunity cost of holding nonearning assets. On this basis the evaluation of the defensive or liquid position of a firm should be made by expressing the stock of liquid assets as a function of the projected need for liquid assets.[6]

Risk Management Implications of This Balance. Reducing the total amount and variability of an organization's needs for cash allows it to decrease its liquidity and increase its operating efficiency. Some of this liquidity represents cash needed to restore retained accidental losses. Therefore, an organization can reduce its need to be liquid by the following:

- Reducing the frequency and severity of these accidental losses
- Transferring, rather than retaining, more losses, thus shifting to the transferee the uncertainties of the timing and amounts of funds needed to finance recovery from these losses
- Arranging in advance appropriate sources of cash to pay retained losses

The first of these three strategies, reducing actual losses, is explored in the ARM 55 text, *Essentials of Risk Control.* The other two strategies are briefly summarized here and elaborated on in other chapters of this text.

Balancing Retention With Transfer. To the extent that an organization shifts to an insurer or other transferee the financial burden of its losses (and if the transferee remains able and willing to pay losses as the transferor expected), the variability of the organization's risk financing cost is reduced. One of the chief benefits of insurance and other reliable risk financing transfers traditionally has been that the insured can replace the highly uncertain cost of retained losses with a much more predictable outlay for insurance premiums. Insurance decreases the insured's uncertainty or, equivalently, reduces the variability of its cash outlays to finance recovery from accidental losses. Thus, quite apart from overall cost considerations, insurance allows an insured to reduce the cash or near-cash assets it might maintain as a safeguard against uncertain losses, thereby reducing liquidity and, consequently, increasing its operating efficiency.

Simultaneously, however, insurance tends to increase the long-term aggregate cost of paying for losses because premiums for protection can be expected to cover not only the insured's losses but also the insurer's loading for its operating expenses and anticipated profit. Thus, although insurance tends to *reduce the variability* of risk financing costs (at least when insurance markets themselves are orderly), it also tends to *raise the total* of these costs unless the insured would have spent more than the amount of the insurer's loading to replace services the insurer would have restored. Therefore, the overall effect of insurance on an insured's need to be liquid—to pay either retained losses or insurance premiums—may not always be clear.

Financing Retained Losses. An organization may unknowingly or knowingly retain losses. An organization may ultimately use its own funds to finance losses from particular exposures because the organization is unaware of the exposure until a loss occurs, or because the insurer or other transferee does not pay losses as the transferor organization had expected. Both possibilities suggest some deficiency in the organization's risk financing program. Nonetheless, some losses that are unknowingly retained are probably unavoidable. This possibility should be kept in mind when considering how much of which losses the organization knowingly chooses to retain.

An organization consciously choosing to retain losses from some exposures needs to decide (1) the amount of losses, (2) from which exposures it wishes to retain, and (3) how to generate funds to restore these losses. These decisions should be influenced by cash flow considerations and the need to make optimum use of funds.

Conversely, an organization may knowingly retain losses because it (1) cannot or chooses not to obtain any insurance or other risk financing transfer for these losses; (2) chooses to retain relatively small losses (and to insure or otherwise transfer larger ones) through per loss deductibles, aggregate deductibles, or excess insurance (or other transfer) arrangements; or (3) suffers a loss that exceeds the amount of insurance (or other risk financing transfer) the organization has obtained. An organization's senior management and its risk management professional should choose, for the exposures it knowingly retains, retention techniques that tend to match the availability of cash to pay for losses with the need for cash for this purpose. Whoever is matching the two variables needs to consider the amounts of cash needed and the timing of these cash needs.

With respect to the amount of cash needed, sound risk financing seeks to limit the size of cash outlays for retained losses by the following:

- Identifying and analyzing loss exposures as thoroughly as is feasible in order to minimize unknown retentions
- Defining clearly, in cooperation with insurers or other transferees, the kinds and amounts of potential future losses the transferor chooses to retain with the terms of its transfer arrangements
- Carefully selecting annual aggregate deductibles so that an unexpectedly large number of small losses within per loss deductibles does not generate an accumulation of retained losses that exceeds the transferor's anticipated total retention
- Where insurance or other transfer is selected, obtaining adequate limits of insurance to equal or exceed maximum foreseeable losses (thus minimizing unanticipated retained losses that go beyond insurance limits)

Having made these efforts to identify and limit the amounts of the losses it will retain, an organization's risk management professional should then focus on selecting retention techniques that can be expected to generate funds at the *time* they are needed for retained losses. Here, the risk financing program should reflect a principle that insurers have long recognized: the total ultimate amount of a loss is usually payable not at the moment a loss occurs or is reported, but instead, over a considerable amount of time. During this time, the insurer or an organization insuring its own losses can generate the funds as needed for actual payout. Insurers' experience indicates that different types of losses entail different "payout patterns." For example, although most property losses are restored within six to eighteen months after the fire or other peril causing them, settlements of liability losses are often spread over a decade with only 50 to 60 percent of the ultimate total of the verdict or settlement plus defense costs actually being paid in the first two or three years after the claim has been made.

Since funds for the total amount of most retained losses are not needed as soon as the loss occurs or is reported, substantial portions of these funds can be used for various investments that may be less liquid and higher-earning than cash or demand deposits in a bank. Only funds needed immediately must be held in demand deposits or diverted from current revenues. Funds needed in three or four months may, for example, be generated from normal sales of merchandise or finished goods. Funds needed only six months or a year after a loss may be secured from such sources as maturing certificates of deposit or other short-term securities. Funds needed in perhaps three to five years may be taken from a specially funded reserve or held in the organization's affiliated subsidiary or "captive" insurer until ultimately needed.

In short, having once limited the extent of retained losses through appropriate, reliable insurance and other transfers, an organization can structure the sources from which it derives funds to pay for any remaining retained losses in ways that minimize its liquidity needs and allow it to increase its rate of return on funds which, ultimately, will be paid out for retained losses. As throughout general managerial finance, matching the timing and amounts of cash availabilities to the timing and amounts of cash needs contributes to the optimum use of funds.

Flexibility of Cash Sources and Needs. Throughout managerial finance, the matching of cash sources with cash needs implies that short-term cash needs typically are fulfilled from highly liquid sources of cash and long-term needs are met from less liquid sources. For example, a manufacturer or a retailer normally expects to purchase raw materials or merchandise inventories using recently generated revenues as part of a regular, short-term cash flow cycle. Funds for long-term projects, such as constructing a building or developing a new product, usually come from long-term debt or equity capital. Such pairings of sources and uses of funds facilitate financial planning and reduce the likelihood that an organization will be without necessary funds when needed.[7]

Within these general patterns, however, an organization can be even more financially flexible if its senior management recognizes that one source of cash can meet several cash needs and that one cash need can be met from several sources.

These possibilities also apply to risk financing, allowing the risk financing program as a whole to withstand unexpected accidental losses by being able to call upon a variety of sources of funds. For example, being able to call upon one source of cash to meet several needs implies that an organization's current revenues, its available lines of credit from financial institutions, and perhaps its ability to raise funds in the capital market can be drawn upon, if necessary, to finance recovery from an accidental loss. Insurance, cash on hand, or funded reserves need not be the only sources of risk financing funds. Similarly, recognizing that one cash source can meet several cash needs should open the minds of an organization's senior management and its risk management professional to the possibility of using, for risk retention purposes, some portions of funds originally slated for some other purpose. For example, an organization that has raised long-term debt or equity capital to finance expansion may find it appropriate to channel some of these resources into funded reserves or into some form of captive insurer. As later explained in Chapter 2, different forms of captive insurance may be neither wholly insurance nor wholly retention, but possess elements of both.

This flexibility in cash sources and needs does not imply that all cash sources are always available to meet all cash needs or that cash to meet any particular need can always be taken from any source. Ideally, cash needs and corresponding sources should be planned, and these plans should be followed to achieve anticipated rates of return and levels of operating efficiency. Furthermore, funds earmarked for particular purposes, such as to retire maturing debt or to pay for particular kinds of anticipated losses, should be safeguarded so that long-term plans are not disrupted for transient purposes. Nonetheless, these plans for the use of the funds should not be overly rigid and should not automatically bar creative risk financing arrangements. Orderly flexibility is the key to a well-balanced position in managerial finance for risk financing and other purposes.

Conflicting Objectives: Optimizing Management

An activity that has two or more goals must often strike a balance between them, achieving each goal in part but none of them in full, because fully meeting one goal would require the unacceptable sacrifice of the others. For example, engineers designing an automobile often must strike a balance between speed and fuel efficiency because the fastest cars are too inefficient and the most efficient cars are too slow for normal use. Similarly, making the best use of risk financing funds may require careful planning and the ability to depart from those plans when unexpected opportunities or challenges arise. Partially fulfilling two or more objectives rather than one objective in full requires *optimizing,* rather than maximizing, management.

Risk financing seeks a number of pre-loss and post-loss objectives that should be consistent with the organization's overall mission. However, risk financing objectives may conflict with organization objectives and with other risk financing objectives—usually in the following ways:

- Among risk financing objectives, financial security generally conflicts with low cost.

- Risk financing needs for funds often conflict with other needs for funds within an organization.
- Among risk financing options, insurance often is a good first choice and a good last choice, but it is seldom the one best choice.

Financial Security Versus Operating Efficiency. A pre-loss objective of risk management and an important post-loss concern is minimizing the cost of financing recovery from accidental losses, that is, to divert as few as possible of the organization's resources to risk financing. Reducing the commitment of these resources also should lower the organization's overall cost of risk. At the same time, however, a crucial post-loss risk financing objective is to ensure adequate funds for at least the survival of the organization, and more realistically, for stability, earnings, or growth objectives in the wake of the most severe loss or combination of losses that the organization can reasonably expect to withstand.

The likely conflicts among these objectives reflects the inherent conflict between the financial security provided by a risk financing technique and that technique's cost. The *financial security* provided by a risk financing technique is the probability that the technique will make available the amounts of funds called for in the organization's risk financing plan at the time and under the conditions the plan specifies. The cost of a risk financing technique is its affect on the expected present value of the organization's future net cash flows (relative to other risk financing options).

Achieving a high degree of financial security allays senior managers' and owners' uncertainties about the future of the organization following major losses. This sense of security usually requires more dependence on insurance or other highly reliable risk financing transfers than it does upon retention, especially the less formalized retention techniques of current expensing of losses or using unfunded reserves. However, insuring tends to be more expensive in the sense that it requires more of the resources that might be used for "normal" productive activities than does retention. In fact, most proposals for increasing an organization's risk retention stress the cost savings these proposals can be expected to generate. In short, achieving the greater financial security and lowered uncertainty provided by reliable insurance (and other risk financing transfers) costs money. Therefore, a risk financing program that seeks both financial security and operating efficiency strives for inherently conflicting goals, neither of which any program can fully satisfy. A sound risk financing program strikes a balance that creates the fullest feasible attainment of both objectives. As conditions change, particularly as an organization's loss exposures evolve and as the relative costs of insurance and other risk financing techniques shift, the "right" balance between retention and transfer or other devices is also likely to change.

Risk Financing Versus Other Organizational Needs. The financial and other resources available to virtually every organization are limited relative to its goals. An essential function of all management is to allocate an organization's limited resources among its seemingly unlimited needs.

Financing recovery from accidental losses is a fundamental need of every organization. Without appropriate funding, no organization can expect to survive serious accidental losses. Indeed, without sound risk financing to restore assets and activities impaired by accidental losses, every organization can expect these losses eventually to jeopardize its productive capacity and, ultimately, its survival. Nonetheless, devoting resources to risk financing reduces resources available for other organization purposes—a fact that a risk management professional's colleagues are very likely to point out during an organization's budget discussions.

Successfully implementing a risk financing program requires securing the active cooperation of managers throughout an organization. Therefore, although the risk management function theoretically competes for organization resources with such other functions as production and marketing, the managers of these functions should not compete with each other. They should understand that cost-effective risk financing of recovery from losses to any department is essential to the well-being of all departments and the organization as a whole. A function that is not restored can only fail to meet output or other goals on time at reasonable cost, thus draining the organization. Proper risk financing should, therefore, be supported in all levels of management throughout an organization.

Insurance as a Risk Financing Choice. Analyzing the role of insurance in a sound risk financing program brings to light many of the potentially conflicting objectives of risk financing. It also reveals the optimizing decision making on which such programs depend. This chapter has briefly explained, and this entire text will examine in some detail, the paradox of insurance—why it is true that insurance is a good first choice and a good last choice but hardly ever the best choice for an organization's risk financing program.[8]

Insurance is a good first choice in at least two senses. It is clearly the preeminent, most popular risk financing technique. When any business executive recognizes an exposure to accidental loss and must approve a choice of funding techniques for paying those losses, it is likely that the executive will first choose insurance. Furthermore, in terms of their daily work, most risk management professionals spend most of their time on insurance-related matters. So, in the practical sense of what the vast majority of these professionals actually "do," insurance is a genuine first choice.

In addition, insurance should come first among financing techniques in a managerial decision-making context. Whenever an organization acquires new or partially unknown loss exposures, for example, when it buys a subsidiary or some real estate or starts making or selling a new product, a valid strategy is to be "safe rather than sorry." So the decision is made to insure the exposure first, whatever it may be. Any insurance that turns out to have been unnecessary can later be canceled. The underlying purpose here is to blanket any unknown exposures with insurance protection as soon as possible, leaving until a later time a more analytical approach to deciding which exposures to insure and which to treat through other risk financing techniques.

There are also two good reasons why insurance should be the last choice in a sound risk management program. First, good risk control, by stopping losses from happening or by keeping them small, is usually preferable to risk financing, which only pays for losses *after* they happen. Risk control safeguards existing assets and activities, reducing the need to devote risk financing dollars or other resources to restoring them. Ideally, good risk control minimizes risk financing costs.

The second reason insurance is an appropriate last choice among risk financing techniques is that it is a relatively costly source of funds for all but the largest, most unpredictable losses. For losses an organization can absorb internally or within its economic family, or for losses the organization can restore with funds borrowed on a short- or long-term basis, these noninsurance funding alternatives are likely to be less costly. They do not require paying the insurer's operating expenses or allowance for anticipated underwriting profit.

These operating expenses and profit are clearly necessary and deserved by insurers for the catastrophe protection and essential services they provide—especially for loss control and claims management. However, for an organization that does not need these services or that can obtain them at less cost elsewhere, insuring less-than-catastrophe losses can be difficult to justify to cost-conscious executives or to owners who are willing to shoulder the responsibility of integrating risk financing with their general financial management.

For any loss exposures that may generate large losses, insurance should be a part of almost every organization's risk financing program. Insurance can be expected to provide the most real protection for the fewest dollars, especially when it is coupled with good risk control to reduce losses and proper use of other risk financing techniques that are appropriate for smaller losses. The combination of these techniques is what makes insurance seldom the one best risk financing choice but almost always an essential part of every sound risk financing program.

SUMMARY

Risk financing is the planning, organizing, directing, and controlling of the sources and uses of the funds an organization uses to finance recovery from accidental losses. Risk financing requires making decisions about the sources and uses of these funds by (1) identifying and analyzing the needs for funds to pay for potential losses; (2) examining the alternative sources of these funds; (3) selecting the most promising sources; (4) implementing arrangements to secure these funds; and (5) monitoring the results of these chosen arrangements.

Every organization's risk financing decisions, like all its other choices about using financial and other resources, should be guided by that organization's mission statement, or brief set of fundamental objectives. These basic organizational objectives should be supported by functional objectives. For any organization's financial activities, these should include forecasting needs for funds, obtaining these funds, managing their use, and responding to special needs. Each of these functional objectives for overall financial management has its risk financing counterpart. Similarly, the specific objectives for financial management—cost of funds, liquidity, solvency, and legality—are supported by several operational objectives for risk financing: survival of the organization, operating efficiency (for profit or other central missions), tolerable uncertainty for management, continuous operations, stable earnings, growth, humanitarian goals, and compliance with the law. Thus, the operational objectives of risk financing should support the operational and functional objectives of an organization's financial management. The functional objectives of financial management should serve, in turn, the organization's overall mission.

Striving to achieve these objectives within the limits of its financial resources often forces an organization to balance some conflicting goals in designing its risk financing program. These include the conflicts among liquidity, financial security, and cost in choosing whether to retain or to transfer the financial burden of an organization's potential accidental losses. To resolve such conflicts, most organizations rely on a program of both retention and insurance that is, for each particular organization, properly balanced.

Chapter Notes

1. The concept of the cost of risk was introduced in the late 1970s by the Risk and Insurance Management Society in New York City, with the technical assistance of Risk Planning Group of Darien, Connecticut. The Society has published survey data on the cost of risk for a particular sample of firms in industries in its periodic *Cost-of-Risk Survey.*
2. This reasoning is elaborated on in many standard financial management, corporate finance, and managerial finance texts. See, for example, J. Fred Weston and Eugene F. Brigham, *Managerial Finance,* 7th ed. (Hinsdale, IL: Dryden Press, 1981), pp. 3–9.
3. This reasoning is amplified in many public finance texts. See, for example, John F. Due, *Government Finance: Economics of the Public Sector,* 4th ed. (Homewood, IL: Richard D. Irwin, Inc., 1968), pp. 4–7.
4. This set of requirements for survival is drawn from Bob A. Hedges and Robert I. Mehr, *Risk Management: Concepts and Applications* (Homewood, IL: Richard D. Irwin, Inc., 1974), pp. 29–34.
5. Frank E. Bird, Jr., and George L. Germain, *Practical Loss Control Leadership: The Conservation of Property, People, Process, and Profits* (Loganville, GA: International Loss Control Institute, 1985), pp. 329–346.
6. Ezra Solomon, *The Theory of Financial Management* (New York: Columbia University Press, 1963), pp. 148–149.
7. James C. Van Horne, *Fundamentals of Financial Management* (Englewood Cliffs, NJ: Prentice-Hall, 1971), pp. 46–68.
8. George L. Head, "First Choice, Last Choice," *The National Underwriter* (Property-Liability/Employee Benefits Edition), 1 June 1987, p. 49.

CHAPTER 2

Examining Risk Financing Options

In order to help an organization achieve its fundamental mission, as well as its related functional and operational objectives, a risk financing program must be tailored to the characteristics of the loss exposures facing the organization, the characteristics of the organization itself, and the conditions of the risk financing, product, and financial markets in which the organization operates.

This chapter catalogues the distinguishing features of specific risk financing techniques. Also included are descriptions of the characteristics of (1) the loss exposures, (2) the organization itself, and (3) the various markets in which the organization operates that should be considered when making tentative choices among these risk financing alternatives. These choices remain tentative until, as described in later chapters, the organization's risk management professional and other executives can evaluate all considerations that arise in implementing and monitoring what appear to be the proper risk financing techniques. Thus, this chapter examines both major risk financing options and the factors relevant to deciding among them. Subsequent chapters describe how to apply each risk financing option in appropriate situations.

FUNDAMENTAL DISTINCTIONS AND DEFINITIONS

Each risk financing technique involves a planned source of funds with which an organization may finance recovery from accidental losses.

The Retention/Transfer/Hybrid Distinction

The sources of funds from which an organization may plan to finance recovery from accidental losses may be broadly classified as

(1) retention, (2) transfer, or (3) a hybrid that combines elements of both retention and transfer. All retention techniques draw on funds originating within the organization or its economic family. Therefore, the financial burden of retained losses, which often fluctuate greatly from year to year, usually falls on the organization. In contrast, transfer techniques include sources of funds originating outside the organization whose losses are being financed. Consequently, the organization's cost of funds obtained through transfer usually does not vary with the organization's loss experience during that period (although costs of using risk transfer may vary because of other factors). For example, paying for losses as current expenses is a basic form of retention, while purchasing guaranteed-cost insurance is a basic form of transfer. A number of more complex risk financing techniques combine elements of retention and transfer, leading to "hybrid" crosses between retention and transfer.

Consistent with the classification of risk financing techniques in Chapter 1, all of the risk financing techniques listed under "internal" in the source of funds of Exhibit 2-1 are considered *retention*: current expensing, unfunded reserves, funded reserves, borrowing, and paying losses through wholly owned affiliates ("single-parent captive insurers"). Similarly, all of the risk financing techniques that rely on external funds are considered *transfer*: guaranteed-cost insurance, participating (or dividend-paying) insurance, deferred premium plans, lagged premium plans, discounted ("net present value," or NPV) premium plans, and noninsurance contractual transfers for risk financing. *Hybrid* plans rely on a combination of internal and external sources of funds. They include retrospectively rated insurance, compensating balances plans, high-deductible plans, and multiple-parent (or "group") captive and pooling arrangements.

There is another fundamental distinction between risk financing through retention and through transfer. Because retention relies on internal funds, the costs of retention are typically experience-responsive during the accounting period in which the losses occur. Conversely, because transfer relies on external funds, the costs of transfer are typically *not* experience-responsive during the accounting period in which the losses occur. The costs of hybrid techniques tend to be less experience-responsive than those of retention but more experience-responsive than those of transfer.

Planned/Unplanned Distinction

Risk financing techniques are planned sources of funds to pay for accidental losses, sources that an organization's risk management professional and other senior executives can reasonably manage. However, under unusual circumstances, the funds to pay for a loss may come from

Exhibit 2-1
Classification of Risk Financing Techniques

Retention (Internal Funds)	"Hybrid" (Internal/External Funds)	Transfer (External Funds)
Current expensing	Retrospectively rated insurance	Guaranteed-cost insurance
Unfunded reserves	Compensating balances plan	Participating insurance
Funded reserves	High-deductible plans	Premium payment plans
Borrowing	Pooling arrangements	Deferred premium plan
Single-parent captives	Multiple-parent captives	Lagged premium plan
		Discounted (NPV) premium plan
		Noninsurance contractual transfer for risk financing

unplanned sources that could not have been anticipated. For example, an organization may incur a loss that entitles it to governmental disaster relief or gives it the right to bring a civil lawsuit because the organization has suffered a legal wrong.

A person or an organization that commits a civil wrong—a tort or a breach of contract—against another person or organization may be held legally liable to pay money to the victim(s) of its wrongdoing. This legal obligation to pay money damages may arise from a court verdict, from a negotiated settlement between the wrongdoer and the victim(s), or under the terms of a statute (such as a state or federal antitrust law, which often calls for a violator to pay treble damages to the victims). Moreover, some contracts contain an agreement, called a "*liquidated damages* provision," through which the contracting parties agree on the amounts of money each will pay the other as compensation for breaching their agreement. All these types of payments from wrongdoers to victims are potentially important sources of risk financing funds for victims, particularly those who have suffered property damage or bodily injury because of a wrongdoer's improper conduct.

However, such monetary payments from wrongdoers are not reliable sources of funds for any well-managed risk financing program. Such legal recoveries from wrongdoers should *not be included in planned sources of risk financing* funds for four reasons:

1. Most losses that individuals or organizations suffer do not arise out of the acts of wrongdoers.
2. Even if another person's or organization's wrongdoing is the cause of a loss, the wrongdoer may be able to avoid liability because of effective negotiation, a strong legal defense, or the uncertainties of the litigation process.
3. The victim of another's wrongdoing may incur such high costs in pursuing a claim that the net recovery from the wrongdoer (the amount of the negotiated settlement or verdict minus the victim's cost of securing it) may not be significant; it certainly is not predictable.
4. If a victim's loss resulting from a wrongdoer's action is also covered by the victim's insurance or other contractual source of indemnity, the insurer/indemnitor is very likely to become subrogated to the victim's rights of recovery against the wrongdoer so that the insurer/indemnitor—not the victim—receives compensation from the wrongdoer.

In short, legal recoveries from civil wrongdoers may best be viewed as windfalls, not reliable components of a planned risk financing program.

ALTERNATIVE RISK FINANCING TECHNIQUES

The discussions under the following headings, elaborating Exhibit 2-1 by describing each of the risk financing techniques identified therein, make clear that the customary distinction between, on the one hand, *retention* (or internal financing of accidental losses at a cost that varies with, or is responsive to, loss experience) and, on the other hand, *transfer* (external financing at a cost that does not vary with, or respond to, loss experience) is overly simplistic. Numerous risk financing techniques are neither retention nor transfer but are, instead, a blend, or "hybrid," of both retention and transfer.

Because of frequent innovations by insurers and the larger insurance brokerage and agency organizations attempting to compete for insureds by offering new "wrinkles" in risk financing, a complete catalogue of all possible risk financing techniques and combinations of techniques is difficult to assemble. Furthermore, because different insurers and other vendors attach proprietary trade names to their risk financing offerings, such a catalogue would require constant updating. Therefore, the following discussion describes and gives the most common labels to the generic forms of (1) retention, (2) transfer, and (3) hybrid techniques.

Retention Techniques

When an organization relies on retention to finance recovery from its own losses (or those losses of others for which it is responsible), the organization draws on funds from within the organization itself or from within its economic family. Under the retention techniques—current expensing of losses, the use of unfunded reserves, use of funded reserves, borrowing, and financing losses through a single-parent captive—the cost of losses and related administrative expenses, often called loss adjustment expenses (LAE), is borne entirely by the organization retaining the losses. Consequently, the organization's current cost of risk financing through retention techniques fully reflects the frequency, severity, and related administrative expenses of the retained losses.

Many risk management scholars and practitioners distinguish between *active* and *passive retention*, or synonymously, between *planned* and *unplanned retention*. These labels describe the degree of conscious planning that goes into an organization's retention of a given loss exposure. By definition, passive or unplanned retention occurs when an organization retains any exposure of which it is unaware or for which it has chosen to make no plans for financing potential losses. In contrast, planned or active retention requires both a thorough recognition and a careful analysis of a given exposure as a basis for consciously choosing to retain a given amount of potential losses from that exposure.

Every loss not covered by a risk transfer to an insurer or other transferee/indemnitor is, by definition and as a matter of practical reality, retained. Some losses possess certain characteristics that make retention either viable or necessary. Examples of situations involving such characteristics include the following:

- The peril that caused the loss was not transferred because of a conscious decision or a lack of awareness on the part of the insured organization.
- The peril that caused the loss was uninsurable or untransferable.
- The loss was not within the scope of the organization's insurance contract or other contractual transfer.
- The size of the loss was such that it:
    - Was within a deductible in the organization's insurance.
    - Exceeded the limits of the organization's insurance so that the excess had to be paid directly by the organization.
    - Exceeded the ability of the indemnitor, who was obligated to pay the loss under an insurance contract, other contractual transfer, or civil court judgment.

An essential function of risk financing is to provide funds for recovery from all possible accidental losses the organization seeks to survive.

(If an organization decides not to attempt to finance recovery from a particular accidental loss—for example, by not repairing or replacing damaged property or by not reopening for business following severe damage that has closed its premises—then no risk financing is needed to pay for any return to pre-loss normalcy.) Therefore, in planning how to finance losses, every possible loss from which the organization may wish to recover should be paired with at least one financing technique (together with at least one risk control technique, discussed in ARM 55, to reduce the frequency or severity of the losses for which financing is needed).

The need to classify retention techniques by the characteristics of the losses to which they apply arises because all risk financing techniques are inherently limited. Insurance and other transfer contracts may cover only some losses (such as direct losses, but not the loss of income) only at certain locations or during specified time periods. Other insurance and noninsurance contracts may be subject to similar restrictions, such as when a lender is obligated to extend credit to a borrowing organization only if certain types of accidental losses occur. Retention again becomes the financing method for losses not otherwise financed and is thus the "catchall" financing technique.

Specific techniques of retention include the following:

- *Current expensing* of losses draws on funds that an organization presumably has on hand or in the bank accounts used in its daily operations to restore losses that are charged as expenses of the current accounting period. Reserves are not drawn on, and the cost of these losses is not apportioned beyond the current accounting period.
- Relying on *unfunded reserves* is similar to current expensing of losses in that the organization draws upon its current operations to generate funds; however, it is unlike current expensing in that the organization has previously established an unfunded account (in the form of a liability or a reduction in the value of an asset, much like recognizing depreciation expense) to which it makes periodic additional entries to recognize the likelihood of future (or present but unreported) losses.
- Using a *funded reserve* is comparable to relying on an unfunded one, except that the organization actually sets aside, before any loss occurs, funds in a bank account or some portion of its own assets from which to draw cash when needed to pay losses.
- *Borrowing* entails the use of an organization's credit to raise funds needed to restore losses either by arranging a line of credit for this purpose before any losses occur or by negotiating a loan shortly after a loss occurs. Because borrowing draws

upon an organization's own credit resources, this technique (like all retention) uses funds the organization could have devoted to other purposes.

- Financing recovery from an organization's losses through a *wholly owned affiliate* (*single-parent "captive insurer"*), which some organizations of substantial size establish to formalize their retention programs by contracting with this subsidiary for it to collect periodic payments from the parent, issue documents that specify the subsidiary's duties to pay particular types of the parent's losses, and pay these losses to or on behalf of the parent when appropriate. Such a wholly owned affiliate provides retention for its parent because its funds come from the parent and there is no transfer of risk outside the parent's economic family; a "multiple-parent captive," which to some degree pools losses among its several owners, is a "hybrid" risk financing technique for all of them.

Notice that this list of retention techniques does not include "self-insurance."[1] "Self-insurance" has so many diverse uses that it is not, by itself, an analytically meaningful term. In much casual conversation and writing, it denotes any form of retention and, therefore, in those contexts it is often synonymous with retention. However, in other contexts self-insurance is more restrictively defined to include only those retention programs characterized by *one or more* of the following features:

- A sufficiently large number of independent loss exposures to make the organization's aggregate losses from these exposures highly predictable
- An established fund to which the organization makes regular contributions and from which losses are paid, much as they would be in a commercial insurance arrangement
- A formalized captive insurance program
- All of the features that the statutes of any state require of an organization that wishes to qualify as a self-insurer of workers compensation or other specified types of exposures in that state (and, thus, to be exempt from requirements to buy commercial insurance or to establish other financial responsibility acceptable to that state for these exposures)

Because it is sometimes difficult and even impossible to determine how self-insurance is being defined, the term is best avoided or defined very carefully when it must be used.

Self-insurance is also criticized as being an oxymoron, a self-contradictory term. Insurance is best defined (as it will be in Chapter 5) as including two elements: (1) the pooling of a large number of substantially identical loss exposures so that aggregate losses can be predicted with tolerable certainty; and (2) the transfer of the financial burden of these losses from a large number of insureds to any insurer. Thus, insurance requires two distinct parties—a transferor/insured/indemnitee and a transferee/ insurer/indemnitor. Because one party fulfills both functions, the term "self-insurance" is often held to be philosophically contradictory.

Another, more practical difficulty with the concept of self-insurance is that many executives unfamiliar with the complexities of risk financing are likely to assume mistakenly that a self-insurance program offers as much protection as does commercial insurance. However, when "self-insurance" is used as a general term for any form of retention, a self-insurance program may be no more financially secure than current expensing of losses.

Transfer Techniques

The retention techniques just described (1) draw on funds originating within the organization suffering the loss (or that organization's economic family) and (2) place the entire burden of actual losses on that organization. In contrast, the transfer techniques about to be described (1) draw on funds originating outside the organization suffering the loss (and from beyond its economic family) and (2) impose a fixed cost on the organization that is not responsive to that particular organization's specific loss experience during the year in question. The risk financing techniques that fulfill these two criteria are (1) guaranteed-cost insurance, (2) participating (dividend-paying) insurance, (3) premium payment plans, and (4) noninsurance contractual transfers for risk financing.

Notice that the second distinguishing characteristic of transfer techniques is that their cost to an insured does not vary with that particular insured's individual loss experience during the year in question. Rather, the cost of all traditional forms of insurance, even guaranteed-cost insurance, varies with insureds' *collective* loss experience *over the long run*. Indeed, the essence of traditional guaranteed-cost insurance is the pooling and spreading of the cost of all insureds' aggregate loss experience over the entire group of insureds over the long run. Thus, as these aggregate losses shared among insureds increase or decrease in frequency or severity from year to year, the premium rate charged all insureds for this coverage also tends to increase or decrease. These premium rate changes for entire groups or classes of insureds differ significantly from loss-sensitive premium rating plans and other features of "hybrid" risk financing techniques that adjust each policyholder's current premium based only on that particular insured's individual loss record.

Guaranteed-Cost Insurance. *Guaranteed-cost insurance* is a type of commercial insurance for which the insured pays a premium at the beginning of each (usually annual) policy period that is guaranteed not to change or be adjusted during that period. *Commercial insurance* is a contract whereby an insurer, in exchange for a premium paid by or on behalf of an insured, promises to indemnify that insured for losses that fall within the scope of coverage of that policy.

Guaranteed-cost commercial insurance is the most typical, and the most traditional, type of insurance contract—the type most frequently referred to simply as "insurance." As later explained in Chapter 5, the scope of the coverage provided by a commercial insurance policy is defined in terms of the perils, property or other things of value, persons or interests, types of losses, time periods, locations, and dollar amounts of coverage that the policy provides. The insured's premium for guaranteed-cost insurance is thus fixed at the beginning of each policy period and is not adjusted for the insured's loss experience during that policy period, for the insurer's administrative costs associated with that policy, or by any dividend paid to the insured at the end of that policy period.

Some guaranteed-cost commercial insurance policies specify premium rates for more than one annual or other policy period. However, these policies are becoming less popular with insurers as they seek ways of raising their premium income to balance rising levels of insured losses. As defined here, guaranteed-cost commercial insurance is also *nonparticipating* insurance, that is, pays no dividend to insureds at the end of each policy period based on their collective loss experience or on other variables. In short, for guaranteed-cost insurance, the premium the insured pays at the beginning of each policy period is guaranteed to be the unchanging, final premium for coverage during that period.

The premium for guaranteed-cost commercial insurance is determined by the insurer's projection of the collective loss experience during the policy period for all insureds that are charged that premium. This premium is the manual premium that the insurer charges all insureds in that particular class. (The manual premium can be adjusted upward or downward for future periods based on the past collective experience of all insureds in each rating class.) Beyond expected aggregate losses, the manual premium also includes charges for the insurer's operating expenses and the projected underwriting profit. The manual premium also often reflects the insurer's estimate of the investment earnings it will generate by investing its premium income (less immediate operating expenses) from the time the premium is received until this money is needed for paying losses. The money thus invested constitutes the insurer's reserves, consisting principally of (1) loss reserves (funds held to pay expected, insured but as yet unpaid losses that have been incurred or will probably be incurred); and (2) unearned premium reserves (funds held to return to insureds the unexpired portion of the premium on any policy that may be canceled or to pay a reinsurer to assume the insurer's liabilities under any given insurance policy).

Participating Insurance. Some property/liability insurance contracts pay "dividends" to all the insureds in a given manual premium rating class based on the collective experience of that class during the policy period that has just ended. Each insured is said to "participate," with all other insureds in the class, in the aggregate underwriting results of the class. The lower the insured losses in each class, the lower the insurer's loss payments and other expenses attributable to that class will be. The higher the insurer's investment earnings on reserves allocated to that class, the greater the end-of-period "dividend" for each insured member of that class is likely to be. Participating insurance is said to give each insured some incentive to control losses and the other costs of providing insurance. Insurers issuing such participating policies usually wish to pay some dividend to all insureds regardless of the group's loss experience. Therefore, the initial premium charged these insureds is often higher than the premium for comparable "nonparticipating" coverage from which insureds expect no "dividends."

Participating coverage is not guaranteed-cost coverage because each insured's cost of insurance will vary depending on the amount of the "dividend" that insured receives. Neither is participating insurance individually experience-sensitive, however, because any one insured's loss experience is not likely to affect significantly the amount of the dividend each participating insured receives. The cost of participating insurance thus responds only to the aggregate experience of the class, and even then is experience-responsive only to the extent the insurer chooses to adjust the dividend paid to all insureds in the class.

Premium Payment Plans. Guaranteed-cost commercial insurance has two principal potential disadvantages for an insured. First, the insured loses some or all of the potential investment earnings on premium dollars during the interval between payment of the premium at the beginning of the policy period and the time—months or years later—that the insured's losses are paid. Second, because the premium is fixed for each policy period, no insured receives any special financial reward for favorable loss experience, that is, lower than average loss frequency or severity, during that policy period. In response to the first of these disadvantages, insurers have developed *premium payment plans* that do not require an insured to pay the entire premium at the beginning of the policy period.

In response to the second concern, that insureds are not "rewarded" for minimizing losses, insurers have developed—and continue to experiment with—a number of "loss-sensitive" rating plans that reduce insurance costs for individual insureds with better-than-average loss experience. The payment plans are a variation on guaranteed-cost commercial insurance and are treated in the following paragraphs. Loss-sensitive rating plans will be treated shortly as forms of "hybrid" risk financing that are neither entirely retention nor entirely transfer.

Premium payment plans involve modifications in the traditional method of premium payment that requires premiums to be paid at the beginning of the coverage period. Included in these types of plans are the deferred premium plan, lagged premium plan, and discounted premium plan.

Note on "Cash Flow" Plans. Considered as a group, cash flow plans and experience-sensitive plans *decrease* the expected present value of an insured's cash outflows for insurance (thereby *increasing* the expected present value of the insured's overall net cash flows if other factors remain unchanged). Experience-sensitive plans place upper limits on the insured's risk financing costs if its accidental losses happen to be frequent or severe, but also usually require payments of minimum premiums even if the insured has no losses. Under experience-sensitive plans, the (1) use of funds that otherwise would initially be paid out as insurance premiums, (2) reduced risk financing costs if loss experience is favorable, and (3) investment earnings on loss reserves are all characteristics of traditional forms of retention. The upper and lower limits on risk financing costs under these plans if loss experience is either extremely adverse or extremely favorable constitute the "insurance element" of these plans. Such an insurance element is a key characteristic of traditional forms of transfer for risk financing. Thus, experience-sensitive plans combine elements of retention and transfer, merging in practice the two conceptually distinct families of risk financing techniques.

As used in conversation, "cash flow plan" is an imprecise term applied in various contexts to many insurance-based risk financing plans, under some of which premiums are experience-sensitive and under others they are not. In its more exact sense used here, *cash flow plan* refers only to modifications in the traditional method of premium payment that requires premiums to be paid at the beginning of coverage periods. By deferring the cash payment of a portion or all of a premium through such a cash flow plan, an insured can use these deferred dollars until they must finally be paid as premiums.

The following paragraphs describe a variety of payment plans in the more precise, restrictive sense: plans that modify the schedule of the insured's premium payments.

Deferred Premium Plan. Deferred premium plans are an alternative to paying an entire annual (or any other periodic) premium at the beginning of a coverage period. They allow an insured to pay fractions of this premium each month or quarter, or at other specified intervals. Such a payment schedule gives the insured longer use of portions of the premium, thus decreasing the present value of premium outlays. In exchange for the right to defer premium payments, the insured must often pay the insurer interest on the unpaid portion of the premium or an additional processing fee for each separate partial premium payment. For premium deferral to increase the net present value of an insured's net cash flows, the after-tax interest rate on this "loan" from the insurer should be less than the after-tax rate of return the insured generates from using the unpaid portion of the premium in its own operations.

Lagged Premium Plan. Some types of insurance on exposures with fluctuating values (such as merchandise inventories or gross business receipts) require insureds periodically to report actual values and then to pay premiums based on these reported values. Premiums for such *reporting form coverages* are typically payable within thirty days from the end of the period for which values have been reported and coverage has been in effect. By extending the deadline for premium payments to sixty, ninety, or more days beyond the end of this coverage period, an insurer may grant an insured more time to use dollars that would have otherwise flowed to the insurer. In effect, lagged premium payments grant the insured an interest-free loan (as long as premium rates are not raised to compensate for the deferral of premium payments).

Discounted (Net Present Value) Premium Plan. Regardless of whether the premium for property and liability coverage is computed on a guaranteed-cost or any loss-sensitive basis, the premium normally anticipates that the insurer will establish reserves for unearned premiums and for losses and will benefit from investment earnings on funds in these reserves. Many insureds question whether an insurer is entitled to any or all of these investment earnings on funds that, in their view, the insurer has not yet "earned" by either paying losses or providing protection during loss-free periods.

In response to this attitude, some insurers project their expected earnings from these invested reserves and credit insureds with all or a portion of these investment earnings. Such credits reduce the policyholder's insurance costs by lowering the premium to the present value of what the premium would otherwise have been if it were discounted at the after-tax rate of interest the insurer anticipates on its invested reserves. A higher discount rate (and a greater portion of investment earnings that the insurer agrees to credit to the insured) means a lower discounted premium for the insured.

Noninsurance Contractual Transfer for Risk Financing. Under the general common law of contracts, the parties to any contract have substantial freedom to apportion among themselves exposures to potential loss by agreeing that one party will be responsible for particular activities and will, therefore, bear the costs of loss associated with those activities. This apportioning of *exposures* to loss that may occur is a *contractual transfer for risk control.*

In contrast, a *noninsurance contractual transfer for risk financing* is an agreement between the parties to a contract that stipulates that one party (not acting as an insurer) will indemnify another contracting party for specified types of *actual losses* growing out of their contract or will hold that party harmless from specified types of claims that may arise out of their contract. In such an arrangement, the party agreeing to indemnify or hold another harmless is the *transferee/indemnitor*, and the party protected by the contractual transfer is the *transferor/indemnitee.* Such a contractual transfer for risk financing is, in theory, comparable to a commercial insurance contract, except that the transferee/indemnitor is not acting as an insurance company. Noninsurance contractual transfers for risk financing generally fall into two categories: indemnity agreements and hold-harmless agreements.

Indemnity Agreements. In general, any party to a contract has the right by common law to agree to pay or indemnify the other party for any losses the latter may suffer in carrying out the terms of the contract. Thus, the range of transactions in which such noninsurance contractual transfers appear is extremely broad. However, the common law of contracts and the statutes of some jurisdictions limit a given party's right to agree to pay another's loss. Indemnity agreements are therefore classified in terms of both (1) the types of transactions in which they are likely to appear and (2) the extent to which they obligate the indemnitor/transferee who would otherwise be excused by common law.

Hold Harmless Agreements. Indemnity agreements may provide a transferor with funds for restoring any type of accidental loss to property, net income, liability claims, or the loss of the services of the transferor's key personnel. Indemnity agreements dealing only with the transferor's liability losses growing out of the activities under the contract between the transferor and transferee are often loosely called "hold harmless agreements." Under a hold harmless provision, the transferee agrees to hold the transferor harmless from specified classes of liability claims by providing the transferor with funds to pay (or by paying on the transferor's behalf) for legal defense, verdicts and settlements, court costs, and other expenses related to the types of claims encompassed by the agreement.

The fact that the transferee/indemnitor is not an insurer can be very important in practice. From the standpoint of the transferor/indemnitee, the financial protection afforded by a noninsurance contractual transfer is often less reliable than commercial insurance coverage because a commercial insurer typically has the following characteristics:

- It possesses greater financial resources, structured primarily for the purpose of indemnifying others for loss rather than for conducting some other business of the transferee.
- It needs to maintain a more impeccable reputation for leaving no properly transferred loss uncompensated.
- It devotes greater attention to the wording of contract provisions describing precisely the nature and extent of its duty to pay the transferor's losses.
- It adheres to more stringent regulations of contractual provisions and the procedures for paying losses when due.

In some very significant cases, however, a risk financing transfer to a noninsurer may be more reliable than commercial insurance. This is likely to be true in the following cases:

- Some unusual loss exposure or operating characteristic puts the transferor/indemnitee's risk financing needs outside the scope of typical insurance contracts.
- The transferee's degree of commitment to fulfilling all the terms of its general business contracts with the transferor motivates the transferee to provide full indemnity when a commercial insurer might question the indemnitee's rights to payment.

Hybrid Risk Financing Techniques

As depicted in Exhibit 2-1, retention techniques draw on an organization's internal funds to pay for losses, and the cost of these funds to the organization is highly experience-responsive. In contrast, transfer techniques draw on funds from sources outside the organization, and their cost to the organization is not experience-responsive. Hybrid risk financing techniques represent a cross between retention and transfer. Thus, as shown in the middle column of Exhibit 2-1, hybrid techniques draw on sources of funds that are both internal and external to an organization and whose costs are somewhat experience-responive.

Retrospectively Rated Insurance. Two loss-sensitive rating plans for determining insurance premiums are called retrospectively rated plans because the insured's premium for coverage during a particular period is based on the insured's loss experience during that *same* policy period. Subject to a maximum and a minimum premium, this final premium amount rises or falls directly with the insured's current loss experience. Losses can be limited so that only a portion of each loss, perhaps the first $100,000, is used to calculate the premium. One of these two types of retrospectively rated plans is based on an insured's losses *incurred* (paid plus reserved losses) during that period; the other is based on the insured's losses *paid* during the period. A retrospectively rated plan is a hybrid risk management plan because it combines elements of basic retention and basic transfer. To the extent that the premium is based on actual incurred losses, the source of funds is internal to the insured organization. To the extent that individual losses are limited when computing premiums and the entire premium is subject to a maximum amount, the source of funds is external to the organization.

Compensating Balances Plan. Many commercial banks require their business borrowers to leave on deposit specified minimum balances that pay no interest to depositors but on which the banks are able to earn interest. This effectively reduces the true amounts these businesses are able to borrow from their banks, increasing the borrowers' costs of loans. These balances are often known as *compensating balances,* indirect payments to banks for serving their commercial customers. For example, assume that Floors Incorporated is considering a loan from Central Bank for $1,000,000. Central Bank will charge 6 percent annual simple interest, or $60,000 a year, and require Floors Incorporated to maintain a 1 percent compensating balance. Floors Incorporated would thus be required to maintain a $10,000 noninterest-bearing account with Central Bank if the loan is approved. Floors Incorporated would then be paying $60,000 annual interest for the use of $990,000 (or $1,000,000 minus $10,000), which would be an effective annual interest rate of about 6.06 percent (or $60,000 divided by $990,000).

Some insurers offer insureds opportunities to "liberate" at least a portion of these mandatory compensating balances by using insurance premiums to offset some of the requirements established by the bank. These insurers agree that all or most of the premium an insured pays the insurer will be deposited by the insurer in the insured's bank and, by agreement with the bank, will be considered to be part of the insured's compensating balance. This allows the insured initially to reduce its actual compensating balance by the amount of the deposited insurance premium. Therefore, if Floors Incorporated were also about to purchase an insurance policy from Everyman's Insurance Company for an annual premium of $5,000, Central Bank and Everyman's Insurance might agree to let Floors Incorporated offset part of its compensating balance requirement with a portion of the premium. Such an agreement might have Everyman's Insurance deposit $4,000 of the $5,000 premium into a separate, non-interest bearing account at Central Bank. Central Bank would agree to consider this $4,000 part of Floors Incorporated's $10,000 compensating balance. Thus, Floors Incorporated would now have to deposit only $6,000 into its compensating balances account at Central Bank. Floors Incorporated would then be paying $60,000 annual interest for the use of $994,000 (or $1,000,000 minus $6,000), an effective interest rate of about 6.04 percent (or $60,000 divided by $994,000).

Any insured losses the policyholder later incurs are then paid out of the deposited premium, thus forcing the insured to replenish its compensating balance by the amount of the paid losses. In this example, Floors Incorporated would be responsible for replenishing its account with Central Bank if Everyman's Insurance used a portion of the deposited premium to cover a loss to Floors Incorporated. As long as insured losses paid by the insurer from this deposit do not exceed the premium first deposited in the insured's bank, the insured can use some of the funds that would have otherwise been paid as insurance premiums, much as if the organization had initially retained these losses. So if Floors Incorporated experienced no covered losses, it would enjoy full use of the $4,000 it did not have to deposit with Central Bank. If $2,000 is paid by Everyman's Insurance for a loss to Floors Incorporated, the insured would be required to deposit an additional $2,000 into its compensating balance account at Central Bank. The effect that this additional deposit would have on the interest rate Floors Incorporated paid for its loan from Central Bank would depend on when it had to replenish the $2,000 to its compensating balance account.

Compensating balance programs are similar to retrospectively rated plans and are therefore considered to be hybrid risk financing plans. The insurer subtracts from the premium amounts for administrative expenses, claims handling, loss prevention, state taxes, perhaps other expenses, and any excess losses that are transferred to the insurer. The remainder of the premium goes into the compensating balance and is used to pay retained losses.

High-Deductible Plans. Under a high-deductible plan, an insurer issues a policy and provides excess coverage and service. Within the deductible amount, the insurer agrees to pay losses and is reimbursed by the insured organization. A small loss fund may be used by the insured to pay losses within the deductible; however, the insured gains the benefit of cash flow on most of the loss reserves for retained losses within the deductible layer.

High-deductible plans are available in many lines of insurance, such as automobile and general liability. Recently, high-deductible plans have become popular with workers compensation coverage, although in the past states did not allow workers compensation deductibles.

Compared with retrospectively rated plans, high-deductible plans may provide savings in premium taxes and residual market loadings, which are both based on the amount of premium. The premium is much lower with a high-deductible plan than with a retrospectively rated plan: under the latter, the premium is based on retained as well as transferred losses; under the former, the premium is based only on transferred losses and the cost of services.

Multiple-Parent Captive and Pooling Arrangements. A risk financing affiliate jointly owned by several parents and a pool are two very closely related hybrid risk financing techniques. These group captives and pools involve more structured risk financing than the elementary forms of retention, yet both give an organization more control over its risk financing program than transfer through commercial insurance.

A wholly owned, or *single-parent,* captive is a form of risk *retention* for the one organization whose losses it finances. A *multiple-parent,* or group, captive provides *hybrid* risk financing for each of its parents. A single-parent captive provides no opportunities for transferring the financial burden of losses beyond the economic family of its single parent. A group captive does offer some opportunities for transfer beyond the economic family of each of the multiple owners of this captive, although these opportunities become limited when the several parents have other close financial interrelationships.

However, both single-parent and group captives may open avenues for drawing on some external sources of risk financing funds—may take on some characteristics of transfer—by purchasing excess insurance or reinsurance for losses beyond the captive's retention. Thus, by combining several conceptually distinct risk financing techniques with risk financing arrangements through an affiliated subsidiary, one or more parent organizations may intertwine retention and transfer of the financial burden of specified losses.

A captive organized to meet the risk financing needs of only the one organization that founded and fully owns it (its single parent) is also different from a pool. In a pool at least two organizations join to form a single entity through which they finance recovery from specified losses of all of the organizations involved. However, the distinction between a single-parent captive and a pool dissolves with a group captive, which has several parents. It is therefore difficult to define the point at which adding more parents to a captive creates a risk financing mechanism that managerially functions as a pool.

For income tax purposes, the distinction between a captive and a pool is crucial: both federal tax and state insurance regulators typically view a single-parent captive as a risk retention device, but frequently consider a pool as a risk transfer mechanism. If a risk financing arrangement is considered a retention device, then the following are true from a tax and regulatory perspective:

- Any transactions between a parent and a captive are not insurance; as a consequence to the captive, no insurance premium taxes are payable, and the indemnitor is not regulated as an insurer.
- Periodic or other payments that the parent makes to the captive are not tax deductible to the parent as business expenses for insurance premiums.

On the other hand, if a risk financing arrangement is considered a transfer device, then the following are true:

- The enterprise formed by the pool is usually considered insurance and must typically pay premium taxes and be subject to state insurance laws.
- Payments made by each participant to the enterprise are typically tax deductible to that participant as insurance premium expense.

Given these facts, the line between a wholly owned captive as a risk retention mechanism and a group captive or a pool as a risk transfer mechanism is significant in determining the after-tax cost of various risk financing alternatives and in assessing the degree of regulatory freedom available to those who finance loss exposures through the mechanism in question. Locating the side of this line on which each specific risk financing arrangement falls is made more difficult because of the growing popularity of multiple-parent captives, whose tax and regulatory status is uncertain in many jurisdictions. As explained further in Chapter 10, which discusses the accounting and tax aspects of risk financing, the tax law distinction between retention and transfer may oversimplify a complex reality that includes numerous risk financing hybrids.

FACTORS TO CONSIDER IN EVALUATING RISK FINANCING ALTERNATIVES

To finance recovery from any given loss, an organization typically draws upon several risk financing techniques, some involving retention, some involving transfer, and perhaps some combining retention with transfer. Some form of retention, planned or unplanned, is the most widely used technique—because every loss not covered by a risk transfer to an insurer or other transferee/indemnitor is retained. Some form of retention is thus by default the most popular risk financing technique.

Several risk financing techniques may be used to finance recovery from any given loss. For example, an organization may insure its warehouse for $5 million against only direct fire loss, subject to a $10,000 per-loss deductible. If no other insurance or other contractual transfers apply, this organization has consciously decided to retain up to $10,000 of direct damage from each fire. However, the organization may not be aware that it has also retained the exposures to loss of revenue from the sale of goods damaged in a warehouse fire, the costs of finding and renting a temporary warehouse, and the costs of rebuilding the warehouse to meet possibly stricter building code requirements enacted since the original warehouse was built. Furthermore, if the warehouse is worth *more* than $5 million, say, $7 million, the top $2 million of loss is retained—consciously or unconsciously—if the warehouse is completely destroyed. In addition, the organization has retained—again, knowingly or unknowingly—the full amount of any losses from perils other than fire.

Within the planned retention of recognized exposures, an organization faces some exposures it must retain and others it may choose to retain or transfer. Required or *mandatory retentions* typically include exposures for which insurance or other contractual transfer is unavailable (nuclear damage or war risks, for example) or for which the law prohibits insurance (such as criminal fines or punitive damages for particularly heinous torts). Some exposures—such as liability for professional misconduct or some intentional torts—may be insurable in theory but not in fact because insurance marketing conditions can make insurance unavailable or unaffordable. When an organization has no transfer options, retention is mandatory—no decisions are needed or possible (short of perhaps entirely avoiding the exposure). In the second category, the choice to retain or transfer exposures, an organization has various options. Some retention options are available, for example, to insure or retain property damage, net income, liability, and personnel losses to the organization. For other exposures, such as liability for damage to others' property in the organization's custody, at least three choices are available. The organization may choose (1) transfer through its own insurance, (2) noninsurance contractual transfer of the exposure to the owners of such property, or (3) some form of retention. In these and other cases of *optional retention,* the organization must choose whether to retain or transfer the exposure and, if retention is chosen, how much of the exposure to retain.

When a risk management professional speaks of choosing to retain an exposure or of managing a risk retention program, the reference is generally to optional retention. This does not mean, however, that the organization's mandatory retentions are irrelevant in light of its optional retentions. In fact, the extent of an organization's mandatory retentions—the maximum frequency or severity of the losses it potentially may be required to finance itself—limits the organization's ability to undertake optional retentions. The uncertainties and fluctuating net cash flows of an organization's normal business operations may also limit its ability to practice optional retention. Because every organization can retain only a limited number of exposures to accidental or business losses without endangering its solvency, large mandatory retentions reduce opportunities for optional retention.

For example, an organization that faces slight products liability or environmental liability hazards may choose to be a workers compensation self-insurer under the laws of several of the states in which it operates. However, if a major new product line poses products liability hazards that insurers refuse to accept, if this new product may prove unpopular in the market, or if the organization discovers a very large, uninsurable environmental pollution liability exposure (such as many previously undiscovered, underground storage tanks that once held toxic substances), the organization's total capacity for retaining exposures to accidental or business losses might be severely strained. Thus forced to retain products and environmental liability exposures it had previously considered insignificant, the organization might well decide to insure rather than retain its workers compensation exposures.

When an organization has the option of consciously deciding among various forms of retention, transfer, or hybrid techniques to finance recovery from an anticipated accidental loss, the factors that the organization's management should consider in evaluating the alternatives include the characteristics of the exposures to losses from which recovery is to be financed, the characteristics of the organization itself, and the characteristics of the markets in which the organization operates. These three sets of factors are charted in Exhibit 2-2 and discussed on the following pages.

Characteristics of Loss Exposures

Risk financing techniques should naturally be in place before the losses they are designed to pay occur. Therefore, with respect to the nature of losses, it is the characteristics of the loss *exposures*, the possibilities of loss—*not the actual losses* themselves—that a risk management professional must consider. These characteristics include loss frequency, loss severity, and the loss estimation patterns these exposures are likely to generate. The characteristics of the exposures provide the best estimates of the characteristics of the actual losses that will need to be paid.

Loss Frequency/Severity. Exposures with high loss frequency and low loss severity are typically deemed the most attractive for retention. A high frequency of losses (not just a large number of exposure units that may produce only a few losses) results in better predictability of loss experience. Low severity means that there is little chance that any

Exhibit 2-2
Factors for Evaluating Risk Financing Alternatives

Characteristics of Loss Exposures	Characteristics of Organizations	Characteristics of Markets
Loss frequency	Financial condition	Insurance markets
Loss severity	Attitudes of management	Product markets
Loss and claim estimation patterns:	Administrative ability in risk financing	Financial markets
Reporting	Ability to adapt to change	
Development		
Payout		
Closure		
Reserving and earnings		

catastrophic losses will be beyond the organization's financial capacity to pay. These types of exposures belong in cell 3 of Exhibit 2-3. Because of the high frequency of such claims, losses from these exposures are often anticipated and funded in advance, although some organizations choose to pay such losses from current revenues or assets as they occur.

Exposures generating high severity losses with a low frequency of occurrence are the least desirable to retain. Insurance is best suited for financing the often catastrophic losses from high-severity, low-frequency exposures, which belong in cell 2 of Exhibit 2-3. Organizations with high-severity and high-frequency losses (cell 1) are, from a practical standpoint, nonexistent—they could not stay in business with such losses. Low-severity losses with a low frequency of occurrence (cell 4) are not generally significant concerns. These small, infrequent losses are generally retained and financed with current assets.

Loss Estimation Patterns. The occurrence of an accident that causes a loss does not generate an immediate need for a cash outflow to pay for that loss, whether transferred or retained. Several crucial types of events almost always occur between the accident and the payments that finance recovery from that loss. The typical patterns of these events—particularly the timing and regularity with which they occur—significantly influence an organization's ability to predict the numbers and amounts of payments needed to budget or to pay for specific types

Exhibit 2-3
Impact of Frequency and Severity on Risk Retention Decision

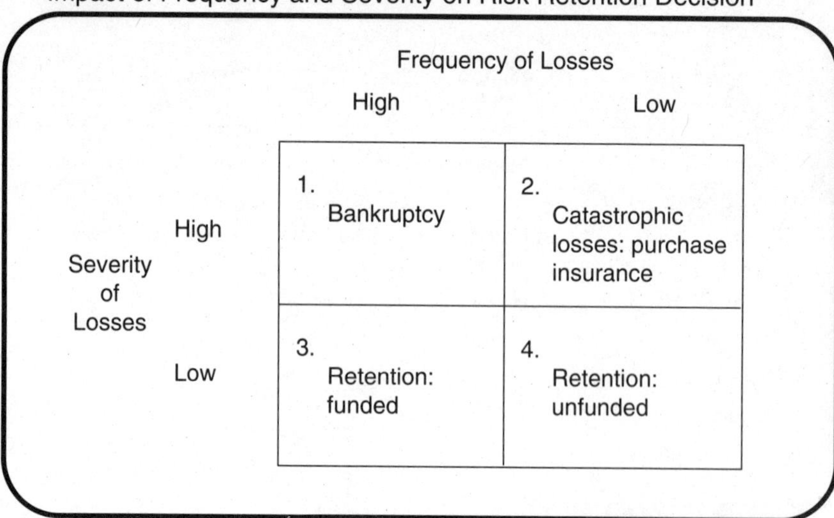

of losses. Hence, the organization's choice of what is, for it, the most promising risk financing technique for these losses also depends on these patterns.

Frequency of Losses
High
Low
Severity of Losses
High
Low
1. Bankruptcy
2. Catastrophic losses: purchase insurance
3. Retention: funded
4. Retention: unfunded

Any specified loss exposure or group of loss exposures may or may not generate any actual accidents during a particular period, such as a month or year. The number of any such accidents and the size of the resulting financial losses depend on the loss frequency and loss severity distributions associated with these particular loss exposures. Assuming a particular set of accidents occurring in a given time period generates a given number of specific instances of physical damage, bodily injury, or loss of income or of key personnel to an organization or for which that organization is legally responsible, the ultimate dollar cost of financing recovery from the resulting losses is determined by five types of patterns. These patterns are especially important in forecasting the timing and amounts of payments that will need to be made for any particular type of accidental losses arising out of a given set of loss exposures. These five types of patterns are as follows:

1. Loss reporting patterns
2. Loss development patterns
3. Claim payout patterns
4. Claim closure patterns
5. Reserving and investment earnings patterns

The first two patterns involve *losses*, the second two apply to *claims*, and the fifth takes account of *earnings on reserves* set aside to meet these claims—earnings that may partially offset the claims. In this context, a *loss* is the financial consequence of an accident, a measure of indemnity expressed as the dollars of compensation that would be needed to pay for full recovery from that loss. In contrast, a *claim* is a demand for compensation for the financial consequences of a given accident—a demand that may be made either (1) for transferred losses against some transferee (such as an insurer, a wrongdoer, or an indemnitor under a noninsurance contractual transfer for risk financing) or (2) for retained losses against the organization itself or some member of its economic family. Any funded reserves established by an insurer, another indemnitor, or an organization retaining its own losses, whether for reported or for anticipated unreported or future losses, should generate some investment earnings. The earnings on these reserves can be used to lower the cash outlays that would otherwise be required to pay for any given loss.

For any given accident, the related claim(s) may be more or less than, or may equal, the resulting loss(es). The claim is larger if it includes compensation for noneconomic losses, such as for "pain and suffering" in a liability claim, or if the claim includes punitive or exemplary damages intended to deter the wrongful conduct that brought about the accident and resulting loss. Even if the amount of compensation an organization pays to claimants or itself receives for a loss exactly equals the loss (the insurance ideal of precise indemnity), the true amount of the claim is typically larger than the claimant's or the organization's actual loss. This is because the costs of settling the claim, known as *loss adjustment expenses* and including expenses for investigating the loss and documenting the claim (especially a disputed claim), must be paid as part of the claim even though these costs are not included in the loss itself.

The claim may also be less than the loss if, for example, an organization decides not to fully restore damage to its own property (the claim being less than the loss by the reduction in the value of the unrestored property), or if the applicable insurance or compensation available from any other indemnitor falls short of the amount of the loss. For claims that reach litigation or settlement negotiations, the amount the claimant receives may be the result of a compromise, and may be well below the claimant's actual economic losses. However, the loss adjustment expenses for disputed claims (especially legal expenses) often swell the claim to much more than the claimant's loss.

An organization must be prepared to pay the amounts of claims (plus loss adjustment expenses), not the amounts of actual losses, through retention, transfer, or some hybrid risk financing, to finance recovery from its own and others' accidental losses. Claims need not equal losses, but losses are the major determinant of claims. Since some claims (such as to replace merchandise stolen from a jewelry store) are usually paid in a single lump sum, and other claims (wage replacement payments, for example) must be paid in a long series of installments, the risk financing requirements of each claim should be separately analyzed in terms of each of the five loss estimation patterns. These patterns are listed above and briefly described in the following paragraphs, which focus on concerns relevant to whether a given organization should retain or transfer the financial burden of these losses. Although no one pattern is decisive, these patterns collectively are very important to the retention/transfer decision.

Loss Reporting Patterns. The mere occurrence of an accident has little risk financing significance until that accident and some indication of the resulting losses are reported to an appropriate risk financing manager of the organization suffering the losses. For many accidents and losses (like building fires, and most automobile accidents and armed robberies), such reporting is virtually immediate, both to the organization involved and to any insurer or other transferee/indemnitor that may be obligated to pay for the losses. In other cases, very significant time intervals may elapse between the occurrence of an accident and the organization's (1) learning that an accident has occurred, (2) realizing that the accident has caused some meaningful losses, and (3) reporting to an insurer or other transferee/indemnitor that either an accident or a loss has taken place.

These intervals are the subject of loss reporting patterns, which indicate—for a given type of loss, such as fire damage, automobile collisions, or products liability claims—the percentage of either the number or of the ultimate value of all the losses that have been reported to an organization's management (for a retained loss) or to its insurer (or other indemnitor, for a transferred loss) at various time intervals after the accident that caused the loss have occurred. Knowing these patterns helps an insurer or other organization make projections based on the numbers and amounts of loss reported as of a given date to estimate the number and the ultimate values of its actual losses, to date.

For example, assume that an organization's or an insurer's records indicate that, for automobile bodily injury claims, 75 percent of the number of all claims are reported within six months of their occurrence, and 95 percent are reported within twelve months. Further assume that the aggregate value of the claims reported after six months has proven to average 65 percent of the ultimate aggregate value of all claims, and—after twelve months—87 percent of the ultimate aggregate value.

Thus, if a large moving and storage company's risk management department had received reports, by September 30 of one year, of nineteen such automobile bodily injury liability claims, having an estimated aggregate settlement value of $1,200,000, and growing out of its activities in March of that year (activities six months earlier), then this loss reporting pattern would suggest that the company would actually incur a larger number of losses, determined by the following equation:

$$\frac{19 \text{ (reported claims)}}{0.75 \text{ (percentage of claims reported after 6 months)}}$$
$$= 25 \text{ (number of estimated claims, to the nearest whole number)}$$

The ultimate aggregate settlement value of the March claims can be calculated as follows:

$$\frac{\$1{,}200{,}000 \text{ (estimated aggregate settlement value)}}{0.65 \text{ (aggregate value of claims reported after 6 months)}}$$
$$= \$1{,}846{,}153.85 \text{ (estimated ultimate aggregate settlement)}$$

The estimated ultimate aggregate settlement value is then rounded to the nearest $10,000, or $1,850,000.

If, after twelve months, the company had received reports of only twenty-one March claims, then valued at $1,750,000, its revised estimates of the actual number of claims incurred from the previous March would be determined as follows:

$$\frac{21 \text{ (reported claims)}}{0.95 \text{ (\% of claims reported after 12 months)}}$$
$$= 22.11 \text{ (number of estimated claims, rounded to 22)}$$

The estimated ultimate aggregate value of the claims reported after twelve months is calculated as follows:

$$\frac{\$1{,}750{,}000 \text{ (value of reported claims)}}{0.87 \text{ (\% of ultimate aggregate value reported after 12 months)}}$$
$$= \$2{,}011{,}494.25 \text{ (estimated aggregate value)}$$

The estimated aggregate value is then rounded to the nearest $10,000, to arrive at a figure of $2,010,000.

This illustrative loss reporting pattern is highly simplified in at least three ways. First, it is very condensed, involving only two estimates of the actual number and ultimate value of incurred reported and unreported losses, at six and twelve months, after which few losses remain unreported. Second, the two estimates of unreported losses are reasonably consistent, both in the number and the ultimate value of losses. Third, a very high percentage of the losses can be quite accurately evaluated within a year. If it remains stable for several years, this particular pattern makes losses predictable, and in the aggregate budgetable, on the basis of information reported within six months of the accidents that generate the losses. Such a pattern, if stable, is well suited to this organization's retention, instead of transfer, of the costs of these losses.

A loss reporting pattern for which any of these three features were reversed would tend to make unreported losses more significant or more difficult to forecast, thus reducing the feasibility of retention. If a substantial portion (either in number or value) of the losses that occur in a given time period remains unreported for several years, there is much uncertainty about the losses that were actually incurred in that period—uncertainty that may make an organization's management reluctant to retain this distant, indefinite obligation that may arise ten or fifteen years hence, when the organization's fortunes or leadership (and therefore ability or willingness to retain losses) may have changed dramatically. Moreover, if there is no well-defined, stable loss reporting pattern, so that the few available statistics suggest widely differing estimates of unreported losses, an organization's management has little reliable information for making a prudent retention decision. Under any of these conditions that enhance the significance or unpredictability of unreported losses, greater reliance on transfer to an insurer or other indemnitor tends to become an increasingly attractive risk financing option.

Loss Development Patterns. Loss development (sometimes called "case development" or "claim development") patterns deal with predictable ways the size, or severity, of a particular type of loss tends to change— almost always to increase, rarely to decrease—over time until the claim has been paid (or the case or claim has been settled).

Losses and the related claims for compensation from a given accident tend to increase for a variety of reasons. These include the tendency of (1) damaged property to deteriorate further unless it is promptly repaired or replaced; (2) an injured person's health to decline without timely medical attention; (3) a liability claimant's attitude to become more hostile if the settlement of a legal claim seems poorly handled or unduly delayed; (4) a net income loss to increase at an increasing rate as the projected date for returning to normalcy is postponed; (5) the loss adjustment expenses for either a retained or a transferred loss to increase with the time needed to reach final settlement, especially if legal disputes arise; and (6) inflation to raise the current dollar cost of financing recovery from loss. Therefore, as will be illustrated in Chapter 9, the frequent joint effect of these and other factors is to raise the ultimate value of a claim by a significant number of percentage points a year, with the percentages differing depending on the type of claim, the time that has elapsed since the accident that has caused the loss, and changing economic conditions.

Because losses tend to increase with time, retention is usually less attractive, and transfer is more attractive, than if losses did not change (or even decreased) between the accident and payment of final indemnity. Loss development patterns, like loss reporting patterns, create uncertainty that many organizations' management is often eager to transfer to an insurer. This is particularly true if the information available to an organization for a relevant loss development pattern is fragmentary or points to no stable loss development pattern on which the organization's management feels it can comfortably rely.

In some situations, however, loss development considerations may favor retention over transfer. Organizations whose management believes that it, or some third-party claims administrator, has specialized expertise, negotiating skills, or other abilities that enables it to control loss development factors more rigorously than can an insurer or another transferee/indemnitor may choose to retain those types of losses for which special abilities can be most advantageously applied. Other organizations may be in the unusual position of having excess cash whose best use is as very profitably invested reserves for the organization's own incurred or anticipated future losses. If these losses and their development patterns can be reliably forecast, such an organization can find retention less costly than transfer.

Claim Payout Patterns. Claim payout patterns, like claim closure patterns (discussed below), deal with patterns of payments for losses rather than with the losses themselves. In this context, claims are paid for both transferred and retained losses. (For retained losses, the organization suffering the loss can best be considered to be paying itself when it uses its own funds to finance recovery from the loss.) If, however, an organization decides not to attempt to seek recovery from a loss—that is, chooses simply to accept the loss and not try to regain its pre-accident position—then no claim payout occurs. In all other cases, some claim payout pattern becomes relevant to the decision whether to retain or to transfer the financial burden of potential losses.

Claim payout patterns describe the arrangement, in time and by relative size, of the payment(s) made to finance recovery from specified types of losses, whether financed through retention or transfer. Each pattern begins with the first payment for a given loss, regardless of when the accident producing the loss occurred or was first reported to the organization or the transferee for financing recovery from it. When a loss is paid as a single payment, the payout "pattern" is simply a single point representing the one payment made at some specified time after the accident that caused the loss occurred. However, when a loss is paid through a series of payments, they fall into one, or a combination, of three basic patterns:

- *Short:* In a short payout pattern, losses are paid relatively quickly after they have been reported. Property, net income, and many life and health losses are likely to produce such payout patterns. (Liability losses, in contrast, are characterized by lengthy payout patterns.) Losses associated with short payout patterns are generally easy to value, and they result in relatively quick settlements with no future payments.

- *Annuity:* In an annuity payout pattern, periodic payments are made for a specified number of years or for the life of a claimant or other individual. Although this pattern is normally similar to a long payout pattern because the payments are made over a number of years, claims involving annuities have a defined end. Annuities are commonly used in workers compensation and other bodily injury cases. The use of *structured settlements* in liability claims also results in more annuity payouts.
- *Long:* A long payout pattern extends over a number of years and often results from accidents that generate claims for payments to many claimants. Therefore, unlike an annuity payment pattern, a long payment pattern is not limited by the life of any individual or clearly identifiable small group of single claimants. Events that cause injury to widespread groups of claimants who, for example, are injured by a defective model of a particular product or by environmental pollution give rise to long payment patterns. This payment structure often amalgamates compensation for bodily injury, property damage, loss of income, and perhaps less tangible harm.

In practice, a payout pattern can combine any of the elements from these basic patterns. In addition, because these patterns apply only after payments for losses growing out of an accident have begun, they may be preceded by a lengthy interval between the occurrence, the report of a loss, and the negotiation of a claim. For example, a medical malpractice claim could first be reported ten years after the event occurred and could be resolved with a structured settlement that includes an annuity for the life of the claimant.

The payout pattern associated with a specific exposure influences the desirability of retaining that exposure. There are, however, two distinct views regarding the attractiveness of long and short payout patterns. One potential benefit of retaining exposures with long payout patterns is the interest and other income that can be made on the money that is held by the organization to make future payments on presently incurred reported and/or unreported claims. For example, if an event in 19X0 results in a liability of $1 million that is paid over a period extending from 19X2 to 19X9, the present value of the liability in 19X0 is significantly less than $1 million because of the time value of money.

There are also disadvantages to long payout patterns. First, the ultimate value of a liability claim will normally increase the longer it remains outstanding, or "open." An event reported in 19X0 that may be worth only $1 million then could grow to several million dollars by 19X9 because of (1) economic and legal inflation and (2) aggravation of the harm that first gave rise to the claim. Second, loss exposures with long payout patterns are characterized by much more uncertainty in terms of frequency and severity than are those with short payout patterns. Organizations retaining exposures are not usually comfortable with a high degree of uncertainty regarding future payments for known or unknown losses.

As a result, exposures with short payout patterns are generally viewed as more desirable candidates for retention. However, the uncertainties involved in long payout patterns should not discourage retention. If an organization keeps good records of its losses and has a sufficiently large exposure base or can obtain credible loss data elsewhere, loss frequency and severity and payout patterns can be forecast with considerable certainty.

Claim Closure Patterns. The claim closure pattern for any particular type of loss indicates the time required, after losses have been reported, to close claims for that type of loss, either by making the last payment needed to finance recovery from the loss or by determining that no payment is required (because, for example, an organization is not legally responsible for the loss in question). In general, claims with typically short payout patterns are closed more quickly than those with long or annuity payout patterns. Notice that the claim closure pattern for a given type of loss is normally longer than the payout pattern because the closure pattern includes investigative and negotiation activities that usually take place before any loss payments begin. Also, small claims and those that involve no disputes are closed much more quickly than larger, disputed claims, particularly those involving bodily injuries calling for medical or income replacement payments over extended periods.

Claim closure patterns usually take account of both the number and the value of the claims closed. For example, for automobile bodily injury liability claims, 55 percent of the ultimate number of claims arising from accidents that occur in a given year, accounting for about 25 percent of the aggregate ultimate value of such claims, will have been closed within twelve months after the occurrence of the accidents generating them. After sixty months, 95 percent of the number of claims, accounting for 70 percent of the aggregate ultimate value of all claims arising five years ago, have typically been closed.

In contrast, for retained claims for damage to an organization's own property, 98 percent of the number of all claims (accounting for nearly

90 percent of the value of all such claims) may be reported to the organization's management within three months of their occurrence. The 2 percent of the number of claims still open are probably for losses not yet reported, and the 10 percent of the ultimate value of the claims is likely to consist mainly of payments still to be made to contractors and suppliers on longer-term construction or repair contracts.

The closure pattern for claims from a given type of loss may have several risk financing implications. An extended closure pattern, like a long payout pattern, may favor retention over transfer by allowing an organization considerable time to mobilize internal funds to pay the claim, particularly if it is payable in installments. Meanwhile, similar to long payout patterns, the organization may make productive internal use of the undisbursed portion of these funds. On the other hand, a long closure pattern coupled with a claim development pattern that indicates rapid growth of the claim over time suggests the need to close the claim promptly. In such cases, an insurer may be better positioned than an insured organization to manage and pay the claim. As with other patterns, the clarity, detail, and stability of claim closure patterns greatly enhances their value to an organization's management in making sound retention/transfer risk financing decisions. In contrast, vague, shifting patterns provide little reliable information to management.

Reserving and Investment Earnings Patterns. The four loss estimation patterns just described—focusing on loss reporting, loss development, claim payouts, and claim closure, together with loss frequency and severity patterns—collectively determine the present value of the payments, along with payments for loss adjustment expenses, that need to be made to finance recovery from losses generated during a specified time period by a given set of loss exposures. The amount of funds that needs to be made available, through retention or transfer, to pay these claims depends in part on a fifth set of patterns dealing with reserving and investment earnings.

To the extent that a claim for a loss that an organization has incurred is covered by that organization's commercial insurance, the insurer is legally required to establish loss reserves equal to the insurer's estimate of the present value of the future payments (plus future loss adjustment expenses) for that claim. The higher the rate of return that can be earned on funds set aside as a reserve for paying a given loss at some set time in the future (either as a single indemnity payment or in a series of payments), the lower the present amount of the reserve needs to be—that is, the greater the portion of the loss that can eventually be paid with future investment earnings. For example, suppose an insurer expects to pay a $10,000 claim at the end of five years. If the rate of return earned on loss reserves is 7 percent per year for the next five years, the insurer must reserve $7,130 now, leaving $2,970 to be earned as interest on this reserve. If, however, the rate of return is 12 percent annually, the insurer needs to reserve only $5,674 today in order for the remaining $4,326 to accrue as interest. The present value of a single payment of $10,000 to be made five years from now, discounted at 12 percent, is $5,674. Conversely, as an insurer's present loss reserve relative to the future value of payments for a given claim increases, the rate of investment earnings the insurer must generate to assure payment of that claim decreases. Thus, if this same insurer, still facing a $10,000 claim at the end of five years, has already reserved $8,500, the rate of return that must be earned to generate the remaining $1,500 over the next five years is 3.3 percent annually. On the other hand, if this insurer has reserved only $4,000 to date, the rate of return required to generate the remaining $6,000 is 20.11 percent; $4,000 invested for five years at a 20.11 percent annual rate of return earns $6,000.

For insured losses, the insurer may exercise considerable discretion in setting the amounts of loss reserves, using any of several individual-case or aggregate valuation formulas that the National Association of Insurance Commissioners has approved for valuing loss reserves. For an insured, the insurer's loss reserving procedures may provide several offsetting advantages and disadvantages. If the insurer follows conservative reserving policies (resulting in ample reserves), the insured can be confident of the insurer's financial strength and reliability in paying these claims; however, ample reserving tends to increase the premiums the insured must pay for coverage because the insurer must channel more premium dollars into reserves than if reserving were less adequate. Conversely, establishing less adequate present reserves (perhaps on the assumption of high future rates of investment return on smaller present reserves) allows an insurer to charge lower premium rates but increases the probability that the insurer will become insolvent, unable to pay insureds' claims.

An organization paying its own losses through some form of retention faces many of the same conflicting concerns. Using its own or borrowed funds to establish ample reserves tends to assure payment of claims but diverts cash from the organization's regular, presumably more productive, internal operations into relatively lower-earning financial investments. Funding less adequate reserves, however, reduces the portion of any claim that can be financed through investment earnings and increases uncertainty about the organization's being able to pay retained claims without great financial strain when they fall due. These and other aspects of paying losses through funded reserves will be explored further in Chapter 3.

Characteristics of Organizations

The characteristics of an organization that significantly influence its decisions whether to retain or transfer the financial burden of loss exposures can be grouped into four categories: (1) financial condition, (2) the attitudes of management, (3) the administrative ability of the organization with respect to risk financing, and (4) ability to adjust the retention/transfer balance as conditions change.

Financial Condition. An organization's ability to retain losses increases as the levels and stability of the following increase:

- Net worth
- Monthly and annual net cash flows
- Available credit
- Earnings
- Investment opportunities
- Asset liquidity (the speed and certainty with which assets other than cash can be converted to a predetermined amount of cash at any time, even under the most adverse circumstances)

Each of these sources can generate funds to finance recovery from accidental losses. An increase in any of them, therefore, puts an organization in a better position to choose additional optional retentions.

There are no generally accepted risk management guidelines for optimal levels of these financial variables that apply to all organizations and give ready and reliable rules of thumb for combined levels of mandatory and optional retentions. Some financial conditions do, however, make an organization more able to undertake substantial retentions. For example, if an organization is strong in terms of its net worth in the context of its industry—for instance, if a particular industry's average ratio of net worth to total liabilities is 0.90—an organization with a ratio of 1.40 is probably in a good position to consider increasing its retentions.

The letter of credit capacity of an organization is also important in the decision to employ a risk financing technique. Many techniques, such as a retrospectively rated plan where payment is made to the insurer based on paid losses, require that a letter of credit be executed in the insurer's favor so as to secure future estimated loss payments. When an organization has limited credit capacity, it may also have limited feasible risk financing techniques.[2]

Reliable net cash flow is extremely important to an organization that attempts to pay for accidental losses out of ordinary operations. An organization with an irregular cash flow, often caused by large seasonal concentrations of cash receipts and cash shortages, cannot rely on its current income to finance recovery from losses because they might call for payments during low-cash periods. An organization with this type of cash flow should set up a reserve funded with liquid assets. Such an organization might also establish a line of credit to handle losses during low-cash periods. When considering this alternative, an organization should take care not to assume unwisely that credit will always be available when needed. If an organization waits until a loss occurs before obtaining credit, it could be refused or required to pay a particularly high interest rate.

In planning for retained losses that may need to be paid during low-cash periods, a risk management professional should recall that there may be a substantial amount of time between the occurrence of a loss, determination or negotiation of the amount of that loss, and the actual disbursement of cash to finance restoration. It is at the time when losses are restored, not necessarily when they occur, that cash is needed.

An organization with wide swings in its earnings pattern should probably avoid substantial retentions unless those swings are a normal, predictable part of a business cycle. In an industry with such "stable" earnings cycles, funded reserves or credit could be arranged to facilitate retention of accidental losses that become payable in low-earnings periods. The senior management of many organizations often sets a working limit of "X cents" per share on the amount of uninsured accidental losses they are willing to accept and report to stockholders and to the financial community. These executives often voice their concerns in statements like "we cannot have uninsured losses of more than X dollars this fiscal year. Otherwise, our earnings per share and the price of our stock will drop so far that our stockholders will be hurt." In a cyclical industry, "X cents" may be larger during business upswings than during downswings.

An organization that retains losses should attempt to earn the highest return possible on the cash that will eventually be needed for claim payments. Some organizations invest such cash in the ongoing operations of the organization. Although this strategy can produce the greatest return on total invested capital, it can also create difficulties with liquidity since assets such as equipment cannot usually be readily sold or mortgaged to pay claims. Assets held to pay claims should ideally be kept in very liquid forms, but this degree of liquidity requires that high earnings on these funds be sacrificed. To offset the low earnings generated by highly liquid investments, the balance of the organization's commitments to financial assets should earn an above-average rate of return.

Attitudes of Management. One of the fundamental objectives of all risk management is to reduce the adverse effects of uncertainty on an organization and its managers so that they are no longer deterred from participating in activities that are beneficial but carry some degree of risk. Managers and especially senior executives must feel reasonably confident that their decisions are correct and that their actions will not, because of unforeseen accidental losses, jeopardize the organization's efficiency or survival. As one noted authority has observed, sound risk management allows executives to enjoy "a quiet night's sleep."[3]

Some executives "sleep" more soundly, endure more stress, and tolerate more uncertainty than do others. Increasing an organization's retentions increases the variability in its cash outflows for retained losses, thus creating more uncertainty about future net cash flows. Projections of future net cash flows become more uncertain because of possible retained accidental losses. For any given level of retention and resulting variability in future net cash flows, some managers will feel more uncertain than others. Therefore, to avoid the paralyzing effects that loss-related uncertainty may have on senior management, an organization's aggregate levels of retention are determined in part by management's tolerance. Furthermore, lower echelon executives are also entitled to be reasonably free from uncertainty, so their tolerance levels should also be considered in determining department retentions.

Tailoring an organization's department and overall retentions to executives' tolerance of uncertainty may either mean changing retention levels or "adjusting" managers' tolerance. If a given set of deductibles or SIRs increases an organization's financial efficiency by reducing its cost of risk in an accounting sense, but the organization's managers feel uncomfortable with such high retentions, one solution may be to educate these managers more fully in the organization's exposures and loss history so that they feel less uncertain. Such a strategy may help the organization to lower its cost of risk and more fully attune its management to the importance and benefits of sound risk financing.

Administrative Ability in Risk Financing. Organizations that begin a new or substantially increased retention program may overlook the many potential difficulties of paying for losses with their own funds. These difficulties range from inaccurately recognizing and valuing losses, through poorly negotiating the settlement of claims, to failing to establish the proper reserves for a wide range of losses. In addition, various filings are usually required by state authorities. Dealing with these obstacles requires considerable expertise. Many organizations do not have and cannot readily hire employees or outside experts with such talents. In such circumstances, switching from insurance to retention is likely to deprive an organization of the insurer's claims administration expertise it once enjoyed but perhaps did not fully appreciate. Without effective administration, any unexpectedly severe or numerous claims may mean eventual failure for any retention program.

Ability To Adapt to Change. Maintaining opportunities to return to insurance is one example of the more general ability to adapt a risk financing program to change. Adaptability is essential because choosing the best risk financing techniques at any time depends on a complex set of factors. These include changes in the organization's loss exposures, in the characteristics of the organization, and in the relative cost and availability of alternative risk financing techniques. Furthermore, a change in an organization's risk financing choices may be only one of many changes the organization wishes to make at a particular time so that it can, for example, introduce a new product, acquire or merge with another organization, or enter international markets for the products it sells or the raw materials it buys.

It is therefore crucial that an organization's choice of optional retentions does not preclude other adaptive changes in its financial and operating profile. For example, an overcommitment to retention, particularly through funded reserving, may consume such a large portion of an organization's financial resources that it cannot finance new activities or acquisitions that would benefit the organization. Furthermore, excessive unfunded retentions, such as exposures to products or pollution liability or to unfunded prior-service pension benefits for retiring employees, may make an organization unattractive as a merger or acquisition candidate. In essence, commitments to risk retention should not be so slight or so extensive that the organization is financially unbalanced and inflexible.

Characteristics of Markets

An organization's choices of risk financing techniques may change from time to time with changing conditions in the markets for insurance and other risk financing techniques, in the markets where the organization sells and buys its products, services, raw materials, or other productive factors, and in the financial markets through which the organization obtained capital.

Insurance Markets. Property-liability insurance premium rates normally move in cycles. When rates fall as insurers compete for new insureds and added coverages, insurance becomes a more attractive risk financing technique for most organizations. Retention thus becomes correspondingly less cost effective. In these times most organizations tend to reduce their optional retentions. Conversely, when premium rates rise in the opposite phase of an underwriting cycle, organizations tend to increase optional retentions. Despite insurance executives' repeated assertions that "this cycle has been the worst yet—this will never happen again," the same patterns in underwriting cycles have persisted for several hundred years. Therefore, they should be expected, and risk management professionals should be ready to respond to them by adjusting the organization's retention/transfer risk financing mix accordingly.

Residual market loadings on premium and premium taxes may also have an effect on the retention/transfer decision. If an organization can retain risk and lower a premium payment, such as with a high-deductible plan, then it can probably achieve a saving in residual market loadings and premium taxes. This cost saving makes the retention of losses more attractive.

There is, however, the problem of overadjusting or underadjusting the retention/transfer mix. Insurers and their marketing intermediaries are equally aware of underwriting and premium rate cycles. Hence, these insurers and their representatives are likely to be skeptical about the insurance requests of an organization whose insurance/retention decisions simply mirror underwriting cycles. To maintain good working relationships with insurers and their underwriters, a risk management professional should strive to maintain coverages on a reasonably consistent basis throughout an underwriting cycle—to remain with its organization's insurers through good times and bad just as an insured organization expects its insurers to remain with it through periods of favorable and unfavorable loss experience.

Product and Productive Factors Markets. A sound risk financing program can be important to an organization in maintaining a favorable image in the markets in which it sells its products and in the capital markets in which it raises funds. A clearly improper or unbalanced risk financing program can, in at least some circumstances, cause consumers or other buyers to shun an organization's products or services. Thus, consumers may be reluctant to purchase the goods of a manufacturer that has been nearly bankrupted by an adverse, highly publicized products liability verdict. The public may also lose faith in an organization that the press has reported to be unable or reluctant to meet such commitments as pension obligations under a self-insured employee benefits program.

Financial Markets. Similarly, financial analysts and securities dealers in the stock and bond markets may recommend that their clients avoid investing in an organization whose risk financing program appears to be overbalanced in the sense that it (1) too heavily relies on insurance, thus raising its overall cost of risk beyond the industry norm or (2) too heavily relies on retention, which, if loss experience were adverse, could jeopardize the organization's survival and thus the investors' capital.

The basic, but not always apparent, guideline that can be inferred from these negative responses to extremes in risk financing is to avoid them by steering a middle course between retention and transfer. The difficulty with this guideline is that an organization's risk management professional cannot be sure when, or if, individuals in product or capital markets will ever judge an organization's risk financing program to be balanced. To further complicate the situation, confidence once lost can be difficult to regain, even with the most prudent risk financing program.

SUMMARY

This chapter describes the alternative risk financing techniques upon which an organization may rely and the factors it should consider in choosing among those techniques where, in fact, it has a choice. Exhibit 2-1 gives a listing of these risk financing alternatives, and Exhibit 2-2 outlines the factors that should be considered in choosing among them. Hence, these two exhibits effectively summarize this chapter.

More specifically, Exhibit 2-1 indicates that every risk financing technique that any organization may use as a source of funds to finance recovery from any type of loss belongs in one of three categories: retention, transfer, or a hybrid combination of retention and transfer. Retention techniques, which involve calling on sources of funds that are within the organization or its economic family and impose costs that are highly responsive to the organization's specific loss experience, include current expensing of losses, unfunded loss reserves, funded loss reserves, using borrowed funds, and paying losses through a wholly owned captive. Transfer techniques, which draw on sources of funds that are external to the organization suffering the loss and generate risk financing costs that are not responsive to the organization's particular current loss experience, encompass guaranteed-cost insurance, participating (dividend-paying) insurance, premium payment plans that modify an insured's premium-payment schedule without being responsive to any insured's specific loss experience (such as deferred premium plans, lagged premium plans, and discounted premium plans), and noninsurance contractual transfers for risk financing.

Hybrid risk financing techniques combine characteristics of retention and transfer. They include retrospectively rated insurance, compensating balances plans, high-deductible plans, and multiple-parent captives and pools. The specific risk financing techniques shown in Exhibit 2-1, although widely used now, may change with innovations in risk financing products.

The factors shown in Exhibit 2-2 that an organization's management should consider in deciding which losses, or portions of losses, to finance through retention and which losses to finance through transfer relate to the characteristics of the exposures that generate the losses, the characteristics of the organization suffering the losses, and the characteristics of the markets in which the organization operates. The characteristics of the loss exposures include the frequency/severity of those losses and the loss and claim estimation patterns for loss reporting, loss development, claims payout, claim closure, and loss reserving practices and investment earnings on these reserves. The important characteristics of the organization are its financial condition, the attitudes of its management, its ability to administer a potentially complex risk financing program, and its ability to respond to changes in its risk financing needs and opportunities. Market characteristics relate to the conditions in insurance markets, product markets, and financial markets that affect the organization.

Every organization faces many loss exposures, has many risk financing choices with which to finance recovery from the losses these exposures generate, and must weigh many factors in making the choices that, for it at a given time, are the most promising. Because of the number of choices and decision factors, and because every organization's exposures and risk financing marketing conditions are constantly changing, evaluating and selecting risk financing techniques is a continuous process.

Chapter Notes

1. Robert C. Goshay, *Corporate Risk Retention and Self-Insurance Plans* (Homewood, IL: Richard D. Irwin, Inc., 1963), Chapter 2.
2. Patrick M. Lynch and Timothy J. Metke, "A Strategic Approach to Designing the Optimal Primary Casualty Risk Financing Program," *CPCU Journal* (December 1991), pp. 211-212.
3. Robert I. Mehr and Bob A. Hedges, *Risk Management: Concepts and Applications* (Homewood, IL: Richard D. Irwin, Inc., 1974), p. 6.

CHAPTER 3

Retaining Losses Through Current Expensing, Reserving, and Borrowing

The most elementary way for an organization to retain a loss exposure is to pay for losses from its present financial resources. This method is generally the most inexpensive, administratively simplest, and least regulated approach to risk financing. The four techniques that an organization may use to restore any accidental losses with its own funds are (1) current expensing of losses, (2) relying on unfunded reserves to pay for losses, (3) drawing on funded reserves to finance recovery from losses, and (4) borrowing funds to pay for losses.

These four retention techniques are often used to finance recovery from losses that are smaller and more predictable than the losses that organizations typically attempt to transfer. These four techniques typically form the "foundation layer" of a sound risk financing program.

These four retention techniques all draw on cash or borrowing power that an organization already possesses. Paying for losses with cash on hand or borrowed funds is often called "self-insurance." However, "self-insurance" is an imprecise term in the risk financing marketplace; it may also be the label for other risk financing mechanisms cataloged in Chapter 2. The one properly precise use of "self-insurance" (and of such related terms as "self-insure" and "self-insurer") is in the context of state and federal statutes and regulations that specify how an organization may retain loss exposures for which these jurisdictions require most organizations to purchase insurance. For example, to assure that injured employees, persons hurt in automobile accidents, and owners of pollution-damaged properties are paid their valid claims, state and federal statutes often require most businesses to obtain at least specified minimum amounts of workers compensation, automobile liability, or (for firms in some industries) environmental liability insurance. However, as explained later in this chapter, many of these statutes also specify conditions under which some especially large or financially strong organizations may, if they choose, retain or "self-insure" these exposures.

This chapter describes the operation, appropriate uses, and limitations of current expensing, unfunded and funded reserving, and borrowing to pay for losses. This chapter also applies the factors, introduced in Chapter 2, that should be considered in selecting each of these four retention techniques and in determining the size of the losses for which some retention techniques should be used (and above which other, more formalized retention or transfer techniques should be applied). Estimating the size of the largest accidental losses an organization can finance through these retention techniques is essential in selecting deductibles for the organization's insurance policies. The last section of this chapter discusses deductible selections.

RETENTION TECHNIQUES

Retention techniques are among the simplest risk financing mechanisms because they involve no elements of transfer. Retention techniques are generally preferable to both transfer and hybrid risk financing techniques. Where retention is feasible, it tends to be less expensive and more reliable than either transfer or hybrid techniques, thus enabling an organization to better control its overall risk financing costs. In addition, retention techniques frequently become an organization's "default" or "residual" risk financing options when no other choices are recognized or available.

General Benefits of Retention

A central, perhaps the central, challenge of risk financing is that the costs of an organization's accidental losses are usually more difficult to forecast and to budget than its other costs for raw materials, labor, supplies, taxes, and other normal business expenses. This unpredictability—and the possibility that cash may not be available when needed to finance recovery from accidental losses—is generally said to be the factor that sets risk financing apart from an organization's other financial management challenges. An organization that is able to forecast its needs for funds to finance recovery from its accidental losses and to provide those funds when needed—that is, an organization that can safely and reliably retain its own losses—can treat risk financing costs much like all its other expenses. For such an organization, risk financing costs become as readily manageable as, say, the costs of raw materials, utilities, or transportation.

Planned, intentional, safe, and reliable retention of major losses is difficult to achieve. In order to knowingly choose to retain all or a given part of the losses from a specified exposure, an organization must (1) recognize that exposure, (2) have the freedom to choose whether to retain losses from that exposure, (3) command the financial and managerial resources needed to make the costs of losses from that exposure as readily predictable and manageable as its other normal operating costs, and (4) be able to limit its outlays for retained losses to acceptable levels. This chapter explores the conditions that facilitate such retention. An organization that can meet these conditions is able to predict, control, and ideally reduce its risk financing costs as readily as its other expenses.

Retention as a Default or Residual Technique

Retention techniques tend to become an organization's default or residual risk financing techniques more often than do any transfer or other retention. A risk financing technique becomes operative automatically, or *by default,* when an organization makes no other conscious risk financing plans for a particular exposure. An organization must rely on default or residual financing for any loss arising from an exposure of which it was not previously aware.

On the other hand, an organization's executives may be keenly aware of a loss exposure and actively seek some insurance or other transfer or retention mechanism. Absent such financing, retention is the organization's only practical alternative. Under these circumstances, retention becomes the *residual* risk financing technique.

The elementary forms of retention, especially current expensing and borrowing, are most likely to be default risk financing techniques because they typically require less pre-loss thought and action by an organization's management than funded or unfunded reserves. For example, an organization may have to depend on current expensing or borrowing as default risk financing for losses arising from an exposure that its risk management professionals failed to address because they (1) did not recognize any possible losses or (2) mistakenly thought the losses were covered by an existing insurance policy or noninsurance risk financing transfer agreement.

Another possibility is that the organization will have to depend on one or more retention techniques as residual sources of financing because the other techniques the organization consciously planned to use proved inadequate or unreliable. Perhaps an insurer or other transferee/indemnitor went bankrupt or wrongly denied a valid claim. Perhaps the amount of the insurance or other indemnity agreement through which the organization thought it had arranged protection proved inadequate for a large individual loss or a rapid series of smaller losses. Perhaps the "captive" insurance subsidiary the organization recently established is not yet functioning effectively enough to pay a particular loss. Arranging for seemingly adequate risk financing before a loss does not guarantee its performance in the wake of a loss. When planned arrangements fail, residual risk financing may be an organization's only recourse.

Specific Retention Techniques

As mentioned earlier, the specific techniques for retention are current expensing, unfunded reserves, funded reserves, and borrowing. Although all forms of retention have much the same overall effect on an organization's financial position, they affect different sections of its financial statements. Current expensing of losses uses ready cash, a current asset on the organization's balance sheet. Borrowing generates funds by increasing the organization's short-term or long-term liabilities. Establishing an unfunded reserve creates a liability on the organization's balance sheet, a liability that is reduced as losses are paid with the organization's own unallocated cash. A funded reserve operates similarly except that, with a funded reserve, part of the organization's own cash or other current assets is set aside or segregated in a separate account specifically earmarked to pay for some particular type of accidental losses.

Current Expensing of Losses. Current expensing of losses occurs when an organization uses the cash in its general checking or savings account to pay for usually minor losses. These expenditures are treated as current expenses, which are tax-deductible in the period when paid. There is typically no accounting or other attempt to anticipate such losses or to spread the payment of these losses over more than one accounting period. Hence, such payments are current expenses charged against current revenues.

The impact of the current expensing of a $10,000 loss on an organization's financial statements is shown in the "Current Expensing" column of Exhibit 3-1. Before the loss occurs, the balance sheet shows $30,000 in the cash account and $65,000 in the capital account. The income statement reflects general expenses of $60,000. After the loss has been expensed, the cash account has dropped to $20,000, and the capital account, to offset the decrease in assets, has fallen to $55,000. The general expenses have increased to $70,000 (the original $60,000 plus the $10,000 retained loss).

Many of the losses normally paid in this way are too small to affect the organization's operating results significantly. Thus, any organiza-

Exhibit 3-1
Illustration of Specific Retention Techniques

	Before Loss	After Loss			
		Current Expensing	Unfunded Retention	Funded Retention	Borrowing
Balance Sheet					
Assets					
Cash	30,000	20,000	20,000	30,000	30,000
Investments (a)	55,000	55,000	55,000	55,000	55,000
Reserve Investments (b)	15,000	15,000	15,000	5,000	15,000
Fixed Assets	60,000	60,000	60,000	60,000	60,000
Total Assets	160,000	150,000	150,000	150,000	160,000
Liabilities + Capital					
Short-Term Debt (c)	20,000	20,000	20,000	20,000	30,000
Unfunded Reserve	10,000	10,000	0	10,000	10,000
Funded Reserve	15,000	15,000	15,000	5,000	15,000
Long-Term Debt (d)	50,000	50,000	50,000	50,000	50,000
Capital	65,000	55,000	65,000	65,000	55,000
Total Liabilities + Capital	160,000	150,000	150,000	150,000	160,000
Income Statement					
Income					
Sales	100,000	100,000	100,000	100,000	100,000
Investment Income	5,500	5,500	5,500	5,500	5,500
Reserve Invest. Income	1,050	1,050	1,050	350	1,050
Total Income	106,550	106,550	106,550	105,850	106,550
Expenses					
General Expenses	60,000	70,000	70,000	70,000	70,000
Interest Expenses	7,900	7,900	7,900	7,900	9,100
Total Expenses	67,900	77,900	77,900	77,900	79,100
Income Before Taxes	38,650	28,650	28,650	27,950	27,450
Taxes (e)	13,528	10,028	10,028	9,783	6,108
Net Income	25,122	18,622	18,622	18,167	21,342

(a) earning 10%
(b) earning 7%
(c) costing 12%
(d) costing 11%
(e) 35%, rounded to nearest $

tion—large or small—would almost certainly treat as a current expense the cost of replacing an ordinary broken window pane or the cost of a blown tire on a delivery van. A larger organization, having a higher threshold of accounting and "materiality," might also treat as a current expense the considerably higher cost of replacing a special stained glass window that had been broken or the cost of purchasing a new van to replace one that had been destroyed. For smaller organizations, the latter two costs would be more significant relative to their accumulated assets and current income. For such smaller organizations, therefore, the latter two losses would be more material, and would probably call for some more formalized form of retention or even some risk transfer through commercial insurance or some other mechanism.

Unfunded Reserves. From a cash flow standpoint, paying losses through an unfunded reserve is essentially the same as current expensing of losses. However, from an accounting perspective, establishing an unfunded reserve involves creating a liability account, similar to a merchant's reserve for customers' uncollectible accounts. Customers' accounts become uncollectible bad debts at random times—much as accidental losses often seem to follow no recognizable pattern. To provide some regularity to the accounting recognition of these losses (from bad debts or from retained accidents), the management of an organization may establish an unfunded reserve designed to anticipate the losses that have occurred, but that may or may not have been reported, during a given accounting period. Additions to these unfunded reserves attempt to recognize in a structured, orderly way the anticipated costs of these losses, and often include the administrative expenses of "adjusting" or arranging for the payment of these losses. For example, the "Unfunded Reserve" row of Exhibit 3-1 shows that, prior to any loss being reported, the organization suffering that loss has established an unfunded reserve of $10,000 for such losses.

Losses handled through an unfunded reserve are typically larger or more significant to the organization than losses treated as current expenses, but they are not so large as to require the creation of a separate funded reserve of cash.

When an organization relies on unfunded reserves, it makes an accounting entry (an allocation, not an actual transfer of funds) at the beginning of each accounting period to the liability account equal to the anticipated amount of the organization's losses of a given type during the accounting period. The periodic additions to this liability account reduce the organization's net worth (its total assets minus total liabilities). As losses are paid during the period, they are deducted from this account.

The "Unfunded Reserve" row of Exhibit 3-1 shows that once the expected $10,000 loss has been reported, it is paid out of the unfunded reserve with cash. This is reflected in the $10,000 decreases in both the cash and the unfunded reserve accounts. Since the loss has been paid during the current accounting period, it increases current general expenses to $70,000. Just as in current expensing, the loss is deducted from current revenues, but, due to prior planning in this case, the capital (or net worth) account is not affected.

At the end of each accounting period, one possible accounting procedure is to return any balance remaining in the reserve to the organization's general unallocated funds, close the reserve, and then establish a new funded reserve for the next accounting period. A second possible procedure is to keep the previous period's reserve open but to replenish it with another accounting entry sufficient to bring the reserve to a level presumed to be adequate for losses and loss adjustment expenses anticipated for the next accounting period. These two procedures have equivalent effects in matching anticipated retained losses to revenues for the same period. This system thus gives some period-to-period regularity to the recognition of these losses even though losses may actually fluctuate substantially.

For income tax purposes only, actual expenditures for losses, not additions to or withdrawals from loss reserves, normally count as tax-deductible expenses. Loss adjustment and other related administrative expenses are also typically tax-deductible when incurred. In short, managerial accounting allows unfunded reserves to pair together average accidental losses with revenues earned, spread monthly or quarterly over a fiscal year. Tax-accounting focused on actual expenditures does not allow this kind of spreading over the fiscal year or among several years.

Funded Reserves. A funded reserve, like an unfunded reserve, is a liability account. An important difference between the two is that a funded reserve contains cash or other liquid financial assets set aside to pay the losses, as they occur, for which the reserve was established. In the example in the "Funded Reserve" row of Exhibit 3-1, before any losses occur, assume the organization has established a funded reserve of $15,000 in investments earning 7 percent (as opposed to the average of 10 percent earned on the organization's other operations and investments).

An organization retaining losses through a funded reserve usually deposits into the reserve at the beginning of an accounting period money equaling the expected value of losses for the accounting period. If the reserve has a positive or negative balance resulting from accumulated deposits and loss payments from previous accounting periods, some other lesser or greater amount may be deposited that, together with any funds remaining in or owed to the reserve from a previous accounting period, should be sufficient to pay losses for the upcoming period. As losses occur, funds to pay for them are withdrawn from the funded reserve and paid out in cash.

Funds an organization deposits as additions to funded reserves normally are not tax-deductible to the organization when deposited, but amounts an organization pays to finance recovery from losses (plus related adjusting and administrative expenses) are deductible to the organization in the period when paid. Thus, as shown in the "Funded Reserve" row of Exhibit 3-1, when the $10,000 loss occurs, it is paid out of the funded reserve by liquidating some of the earmarked investments. The impact on the income statement appears (1) in the reserve investment income account, where only $5,000 of reserve investments remain to earn interest, and (2) in the current general expenses, which increase by $10,000—the amount of the loss, not the amount in the reserve.

With respect to these particular managerial accounting and tax effects, therefore, a funded reserve is not significantly different from an unfunded one. Funded and unfunded loss reserves can differ substantially, however, in their cash flow effects for an organization retaining losses through these reserves. An unfunded reserve typically has the same cash flow effects as the current expensing of losses. In contrast, a funded reserve requires setting aside in cash or other liquid financial assets funds that may possibly be significant to the organization's overall operating results. Funds set aside as reserves are typically taken out of the normal stream of the organization's operations and placed in investments that generally earn a lower rate of return than those devoted to the organization's normal operations.

Funded reserves have two cash flow consequences. First, the funds placed in such reserves do earn an identifiable return, and these earnings are taxable to the organization (if the organization itself is subject to income taxes and if the investment income is not otherwise tax-free, as is municipal bond interest income). Second, these investment earnings are usually less than the same funds would earn if they were employed in the organization's normal activities. Therefore, relying on a funded reserve to pay for specified types of accidental losses tends to reduce the organization's overall profitability or operating efficiency.

The disadvantage of typically lower earnings on reserved funds can be offset by the greater financial security of this retention technique compared to current expensing or unfunded reserving. Advance funding provides more assurance to the organization's management that the funds will be available when needed to pay for accidental losses may have to be deferred. When an organization relies on current expensing or unfunded reserving, a large retained loss or a series of smaller retained losses within a short period can be very disruptive. Normal operations may have to be severely curtailed and all or some payments of normal expenses may have to be deferred. With funded reserves, however, the likelihood of business disruptions after an accident can be greatly reduced, especially if the reserves are adequate. Thus, to achieve greater stability of operations and earnings despite retained accidental losses, some organizations choose to sacrifice some profits or efficiency by accumulating significant funded reserves for anticipated retained losses, even though additions to these reserves normally are not tax-deductible expenses.

For a funded reserve to be financially sound, three conditions must be met. First, the funded reserve must be sufficiently well established for it to hold funds adequate to pay actual retained losses. A large loss occurring just a few months after a funded reserve has been inaugurated may greatly exceed the accumulated fund, forcing the organization to rely on some other risk financing technique—typically some form of current expensing, perhaps in combination with borrowing, to pay for the large retained loss. Second, once the reserve has grown to adequate size, sufficient funds must be maintained to pay for the anticipated actual losses. As such a reserve becomes substantial, an organization's management is often tempted to withdraw funds from it for purposes unrelated to risk financing. Such withdrawals can jeopardize the security of the organization's overall risk financing program. Third, the assumptions and computations that determine the periodic payments to add to the fund must be sufficiently precise to anticipate (1) the actual level of "normal" losses to be retained, (2) the investment earnings that add to the fund, and (3) the loss adjustment expenses and other managerial costs of paying losses through the funded reserve. If either the periodic contributions to the fund or its earnings are not sufficient to pay the losses that occur and related operating expenses, the funded reserve may prove inadequate or unscheduled additional contributions to it may be necessary.

Borrowing To Pay for Losses. An organization can also retain losses by borrowing funds in the amounts needed to pay for those losses when they occur. Instead of its cash, the organization may use its credit to generate the required funds. There are many ways an organization can draw on its credit to pay for either large or small accidental losses, but the three most common are (1) borrowing from a bank with which the organization has established a line of credit, (2) issuing bonds so that bondholders' funds effectively finance recovery from some accidents, and (3) delaying payments to an organization's trade creditors. Such borrowings may be arranged either before or after the accidents that the borrowed funds restore. Depending on the organization's borrowing capacity when these arrangements are made, borrowed funds may finance recovery from losses of any size or frequency. In the example in the "Borrowing" column of Exhibit 3-1, the organization has arranged for a line of credit to finance losses equal to or less than $20,000 as these losses occur. The cost of borrowing these funds is assumed to be 12 percent, the interest rate the organization is currently paying on its short-term debt.

For an organization that makes borrowing a significant source of risk financing funds, there are both advantages and disadvantages to negotiating credit arrangements before major accidental losses occur. An advantage of pre-loss arrangements is that the organization will probably be able to arrange for larger amounts of borrowing, perhaps at lower rates of interest, before a major loss prompts lenders to question the organization's ability to repay any borrowed funds. Furthermore, the organization may be in a stronger negotiating position, and more able to be patient with lenders, before a major loss creates a financing crisis.

On the other hand, it is only after a loss that an organization and its potential lenders can know the extent of the organization's risk financing needs arising from that loss. Moreover, in the wake of a major loss, lenders may be more willing to advance borrowed funds to finance recovery so that the organization can continue operations and repay debts the organization already owes to these lenders.

Borrowing creates a number of cash flow and income tax consequences for the lender, both after and possibly before an accidental loss occurs. Before a loss, an organization that arranges a line of available credit usually pays the bank or other lender a one-time fee for the line of credit plus a nominal interest charge on the amount of the line of credit. Such fees and interest payments are tax-deductible cash outflows for the organization. There may also be other administrative costs associated with establishing and maintaining such lines of credit or other pre-loss borrowing arrangements.

After a loss, the amount borrowed to finance recovery is a temporary cash inflow to the organization, but it is not taxable income. However, amounts paid out to finance recovery from accidental losses are typically tax-deductible expenses to the organization, as are any interest payments or other costs the organization incurs to obtain the borrowed funds. Thus, a tax-paying organization that uses borrowed funds to finance recovery from retained losses is likely to incur two tax-deductible expenses: (1) the amount of the accidental loss (computed under the tax regulations applicable to casualty losses) and (2) interest and other administrative expenses associated with the loan. However, if the organization deposits borrowed funds for a brief period into an interest-bearing account before paying them out, the interest earned is taxable.

For example, in the "Borrowing" column of Exhibit 3-1, the borrowed funds are used immediately to restore the $10,000 loss. The organization's short-term debt increases, therefore, by $10,000. The cash account also actually increases by $10,000 from the loan and then decreases by $10,000 to pay for the loss, thus creating no net change in assets on the balance sheet. The balance sheet capital account decreases by $10,000 to balance the payment of the loss. The income statement reflects the loss through an increase of $10,000 in current general expenses and also shows the costs of borrowing as an increase in interest expenses.

Borrowing is a form of risk retention, not risk transfer. Even though borrowed money originates with a lender outside the organization, borrowing has two crucial characteristics of retention. First, borrowing to pay for accidental losses almost always reduces the borrower's credit capacity to borrow for other purposes. Second, borrowing creates no transfer of risk, no shifting of uncertainty about the number or size of any accidental losses. Instead, when an organization borrows funds to pay for accidental losses, the organization's costs vary directly with these losses. Unlike most insurance premiums, the cost of borrowing to pay for losses equals the amount of these losses plus interest and any loan service charges. Therefore, the risk associated with the fluctuating cost of accidental losses remains with the borrower.

Advantages

The major advantages of retention techniques are that in comparison with transfer and hybrid techniques, they usually they are administratively less complex to implement, are often subject to fewer detailed governmental regulations, and have a lower long-run average cost for organizations with reasonably predictable loss experience.

Administrative Simplicity. The more basic techniques for retention tend to be simpler to administer than either transfer techniques or the hybrid techniques that mix retention and transfer. Retention usually involves only one entity financing recovery from its own losses or claims against it. Retention thus requires no contract between entities with competing interests or differing expectations or perceptions. A partial exception arises with funded reserves, which normally involve some definite procedures for depositing and withdrawing money to and from specified accounts. Thus, largely because of their informality, these retention techniques are relatively easy to manage.

Relatively Little Regulation. With the notable exception of statutory "self-insurance" arrangements for retaining particular exposures under various state and federal statutes, retention techniques tend to be less regulated than other risk financing alternatives, especially insurance and other risk control and risk financing transfers. Retention requires less regulation because, in many cases, the organization retaining its own loss exposures is the only entity whose interests are affected by the wisdom or the adequacy of the retention arrangements. If the retention program fails, the bulk of the adverse consequences usually falls mainly on the retaining organization. Even with respect to employee benefits, where the interests of employees and their dependents clearly are affected, an employer using its own funds to finance the benefits has very substantial freedom in designing and funding these plans.

Lower Long-Run Average Cost. For those losses that an organization can safely retain, retention often tends to be less costly in the long run than either risk transfer or hybrid risk financing. Retention, where it is feasible, tends to save an organization risk financing dollars that would otherwise cover insurers' and intermediaries' operating expenses and profits, insurance premium taxes, and the costs of complying with many regulatory requirements.

However, retention also imposes its own costs: potentially destabilizing fluctuations in cash outflows to pay for losses (outflows that may be much larger in a given accounting period than insurance or another risk financing technique would have cost), and the organization's own expenses for providing internally or purchasing elsewhere the claims administration, loss control, or other services that an insurer would have provided to the organization at no extra cost beyond the insurance premium.

Nonetheless, on balance, retention is usually less costly in the long run than other risk financing techniques for an organization that can count on fairly predictable losses and on cash flows to pay for them and that can do without or economically replace services that insurers or other transferees would have provided.

Government Requirements

Although freedom from regulation is often an advantage of retention, federal and state regulation of an organization's retention programs can be extensive when an organization seeks to retain an exposure for which the federal or state government normally requires the purchase of insurance. An organization's efforts to retain its workers compensation, automobile liability, products liability, or environmental pollution liability exposures are prime examples of where regulation can be complex. The public policy reason for requiring all organizations to buy these types of liability insurance is to assure that those whom the organizations' activities harm receive adequate compensation. This duty to compensate exists regardless of whether an organization purchases insurance or wishes to rely on its own internal financing through retention.

Therefore, the federal government and numerous state governments have established standards for becoming an authorized or "qualified" self-insurer of these exposures. These regulatory standards are designed to provide the same financial security for potential claimants as if the "self-insuring" organization had purchased the coverage that is mandatory for other organizations.

Thus, for these particular types of liability exposures, with significant variations among jurisdictions, these regulations of retention or "self-insurance" programs are likely to stipulate:

- The minimum size of the organization that seeks to qualify to retain, or "self-insure," its exposures rather than purchase commercial insurance.
- Licensing requirements for all qualified "self-insurers," including periodic relicensing of these organizations.
- Funding arrangements designed to be actuarially adequate to meet actual or potential workers compensation, automobile, or other designated liability claims against the "self-insuring" organization.
- Requirements to report to designated federal and state government agencies, focusing not only on the financial strength of the "self-insurer" but also on the underlying soundness of its management.
- Purchase of excess insurance by the "self-insurer" to cover claims and claims-related expenses that may, in either individual cases or in the aggregate, surpass the "self-insuring" organization's capacity to pay claims to others.
- Payment by "self-insuring" organizations of taxes and assessments levied in many, but not all, states on the basis of premiums received or losses paid just as if each "self-insurer" were an insurer. These payments strive to assure that the state and federal jurisdictions do not lose the tax revenue they have otherwise received from the insurance transactions.

Different jurisdictions impose different statutory requirements on organizations that seek to qualify as "self-insurers" of loss exposures for which most organizations are required by statute to purchase insurance. Many jurisdictions do not permit any "self-insurance" of particular exposures. The prohibition against "self-insurance" or other retention programs may reflect the legislative judgment that only commercial insurance can provide sufficiently secure promises of compensation to those suffering work-related, automobile, or other specified injuries.

CHOOSING AMONG THESE RETENTION TECHNIQUES

As explained under the previous heading on the advantages of retention, the theoretically ideal risk financing program would enable an organization to treat its risk financing costs like any of its other readily predictable, normally budgetable expenses. Even though the random nature of the costs of accidents makes this ideal difficult to achieve, an organization wishing to control its overall risk financing costs should seek to retain as much of its risk financing expenses as it safely can. Furthermore, among the available retention techniques, an organization can typically reduce its risk financing costs if it can rely on the administratively simpler retention techniques, such as current expensing of losses or unfunded reserving, rather than having to turn to the more administratively complex retention techniques of funded reserving or borrowing. In short, retention, where it is feasible, is typically preferable to transfer; among retention techniques, a simple form of retention is preferable to a more complex one provided that the risk financing techniques upon which the organization does rely can be counted on to generate funds to pay for every accidental loss an organization may suffer.

As will be illustrated shortly in connection with Exhibit 3-2, successfully using retention—particularly in its simplest and least costly forms—requires overcoming conditions within an organization that arise from the loss exposures the organization faces or exist in the risk financing markets in which the organization operates. These conditions often force an organization to knowingly or unknowingly use some form of transfer or some hybrid risk financing technique rather than making a conscious choice to entirely retain all of a given exposure to accidental loss.

Theoretically, any retention technique can be used to pay for any type of retained loss. As the following example illustrates, however, risk financing often involves a combination of various forms of retention, hybrid techniques, and transfer.

Assume that a manufacturer suffers serious fire damage to one of its three factories. Most of the property damage to the factory is covered by fire insurance, except for a deductible of $500 for each item of factory machinery damaged in the fire. However, the manufacturer's business interruption insurance was written to cover a maximum of only six months' loss of gross earnings, and the actual factory downtime extended to eight months. Assume that this manufacturer also suffers a major net income loss. It may, consciously or by default, retain portions of the resulting losses by absorbing as a current wage and salary expense the value of executive and other personnel time devoted to assessing the fire damage and planning a prompt return to production. The manufacturer may also charge against an unfunded reserve for property damage the uninsured portion of the fire damage to the factory machinery ($500 for each of the seventy-five damaged machines). Furthermore, it may absorb (as a decrease in anticipated revenues) the portion of the resulting net income loss attributable to the seventh and eighth months of interrupted operations. The manufacturer may also retain other portions of its net income loss by not paying its raw materials and other suppliers with its usual promptness. In effect, by slowing payments to creditors, the manufacturer borrows from the suppliers the portion of its trade balances that it normally would have paid during these months. This delay in payment reduces the organization's ability to obtain further supplies on credit during this period. The manufacturer also transfers to its property and business interruption insurers major portions of the physical damage and net income losses from this fire. These risk financing transfers, however, were exceptions—in terms of types of losses if not in dollars of loss. Except where this manufacturer made specific arrangements to transfer the financial burden of these losses, the manufacturer retained all of its losses.

The risk financing professional of a well-managed organization chooses particular retention techniques to pay for specified types of retained losses. Under risk financing programs that are less well-managed, residual or default financing techniques tend to dominate.

In order to choose which, if any, of the four retention techniques—current expensing of losses, relying on unfunded reserves, relying on funded reserves, or borrowing risk financing funds—an organization should consider all of the decision factors presented so far, as well as cash flow predictability. The discussions under the following two headings present these decision factors as, first, sets of conditions that need to be met to facilitate retention and, second, a decision model for enhancing the predictability of an organization's cash flows.

Decision Factors

The factors an organization should consider in deciding whether retention is appropriate, and if so, which retention technique to use, have been described in Chapter 2 and earlier in this chapter. The purpose of the current discussion is to present a framework for simultaneously considering these various factors as they create conditions that must be met in order for an organization to retain successfully the losses from a particular exposure. This discussion brings together the factors for evaluating risk financing alternatives from Chapter 2, the catalog of risk financing techniques from Chapter 1, and the reasons for risk retention also presented in Chapter 1. This framework recognizes that retention occurs by default unless transfer is chosen and that, by implication, an organization's profitability/efficiency (as represented by net cash flows) is the fundamental decision criterion for making risk management decisions.

These factors and the alternative choices are presented in Exhibit 3-2, which consists of five concentric circles that may be viewed as a maze through which an organization's risk management professional must guide the organization if it is to safely rely on retention as the principal risk financing technique for a given loss exposure. Escaping from the center of the maze and reaching the retention options that form the outermost circle, or boundary, of the maze require meeting the conditions for intentional and reliable retention that are imposed by each of the inner rings of the maze.

The innermost circle, numbered 1, depicts the characteristics of an organization that Chapter 2 cited as factors for evaluating risk financing alternatives—that is, financial condition, management attitudes, administrative ability, and ability to adjust the organization's mix of risk financing techniques. If any one of these four characteristics of an organization precludes it from consciously retaining the losses from a particular exposure, then the organization must either find a way to transfer the financial burden of these losses, use some hybrid risk financing technique, or leave these losses unmanaged, outside the scope of its organized risk financing plans.

If the characteristics of the organization enable it to consider conscious retention of given losses, then the organization's risk management professional must next consider the factors in circle 2 of Exhibit 3-2. The factors in this circle relate to the characteristics of each loss exposure that the organization is considering retaining. These factors include loss frequency, loss severity, the predictability of both loss frequency and severity, and loss estimation patterns for estimating an organization's cash flow needs to pay for retained losses (that is, data on loss reporting, loss development, claim closure, and claim payout patterns).

If the characteristics of the loss exposures the organization may choose to consciously retain are consistent with or would facilitate such retention, then the organization's risk management professional should next consider the reasons for retention that are presented in circle 3 of Exhibit 3-2. In this third circle, an organization's risk management professional should seek knowing, voluntary retention. Doing so, however, requires avoiding other essentially unmanaged or involuntary and unintentional reasons that may force unwanted retentions.

Thus, to steer an organization into knowing, voluntary retention, its risk management professional must avoid unplanned or unmanageable

Exhibit 3-2
Decision Factors for Risk Financing Alternatives

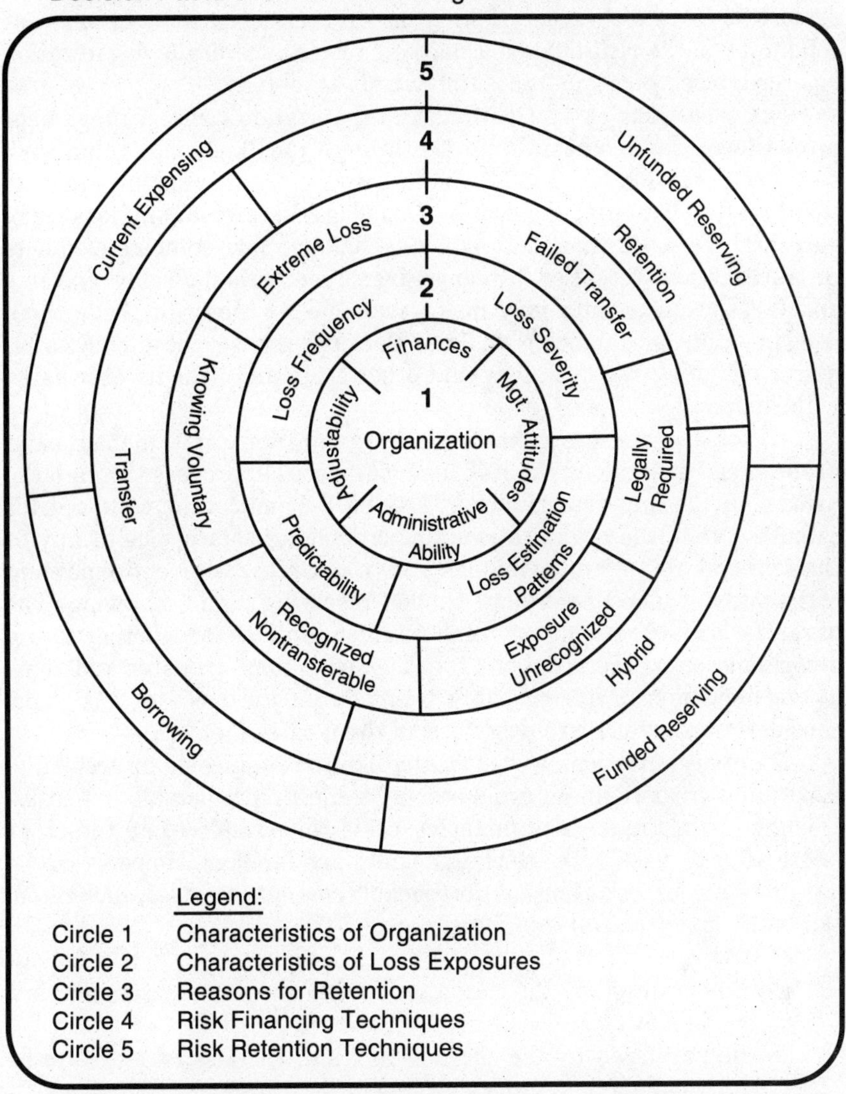

Legend:

Circle 1	Characteristics of Organization
Circle 2	Characteristics of Loss Exposures
Circle 3	Reasons for Retention
Circle 4	Risk Financing Techniques
Circle 5	Risk Retention Techniques

Source: Alice Ann R. Head, RN, CHRM, "Risk Financing Decision Factors Chart," *National Underwriter,* Property & Casualty Edition, June 8, 1992, pp. 18, 20.

retention of (1) losses that are so extremely large they exceed the limits of the organization's insurance or other risk financing contracts, (2) losses the organization has failed to transfer because of some other defect in an attempted transfer, and (3) losses from exposures that the organization's management has not recognized. In addition, the organization may be required to retain some losses that statutes or contracts require it to retain rather than transfer the losses that, because of conditions in the risk financing markets or elsewhere, the organization has recognized but cannot cost-effectively transfer.

For those loss exposures that an organization's risk management professional can successfully guide through the "knowing, voluntary" sector of circle 3 in Exhibit 3-2, the fourth circle in this exhibit presents the three fundamental choices for financing losses from any loss exposure: transfer, retention, and hybrid techniques that combine elements of transfer and retention. At any given time, risk financing markets and legal requirements may make available a variety of these three fundamental risk financing choices. Deciding among these choices requires weighing the cash flow and other costs and benefits associated with each option.

If, for a given loss exposure, an organization's risk management professional has guided the risk financing decision process through the "maze" of the first four circles of Exhibit 3-2 and continues to opt for retention, then the organization's management has a choice of any of the four risk retention techniques shown in circle 5: current expensing of losses, unfunded reserving, funded reserving, and borrowing. The organization's choice among these retention options, or whether to use a combination of these options together with some transfer and some hybrid techniques, will probably be made on the basis of cash flow considerations, which are described in the next section.

Many organizations would ideally like to retain costs of accidental losses and treat them as ordinary, quite highly predictable expenses. Doing so would make risk financing costs comparable to all the other "normal" expenses with which managers are familiar. However, to be able to retain losses as normal, foreseeable current expenses, such retention must meet the following criteria:

- Be permitted by the characteristics of the organization (circle 1 in Exhibit 3-2)
- Be permitted by the characteristics of the loss exposure to be retained (circle 2 in Exhibit 3-2)
- Be permissible and cost-effective under the current legal restrictions and risk financing market conditions (circle 3 of Exhibit 3-2)
- Be more cost-effective than some form of voluntary transfer or hybrid risk financing (circle 4 of Exhibit 3-2)
- Be more cost-effective than unfunded reserving, funded reserving, or borrowing as a form of retention (circle 5 of Exhibit 3-2)

Cash Flow Predictability

An organization that generates a larger, more stable, and more predictable stream of net cash flows is more profitable and more efficient than an organization whose net cash flows are smaller, less stable, or less predictable. In risk financing, an organization's loss experience and its choices of risk financing techniques affect both the size and the predictability of its net cash flows. The discussion here focuses on how choices of risk financing techniques, particularly risk retention techniques, influence the predictability of an organization's net cash flows. One of the fundamental purposes of all risk management, especially risk financing, is to reduce the unplanned, disruptive effects of accidental losses on an organization's finances and operations.

Exhibit 3-3 compares an organization's choices of risk financing, particularly risk retention, techniques to a cross-sectional view of a recirculating fountain of recurring cash flows. In this fountain an organization's loss exposures are similar to the water, and the steps they flow down are like the risk financing alternatives among which the organization may choose. The circulating process begins on the right side of the exhibit with all the organization's exposures to accidental losses flowing up into the organization. Because retention is the default risk financing technique, every organization begins its risk financing program retaining all exposures. Thus, when the loss exposures first affect the organization by flowing into the fountain through the vertical pipe on the right, they first rest entirely on the top, "organization," level of the fountain. Here, the organization fully retains all its loss exposures, having made no other arrangements for financing any resulting losses, and the predictability of the organization's net cash flows from risk financing is minimal.

To increase the predictability of its net cash flows, the organization's management now faces a number of risk financing choices, corresponding to the downward steps. The first downward step, step 1, is transfer. Because the cost of transfer (principally commercial insurance) is fixed during any given period, relying solely on transfer greatly increases the predictability of the organization's net cash flows related to risk financing. If the organization could transfer all its loss exposures to reliable insurers, it would eliminate virtually all the unpredictability of its risk financing costs. In the context of Exhibit 3-3, full insurance of all potential accidental losses could be achieved only by erecting a high wall at the left edge of the "transfer" step so that no loss exposures could flow off this step onto lower steps that are associated with risk financing techniques whose cash flow predictability is less.

No organization can insure all its exposures to loss. Therefore, some exposures flow down to the next step, step 2, which represents "hybrid" risk financing techniques that combine retention with transfer. These techniques provide some additional predictability to risk financing cash flows, although not as much predictability as transfer. If an organization were able to deal with all its loss exposures through transfer and hybrid techniques, its risk financing costs would still be highly predictable. In practice, however, some loss exposures still flow over the "hybrid" step onto the still lower "retention" steps. The two steps over which exposures flow before reaching the retention steps remove some of the unpredictability from (or add to the predictability of) the organization's risk financing costs. Each lower step adds something, but progressively less, to the predictability of the losses that flow over it, and the line that slopes downward and to the left over the steps in the fountain depicts decreasing marginal predictability of cash flows at each step.

Exhibit 3-3 contains four steps for specific types of retention, steps 3 through 6. These steps array the four forms of retention in decreasing order of their power to increase the predictability of an organization's risk financing costs. Thus, borrowing (with its fixed interest cost and repayment schedule) generally but not always imposes costs that are more predictable than the costs of operating a funded or unfunded reserve. Current expensing of losses, the most basic form of retention, typically adds little if anything to the predictability of an organization's risk financing costs. For some organizations, however, under some unusual circumstances, the different forms of retention may rank differently in their respective individual abilities to make risk financing costs more predictable.

In short, as loss exposures flow down the fountain, each step they travel over adds progressively less to the predictability of the organization's risk financing costs. Only by holding loss exposures at relatively high steps in the fountain can an organization achieve high predictability of its risk financing costs. In virtually every organization, some exposures flow to the current expensing step, leaving some unpredictability in the organization's net cash flows from accidental losses.

Once an organization has made its risk financing choices, the organization's management must assess through experience the results of those decisions. Within the fountain portrayed in Exhibit 3-3, this assessment occurs at the end of an accounting period for exposures to be recirculated during the next accounting period. Through this assessment, the organization's management should evaluate its current risk financing techniques in light of its past loss experience and anticipated exposures. The level and predictability of the organization's risk financing costs may or may not have been acceptable during the past accounting period(s). If costs were unacceptably high or unpredictable, the organization's management may choose to lower its loss exposures, improve risk control, or alter its mix of risk financing techniques to try to finance

Exhibit 3-3
Risk Financing Techniques and Cash Flow Predictability

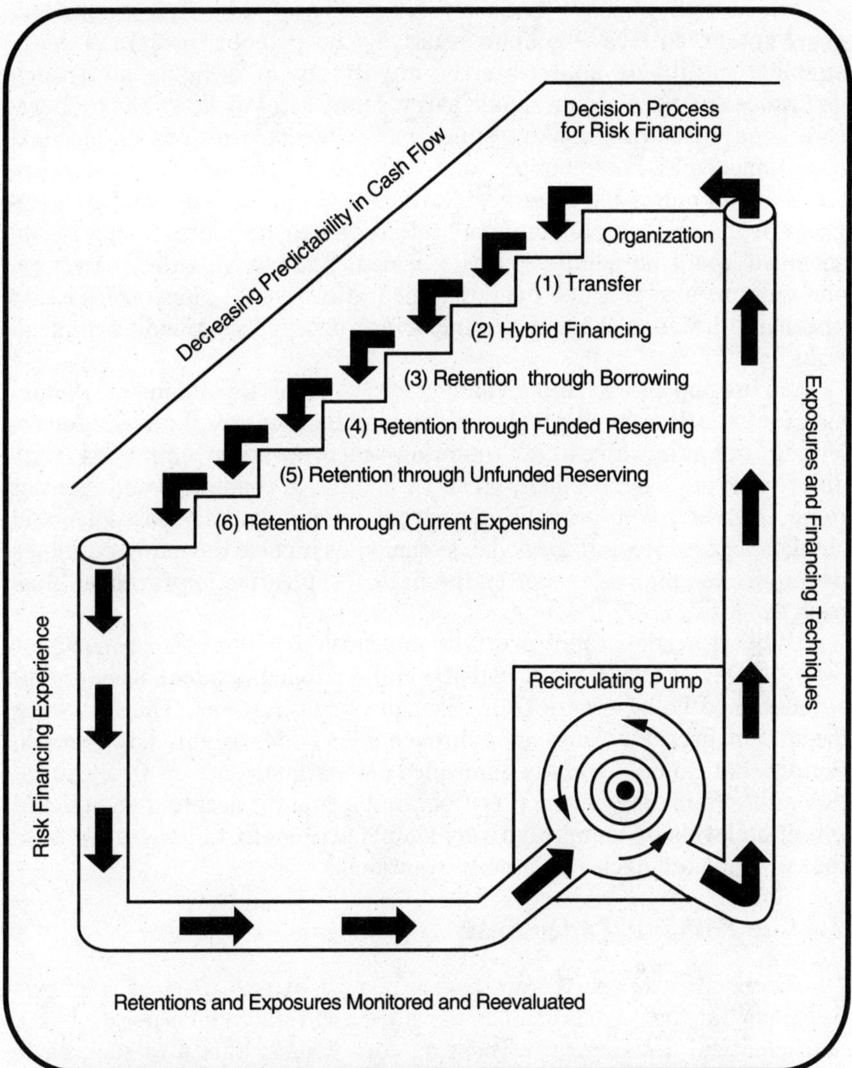

Source: Alice Ann R. Head, RN, CHRM, "Risk Financing Techniques and Cash Flow Predictability," *National Underwriter,* Property & Casualty Edition, forthcoming.

losses at higher steps of the fountain during upcoming accounting period(s). By repeating this process over several accounting periods, senior management should be able to enhance significantly the predictability of the organization's risk financing costs.

SELECTING RETENTION LEVELS

Even executives who know relatively little about formal risk management intuitively appreciate the importance of deciding how much insurance an organization should carry. Many rules of thumb have therefore been offered for making quick but accurate decisions on optional retention levels. For example, many insurance representatives and financial columnists have suggested that an organization restrict its aggregate mandatory and optional retentions to no more than various specified small percentages of its assets, net worth, sales, earnings, and current assets. Such oversimplified, "universal" rules are usually unreliable because they ignore important differences among organizations.

At the opposite extreme, many decision theorists and financial management scholars have developed complex mathematical models for selecting optimum levels of retention—incorporating equations with different types of exposures, levels of insurance premiums and interest rates, insurance and product market conditions, liquidity positions, and similar factors. Most of these decision models involve too many variables or require too high a level of mathematical sophistication for most business executives.

What is needed, therefore, is an approach to making decisions about retention levels that is both realistic and flexible and adequately understandable to be of practical use in most organizations. The following discussion presents such an approach by (1) describing how several factors that cannot be easily quantified place constraints on an organization's retention options and (2) presenting a rule for deciding on optional retention levels by using relatively simple arithmetic to generate charts that present the decisions about retentions.[1]

Factors Difficult To Quantify

There are various factors that are most often a part of retention decisions but that are difficult to measure and thus to incorporate into a mathematical decision rule. These factors usually relate to such basic goals of risk management as minimizing managers' uncertainty, maintaining continuity in an organization's operations, safeguarding the stability of earnings, and fulfilling the organization's humanitarian objectives. In addition, many organizations find that their retention choices are often restricted by "retention norms" within their industry and by insurers' willingness to offer a variety of retention options.

Tolerable Uncertainty. Managers' reluctance to undertake new ventures can be important in determining whether an organization assumes any optional retentions beyond its mandatory ones arising out of exposures it cannot transfer. What has been said about tolerating uncertainty in connection with *if* an organization should undertake optional retentions is equally valid with respect to *how much* of such retentions it should assume.

As an organization chooses to raise its retentions, some point of resistance is almost surely reached—a point at which key executives are no longer willing to assume uninsured exposures (or to remove existing insurance from present exposures), no matter how significant the premium savings or reductions in overall costs of risk may be. This reluctance comes from an understandable fear that having too little insurance can jeopardize the organization's future or management's continued employment. Therefore, when a decision about retention is being made, the level of tolerable uncertainty can lead executives to reject or accept any further optional retentions, or to reject or accept a portion of optional retentions.

Continuity of Operations. An organization that emphasizes uninterrupted operations needs assurance that it will have enough cash in almost any foreseeable disaster to maintain at least essential activities at its present location or in a temporary facility. A hospital, university, or newspaper is a good example of such an organization. This type of organization typically needs more funds sooner after a major loss than if it were willing to tolerate any business interruption. Unless the organization's executives have good reasons for believing that they will have enough cash to maintain continuity, insurance or some other highly reliable risk financing transfer is essential. In this case, the decision would be to rely on transfer rather than retention.

Stability of Earnings. One of the truly classic descriptions of the merits of insurance is that appropriate coverages allow an insured to substitute a known cost (a periodic insurance premium) for a highly uncertain cost (one or more uninsured losses of unpredictable severity). A logical extension of this idea is that insurance allows an organization to stabilize its reported expenses during any accounting period because it can be sure that its insurers, and not its earnings statement, will absorb—and provide funds for restoring—any accidental losses that would otherwise produce unacceptable fluctuations in its earnings stream. For instance, maintaining $X per share limits an organization's aggregate mandatory and optional retentions for any given accounting period. Because this limit applies to the total retentions, any decision about *optional* retentions needs to be based on a careful evaluation of expected losses from *mandatory* retentions. It is therefore possible that no optional retentions are feasible.

Humanitarian Objectives. The risk management program of any organization needs to accommodate its senior executives' perception of the organization's social responsibility or their need to maintain a favorable public image. They may view excessive retention as socially irresponsible or as detrimental to the organization's image. For example, if an organization elects to retain levels or types of losses whose restoration it cannot immediately finance, a major disaster may damage third parties whom the organization should but cannot compensate. Because of such excessive retention, this organization would have skirted its social responsibility and damaged its public image.

In addition, operating efficiency (or profit) may conflict with humanitarian concerns. Assume, for example, that Company A manufactures a vaccine that prevents a childhood disease. The vaccine is 99.8 percent effective; however, there is a 0.2 percent chance that severe brain damage, or even death, may strike children to whom the vaccine is administered. Assume further that federal food and drug authorities determine that the benefits of preventing this disease outweigh the small chance of serious injury to children. A national vaccination program is consequently initiated, and Company A is the only manufacturer of the vaccine. Company A then finds that liability insurance for this vaccine is extremely expensive and it undertakes a variety of other risk financing measures. First, it establishes a per-patient retention that seems affordable. Above that amount the company seeks insurance but finds that the likely insurance cost will make the vaccine unprofitable to manufacture. At the same time it is possible that full retention would mean bankruptcy if there were several severe vaccine-related liability claims.

Several humanitarian issues emerge in this scenario. Although the vaccine is crucial, what is the company's obligation to produce and sell it? Should it sell for a loss? Should the company purchase insurance regardless of cost and raise the price of the vaccine accordingly? Should the company decide that its business risk is too great and simply stop production of the vaccine? These risk financing and related business decisions cannot be made on the basis of a quantitative analysis only.

Industry Comparisons. Some executives may wish to be guided in their retention decisions by what they see as the "collective wisdom" of their competitors. Therefore, these executives will seek data on the types and amounts of losses that other similar firms have retained. Such data have been gathered through cost of risk surveys compiled and published by the Risk and Insurance Management Society. In addition, trade and professional organizations affiliated with particular industries sometimes gather insurance and other risk financing data from their members and publish composite results. Industry-conscious executives then tend to follow these examples to the extent that the insurance market permits.

This approach to selecting retention levels has merit to the extent that (1) some true industry norm actually exists and has a rational basis and (2) any organization's significant deviation from standard industry practice might raise concerns among insurers or in the financial markets about the soundness of the organization's risk financing program. However, this approach to retention decisions becomes dubious when (1) the supposed industry norm is merely an arithmetic averaging of highly varied retention decisions, (2) insurance or financial markets for the organization are not particularly sensitive to its risk financing decisions, and (3) the approach focuses on the activities of others, thus ignoring important features of the organization's loss exposures or other opportunities for risk financing innovations.

Availability of Retention Options. Most of an organization's conscious decisions about optional retentions arise in connection with deciding what amounts of losses not to insure. Thus, an organization chooses an optional retention when it selects the amounts of any per-loss or annual aggregate deductibles in its insurance policies, the amounts of any "self-insured" retentions (SIRs), the attachment points for its excess insurance, or the upper limits of particular insurance coverages. In making these decisions, the organization consciously chooses to retain those portions of any loss that fall (1) within a deductible, or SIR, (2) beneath the attachment point of any excess insurance, or (3) above the upper limits of all its available insurance.

In making these choices, an organization is almost always limited by the options that insurers are willing to offer. Based on its premium rating systems, underwriting standards, and reinsurance arrangements, an insurer usually sets schedules of deductible credits and minimum and maximum amounts of coverage that the insurer's underwriters and marketing intermediaries cannot readily modify. These schedules may not allow a given insured organization to obtain precisely the amounts of insurance or exactly the deductibles it wishes. The organization may then have to purchase an amount of coverage that only approximates what it wishes or it may have to deal with another insurer.

As an example, assume that an insurer offers comprehensive liability insurance in alternative face amounts of $1 million, $5 million, $10 million, or $50 million. The $1 million of coverage requires no SIR, but the three larger alternative face amounts carry mandatory per-occurrence SIRs of $50,000, $100,000, and $500,000, respectively. Assume further that a particular manufacturer wishes to purchase $30 of coverage with an SIR of $25,000 per occurrence. To obtain coverage from this insurer, the manufacturer will need to change its coverage/retention desires or convince the insurer to modify its coverage/retention offerings. If neither compromise is possible, this manufacturer needs to seek coverage elsewhere or go without insurance.

Decision Models

Although each of the factors described in the preceding paragraphs has an important bearing on the extent to which an organization chooses to retain loss exposures, none (with the possible exception of standard industry practice) generates a decision rule for selecting a particular dollar amount of retention above which insurance or some other transfer technique presumably becomes operative. At most, the preceding factors constrain an organization's retention decisions. However, within these constraints, an organization's risk management professional is obligated to select certain exposures and the portion of each exposure for which retention appears to be the best risk financing alternative. A risk management professional thus needs some decision process or rule by which to make and justify optional retention decisions.

Two decision rules are provided by (1) cash flow analysis and (2) a simplified version of the classic profit-maximizing (cost-minimizing) model.

Cash Flow Model. Cash flow decision rules can be used to select the risk management techniques that most enhance an organization's operating efficiency. In essence, an organization should select that combination of (1) assets/activities and (2) risk management techniques for these assets/activities that maximizes the present value of its expected future net cash flows.

This rule becomes germane for retention decisions because an organization's selection of the exposures and loss levels it will retain affects the expected present value of its future net cash flows as much as any other risk financing decision. Thus, increasing retentions has the following cash flow effects:

- Decreasing insurance premiums that would otherwise be paid
- Increasing expected cash outflows for retained losses (to the extent that increased attention to risk control fails to reduce the organization's actual losses)
- Increasing cash outflows for claims administration
- Increasing cash outflows for risk control
- Increasing administrative cash outflows for operating any of the more complex risk retention techniques (such as funded reserves or captive insurers)
- Increasing management's "cost of worry," the amount of money the organization's executives would pay to remove their uncertainty about the actual ultimate value of losses from retained

exposures—that is, to be certain that actual losses will equal the expected value of losses in any given period

The first of these effects, insurance premium savings, is equivalent to a cash inflow generated by added retention; the others are cash outflows. As an organization increases its retentions, the cash inflow from premium savings typically will rise sharply and then begin to level off as insurance premium rate credits for larger deductibles increase, but at a decreasing pace. Similarly, the cash outflows associated with added retentions are slight for small retentions, but they rise more steeply with increasingly large retentions. It usually follows that increasing retentions too much adds progressively less to the expected present value of an organization's net cash flows and, eventually, decreases the present value of expected net cash flows.

Comparing net cash flows (and resulting rates of return) for different retention levels permits zeroing in on the retention level that can be expected to generate the highest expected present value of future net cash flows for a given asset/activity. Based on this decision rule, the retention level that yields the highest expected present value of future net cash flows is the "best" retention choice for that asset/activity.

For instance, consider the full-insurance example shown in Exhibit 3-4 in which an organization fully insures for a $60,000 annual premium its initial $200,000 investment in a project that is expected to generate $60,000 of added revenues and $14,000 of added accidental losses each year. The insurer, anticipating that it will pay 60 percent of its premium income as indemnity for these $14,000 of losses, requires an annual premium of $23,333 (computed as $14,000/0.60). Therefore, as shown in Exhibit 3-4, the organization's after-tax net cash flow from this full-insurance alternative is an expected $30,000 annually, yielding—after income taxes presumed to be 40 percent—an 8.15 percent time-adjusted rate of return on the project.

Assume further that the organization next considers comparable insurance, but is subject to a $1,000 per-loss deductible. As shown in Exhibit 3-5, the organization's insurance expenses may consequently be reduced to a hypothetical $20,000, but the organization can expect to retain formerly insured losses of $1,800 paid out each year and to pay an additional $200 a year in claims administration costs. In addition, the organization's management suggests, after some careful questioning by the risk management professional, that they would pay $500 per year to be certain that their retained losses will, in fact, come to $1,800 annually. Notice that this $500 cost of worry is treated in Exhibit 3-5 as an implicit after-tax expense, not one actually paid with tax deductible dollars. It follows, as shown in the upper portion of Exhibit 3-5, that the annual after-tax net cash flow from the project can be expected to change

Exhibit 3-4
Differential Annual After-Tax Net Cash Flow—Full Insurance

Calculation of NCF

Differential cash revenues		$60,000
Less: Differential cash expenses (except income taxes): Insurance expense		23,333
Before-tax NCF:		$36,667
Less: Differential income taxes:		
Before-tax NCF	$36,667	
Less: Differential depreciation expense ($200,000/10 years)	20,000	
Taxable income:	$16,667	
Income taxes (40%)		6,667
After-tax NCF:		$30,000

Evaluation of this NCF

Factors:

Initial investment—$200,000
Life of project—10 years
Differential annual after-tax NCF—$30,000
Minimum acceptable rate of return—12% annually

Evaluation by the Net Present Value Method:

Present value of differential NCF ($30,000 x 5.650)	$169,500
Less: Present value of initial investment	200,000
Net present value (negative)	($ 30,500)

Evaluation by the Time-Adjusted Rate of Return Method:

$$\frac{\text{Initial investment}}{\text{Differential NCF}} = \frac{\$200{,}000}{\$30{,}000} = 6.667 = \text{present value factor}$$

Interpolation to Find the Exact Time-Adjusted Rate of Return (r):

	Rate of Return	Present Value Factor	Present Value Factor
	8%	6.710	6.710
	r		6.667
	10%	6.145	
Differences:	2%	0.565	0.043

r = 8% + [(0.043/0.565) x 2%]
= 8% + 0.15%
= 8.15%

solely because of the organization's greater retention through a larger deductible, from $30,000 to $30,800 per year. As a direct result, the time-adjusted rate of return on the project rises from the 8.15 percent in Exhibit 3-4 to 8.39 percent a year in Exhibit 3-5.

If the organization raises its retention of losses from this project to a still higher level—for example, a deductible of $5,000 per loss—then its out-of-pocket actual cash outlays are likely to decline even further, but its implicit after-tax cost of worry may well rise, particularly if the organization is small. For example, as suggested by Exhibit 3-6, a $5,000 per-loss deductible may lower insurance costs to only $3,000, but expected costs of retained losses may rise to $12,000. As further consequences of this larger deductible, claims administration and other costs associated with managing these losses may rise to $2,000, giving a total of $17,000 (computed as $3,000 + $12,000 + $2,000) actual expenditures for losses, less than the $23,333 for full insurance and even less than the $22,000 actual expenditures with a $1,000 per-loss deductible. However, as shown at the end of the calculation for net cash flow in the upper half of Exhibit 3-6, the organization's management considers the cost of worry for the larger deductible to be $5,000. Consequently, the appropriate after-tax net cash flow associated with the project insured and subject to a $5,000 per-loss deductible is $28,800, shown in the upper portion of Exhibit 3-6. This yields a time-adjusted rate of return of 7.28 percent a year as shown at the bottom of Exhibit 3-6.

By displaying the consequences of different retentions, these three exhibits begin to zero in on the appropriate optional retention level this organization should adopt on this project. The three exhibits show that among these three options the one that is preferable, the one generating the highest rate of return, is the $1,000 per-loss deductible. The next stop in finding the precise optimum retention would be to compute rates of return for deductibles of, say, $800 and $1,200 per loss. If the rate of return for the $1,200 deductible is greater than that for the $1,000 deductible (and if the rate of return for the $800 deductible is less than that for the $1,000), then the cost effectiveness or operating efficiency of greater retention is still rising at the $1,000 level. Under these particular assumed conditions, therefore, the true maximum rate of return would probably be reached above a retention of $1,000 per loss and below $5,000—perhaps at $2,000 or $3,000 per loss. If, in contrast, the rate of return for the $800 deductible is greater than that for the $1,000 deductible, then the maximum rate of return probably is associated with an optimum choice between the $1,000 and full insurance (that is, $0 deductible). A relatively short series of calculations similar to those in Exhibits 3-5 and 3-6 should soon elucidate the optimum retention level—particularly from among the fairly small number of "round-figure" deductible options the insurance market is likely to offer.

Exhibit 3-5
Differential Annual After-Tax Net Cash Flow—Insurance with $1,000 Deductible

Calculation of NCF

Differential cash revenues		$60,000
Less: Differential cash expenses (except income taxes): Insurance expense	$20,000	
Retained losses	1,800	
Other administrative costs	200	
		22,000
Before-tax NCF:		$38,000
Less: Differential income taxes:		
Before-tax NCF	$38,000	
Less: Differential depreciation expense ($200,000/10 years)	20,000	
Taxable income:	$18,000	
Income taxes (40%)		7,200
After-tax NCF:		$30,800
Less: Cost of worry		500
After-worry NCF		$30,300

Evaluation of this NCF

Factors:

Initial investment—$200,000
Life of project—10 years
Differential annual after-worry NCF—$30,300
Minimum acceptable rate of return—12% annually

Evaluation by the Net Present Value Method:

Present value of differential NCF ($30,300 x 5.650)	$171,195
Less: Present value of initial investment	200,000
Net present value (negative)	($28,805)

Evaluation by the Time-Adjusted Rate of Return Method:

$$\frac{\text{Initial investment}}{\text{Differential NCF}} = \frac{\$200,000}{\$30,300} = 6.601 = \text{present value factor}$$

Interpolation to Find the Exact Time-Adjusted Rate of Return (r):

	Rate of Return	Present Value Factor	Present Value Factor
	8%	6.710	6.710
	r		6.601
	10%	6.145	
Differences:	2%	0.565	0.109

r = 8% + [(0.109/0.565) x 2%]
= 8% + 0.39%
= 8.39%

Exhibit 3-6

Differential Annual After-Tax Net Cash Flow—Insurance with $5,000 Deductible

Calculation of NCF

Differential cash revenues			$60,000
Less:	Differential cash expenses (except income taxes): Insurance expense	$3,000	
	Retained losses	12,000	
	Other administrative costs	2,000	
			17,000
Before-tax NCF:			$43,000
Less:	Differential income taxes:		
	Before-tax NCF	$43,000	
	Less: Differential depreciation expense ($200,000/10 years)	20,000	
	Taxable income:	$23,000	
	Income taxes (40%)		9,200
After-tax NCF:			$33,800
Less:	Cost of worry		5,000
After-worry NCF			$28,800

Evaluation of this NCF

Factors:

Initial investment—$200,000
Life of project—10 years
Differential annual after-tax NCF—$28,800
Minimum acceptable rate of return—12% annually

Evaluation by the Net Present Value Method:

Present value of differential NCF ($28,800 x 5.650)	$162,720
Less: Present value of initial investment	200,000
Net present value (negative)	($37,280)

Evaluation by the Time-Adjusted Rate of Return Method:

$$\frac{\text{Initial investment}}{\text{Differential NCF}} = \frac{\$200{,}000}{\$28{,}800} = 6.944 = \text{present value factor}$$

Interpolation to Find the Exact Time-Adjusted Rate of Return (r):

	Rate of Return	Present Value Factor	Present Value Factor
	6%	7.360	7.360
	r		6.944
	8%	6.710	
Differences:	2%	0.650	0.416

$$r = 6\% + [(0.416/0.650) \times 2\%]$$
$$= 6\% + 1.28\%$$
$$= 7.28\%$$

Simplified Profitability Model. A generalized model for making decisions about optional retention incorporates the preceding factors and uses a basic profit-maximizing criterion (or operating efficiency criterion for a nonprofit organization). First, the appropriate decision variables, or parameters, must be quantified. They must be cast into a suitable decision rule for selecting per-loss deductibles under an insurance policy.

Parameters of a Solution. There are three parameters that, when quantified, determine an optimum deductible. These three parameters are the following:

- A schedule of premium savings and costs of assuming alternative deductibles
- A point of disruption or, as the term will be explained, a financial capacity to absorb losses
- The degree of credibility or confidence an organization's management is willing to assign to its own loss experience

Savings and Costs. The percentage premium reductions offered by an insurer when the insured assumes a deductible should, as explained in the following paragraphs, typically increase at a decreasing rate, reflecting the distribution of loss by size and frequency that forms the basis for the full-coverage premium. These reductions equal the premium when the deductible equals the face value of the policy, that is, when the buyer retains the entire exposure and pays nothing to the insurer. Thus, the general shape of the schedule of total premium credits or savings is shown in Exhibit 3-7 by curve OP, which has a positive slope throughout the graph. For illustrative purposes, Exhibit 3-7 overstates the total premium per period as a percentage of the value of the property insured. This percentage would be represented in the exhibit as the ratio VP/AV. Also, the cost of assuming the deductible is probably exaggerated.

A word of orientation is in order in connection with Exhibit 3-7. The exhibit applies to a single policy period for a property insurance contract. The horizontal axis shows dollars of deductible assumed ranging from none at O to the full property value at V. The object of the model is to choose the optimum point for the deductible on this axis. The vertical axis shows total dollars of premium savings and loss assumption costs. Although neither axis depicts absolute dollar amounts, each is thought of as having an equal scale ranging from zero to the insurable value of the property.

The curve OP is total premium savings at various levels of deductible. The curve CC is total costs of assuming the various possible deductibles (to be explored). For the present, total costs of assuming the

Exhibit 3-7
Premium Savings and Loss Assumption Costs—Single Firm, Perfect Credibility

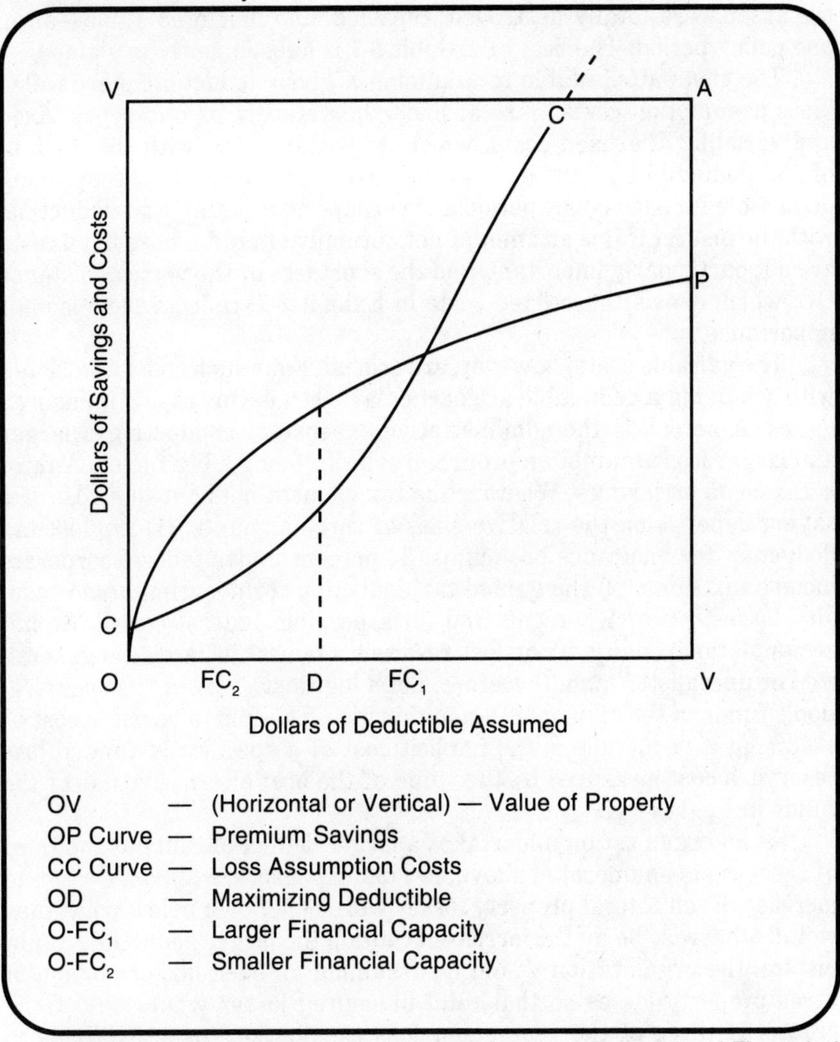

Source: George L. Head, "Optimizing Property Insurance Deductibles: A Theoretical Model for the Corporate Buyer," *The Journal of Risk and Insurance*, vol. 32, no. 3 (September 1965), p. 341.

deductible are assumed to be perfectly predictable, based on the firm's experience to which management is willing to assign 100 percent credibility.

For decision-making purposes it can be assumed that loss assumption costs never exceed the insurable property value, but a theoretical excess is recognized by the dashed extension of the CC curve beyond line VA. Loss assumption costs could fall in this dashed area, for example, if the asset were totally destroyed, replaced, and damaged again—all in one policy period. The rest of Exhibit 3-7 is subsequently explained.

The costs attributable to assuming a given deductible, here called "loss assumption costs," are at least theoretically of two types: fixed and variable. The fixed costs, which do not fluctuate with the amount of the deductible, might include the cost of determining the optimum deductible for each policy period and perhaps negotiating that deductible with the insurer if it is an amount not normally offered. These fixed costs are not particularly important, and the shortness of the vertical distance OC, which shows these fixed costs in Exhibit 3-7, reflects their lack of importance.

The variable costs, however, are crucial. Four such costs associated with assuming a deductible are particularly large. One cost is uninsured losses. A second is the administrative expense of conducting a larger and larger loss assumption program, salaries being a big factor. A third is tax costs or savings. Whether the tax element nets out to a cost or a saving depends on the relative sizes of three amounts: (1) the lost tax deduction for insurance premiums, 34 percent under federal corporate income tax rates; (2) the gained tax deduction for nonreimbursed casualty losses, also 34 percent; and (3) a possible federal excess capital accumulation penalty tax on loss reserves against "hazards too generalized or unrealistic" and, therefore, not a legitimate use of the organization's funds in the opinion of tax authorities. The fourth variable cost of assuming a deductible is the implicit cost of a specifically funded loss reserve, a cost measured by the value of the best alternative use of the funds in the reserve.

As an organization undertakes a larger deductible, all but the third of these costs enumerated above, net tax expense, are almost certain to increase. Even if total property losses were held down below what they would otherwise be by the increased caution the larger deductible might inspire, the organization would be assuming an even larger portion of these property losses so that total uninsured losses would tend to increase. If three of the four major loss assumption costs are likely to increase with larger deductibles, total loss assumption costs are almost certainly going to increase. This, then, is the meaning of the upward sloping CC curve in Exhibit 3-7.

The exact shapes of the OP savings curve and CC costs curve are not crucial, except that OP must increase at a decreasing rate and CC must increase at either an increasing or a constant rate. Although these conditions do not appear to be too much to expect in the real world, some attempt should be made to justify them mathematically.

First, an equitable premium savings curve will increase at a decreasing rate because, for virtually all types of property and liability losses, large losses are less frequent than small ones. Therefore, the height of the OP curve at, say, D in Exhibit 3-7 represents the amount of money that the organization must pay the insurer to cover expected losses equal to or less than OD. If the firm elects to assume rather than insure losses equal to or less than OD, then it can save the amount of premium represented by the height of OP at D.

The precise shape of the loss cost curve depends on the loss probability distribution. For example, the distribution of fire losses has such a strong positive skewness that the very small range in which premium savings rise at an increasing rate can be ignored. Instead a decreasing rate of increase is used throughout. In any case, the premium credits allowed in practice by insurers are not refined enough to reflect this narrow range.

The shape of the loss assumption costs function must increase at a constant or increasing rate. In economic terms, this implies that the deductible-assuming organization has either constant or decreasing returns to scale when it tries to act as its own insurer. Since the organization in question is presumably and principally engaged in some business other than insurance, it may become less and less efficient in that business the more (past some optimum point) it tries to behave like an insurer.

The net savings, premium savings less loss assumption costs, that an organization can achieve by using any given deductible are given by the vertical distance between the OP and CC curves at a point on the horizontal axis corresponding to the amount of the deductible. Geometrically, this maximum distance is at the point at which tangents drawn to each curve are parallel, that is, where the slopes of the curves are equal, roughly at the dashed line D in Exhibit 3-7. Where this line cuts the horizontal axis determines the most economical deductible, if there are not other limitations.

In fact, two other limitations will be developed, one relating to confidence in the prediction of the loss assumption costs curve and the other regarding the firm's ability to absorb a single loss less than or equal to the amount represented by the horizontal distance OD. The basic rule, however, is to choose the deductible that will maximize the excess of premium savings over loss assumption costs.

Financial Capacity. An organization's financial capacity to absorb a series of losses is the first limitation on the basic maximizing rule. Referring again to Exhibit 3-7, if the organization is going to absorb all single losses equal to or less than OD, its financial capacity to absorb a series of losses must be at least equal to OD multiplied by the expected number of such losses. Ignoring for a moment the expected number of such losses (a question of credibility, the third parameter), assume perfect credibility—absolute certainty of no more than one loss equal to OD. If the organization's financial capacity is O-FC_1, it can absorb a loss of size OD and will choose OD as its optimum deductible. (Notice that it will not choose one larger than OD because beyond D the excess of savings over costs declines.) If, however, the capacity of the organization is only O-FC_2, it cannot afford deductible OD and will have to settle for a deductible equal to its financial capacity. Such a deductible maximizes the organization's achievable vertical distance between OP and CC.

Arriving at a value for FC is primarily a matter of judgment. Financial capacity, or the point of financial disruption, is defined as the limit of the organization's ability to absorb loss assumption costs with its own or borrowed funds while avoiding undue disruption of its normal activities. "Undue" is an obvious hedge, given quantitative meaning only by the individual executive. In general, however, the greater the ratio of the current net revenue of the firm to the value of its exposed property, the greater is its financial capacity. Also, the more liquid its assets, the greater is the firm's ability to adjust to short-run adverse loss experience. Probably the most important factor in determining capacity is the ratio of the organization's uncommitted retained earnings and lines of credit to the value of its exposed property. The higher this ratio, the greater is the organization's ability to replace destroyed property without seriously weakening its asset structure.

The use of ratios in analyzing capacity implies that the large organization is not necessarily in a more favorable position to assume a deductible than the small organization. It is the liquidity of the assets and the ratios of income and reserves to assets, not the absolute size of the income or reserves, that determine capacity. (The relative advantage of the large organization increases, however, when credibility of loss experience is considered.)

Credibility or Tolerance of Uncertainty. The CC curve showing loss assumption costs in Exhibit 3-7 assumes perfect credibility, or perfect predictability, of the organization's future retained accidental losses. This unrealistic assumption needs to be eliminated. The CC curve then becomes not a single line but a range of possible values as the curve shifts downward with favorable loss experience in a given time period or upward with adverse loss experience in another time period.

A range of possible loss assumption cost curves can be developed on the basis of historical loss-causing events. A determination of what the loss assumption costs of these events would have been had various deductibles been employed will generate the needed curve. But since history is seldom a perfect predictor of the future, actual assumption costs will almost certainly vary from predicted costs, shifting the CC curve. This variance is a measure of the credibility of the loss assumption costs curve, the credibility being greatest when the variance is least.

Actuarially, the relative variability of losses as a percentage of their expected value is inversely related to the expected number of loss-causing events and directly related to the relative variability in the amount of loss per loss-causing event. Consequently, this relative variability of losses decreases as the number of loss-causing events increases. It also decreases as the dispersion of the dollar amounts of loss decreases as a percentage of the expected losses. Because credibility is the inverse of variability, credibility increases as the number of losses increases and decreases when the percentage deviation of actual losses from average losses is large. Given the proper data, an actuary could assign a credibility rating to any organization's loss experience.

An executive, however is not an actuary and often takes chances few insurance underwriters would. Thus, the relevant standard of predictability for an executive is not solely the mathematically based credibility, but also the degree of uncertainty this executive can tolerate. How big a chance is this executive willing to take? How big a chance does this executive want to take to realize a potentially large profit? If this willingness of the individual executive can be expressed as a Y percent chance that actual losses will fall within an interval of plus or minus $X from the prediction, that is, we can't be more than $10,000 off once every 10 years, then a range of loss assumption costs curves can be statistically specified.

There seems to be a simpler but less high-powered approach to incorporating the tolerance for uncertainty into a rule to guide the corporate insurance buyer. This approach begins with the premise that the greater the executive's willingness to take a chance, the greater is the deductible this executive chooses up to a limit imposed by the organization's financial capacity to absorb perfectly predictable losses. And, of course, in no case will this executive choose a deductible above that which maximizes the excess of premium savings over predicted loss assumption costs.

In other words, financial capacity is a barrier between the executive and the optimizing deductible. If this barrier is raised or lowered according to whether the executive requires more or less certainty, the greater the certainty required, the less will be the deductible chosen. More succinctly stated, one way to reflect the tolerance for uncertainty in the model is to accordingly weight the financial capacity factor. The simplest way to do this is to multiply the FC value by one plus the acceptable level of uncertainty. (For example, the executive willing to take a 10 percent chance multiplies by 1.1).

Decision Rule. Tying together the three parameters—the excess of premium savings over loss assumption costs, financial capacity to absorb loss assumption costs, and tolerance for uncertainty—leads to the general rule for choosing the optimizing deductible. It can be stated as follows: choose the deductible that maximizes the excess of premium savings over loss assumption costs, provided that the deductible does not exceed the financial ability of the firm to absorb expected losses multiplied by 1 plus the acceptable degree of risk.

The following example illustrates this decision rule. If, for a given exposure (such as a building to the fire peril):

D = optimizing deductible
S = total premium savings
C = predicted total loss assumption costs
FC = financial capacity to absorb loss assumption costs
R = acceptable degree of risk $(0 \leq R \leq 1)$

then the optimizing solution is reached when: D maximizes (S−C) and

$$D \leq FC(1 + R)$$

"Equal to or less than" in this case means that the deductible must be equal to or less than the organization's financial capacity multiplied by 1 plus its acceptable degree of risk.

Assume that the property in question is an automobile repair shop whose construction class, occupancy, location and degree of public and private fire protection generate an annual premium rate of $1.49 per $100 of coverage. The schedule of rate credits, resulting total premium savings, and arbitrarily assumed loss assumption costs are shown in Exhibit 3-8. The assets that will be readily available to meet any fire loss during the coming year are predicted to be $13,000. Management is willing to accept no more than one chance in twenty of choosing an uneconomical deductible.

From the table it is clear that expected savings minus costs reach a maximum with a deductible somewhere between $10,000 and $20,000, probably close to $15,000. Given the financial capacity applicable to this exposure of $13,000 and a risk factor of 5 percent, the upper limit on the deductible, FC(1 + R), becomes $13,000 (1 + .05) = $13,650.

If the organization is in a position to bargain for a deductible between $10,000 and $15,000, it will have to more closely examine its savings and costs curves in the $10,000 to $13,650 range (probably with a graph rather than a table) to find the exact optimum point. If the organization can only choose an even deductible listed above, $10,000 is the optimizing choice.

Exhibit 3-8
Indicated Pure Premium Rate Credits and Resulting Savings and Insurance Costs

Deductible	% Credit	Premium Savings	Assumption Costs	Savings minus Costs
$ 0	0	$ 0	$ 10.00[a]	$ –10.00
5,000	19	283.10	190.00	93.10
10,000	25	372.50	260.00	112.50
15,000	31	461.90	330.00	131.90
20,000	37	551.30	430.00	121.30
25,000	43	640.70	610.00	30.70
50,000	64	953.60	1,100.00	–146.40
75,000	78	1,162.20	1,400.00	–237.80
100,000	100	1,490.00	1,800.00	–310.00

[a] The $10.00 would be the fixed-cost element discussed in the text. Note that in practice a great deal of research would be needed to develop a schedule of the organization's actual loss assumption costs.

ESTIMATING APPROPRIATE AMOUNTS OF RESERVES

Retaining the financial burden of potential accidental losses, especially the burden of large individual losses or a great number of smaller losses, can be a significant financial undertaking for an organization. To assess the organization's continuing ability to accomplish this task, the organization's risk management professional should keep its senior management informed about the extent of these obligations—both for specific incurred losses that are known to have occurred and that the organization plans to finance through retention and for losses presumed to have been incurred but not yet reported. (If an organization seeks to become or to remain authorized as a qualified "self-insurer" under federal or state laws pertaining to the retention of automobile liability, workers compensation, or pollution liability claims, the state or federal law governing these "self-insurers" typically requires periodic detailed financial reports to document their continuing ability to pay these retained claims to employees, consumers, and members of the public.)

To estimate the ultimate amount of these retained obligations for such losses, the risk management professional for a soundly managed retention program will probably want to follow procedures like those detailed in Chapter 9 for forecasting an organization's risk financing needs. Therefore, with respect to each of the major classes of significant retained losses, an organization's risk management professional will want to apply the procedures outlined in Chapter 9 for the following:

- Applying appropriate loss frequency and severity distributions to estimate incurred losses from data on reported losses
- Adjusting the reported value of these losses for their likely growth or "development" because of inflation, the effects of any likely litigation related to these losses, and changes in statutory levels of benefits (such as for workers compensation claims) to project the ultimate value of these losses
- Discounting to their present value the adjusted ultimate value of these losses to reflect the amount of money the organization needs to have on hand to pay these adjusted ultimate values (either as lump sums or as periodic payments for loss of income or for medical or rehabilitation services) when these amounts become due

In short, for losses an organization plans to retain, good risk management dictates that the organization should apply to itself the same standards of financial soundness that the organization would apply in choosing an insurer. Just as an organization usually seeks documentation of the financial soundness of its own insurers, so should an organization relying on any of the forms of retention discussed in this chapter seek to assure itself that its plans for retention—whether funded or unfunded—provide the same levels of assurance of payments that it would require of its insurer(s). From the standpoint of a claimant seeking compensation for a liability claim, as well as from a public policy perspective, the most crucial concern is that losses be paid—whether ultimately financed through retention or through some form of transfer.

Therefore, an organization relying on retention needs to be able to assure its managers and owners, and to document to claimants and regulators, that retained losses will in fact be paid as needs for these funds arise. Sound risk management calls for forecasting (and perhaps funding) risk financing needs with equal diligence regardless of whether these needs are met through retention, transfer, or some hybrid risk financing techniques. Thus, the procedures outlined in Chapter 9 for forecasting risk financing needs are equally applicable to all types of accidental losses.

SUMMARY

This chapter examines some of the most crucial decisions that an organization faces when using the four fundamental risk retention techniques: current expensing of losses, using unfunded reserves, relying on funded reserves, and borrowing funds needed to pay for accidental losses. After giving background information on the mechanics of these four retention techniques and their shared characteristics, this chapter analyzes the factors an organization should consider when selecting which retention technique(s) to apply to which losses. It then examines the factors that influence how much of a given loss an organization should plan to retain (while planning to transfer any remaining portion of the loss).

These four retention techniques are similar in their operating mechanics. All of these retention techniques draw on the organization's present financial resources for risk financing funds. These funds may originate from the organization's own operations (with current expensing or unfunded reserving), specially earmarked reserves (with funded reserving), or from creditors (with borrowing).

Each of these sources of funds may or may not be adequate to finance recovery from a particular loss. The adequacy of the funds from any given retention technique depends on the size of the loss, the cash position of the organization at the time the funds are needed, the accuracy with which reserves have been calculated and funded, and the ability of the organization to arrange to borrow the needed funds either before or after the loss.

In general, using these retention techniques has no federal income tax consequences for the retaining organization until a loss is paid, when the loss payment becomes a tax-deductible casualty loss for the organization. Despite some differences in their operation, these four retention techniques are relatively simple to administer and are subject to little regulation in comparison with a more complex hybrid or transfer technique.

The factors an organization should consider when it has a choice among these retention techniques—that is, when retention is optional rather than mandatory—arise from circumstances dealt with in earlier chapters. These factors pertain to characteristics of the organization itself, characteristics of the exposure generating the losses to be retained, the reasons the organization is retaining the loss, and the availability of other risk financing techniques. A crucial consideration in selecting the most appropriate retention technique(s) is the effect that each technique may have on the predictability of the organization's net cash flows. Because increasing the stability and predictability of net cash flows is an important financial objective for many organizations, sound risk financing often calls for giving priority to those retention techniques that add the most to stable cash flows.

With respect to the amounts of loss an organization should be prepared to retain, the risk management professional should ask senior management to consider such nonquantitative factors as management's tolerance for uncertainty, its desire for continuity of uninterrupted operations and stability of earnings, the strength of the organization's commitment to humanitarian (as opposed to profit-seeking) objectives, and the importance that management attaches to any standard practices within the particular industry for appropriate levels of retention. Within these constraints, a risk management professional may develop decision models for choosing optional retention levels that are based on either (1) cash flow considerations that select the level of retention that maximizes the expected present value of an organization's future net cash flow (and, therefore, the rate of return on, or efficiency of, its operations) or (2) simplified profitability analysis, to find the level of retention for any given exposure that maximizes the expected difference between the organization's insurance premium savings and its risk retention costs, subject to the organization's capacity to retain risk.

Chapter Note

1. George L. Head, "Optimizing Property Insurance Deductibles: A Theoretical Model for the Corporate Buyer," *The Journal of Risk and Insurance,* vol. 32, no. 3 (September 1965), pp. 337–346.

CHAPTER 4

Financing Losses Through Captives and Pools

In principle, the management of an organization's risk financing program is simplified and made more logical by distinguishing between risk retention and risk transfer. The logic for this distinction has at least three sources. First, where it relies on retention, an organization must be prepared to generate money internally to pay for losses; where it relies on transfer, an organization must assure itself that the outside sources to which it looks for funds will be able and willing to provide this money in appropriate amounts. Second, retained losses make direct demands on an organization's cash flows; these demands are typically less predictable than the payments the organization makes to transfer risk. Third, any risk transfer can typically be only as reliable as the contract establishing that transfer is enforceable; therefore, through successful risk retention, an organization can become more self-sufficient and confident about its sources of funds.

Yet, in financial reality, this highly logical distinction between retention and transfer often becomes blurred. For example, borrowing funds to pay for losses may appear to be transfer because the money comes from the lender, a source outside the organization. However, this hides the essential fact that borrowing actually reduces the organization's credit resources, cutting its ability to borrow further for other purposes. In the end, the organization has actually retained the loss, since it must draw on its own funds to repay the lender. Further, the ideal line between retention and transfer begins to fade when considering various loss-sensitive insured cash flow plans, which establish the upper and lower limits of an organization's insurance costs while allowing it to secure many of the investment income and control-of-funds advantages that usually characterize traditional forms of retention. In addition, the formation of affiliated insurance subsidiaries to meet the risk financing needs of one or more parent organizations has raised complex, important questions about whether such captive insurers represent retention or transfer. Somewhat similar questions have been spawned by insurance pools and risk retention groups that have been formed in response to the difficulties that some insureds have experienced in obtaining traditional insurance at reasonable cost.

CAPTIVES AND POOLS—DEFINITIONS AND TYPES

A captive insurer (more accurately, an affiliated insurer) and a pool are two very closely related risk financing techniques. Both involve more structured risk financing than do simpler forms of retention, yet both give an organization more control over its risk financing program than does the purchase of commercial insurance. A captive organized to meet the risk financing needs of only the one organization that founded and fully owns it (its *single parent*) is quite different from a group captive or a pool, each of which comprises at least two organizations that join to form a single entity through which they finance recovery from specified losses of any member organization.

In Chapter 2, a single-parent captive is classified as retention, while a group or multi-parent captive is considered a hybrid risk financing technique because it contains elements of basic retention and basic transfers. For income tax purposes, a single-parent captive is considered to be a risk retention device although a multi-parent captive or a pool may or may not be considered one. A pool is not considered a risk retention device if there is risk distribution among the owners/participants.

If a risk financing arrangement is considered a risk retention device, then the following statements are true from a tax and regulatory perspective:

- Any transactions between a parent and the entity are not insurance; as a consequence to the entity, no excise taxes are payable on premiums, and the entity is not regulated as an insurer.
- Periodic or other payments the parent makes to the entity are not tax deductible by the parent as business expenses for insurance premiums.

If a risk financing arrangement is considered a risk transfer device, then the following statements are true:

- The enterprise is usually considered to be engaged in the insurance business and must typically pay premium taxes and be regulated as an insurance company.

- Payments made by each participant to the entity are typically tax deductible by participants as insurance premium expenses.

Given these facts, determination of whether an entity is a risk retention or risk transfer mechanism is significant in projecting the after-tax cost of various risk financing alternatives and in assessing the degree of regulatory freedom available to participants.

For a risk financing pool protecting municipal or other public entities, the tax status of payments are irrelevant to the participant. The pool may or may not be considered insurance, depending on the state enabling statutes, which also determine the degree of regulation. Most public entity risk pools qualify for federal tax-exempt status as instrumentalities of government entities, where they are controlled by and operate solely for the benefit of public entities.

Against this background the following discussion explores the distinctions between captives and pools with an eye to their tax and regulatory status. The present discussion previews the more detailed treatment of income taxes presented in Chapter 10 of this text. Moreover, to keep the present discussion in perspective, two caveats are necessary. First, the decision to create or join a captive or pool—or any other form of risk financing—should be made primarily on the basis of internal financial management and overall operating efficiency, not on its tax and regulatory factors alone. Second, the current discussion presumes that the tax authorities will continue to treat payments for risk transfers as tax-deductible expenses, while treating additions to reserves for retention as non-tax deductible.

Definitions

To distinguish among various types of captives and pools, it is best to examine first the generic differences between all captives and all pools. These differences will also clarify how a captive and a pool differ from a mutual insurance company.

Captive. Because risk financing techniques evolve in response to market forces and tax and regulatory statutes, the definitions of these techniques also change in response to similar forces. The concept and definition of a *captive* has evolved rapidly as organizations seeking to use captives have attempted to develop a more reliable and stable market than has been provided by conventional insurers. One of the best current definitions of captive is that it is a subsidiary owned by one or more parent organizations established primarily to insure the exposures of its owner(s). The words "subsidiary" and "primarily . . . the exposures of its owner(s)" are crucial to this definition.

A *subsidiary* of one or more parents is an organization that may be legally separate from but is managed by its parents. Within the bounds of sound risk financing practice, the activities of a captive are guided by the best interests of the parents in terms of the types of losses financed, ratemaking and underwriting practices, and the captive's strategies for investing its available funds. The captive operates primarily to provide risk financing for its parent(s) in the sense that (1) most of the exposures dealt with through the captive are those of the parent(s), (2) most of the capital for founding the captive comes from the parent(s), and (3) the management of the captive is controlled by persons who are also employees of the parent(s).

Pool. A risk financing pool is one application of the general concept of pooling that is used throughout commerce. As typically defined, a *pool* is an association of persons or organizations formed to combine their resources for some common advantage. By extension, "pool" also may refer to the member participants in or the resources of such an association. In a risk financing context, the common advantages a pool seeks for its member participants relate to cost-effective management of funds for financing recovery from accidental losses. Thus, in this context, a *risk financing pool* may be defined as an association of persons or organizations that combine their resources for their common advantage in managing funds to finance recovery from accidental losses.

By definition, a pool must have more than one participant. Pooling also suggests the creation of an entity that is legally distinct from each of its participants. The implication is that the managers of a pool, perhaps appointed to represent the pool participants, make judgments intended to be independent of the participating organizations and to serve the long-term mutual interests of the group as a whole as distinct from each of its members. In principle, a pool's continuing existence and viable operation are independent of, not controlled by, any one owner.

As a *mutual association,* a pool usually operates on a not-for-profit basis. To further its members' shared risk financing interests, most pools periodically distribute to their participants any excess earnings from underwriting or investment operations that are not needed to support the pool's risk financing activities. Such distributions are usually proportional to the size of the exposures (as measured by loss potentials or premium volumes) of the participants. If underwriting and investment activities do not generate enough funds to sustain the pool's risk financing activities, the participants may be further assessed, usually on the same proportional basis. Decisions on such "dividends" earned or additional assessments typically are made by an executive committee that takes an active, democratically oriented role in the major policy-making decisions of the pool. However, they are not usually involved in its routine daily operations (which are handled by persons paid by and answerable to the pool itself).

Mutual Insurers. Like a pool, a mutual insurer collects funds from many participants. These funds are called premiums or contributions and are used, together with investment earnings on them, to pay insured losses. Also like a pool, a mutual periodically distributes any funds that are excess in the sense that they are not needed to meet participants' risk financing needs. Some mutuals also reserve the right to levy additional assessments against participants if more funds are needed to meet unexpected, especially heavy covered losses; however, for business reasons, few mutuals choose to exercise this right. There is generally no substantive legal doubt that the protection a large mutual organization provides to its participants is risk transfer, that the transaction constitutes insurance, and that payments made by each participant to the mutual are tax deductible to that participant.

The differences between a pool and a mutual insurer are, therefore, matters of degree. The members of a pool are usually limited in number and operate in the same industry or have other substantial common economic interests beyond their participation in this risk financing mechanism. Public entity pools usually operate within one state because they are allowed to exist under an individual state's enabling legislation. They are usually allowed to serve more than one type of public organization, such as counties, school districts, or municipalities. In contrast, a mutual insurer may provide risk financing for many hundreds or thousands of organizations in highly different industries; the participants may have few other common interests beyond their participation in the mutual. Therefore, the insureds in a mutual do not ordinarily engage directly in its management, particularly in major strategy or policy decisions that would typically be of great concern to, and substantially controlled by, the participants in a pool or the parents of a captive. Although the insureds in a mutual theoretically own the enterprise and vote on the appointment of key officers and directors, they normally cannot control this management any more effectively than can the individual stockholders of a widely held public corporation. Because these size and control differences between pools and mutuals are matters of degree, there may be little practical difference between a very large pool and a very small mutual.

Types

The preceding section explained the generic differences between captives, pools, and mutuals. This background provides a basis for distinguishing among the various types of captives and pools.

Types of Captives. Captives are usually classified in terms of their sponsors. They may be pure captives, association captives, group captives, risk retention groups, or rent-a-captive arrangements.

Pure Captive. A pure captive is wholly owned by the single parent for whose benefit it operates. A pure, or *single-parent,* captive—because it provides risk financing for no other entities except its one parent—is the clearest example of using a captive for risk retention, not transfer. (However, note that some risk may be transferred through excess of loss reinsurance of the captive.) From the perspective of financial management, a pure captive provides no economically separate entity to which the parent's loss exposures can be transferred. At most, a single-parent captive can provide a highly structured mechanism for gathering data on loss exposures, levying charges against the various departments and operations within the organization, reflecting their respective exposures, and providing claims management for the parent organization. Properly operated, a single-parent captive can support controlled, effective, and efficient risk retention.

Association Captive. An association captive has more than one parent, all of which belong to a particular industry or professional association and all of which have similar loss exposures and risk financing needs. Many of the early single-industry mutual insurers that sprang up along the Atlantic Coast in the nineteenth century established precedents for modern association captives. When a sufficient number of parents achieve an adequate spread of risk that will generate credible loss statistics, and when captive management is strong enough to make and implement decisions independent of its parents, an association captive can function much like a pool or mutual. If it meets these qualifications, such an association captive can provide risk financing that, from a managerial perspective, is equivalent to risk transfer.

Group Captive. A group captive is similar to an association captive except that it is not sponsored by a trade association or professional society. Its two or more parents consequently do not have such closely similar exposures or comparable risk financing needs. It follows that the participants in a group captive tend to be united solely by their common interest derived from owning the group captive.

The distinction between risk retention and risk transfer is less clear for group captives. In some situations, a focus on tax savings has led tax authorities to examine whether the parents of a group captive (especially those with few members) operate the captive for legitimate risk financing reasons beyond merely seeking income tax deductions for "premiums" they have paid for "insurance" from their captive. These authorities have been reluctant to grant tax deductibility for risk financing arrangements of groups formed primarily to gain tax advantages. These authorities, backed by the courts, have generally held that these groups are really risk retention mechanisms in disguise.

In other cases, especially when the parents have demonstrable risk financing or risk control needs not met by existing insurance markets, group captives have generally been recognized as true risk transfer mechanisms. This is because, first, they were clearly formed and continue to operate for reasons unrelated to taxes, and second, they have been managed independently of the particular interests of any individual participant. Such group captives grew out of the tradition of the industry-centered and community-centered mutuals of nineteenth-century America.

Risk Retention/Purchasing Group. The terms *risk retention group* and *risk purchasing group* originated in the federal Risk Retention Act of 1981, which was passed in response to a "products liability crisis" that arose from the rising costs and decreasing availability of products liability coverage from commercial insurers during the preceding year. This act was written to help organizations in any industry meet their liability risk financing needs by (1) forming their own mutual risk financing organization (a risk retention group) or (2) establishing a buyers' cooperative (a purchasing group) to secure insurance in regular commercial markets for the group on a more efficient and favorable basis than could an individual member. In response to the liability crisis of the mid-1980s, the act was expanded in 1986 to include all types of liability insurance except workers compensation and personal liability.

A risk retention group must insure all of its owners, and all owners must be insureds. As a federal act, the Liability Risk Retention Act of 1986 only requires that a risk retention group be licensed in one state in order to underwrite risks in all states. Thus, a risk retention group can be a group captive with capital stock or a mutual insurer licensed under the laws of a single state.

Organizations that were unable or unwilling to finance their liability losses through risk retention groups were encouraged by the 1981 and 1986 acts to cooperate in making collective purchases of liability coverage from the commercial insurance market. The acts are based on the assumption that a well-managed buyers' cooperative is usually more attractive to insurers than are the members individually because (1) the total premium generated by the cooperative merits more underwriting, rating, and loss control attention than does any single member of the cooperative; (2) the members of the cooperative can obtain better loss control and other risk management services from independent providers than can the individual members; and (3) the cooperative possesses more bargaining leverage with insurers and service providers than do many of its individual members.

Therefore, the Liability Risk Retention Act of 1986 authorizes firms in any industry to form purchasing groups for liability insurance and to otherwise cooperate in managing their liability loss exposures. The act excuses the members of such groups from liability for many forms of collusion under antitrust laws and fictitious group statutes, provided their activities are limited to management of the participants' liability exposures. These exemptions enable these groups to engage with impunity in activities that would otherwise be considered restraint of trade in insurance markets. The number of risk retention and risk purchasing groups has increased dramatically in recent years as insureds have used these risk retention and purchasing exemptions to save on insurance costs and avoid state regulation.

Rent-A-Captive. Some existing pure, association, or group captives are willing to "rent" their facilities—such as underwriting, rating, claims management, and accounting and financial expertise—to other organizations that would like to derive the benefits of a captive but do not want to incur the expenses of forming and capitalizing one. For a fee that usually reflects the amount of effort required to accommodate the "renter," an existing captive agrees to let one or more renters participate in the captive arrangement as if they intended to be permanent parents. Such an arrangement can generate additional revenue and a wider exposure base for the original parents of the captive while allowing new firms to test the wisdom of forming their own enterprises. Some insurance brokerage organizations and insurers have formed captives principally to make rent-a-captive services and facilities available to those clients who want to use the captive risk financing mechanism but find it infeasible to start their own.

An Alternative Classification: Pure and Broad Captives. A *pure captive* is one that provides risk financing only for its parents, regardless of how few or numerous, otherwise related or unrelated, they may be. In contrast, a *broad captive* is one that also provides risk financing for organizations that are not its parents. In short, a pure captive provides risk financing only for its parents; a broad captive meets others' needs as well.

A subsequent section in this chapter describes the advantages of or the reasons for employing a captive. One of these may be to use it as a device for entering the commercial insurance and reinsurance market as a seller of coverages to other organizations. Thus, one reason a parent may choose to form a broad captive is to implement a long-term, general marketing strategy for the parent and its corporate affiliates.

Two other reasons a broad captive may have special appeal relate more directly to an organization's risk financing needs. First, accepting "outside" business may provide an organization's captive with a broader base of loss exposures and a more credible set of loss statistics from which to develop more meaningful premium rates—in short, to form a better *risk pool.* Second, one of the criteria that tax authorities sometimes use to evaluate the independence of an affiliated insurer (and thus the tax deductibility to the parent of "premiums" paid to the captive) is the percentage of outside business the captive underwrites; therefore, providing substantial risk financing for a significant number of outside organizations may enhance a parent's likelihood of being allowed a tax deduction for payments to its own captive.

Types of Pools. The classification of pools is not as complex as that of captives. The tax deductibility of premiums paid by participants to pools for insurance has been largely unchallenged because the participants usually transfer risk to the pool itself. Consequently, several of the basic distinctions among types of captives generally have not been considered relevant when analyzing pools. Such distinctions may be based, for example, on the number of parents or whether they write substantial amounts of insurance on "outside" exposures of entities other than their parents (distinctions once thought useful in obtaining tax deductibility for "premiums" paid to these captives).

Pools are classified in terms of (1) the organizational characteristics shared by their participants, (2) the types of coverage they provide, and (3) whether they operate in the primary insurance or in the reinsurance market. A *municipal pool* provides risk financing for municipalities (and perhaps for other public entities), while a *public utility pool* focuses on the risk financing needs of electric, natural gas, and other utility firms. Similarly, a *products liability pool* provides only (or at least primarily) products liability protection for its participants, while a *malpractice pool* centers on professional liability exposures of its participants.

CAPTIVES AND POOLS—RETENTION OR TRANSFER

For tax and regulatory purposes, a single parent captive is generally considered a retention device and a pool is generally considered a risk transfer device. Captives with multiple parents or covering substantial loss exposures unrelated to a parent may be retention or transfer devices, depending on regulators' and the courts' views of the particular circumstances of each enterprise. Pools clearly have the two hallmark characteristics of insurance: (1) transfer of the financial burden of specified losses from one group (participants/transferors/indemnitees) to a separate, unaffiliated transferee/indemnitor (the pool itself); and (2) the sharing or combining of loss exposures (colloquially, the *pooling of risks*). Even when a pool has as few as two participating indemnitees, it has both of these essential characteristics of insurance and can, at least in principle, therefore be classified as a transfer mechanism. Several currently prominent and highly successful mutual insurance companies serving the general public once began in just this fashion when a few businessowners banded together for mutual protection when they felt that the then existing commercial insurance markets were not meeting their needs. Their small pools grew to become outstanding general insurers.

Just as clearly as pools constitute transfer, *some* captive insurance arrangements are clearly a retention mechanism. For example, when a captive has only one parent, does not purchase reinsurance, and "insures" the loss exposures of no other entity, there is neither any shifting of the financial burden of losses to an economically independent entity nor any pooling of loss exposures. However, if a single-parent, single-indemnitee captive grows in one or both of two directions—by acquiring more parents who are of different corporate or economic "families" or by indemnifying entities that are not its owners—then there is probably an element of risk transfer involved. This growing and diversifying captive begins to take on the characteristics of an insurance company and begins to approach what state and federal statutes term "engaging in the business of insurance."

Determining exactly when such a diversifying captive ceases to be a retention device for one or a few parents and begins to engage in the business of insurance is very important but very difficult. It is important because as long as a captive is a retention device, (1) the "premiums" the parent pays to the captive are typically not tax deductible, (2) the captive does not need to comply with the highly complex and costly regulations by which every United States' and most foreign jurisdictions regulate how an insurer operates, and (3) these jurisdictions normally do not collect insurance premium tax revenues from risk financing mechanisms deemed to be retention. However, once a captive crosses the boundary into transfer by providing "insurance" to a founder or to some other indemnitee, then all three of these conditions are reversed. It is difficult to decide if and when this reversal should be implemented because the precise boundary between retention and transfer is not always clear and because the United States legal system delegates to each jurisdiction much independent authority to resolve for itself the retention/transfer issue. The taxation and regulation of captive insurance arrangements consequently have been the subject of much litigation and numerous administrative hearings, many of which have reached conflicting decisions. Many business executives, scholars, and other observers find these conflicts unfortunate and seek greater certainty in finding and interpreting the applicable statutes and regulations.

DECIDING TO ESTABLISH A CAPTIVE OR POOL

Financing accidental losses through a captive or pool strengthens the risk management programs of an organization only if two conditions are fulfilled. First, the benefits derived from a captive or pool must exceed the costs of such an arrangement and, second, establishing and operating a captive or pool must be feasible in practice for the organizations that found and use it. Thus, the decision to establish a captive or pool requires (1) weighing benefits and costs and (2) determining the practicality of actually operating a captive or pool.

Weighing Benefits and Costs

The decision to inaugurate or to join a captive or pool should be an essentially financial one. Pride or prestige in owning or founding an insurance company or angry frustration with current but probably temporary conditions in commercial insurance markets may not be valid reasons for establishing or joining a captive or pool. Therefore, making a good decision requires an objective analysis of financial benefits and costs.

Benefits of a Captive or Pool. The benefits of forming or joining a captive or pool can be broadly classified as reduced insurance costs, improved net cash flows, more stable insurance markets, improved coverage, fewer regulatory restrictions, improved loss control and claims services, coordination of insurance programs for organizations operating in many jurisdictions, and more ready access to reinsurance and retail insurance markets.

Reduced Insurance Costs. Many organizations with favorable loss experience under commercial insurance often feel that their insurance costs are higher than necessary because commercial insurers' rating systems seem inadequately responsive to a favorable loss record. A captive may improve the perceived rating equity by making each insured's premium more flexible, especially in terms of rate credits. Insurance costs may also be reduced because a captive or pool can achieve greater operating efficiency than can a commercial insurer operating in a broader market. For example, a captive or pool may have greatly reduced marketing costs, thus passing on lower costs than would a commercial insurer to the insured or parent. Moreover, if the parents of a captive or participants in a pool already practice sound loss control or claims administration, the captive or pool need not provide these services, thus enabling it to eliminate the related premium "loadings" a commercial insurer would normally charge all insureds. There may be additional reductions in premium rates because the captive or pool can generate a higher rate of investment income on its unearned premium and loss reserves than commercial insurers can achieve or will credit to insureds as premium savings.

Improved Net Cash Flows. Reduced insurance costs tend to lessen an organization's cash outflows for risk financing. Beyond this one direct cash flow effect, the insurance and reinsurance operations of captives and pools can generate positive net cash inflows for their parents or participants. Money once spent on commercial insurance can stay in the captive or pool regardless of whether it is the primary insurer or a reinsurer of coverages initially placed through fronting insurers, which reinsure with the captive or pool.

To the extent that the captive or pool generates revenue from its underwriting or investment activities that is not needed to support its operations, the revenue can be returned as dividends to the parent or participating insureds, thus providing a new source of cash inflow. (To the extent that the captive or pool cedes coverage and premiums to a reinsurer, allowing cash to "escape," this source of net cash inflow is reduced.) In short, by functioning as their own insurers and keeping funds within their own corporate families, participants in a captive or pool eliminate the net outflow of cash to pay for outside insurance coverage.

More Stable Insurance Markets. The executives of captives and pools recognize their close relationships with their parents and participants; were it not for their special risk financing needs, these captives and pools probably would not exist. Therefore, captives and pools usually strive to be especially reliable sources of indemnity, resistant to the market fluctuations that prompt commercial insurers to alter the prices and availabilities of their coverages. Although captives and pools cannot always meet their parents' and participants' coverage needs, a sense of a common purpose and interests usually leads the management of captives or pools and their insureds to establish mutually satisfactory coverage arrangements.

Moreover, the option of placing its coverages with a captive or pool often gives a parent or participant special leverage in commercial insurance markets. Knowing that a potential insured has a captive or pool alternative, commercial insurers may be willing to offer insurance on more competitive terms to attract or hold business. Whether a potential insured actually intends to use the captive or pool may not matter; a commercial insurer perceiving the captive or pool as a threat to its market share may become more accommodating to insureds.

Improved Coverages. Captives or pools that serve organizations having special risk financing needs are likely to be established in jurisdictions whose insurance codes grant them great freedom to offer broader coverages than are typically available in commercial insurance markets. Captives in particular are able to provide their parents with coverages not usually available in commercial insurance markets, thereby more fully meeting the unique or specific needs of their parents.

Given the special relationship between parent and captive, insurance commissioners often reason that—with respect to the scope of exposures to be transferred—captives and their parents require fewer regulations than do commercial insurers in more generalized markets. Captives (and to some extent pools) have thus been somewhat successful in overcoming regulatory underwriting restrictions to cover some perils that often have highly limited commercial insurability, such as strikes, floods, medical malpractice, and products liability.

Fewer Regulatory Restrictions. A captive or pool and its parent(s) or participants can usually be expected to have a special working knowledge of one another. This knowledge is one of three sources of the freedom that captives, pools, and their insureds enjoy and that those participating in more traditional insurance relationships do not. A second source of freedom is the ability of the parents or participants to select a captive's or pool's legal domicile, the jurisdiction with primary regulatory authority over it. By choosing a domicile whose insurance code best suits the founders' needs with respect to capitalization requirements, coverages, rating plans, and investment practices, founders can free themselves from certain undesirable regulations. (The statutes in any jurisdiction can, however, be revised, thereby creating a less favorable regulatory environment than the founders first anticipated; they may choose to remain in that environment or to dissolve and reestablish their captive or pool in a more favorable jurisdiction.)

A third source of coverage flexibility is an organization's access to reinsurance markets through its captive (or a group of organizations through its pool). As explained in Chapter 6, reinsurers normally deal with insurers and other reinsurers, not directly with insureds. However, by using a captive or pool as its negotiating agent, an organization or group can operate directly in the reinsurance market, entering into reinsurance, excess and umbrella insurance, and retrocession arrangements as a buyer or provider of coverage. The relatively unregulated realm of reinsurance thus permits an organization to obtain coverage from a wide range of insurers and reinsurers. Given this freedom, parents of a captive or the participants in a pool have, in principle, access to virtually any available insurance coverage.

An additional advantage to public risk pools is that enabling legislation, in some but not all jurisdictions, specifically exempts them from state insurance regulations, premium taxes, and solvency guarantee fund contributions as insurers, since they are providing collective services that the individual public entities could not obtain for themselves.

Improved Loss Control and Claims Services. A particular organization or group may feel that it requires a greater degree or special type of loss control or claims management services than seems available at a reasonable price from commercial insurers. Establishing a captive or pool may well be a cost-effective way of obtaining tailored service, especially if the captive or pool generates economies of scale or concentrations of special expertise that the individual organizations could not achieve alone. Moreover, the status of a captive or pool as a "third party," officially organized and staffed as an entity separate from its insureds, is likely to give a captive or pool greater autonomy and authority in dealing with the parents' or participants' personnel and claimants, thus upholding the principles of sound insurance administration with greater objectivity.

Coordination of Insurance Programs in Many Jurisdictions. International and even numerous, widespread national organizations often have difficulty obtaining uniform insurance coverages because insurance codes differ from state to state and country to country. Some jurisdictions require that certain insurance contract provisions follow a prescribed wording. They may also mandate that loss exposures located within their boundaries be insured to specified limits or by an insurer domiciled within those boundaries. The ability to insure, reinsure, or retrocede certain types of risks through a captive or pool—with the captive or pool dealing as necessary with various local insurers and reinsurers—can greatly simplify the design and control of a coordinated insurance program for a far-flung organization. The captive or pool can also administer loss control and claims service programs much more consistently than the organization's (or its insurer's) personnel could from scattered locations. If poorly administered, a multinational or multi-state insurance program can be chaotic; by placing the risk financing challenges in the hands of the competent, central management of a captive or pool can greatly reduce administrative costs and achieve more coherent results.

Improved Access to Reinsurance and Retail Insurance Markets. In addition to allowing an organization or group to secure better coverage for itself, a captive or pool can enable its parents or participants to sell insurance for the underwriting and investment profits this activity may bring. Once a captive or pool has successfully met the risk financing needs of its founders, it may wish to expand its markets to a broader group of organizations or to a wider range of coverages. Broadening its number and range of clients improves a captive's or pool's access to reinsurance and direct excess insurance.

Costs of a Captive or Pool. Establishing a captive or pool requires a commitment of substantial resources in capital, surplus, and personnel. Moreover, choosing to finance recovery from accidental losses through a captive or pool logically entails abstaining from other retention or insurance alternatives. Either of these requirements may impose heavy burdens on an organization in the form of (1) unexpectedly costly or ineffective risk financing and (2) great difficulties disengaging from the captive or pool and returning to more traditional risk financing techniques.

Unexpectedly Costly and Ineffective Risk Financing. The founders of a captive or pool need to anticipate the substantial initial capital expenses of becoming established in a new jurisdiction, for hiring personnel to conduct underwriting and investing operations, and for obtaining the space, equipment, and supplies for daily operations. An organization that is considering joining an existing captive or pool also needs to be prepared to bear its share of these expenses often without any guarantee (or even expectation) that these outlays will be recoverable if the captive or pool is dissolved or if the organization later elects to withdraw from it.

Beyond these initial capital requirements and ongoing expenses, the most significant and least predictable expense for any risk financing program is its outlays for accidental losses. If these losses prove to be much larger than anticipated (especially in the early years or if a captive or pool lacks adequate reinsurance, perhaps because of reinsurer insolvency), the captive or pool may face insolvency or may require infusions of new capital. In either of those instances, a parent of a captive or a participant in a pool is likely to encounter unanticipated demands for more capital as the only alternative to failure, with the concomitant loss of all the initial investment. In addition to loss expenses, any of the normal ongoing insurance costs including loss control, claims handling, ratemaking, underwriting, accounting, and financial management may prove much higher than expected. This can slowly drain the resources of the pool or captive, consequently raising the risk financing costs of each participant or parent. If these costs must increase, then those with favorable loss experience may claim that they are entitled to pay lower assessments than others, perhaps leading to many of the pricing and availability problems that first led to the creation of the captive or pool.

The operating results of a captive or pool may also be disappointing. Starting and managing a property and liability risk financing mechanism so complex that it resembles an insurance company requires a wide variety of actuarial, financial, legal, loss control, underwriting, and general management skills. The cash flow, underwriting, and investment projections underlying the decision to launch or join a captive or pool may have assumed that personnel with these skills would merge into a cohesive team to produce "model" underwriting and investment results. In fact, some of this expertise may be entirely lacking, or those with a crucial skill may not function as efficiently with their fellows as envisioned. For example, the rate charges of captives or pools may prove inadequate, loss control deficient, claims handling erratic, or the senior management of the captive or pool may not receive the expected degree of commitment from participants. For these or other reasons, the captive or pool simply may not produce the results at the costs that were projected when the plan began or when some later members joined the enterprise. Negative possibilities can be minimized by accepting underwriting risks that can be realistically financed, either through existing capital or appropriate excess of loss reinsurance.

Difficulties Shifting to Other Alternatives. Before embarking on a new venture, especially one whose success is directly tied to the skillful management of events so uncertain as accidental losses, it is prudent to consider if other options will be available at a reasonable cost if the enterprise fails or if one of the participants chooses to abandon it. Those who form or join a captive or pool are making long-term commitments to one another and to others who may have claims against the captive or pool. In Chapter 2, the demonstration that accident-related legal claims may take decades to indemnify implies that the commitment cannot simply be financially or ethically abandoned. Therefore, arrangements for (1) allowing any one participant to withdraw or (2) winding up the entire enterprise should be explicitly detailed in the charter, bylaws, or other founding documents of the enterprise and individual participation agreements.

For a single-parent captive, terminating the enterprise or withdrawing from a particular line of coverage is usually relatively simple. This single parent can absorb any outstanding losses once financed through the captive through a more elementary type of retention and search for other financing alternatives for future losses. Liability claims once financed through the captive are automatically transferred back to the parent, which must either accept or attempt to retroactively insure these claims. As long as the parent itself remains solvent, the demise of the captive only forces the parent to temporarily increase its burden of retained losses until it can arrange new risk financing.

In a multi-parent captive or pool, one member's withdrawal—or a unanimous decision to terminate the enterprise—is likely to cause more perplexing difficulties. In these situations care must be taken not only to protect the rights of outside claimants (to whom the withdrawing members may eventually become liable) but also to preserve equities among the departing and remaining members of the captive or pool.

For both these purposes the articles of incorporation, bylaws, or other key documents related to the venture should detail how the assets of the captive or pool, its continuing expenses and income, and its obligations to participants are to be apportioned. The founders of a captive or pool have considerable latitude in determining these apportionments; more important than the precise terms of these apportionments is that the allocations be clear and implemented as stated at the appropriate times.

In order to leave a group captive or a pool, a member may be forced to surrender its ownership interest. Some even have withdrawal penalties as high as 30 percent of the previous year's premiums.

A Note on Taxes. Tax considerations can be advantages or disadvantages for captives or pools depending on the tax statutes and their interpretation in a given jurisdiction at a given time. Some of these considerations include (1) the deductibility from taxable income of parents' and participants' payments to a captive or pool, (2) the obligation to pay premium taxes for having engaged in the "business of insurance," and (3) the tax status of net cash flows that a captive or pool may generate and pay as dividends to its participants.

Current United States federal tax law appears to bestow the advantage of premium tax deductibility where there is risk transfer, but not where there is a retention arrangement. However, these statutes or their interpretation may change. Therefore, rather than conclude that any given tax treatment is or is not a relative advantage of the particular financing technique, the risk management professional should recognize that tax advantages and disadvantages, like other strengths and weaknesses of various risk financing alternatives, should be weighted (ideally, expressed in present values of expected net cash flows) so that they can be considered in the same way as other costs and benefits of risk financing alternatives.

Determining Feasibility of a Captive or Pool

If an organization's risk management professional and its senior executives agree that forming or joining a captive or pool would, in principle, benefit the organization, sound risk financing next calls for a detailed feasibility study. This study should determine whether or not the captive or pool would also be practical in reality.

A proper feasibility study is not a sales presentation. Therefore, a feasibility study that merely documents a previous conclusion is suspect. (In fact, one particularly meaningful criterion for selecting an external expert to lead a feasibility study is how often the expert has recommended *against* a captive or pool, and the reasons for such negative recommendations.) A proper feasibility study should explore with a team of objective experts whether the organization possesses, and can have continuing access to, the financial, managerial, and other resources needed to operate or participate in a captive or pool.

Because establishing a captive or pool entails the regulatory, accounting, and financial complexities of starting an insurance company, any feasibility study should be conducted by a team of specialists. The leader is often someone associated with a risk management consulting or an insurance brokerage firm, or an insurer, many of which also are prepared to manage the ongoing operations of any captives or pools. Before retaining an expert, it is good practice to reach a preliminary agreement with this expert on the scope, purposes, schedule, and cost of the study. More specifically, a full-scale feasibility study should be preceded by general agreement between the interested organization(s) and the outside expert with respect to the following:

- Possible alternative forms of organization for the captive or pool (for example, stock, mutual, or reciprocal).
- Types and amounts of property, liability, net income, or personal loss exposures the organization(s) may wish to finance through the pool or captive.
- Jurisdictions in which the organization(s) may wish the captive or pool to be domiciled.
- Amounts of initial capital and annual expenses the founding organizations envision allotting from their own resources to the captive or pool until it becomes self-supporting.
- Types of services (actuarial, financial, legal, managerial, and the like) the captive or pool will require and the possible sources for them.
- Cost of the feasibility study itself, the procedures for conducting it, the subjects to be included in the study, and a timetable for its completion.
- Whether the ultimate goal of the captive or pool is to grow beyond the needs of its current participants to serve wider markets and eventually to become a general insurance company.
- Benefits anticipated from the study even if it should recommend against establishing a captive or pool. (These benefits might include a thorough analysis of the organizations' risk management programs and recommendations for improvements.)

Based on such a preliminary agreement, representatives from the client organization(s) and the consulting organization should be chosen for the study team. The study should involve two distinct parts: a *risk management analysis* and an *operational analysis.*

The basic purpose of the risk management analysis is to determine the types of losses that could best be financed through the captive or pool. To achieve this purpose, the team must analyze the organizations' loss history, current loss exposures, and the existing means of treating these exposures, including the ability to finance losses through the captive or pool. This information can be a basis for discussions with reinsurers, captive management companies, and other specialists who might provide services to the captive or pool. Moreover, the risk management portion of a feasibility study should better enable each participating organization to view its risk management program as a whole, with or without a captive or pool, rather than merely considering the captive or pool as an isolated project.

The purpose of the operational analysis is to project the costs and benefits the parent(s) or participants could expect from the most reasonable use of a captive or pool and to compare these cost/benefit relationships with those of other risk financing alternatives. To achieve this purpose, price quotations must be secured from reinsurers, captive management companies, and other service organizations for all activities relevant to the operations of the captive or pool. Prices should also be obtained for each of the other risk financing alternatives. The study should structure this information to compare the costs and benefits of alternatives under a variety of scenarios involving expected levels of accidental losses, especially severe loss levels, as well as particularly favorable loss experience. It is not sufficient for a captive or pool to appear feasible under only favorable conditions—it should also appear reliable during the worst foreseeable times.

The final feasibility study should structure its findings and recommendations to include a brief summary and index of the entire report, a detailed discussion of the alternative risk financing techniques and the costs and benefits projected for each, a summary of the legal and tax implications of the captive or pool for the parent(s) or participants, and if a captive or pool is recommended, a sequence and schedule for the steps needed to implement this recommendation.

ESTABLISHING AND OPERATING A CAPTIVE OR POOL

When establishing a captive or pool, risk management professionals and senior executives must make a number of crucial decisions as to the nature and scope of their enterprise. Once the enterprise is established, they must also make numerous decisions about how it will operate on a daily basis.

Establishing a Captive or Pool

The decisions made at the outset about the (1) organizational form, (2) domicile, (3) initial and continuing capitalization, (4) method of providing coverage, and (5) types of coverage provided are among the most important decisions confronting the management of a captive or pool because they shape all its future activities.

Organizational Form. For establishing formal risk financing mechanisms for retention or transfer, property and liability insurance history and traditions provide three basic models: a *stock organization*, a *mutual organization*, and a *reciprocal organization*. They are usually defined in an insurance setting as follows:

- A stock insurer is an incorporated insurer with capital contributed by stockholders to whom earnings are distributed as dividends on their shares.
- A mutual insurer is an incorporated insurer owned by its policyholders to whom earnings are distributed as dividends in some equitable manner.
- A reciprocal (or a reciprocal exchange) is an unincorporated group of individuals or organizations called subscribers who mutually insure one another, each separately assuming individual shares of each insured loss exposure.

With the exception of a single-parent captive, which has only one owner, any other captive or any pool can be operated by its parents or participants as a stock organization, a mutual organization, or a reciprocal.

Before 1970, most captives were formed as stock organizations for any of several reasons. First, the founders' ability to determine who should hold the stock and to prohibit or limit transfers of the stock ensures complete ownership and control of the captive by its parents. Second, a stock organization can be more easily liquidated when it has fulfilled its objectives and is no longer needed; the owners clearly have the right to discontinue their enterprise without raising any regulatory concerns about whether persons or organizations receiving risk financing protection through the enterprise have been equitably treated. Third, for dealing within reinsurance markets, stock organizations of a given capital size are typically regarded as financially more reliable than all but the largest of mutual and reciprocal organizations.

Since the 1970s, mutual and reciprocal forms of organization have become significantly more popular. Especially for association and group captives, the mutual or reciprocal framework has been appealing because of the ability to expand or contract its operations as parents' risk financing needs change and because of the spirit of interdependence—as well as independence from the commercial insurance market—that mutuals and reciprocals typically engender. Furthermore, for any one organization seeking risk financing, a pool or reciprocal is easier to form, enter, or exit than is a stock organization.

Nearly all pools are structured as mutual organizations or reciprocals—very few, if any, begin as stock organizations. Because interdependence is essential to the basic notion of a pool, ownership of the organization by those whom it protects is highly logical; ownership as a stock organization by "outsiders" would tend to subvert the basic spirit of the enterprise. Thus, in addition to the preceding advantages, the members of the pool can also "persuade" other members to adopt sound risk control and other proper management techniques.

Domicile. An organization or group forming a captive or pool has considerable freedom in choosing the legal jurisdiction that will be its "home" in the sense that the captive or pool (1) is first formed in, (2) is regulated primarily by, and (3) is subject to the tax laws of that jurisdiction. A captive or pool need not conduct the bulk of its activities in its domiciliary jurisdiction (in some cases it is prohibited from doing so) as long as it meets the minimum requirements for maintaining a corporate office in that jurisdiction. In a legal sense, such an office need be little more than a mailing address and can, in fact, be maintained by an agent whose primary business is maintaining corporate offices for a large number of captives, pools, or other noninsurance organizations that wish to be domiciled in a given jurisdiction but, in fact, conduct the bulk of their business elsewhere.

The very wide range of domiciles can be broadly classified as *domestic* (located within the United States or other country in which the participants are legally domiciled) and offshore (any jurisdiction that is not domestic). *Offshore domiciles* offer the general advantages of freedom from taxation by the country in which the captive parents or pool participants conduct the bulk of their business (although these offshore sites may have their own special tax and regulatory requirements). In addition, there may be a U.S. federal excise tax for premiums paid from the U.S. to offshore companies. Several states have enacted statutes designed to encourage formation of captives or pools, both to meet the risk financing needs of their own domestic corporations and to gain the revenue and prestige derived from taxing and regulating the captives or pools they might attract from other jurisdictions. During times of rapid captive or pool formation, some jurisdictions compete vigorously for captives to form in their states.

Because captives or pools are best conducted as permanent enterprises, and not as temporary devices for benefiting from fluctuations in commercial insurance markets, an organization or group should choose a domicile best suited to its long-term needs, regardless of which jurisdictions may temporarily be most popular. Therefore, simply for convenience, an organization or group whose operations are concentrated in a particular jurisdiction often will choose it for a domicile regardless of the regulatory, tax, or other incentives available elsewhere. (Most public sector pools serve entities within a single state, so there is only one feasible domicile.)

Other organizations or groups, especially those whose operations already span several countries, tend to explore a wider range of domiciles in terms of the (1) ease of formation, (2) freedom from regulation, (3) operating convenience, and (4) tax advantages. A particularly attractive jurisdiction is one that, with respect to formation, offers the following:

- Low minimum capital requirements initially and as the underwritings of the captive or pool grow
- Rapid formation with few, if any, mandatory waiting periods or "red tape" delays
- Permission for one captive or pool to underwrite coverage against a wide range of loss exposures so that the legal structure of the enterprise may remain relatively uncomplicated

With respect to regulatory freedom, the second important criterion in deciding where to locate a captive or pool, a favorable domicile often is one that does the following:

- Permits and recognizes as "insurance" the writing of a wide range of coverages on loss exposures located throughout the world
- Imposes few or no insurance rate regulations or recognizes diverse premium rating plans for individual insureds
- Allows the captive or pool to invest its reserves and other funds in a variety of financial instruments, real property, and other tangible assets
- Places few restrictions on the movement of or convertibility between international currencies
- Has a tradition of political stability and liberal regulation of business, thus ensuring that current freedoms are likely to remain

Operating convenience, the third criterion, is likely to be greatest in a jurisdiction characterized by the following:

- A strong business infrastructure of insurance, reinsurance, banking, and accounting firms that will be able to supply services or personnel to support the operations of the captive or pool
- A recognition of the economic benefits that the jurisdiction derives from, and a wish to continue to attract, captive and pool operations
- Reliable internal and international communications networks,

especially telephone systems, so that information and funds can be readily exchanged and transferred
- Access to convenient transportation
- A suitable economic and legal environment and culture

In terms of the tax climate, an attractive domicile is one that does the following:

- Levies little or no premium tax on captives or pools
- Requires no, or only a small, annual licensing or other business privilege fee
- Imposes little or no state income tax on captive and pool earnings from underwriting or investment operations

Although a captive or pool should be formed only as a long-term risk financing technique, those responsible for the initial venture should recognize that time may require changes. Economic and regulatory conditions may someday require that the domicile be moved. Such a move may technically require only a few changes in legal forms, addresses, and similar details. Nevertheless, moving a captive may require shifting financial assets from one jurisdiction to another and satisfying various security and other regulations of the jurisdiction from which the move is being made. Therefore, to allow for a possible change in domicile, those choosing the initial home should be sure that it does not unduly restrict the portability of the enterprise.

Initial and Continuing Capitalization. Any risk financing mechanism should have access from its inception to financial resources that can help (1) pay the initial costs of launching the enterprise and (2) absorb unexpectedly high losses, especially during the first few years of operation. Access to ample financial resources greatly increases the likelihood that the enterprise will succeed, and therefore substantially enhances the financial security enjoyed by its "client" parent(s) or participants.

It is for these reasons that the insurance codes of all jurisdictions require an organization that seeks to be recognized as an insurer to begin operations with at least the minimum amounts of paid-in surplus (or for a stock organization, capital and surplus) specified in the applicable code for the kinds and amounts of insurance to be offered. Beyond this initial capitalization, these codes specify minimums below which paid-in surplus must never fall. (If these minimums are not met, the insurance regulator usually has the authority to place the insurer in financial rehabilitation or receivership.) These initial and continuing capital and surplus requirements vary widely from one jurisdiction to another, and within any one jurisdiction the code often specifies different minimums for different types of insurance. Many jurisdictions also establish different minimums for stock insurers, mutuals, and reciprocals, and still other jurisdictions specify separate sets of capitalization requirements for captives as well as for organizations wishing to qualify as "self-insurers" of workers compensation or other loss exposures.

These capital requirements can greatly influence an organization's choice of domiciles. Some organizations may not have or be able to raise the capital they would need to qualify as an insurer in a jurisdiction in which they would prefer to be domiciled. (Even for a single-parent captive, the capital and surplus requirements of a jurisdiction are only one indication of the resources that will be needed, according to sound risk financing, to operate such a captive.)

The types and timing of funding to meet initial and continuing capital requirements also vary. Some jurisdictions require cash, certificates of deposit, or other liquid assets, while others will accept letters of credit or financial guarantee bonds. Some jurisdictions require the entire amount of the initial capital to be deposited with regulatory authorities before a new insurer is authorized to issue its first policy; other jurisdictions establish a schedule that permits particular types of insurers (especially captives and small pools) to begin operations before collecting the minimum capital or surplus that will eventually be required.

In addition to initial and continuing capital, many jurisdictions also impose other financial and investment restrictions on insurers to ensure that they remain able to meet obligations to policyholders; a related requirement is that authorized insurers follow certain auditing and reporting procedures and document their continuing financial solvency for the insurance regulator. For example, most jurisdictions mandate that the permanent minimums of capital and surplus be maintained in specified classes of particularly conservative investments. Each jurisdiction is also likely to establish guidelines for maximum permissible ratios of premiums written to policyholders' surplus, of particular classes of an insurer's investments to its total assets, and of an insurer's net retentions (after deduction of ceded reinsurance) in the aggregate and for any given loss exposure.

The form of organization chosen for a captive or pool influences how it can best raise its initial and continuing capital. Stock organizations obtain their beginning capital and surplus from their owners who do not have to be their insureds. Generation of funds can be on any nonfraudulent basis. Subsequent paid-up surplus consists of what is left of profits after any dividends paid to stockholders—the lower the portion of earnings distributed as dividends, the more earned surplus remains to support risk financing operations. In a mutual or reciprocal organization the initial surplus is generated from funds contributed by the participants. Thereafter, the annual contribution from each parent or participant to the organization's financial reservoir from which losses and operating expenses are paid is affected by its loss exposures, the extent to which these exposures are insured through the captive or pool, the premium rates charged each parent or participant, overall underwriting and investment results, and any dividend returned to that parent or participant.

For a captive or pool operating as a mutual or reciprocal, premium and dividend rate structures followed during its initial years should be actuarially designed to generate and retain surplus by charging rates that are relatively conservative. As a captive or pool matures, its senior management will often choose more refined rating and dividend schedules that reflect each parent's or participant's individual loss experience or loss control efforts.

Premium rates often reflect the extent to which various parents or participants retain loss exposures through different deductibles. The net cost of coverage for organizations that retain more of their exposures can be reduced by a premium rate structure or a dividend scale that rewards greater retention. Because fundamental fairness and shared interests are so essential to the success of a captive or pool organized as a mutual or reciprocal, and because organizations using captives or pools tend to be directly involved in their management, it is crucial that the formulas for raising initial capital, developing premium rates, and distributing dividends be equitable to all participants.

Method of Providing Coverage. A captive or pool may function as a primary insurer, a reinsurer, or as a combination of both in helping its parents or participants meet their risk financing needs. As a primary insurer, the captive or pool receives payments (premiums if the arrangement qualifies as an insurance) from its parents or participants. In return, it issues policies that obligate the captive or pool to pay each parent's or participant's losses as would any commercial insurer. Also functioning as a primary insurer, a captive or pool may reinsure a substantial portion of its primary insurance obligations, again much as any commercial insurer would.

As a reinsurer, a captive or pool may negotiate an agreement with one or more commercial insurers, or *fronting insurers,* to issue policies in each fronting company's name to parents or participants. As shown in Exhibit 4-1, the fronting company then cedes all or most of its primary insurance obligations back to the captive or pool, which acts as a reinsurer. The captive or pool retains both control of and investment earn-

Exhibit 4-1

Typical Relationships of Parent or Participant, Third-Party Claimant, Fronting Insurer, Captive or Pool, and Reinsurer

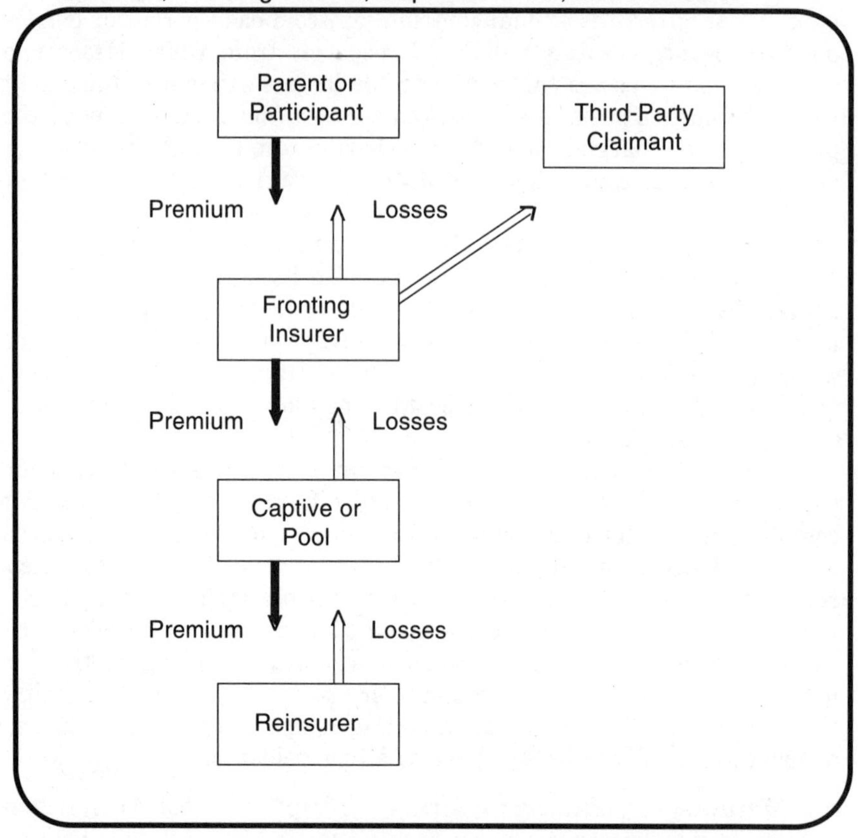

ings from the bulk of the premium initially paid for the primary coverage. If the captive or pool as a reinsurer is not able to retain the entire loss exposures of the parents or participants obtained through such fronting arrangements, the captive or pool may enter into additional reinsurance arrangements to further distribute these exposures throughout the reinsurance market. Because only the fronting insurer and not the captive reinsurer needs to be licensed in a jurisdiction where the parent's or participant's loss exposures are located, fronting arrangements have the additional advantage of permitting a captive or pool to generate underwriting earnings without being licensed in a variety of jurisdictions.

Finally, a captive or pool may act as a primary insurer for some exposures and as a reinsurer for others, thus giving it more flexibility in dealing with the loss exposures of parents or participants. It also has many more strategic options for generating underwriting and investment income from various segments of the primary insurance and reinsurance markets.

Types of Coverage. Most captives or pools provide the types of insurance their parents or participants cannot otherwise easily obtain. Thus, at various times during the past quarter century, most captives and pools have provided liability coverages, particularly for medical and other professional malpractice exposures, workers compensation obligations, and products liability claims. Concurrently, many municipalities and other public entities have experienced serious price and availability problems with coverage for their general liability exposures, which often encompass police, public works, and other activities that tend to generate many large liability claims because of the changing laws of governmental liability.

Beyond meeting their parents' risk financing needs, a growing number of captives (as distinct from pools) have shifted their focus to generating higher profits by gaining more complete control of investable funds for their parents. In this new focus, liability coverages have again proven attractive for captives because of the long periods during which funds in loss and unearned premium reserves can be held as investments.

Captives and pools have also frequently provided life and health coverages to support parents' or participants' employee benefit plans, again because of the opportunities for long-term investment income. However, the federal Employee Retirement Income Security Act (ERISA) places rather strict limitations on the extent to which a captive or pool can act as a fiduciary of funds held for the ultimate benefit of parents' or participants' employees. These restrictions are designed to protect the interests of the employees. They are also designed to prevent a captive or pool from facing conflicts of interest or engaging in "self-dealing" when carrying out its dual responsibilities to these employees and their respective employers.

Using fronting arrangements, captives and pools have frequently offered coverages of exposures that are required by insurance codes in various jurisdictions to be underwritten by an insurer domiciled in that jurisdiction. Workers compensation and automobile liability exposures are often subject to such regulations in states that want to assure that their residents injured on the job or in highway accidents are adequately compensated. One method of meeting these local insurance requirements is to use a domestic insurer as a fronting company with the understanding that it will reinsure this primary coverage through the captive or pool. The net result is that the parents or participants in the captive or pool can both meet the requirements of the local statute and achieve many of the investment and other benefits they could derive from retaining these exposures.

Operating a Captive or Pool

Having established a captive or pool, the founders must decide on a general management framework within which the captive or pool can efficiently conduct its marketing, underwriting and rating, reinsurance, claims administration, loss control, and financial management activities. They must also ensure that these daily operations generate data for evaluating the actuarial, financial, and general management performance of the captive or pool. Those who wish to operate a successful captive or pool must establish regular procedures for performing each of the same functions on which the success of any insurer depends. For some of these functions, the captive or pool will need to rely primarily on its own in-house personnel because of their unique understanding of the captive's or pool's operations. For other activities, outside experts may be indispensable, at least initially. A third set of activities may be jointly performed by internal and external personnel, who are retained as consultants or on some temporary basis. As a preview for much of the following discussion, Exhibit 4-2 indicates how many essential functions within a captive or pool are typically performed by internal personnel, by outside experts, and by both.

General Management Framework. Organized as a stock, mutual, or reciprocal organization, every captive or pool must have a structure of executive and support personnel to conduct its activities.

Single-Parent Captive Management. A captive insurer can be managed by its own executives and personnel or through a contract with an outside management firm. Some single-parent captives are administered through or guided by the parent's risk management or finance department; the parent's risk management professional is often appointed chief executive officer of the captive. In this capacity, this professional may manage the captive on behalf of the parent. For association and group captives, executives and operating staff are often chosen from outside the ranks of the parents' employees, although the overall governing board of such a captive is likely to include risk management professionals from several of the parents.

For many new captives, as well as for those that remain relatively small and informal, the popularity of external management principally stems from the fact that the captive's operations can be conducted more economically by an outside management company. In addition, the presence of an independent management team, none of whom are employed by the parent, has been offered as evidence to the Internal Revenue

Exhibit 4-2
Typical Allocation of Captive or Pool Functions Among Internal, External, and Shared Expertise

Function	Internal	External	Shared
Marketing	X		
Data Collection	X		
Underwriting		X	
Reinsurance & Insurance Brokerage		X	
Contract Insurance/ Coverage Plan Administration			X
Billing/Collections	X		
Claims Administration		X	
Loss Control/Prevention			X
Management Information Systems		X	
Payroll/Premium Audits		X	
Accounting			X
Investment Management			X
Financial Audit		X	
Actuarial Review		X	
Performance Audit		X	
Legal Counsel		X	

Reprinted with permission from V.M. Stephens, et al., eds., *Risk Financing* (Dallas, TX: International Risk Management Institute, Inc., looseleaf revised and updated periodically), October 1983, p. IV.F.10.

Service to support the argument that an association or group captive is an independent entity to which the parents have transferred loss exposures, thus qualifying for income tax deductions for insurance premiums. Such independent management, indicating that the parents are "dealing at arm's length" with the captive, has also been useful in demonstrating to other insurers and reinsurers in the United States and abroad that the captive is a true insuring organization worthy of status as a peer.

Captive management services are readily available from many large insurance brokerage and consulting organizations and from the risk management service departments of major commercial insurers. Captive management services are usually provided on a fee basis, according to the amount of work performed. Some captive management organizations, however, charge a fixed monthly or annual fee plus out-of-pocket expenses.

Management of Group and Association Captives and Pools. The governing body of a group or association captive as well as a pool, usually a board appointed by the members, is responsible for its general operations and financial condition. This responsibility includes determining premium rate levels, securing reinsurance, establishing dividends and earnings distribution procedures, selecting any needed outside providers of actuarial and loss control services, and establishing procedures by which new participants can join or existing participants can withdraw.

Essential to the success of any group plan is every participant's understanding of the mutuality of this risk-sharing arrangement. While hoping for reduced cost and greater premium stability, the participants must be prepared for the possibility of adverse loss experience and fluctuating cost. This commitment to shared risk is particularly vital when many of the participants are small or medium-sized organizations, or persons who are members of a trade or professional association who are not accustomed to underwriting others' loss exposures.

For those unusual situations where extremely adverse covered losses or very poor investment results may render initial capital inadequate, the governing body must be prepared to fund any projected deficit. A group or association captive may ask the members to contribute additional surplus, and a pool may assess members for any shortfall.

Underwriting and Rating. Once a captive or pool has selected the types of coverage it wishes to provide to its parents or participants, it must have access to technical expertise in order to establish the contractual terms for insuring loss exposures and for determining appropriate premiums for this protection. The personnel of the captive or pool may have such underwriting and ratemaking expertise. In most cases, however, it can best be obtained through an insurance brokerage or consulting firm, a risk management service department of a commercial insurer, or from an independent service provider. In addition, the captive or pool must have continuing access to these essential skills.

Any competent outside service provider can normally evaluate the underwriting loss exposures of the captive or pool parents or participants, develop policy forms to meet these exposures (while excluding exposures the captive or pool does not wish to undertake), calculate appropriate premium charges, and develop underwriting guides for placing parents or participants in appropriate rating classes (or, if necessary, denying coverage to some applicants). These developmental tasks require some time and effort for which the service provider will charge either an hourly or a flat fee. If internal personnel are performing these tasks, they should have enough time to complete them carefully.

If a captive does not wish or does not need to qualify as an insurer, then the charges it levies against parents or participants may be structured in any way that is mutually acceptable and financially sound. For such an enterprise, few regulations affect the nature or price of the financial protection provided. In contrast, a captive or pool that seeks to qualify as an insurer under the laws of its domicile must follow underwriting and rating practices that comply with the procedures and the standards of adequacy, equity, and reasonableness of that jurisdiction.

The ratemaking procedures of a sound captive or pool generally follow the procedures of a traditional, commercially insured policy both because these procedures are sound insurance practice and because they are typically mandated by applicable insurance codes. Thus, a captive or pool may charge manual (guaranteed-cost) premium rates or may establish any of a variety of merit rating or loss-sensitive rating plans authorized by the insurance code by implementing regulations for the type(s) of coverage written within the captive's or pool's domicile or, in some cases, the jurisdiction in which the loss exposure is located. Because pools heavily emphasize mutuality and loss sharing, rating plans that apply to pools often emphasize dividends based on group experience.

Such dividends both reward favorable loss experience and reduce parents' or participants' ultimate risk financing cost. In a financial and cash flow context, dividends are partial refunds of risk financing funds from "policyholders' surplus" because the sum of their "premiums" and investment income is greater than the total of losses paid, loss reserves, and operating expenses over one or several calendar quarters or years. Further, the amounts returned as dividends are deemed by the management of the captive or pool to be no longer needed to support any expansion or diversification of the captive's or pool's activities.

Insurance premium rates must be based on actuarial and financial assumptions regarding at least three factors: parents' or participants' loss experience, the captive's or pool's operating expenses, and investment income. Dividends are generated from favorable deviations—lower losses or operating expenses and higher investment income for the captive or pool—from the results projected in premium rate calculations. (Many insurers who wish to pay dividends regularly use loss, expense, and investment income assumptions to determine premium rates so that some minimum dividend will be generated—so that something "extra" will be returned to policyholders. Here, the size, rather than the existence, of dividends depends upon favorable deviations from these assumptions.) As a result of different ratemaking procedures, the following are true:

- Better than assumed underwriting experience generates savings for the captive or pool, which, if not needed to support expanded operations or diversification into other activities, can be returned as dividends to parents or participants.
- Expense savings may result from reduced administrative expenses, more effective loss control, and economies of scale because of collective purchasing from outside service providers.
- The size of dividends generated from investment income depends on the market performance of the captive's or pool's financial assets and the amount of its expenses to support its investment activities.

Once the particular dividend rate for a given quarter or year has been determined by the senior management of the captive or pool, the dollar amount of each parent's or participant's dividend for that period is usually related to its premium volume and/or loss experience.

Dividend policy must address not only the size of periodic dividends but also the classes of parents or participants eligible for them. The charter or bylaws of a multi-parent captive or pool may stipulate that each parent or participant is eligible for dividends that were generated only during its years of membership. Alternatively, each periodic dividend may be based on the cumulative results of the captive or pool since its inception rather than on the loss, expense, or investment experience for individual periods. Also, to encourage continuing membership, the dividend formula for a captive or pool—unlike that of most commercial insurers—may specify that a parent or participant is not eligible for any dividends that become payable after it withdraws—that is, in some captives and pools, dividends are not prorated for the portion of the last dividend period during which a withdrawing parent or participant leaves the captive or pool.

Marketing. Because captives and pools exist to meet the risk financing needs of particular organizations or groups, their marketing activities should be correspondingly targeted and their marketing expenses similarly reduced because their potential clients are readily identified and presumably inclined to use their risk financing services. In fact, a captive with only one or a few parents may have essentially no identifiable marketing activities or expenses. In contrast, a captive or pool with a sizable membership must continue its service, educational, and promotional efforts, often in the form of "membership" drives. These and similar activities attract and hold members who might otherwise seek the apparent benefits of commercial insurance or some other form of risk financing.

Reinsurance. Few captives or pools, like few commercial insurers, have the capital and underwriting capacity to retain the full amount of all loss exposures. Consequently, most captives and pools, especially relatively small ones, need reinsurance to support their underwritings in the same way that commercial insurers also need reinsurance (see Chapter 6).

Reinsurers also provide a captive's or pool's senior and technical managers with useful information about insurance and reinsurance management. Moreover, portfolio reinsurance is useful for a captive or pool seeking to withdraw from a line of risk financing. Because the purchase or sale of reinsurance is an intricate process, most captives and pools must use the expertise available from a reinsurer or a reinsurance broker to represent them as buyers or sellers in reinsurance and retrocession markets.

To achieve these benefits, a captive or pool must have credibility as a buyer and seller of reinsurance. Therefore, the management of a captive or pool should focus on the several factors that reinsurers weigh in determining whether and how much coverage to provide to, or reinsurance to seek from, a captive or pool. Among the important factors generally considered by reinsurers are the following:

- The legitimacy of forming a captive or pool—the most ideal reason being to provide cost-effective risk financing to parents or participants (and not simply to provide income tax advantages)
- The extent of managerial and financial commitment of the parents or participants to maintaining the captive or pool on a stable, permanent basis regardless of price and availability fluctuations in commercial insurance markets
- The adequacy of the financing for the captive or pool and how readily available additional capital will be
- The extent to which the policy forms and underwriting practices of the captive or pool parallel those of the commercial insurance markets (greater similarities typically give reinsurers more faith in the captive or pool)
- The adequacy of the premium rates charged by the captive or pool
- The adequacy of internal technical expertise or of readily obtainable outside expertise
- The general caliber and reputation of the captive's or pool's senior management

Captives and pools have simultaneously needed to convince their present and potential parents and participants that they are special providers of needed protection—sources of risk financing not readily found in other commercial markets. Thus, captives and pools have simultaneously sought to appear reassuringly traditional to the reinsurance markets and refreshingly innovative to those for whom they provide risk financing.

Claims Administration. Prompt payment of claims, as well as vigorous control of the amount of these payments, is extremely important and requires broad technical expertise. Therefore, those who are responsible for managing the claims-handling activities of a captive or pool should be as skilled as commercial insurers in coverage analysis, loss and claim evaluation, and negotiating skills. Moreover, the rising standards of professional liability now being imposed on claims adjusters generally imply that the claims management personnel for a captive or pool must also be able to meet these standards, especially when dealing with third-party claimants who may sue the captive or pool if their claims are not handled according to the common law and fair claims practices acts of their jurisdiction. Therefore, all but the largest captives and pools rely almost exclusively on external legal counsel or other service providers to handle claims investigations, litigation, claims payments, and subrogation activities. Effective cooperation among the parents or participants in a captive or pool, the managers of the captive or pool, and the outside service providers is required. In addition, the specific duties and rights of external claims-handling personnel must be detailed in writing and confirmed or clarified as necessary by ongoing discussions so that claims administration is properly performed.

Loss Control. Risk financing through a captive or pool provides an incentive to practice effective loss control. On the one hand, reducing loss frequency and severity of captive parents or pool participants requires as much expertise as does claims administration. On the other hand, a parent's or a participant's own personnel are in the best position to recognize and, ideally, to eliminate the actual hazards associated with their daily work. Many pools and captives have found that loss control is best performed by a combination of outside technical experts and an organization's own personnel. In an ideal situation, outside experts would consult with supervisory and first-line personnel within an organization to develop customized risk control programs. They could also provide ongoing technical assistance in training, thus developing loss control programs that are both tailored to the exposures common to all members of the captive or pool and to the unique features of each member organization. As with outside claims-handling personnel, external loss control experts should have their duties and rights detailed in writing so that they can more completely meet their clients' expectations.

Exhibit 4-3
Activity Standards for Senior Captive or Pool Management

- Regular delivery to senior management of financial data and information that is comprehensible, timely, and useful
- Adequate opportunity for senior management to discuss operating trends
- Senior management approval of audit policies and periodic review of their implementation
- Joint participation by senior and operating management in developing annual and other periodic budgets
- Proper cash management and handling in cooperation with bank and investment officials to assure proper accounting, availability of funds, and few if any breaches of security
- Periodic senior management review and approval of investments, underwriting, marketing, and other department plans
- Annual senior management selection or confirmation of external auditors, to provide regular, detailed reports
- Senior management review of competitive bidding processes for selecting external service providers

Reprinted with permission from V.M. Stephens, et al., eds., *Risk Financing* (Dallas, TX: International Risk Management Institute, Inc., looseleaf revised and updated periodically), December 1986, pp. IV.D.16, 17.

Financial Management. To be successful, a captive or pool and its parents or participants must both maintain good accounting records that can become the basis for financial management. In order to achieve this, the financial management of a captive or pool is typically shared by the staff and management of a captive or pool and the accounting and financial personnel of each parent or participant. Furthermore, because insurance accounting can be complex, outside service providers, such as insurers or independent firms that serve insurers, are often used. They often help each organization adapt their accounting software to accommodate detailed ledgers, filing structures, and reports that consistently and accurately reflect the transactions and financial condition of the pool or captive. The staff of the captive or pool or an outside service firm typically furnishes monthly balance sheets and statements of operations to the governing board of the captive or pool. These results are also semiannually or annually reported to all parents and participants. The same personnel also prepare information needed for rate filings with state regulatory officials and for completing tax returns and other documents required by state and federal revenue authorities.

Exhibit 4-4
Activity Standards for External Service Providers (or Internal Captive or Pool Departments)

Marketing

- New parent or participant solicitation by direct mail, personal visits, and so on
- Number of educational and promotional meetings
- Quality of promotional materials
- Response to service complaints

Underwriting

- Maintenance of underwriting policy manual and supporting rationale
- Timely rating and pricing proposals for prospective parents or participants
- Maintenance of coverage documents
- Timely rerate renewals to existing parents or participants
- Timely generation of billing source documents
- Management of underwriting support services, such as specialty engineering, underwriting surveys, and so on
- Timely provision of coverage support documents to parents or participants
- Maintenance of exposure summary questionnaire

Reinsurance

- Timely and comprehensive applications for reinsurance
- Advocacy before reinsurance underwriters
- Critical review of reinsurance contracts
- Aggressive reinsurance negotiation on behalf of pool
- Maintenance of reinsurance contracts
- Monitor financial and operating stability of reinsurer insurers
- Timely placement of commercial insurance policies if not available from the pool

Financial Management

- Maintenance of program budget reporting system
- Maintenance of general ledger and check reconciliation
- Production of monthly balance sheets and statement of operations
- Performance of monthly aging of loss drafts
- Timely filing with state regulatory agencies and Internal Revenue Service
- Having timely and accurate cash flow projects
- Preparation of papers for external auditors
- Management and quality control of field adjusters
- Compliance with procedures and controls
- Ensuring procedures and control of field adjusters
- Ensuring promptness and expertise of claims handling

- Maintaining adequate file documentation and proper claims verification
- Maintaining accurate reports of payments and reserves
- Adequacy or excessiveness of payments
- Perform periodic loss reserve adequacy analysis
- Aggressive pursuit of subrogation
- Timely claims notice reporting to reinsurers
- Periodic technical review of high amount claims
- Preparation and maintenance of loss control plan or service
- Development and maintenance of training calendar
- Documentation of loss prevention field visits
- Documentation of quality control reviews of field loss control specialists

Actuarial Activities

- Timely production of experience modification factors
- Documented review of rate adequacy
- Quarterly summary of high amount losses
- Annual summary of loss ratios by parent or participant and by line of coverage
- Annual summary of earned premiums by parent or participant by line of coverage
- Annual claims information details by line of coverage to facilitate actuarial rate adequacy tests and experience modification
- Documentation of captive's or pool's expense ratios by type of insured and in comparison with ratios for commercial insurers

---

Reprinted with permission from V.M. Stephens, et al., eds., *Risk Financing* (Dallas, TX: International Risk Management Institute, Inc., looseleaf revised and updated periodically), December 1986, pp. IV.D.17-20.

Evaluating Performance. As suggested in Exhibits 4-3 and 4-4, an indispensable step in managing any activity—including the operation of a captive or pool—is controlling its performance. This is done by gathering information on activities, comparing this information with standards for acceptable performance, and, where necessary, correcting substandard performance. To ensure proper evaluation and control, the internal management of a captive or pool must have a system for gathering data on performance and must use this data to review the organization's actuarial, financial, and general management. Evaluation and control may be done by the organization's internal personnel, by outside service providers, or jointly by both.

Financial projections, properly made and subject to change by any unforeseen external conditions, can be the performance standards for the captive or pool. In addition to *performance standards,* against which the results of activity are measured, the captive or pool management and the work of outside service providers should be evaluated by *activity standards.* An activity standard is not used to measure results—which may be subject to chance fluctuations, such as unexpected frequencies or severities of accidental losses—but to measure the efforts put forth to seek these results. (Activity standards rely on a belief that good efforts will produce good results.) Because the successful management of a captive or pool often requires cooperation between internal personnel and external service providers, the activity standards that highlight symptoms of inadequate cooperation are extremely important. Exhibits 4-3 and 4-4 summarize some possible activity standards for evaluating the senior management of a captive or pool and of external service providers. The standards for external providers may also serve indirectly as standards for internal departments performing these same functions. If these critical operating functions are not being performed internally as cost effectively as they could be by an external service organization, then the possibility of turning to an external provider should at least be evaluated.

SUMMARY

The distinction that exists in principle between risk retention (internal financing of losses) and risk transfer (relying on external sources) is not always totally clear in practice. Between clear retention (such as using current revenues or funding reserves to pay for losses) and clear transfer (such as commercial insurance or the noninsurance contractual arrangements to be analyzed in Chapter 7) is a relatively narrow but crowded continuum of risk financing techniques that have elements of both retention and transfer. These hybrid techniques have raised questions about the tax and regulatory status of the organizations that use them.

Close to the traditional forms of retention are single-parent captives—risk financing subsidiaries affiliated with individual companies managed primarily to meet that one parent's financing needs. Multiparent captives serve the risk financing needs of many parents that pool their loss exposures and underwriting experience through a hybrid risk financing mechanism that is neither wholly retention nor wholly transfer. Their management is quite independent of the wishes of any one particular parent. Because of this, they begin to look like a more traditional risk transfer operation, which is characterized by the mutual sharing of losses and the clear transferring of the financial burden of those losses to a legally and managerially separate entity.

Closer to traditional forms of transfer are pools. Pools with a substantial number of members are clearly risk transfer mechanisms. They serve only the risk financing needs of the organizations that form them and that participate in their financing and management. Most pool members are within the same industry or geographic territory.

Clearly exemplifying true transfer are mutual insurers with many members. They are characterized by management that is almost totally independent of any one participant, a sharing of losses among participants, and the willingness (or even eagerness) to attract more participants from a wide variety of industries. Several of today's most successful mutual insurers began as what were then, in effect, captives with just one or a few parents (although the term "captive" was then not recognized). As these organizations gained their independence, they became pools and often mutuals (sometimes converting to stock insurance organizations) as they expanded their underwritings to new and more diverse groups. For regulatory, taxation, and managerial purposes, it is often difficult to define the precise point in this growth process when these risk financing mechanisms ceased being devices for retention and became risk transferring insurers.

Deciding when or if a captive or pool has achieved insurer status has not always been easy. However, those groups that have been formed under the federal Risk Retention Act, which enables manufacturers, professionals, and other groups to form risk retention groups or purchasing groups to obtain or provide their own liability coverages, are generally recognized as insurers (or collective buyers of insurance). As such, they have been favorably taxed. In addition, because of the Liability Risk Retention Act of 1986, they have been favorably regulated.

In deciding to use commercial insurance, a captive, or a pool, an organization must weigh their respective benefits and costs. The benefits include reduced (or stabilized) risk financing costs, improved net cash flows, broader insurance coverages, improved loss control and claim services, relative freedom from insurance marketing regulations, improved coordination of insurance programs that span numerous jurisdictions, and greater access to the domestic and international insurance and reinsurance markets. The potential disadvantages of forming and operating a captive or pool include unexpectedly costly or ineffective risk financing, extensive resource commitments to the captive or pool, and difficulties in shifting to other risk financing alternatives. The decision to form a captive or pool should be based on sound internal financial and managerial considerations, not primarily on income tax benefits.

Even if a captive or pool appears to be beneficial, its parents or participating organizations may not possess or have access to the financial resources and types of expertise needed to make a captive or pool feasible. To a great extent, the successful implementation of a captive or pool is determined by basic preliminary decisions that include the organizational form it should take, its jurisdiction of domicile, its initial and continuing capitalization, its method of providing coverage, and the types of coverage it will offer. Any single organization or group that considers launching a captive or pool must be prepared to, in essence, operate an insurance company—to provide the general management framework for an insuring organization, and to secure internally or externally the underwriting, ratemaking, marketing, reinsurance, claims management, loss control, and financial management expertise required of any soundly operated risk financing enterprise.

CHAPTER 5

Transferring Losses Through Traditional Insurance

Commercial insurance may be the most often used risk financing technique, the major source of funds to finance recovery from accidental losses, for most private and public organizations worldwide. For a very large number of relatively small organizations, purchasing coverage from an outside insurer is the most reliable way of arranging for funds to pay for losses, especially those which are large relative to the organization's own resources. Such insurance is also a highly logical first choice for any organization, regardless of its size, when it first encounters new and potentially large exposures through merger, acquisition, or some change in its operations. The strategy is to "insure first, then drop any unneeded insurance later" when the loss exposures become better known and more manageable with other risk financing techniques. Thus, in terms of importance and timing, insurance is for many organizations the best financing technique when nothing else will do.

This chapter examines insurance as a risk financing technique, and the chapters that follow explore each of the other major risk financing techniques. This chapter focuses on primary insurance (excess insurance is dealt with in the next chapter). Primary insurance covers losses either from their first dollar or above a relatively small deductible (ranging from as little as $50 to perhaps $1,000 or $10,000). Excess insurance covers only the upper portions of much larger losses that exceed, for example, $100,000, $1,000,000, or even more, with the insured retaining or separately insuring smaller losses.

This chapter first examines primary insurance, in a managerial and economic context, as a pooling and transfer mechanism among many entities, and then examines it as a legal contract between an insured and an insurer as individual entities. The closing section of the chapter provides a general framework for analyzing the coverage under any given insurance contract and for weighing the relative costs and benefits of many of the coverage alternatives an insured is likely to have when selecting insurance coverages.

FINANCIAL AND MANAGERIAL ASPECTS OF INSURANCE

The insurance industry offers a mechanism for reducing the uncertainties that potential accidental losses pose to specific individuals and organizations by allowing them to pay predictable periodic amounts into a pool of funds from which those relatively few who actually suffer loss can be reimbursed. Therefore, by reducing uncertainty, insurance makes economically feasible some activities that otherwise would be widely considered "too risky" to undertake. By providing the financial protection that makes these ventures more attractive, insurance increases overall productivity. In terms of any particular organization, insurance is one of the several alternative sources of funds on which that organization's management can call to finance recovery from losses that fall within the scope of an insurance policy, up to that policy's limit of liability for each loss.

Considered as a legal contract between an insured and an insurer, insurance has some additional, specific characteristics not shared by other risk financing techniques or by most other general business contracts. Therefore, while insurance policies are subject to the general principles of contract law, they are also subject to some other legal doctrines that are specific to the rights and privileges of the insured and the insurer. Because of these specific doctrines, developed under common law and modified by statutes, insurance contracts have become a special subset of the more general class of indemnity contracts, including, for example, the noninsurance contractual transfers for risk financing to which Chapter 7 will be devoted.

Definitions of Insurance

Insurance is not only a risk financing technique, but also a legal contract. It is therefore useful to think of insurance as (1) a mechanism for pooling and transferring loss exposures within an economy and between organizations and (2) a legal means for financing recovery from losses in which the contracting parties are an indemnitor/transferee (insurer) and an indemnitee/transferor (insured). Economic definitions of insurance usually stress both *pooling* of exposures to reduce uncertainty and *transfer* to shift the financial burden of losses. For example, one classic and widely recognized economic definition of insurance describes it as follows:

> That social device for making accumulations of capital to meet uncertain losses which is carried out through the transfer of the risks of many individuals to one entity or group which functions as the insurer.[1]

Legal definitions of insurance stress the respective binding commitments of the insured and the insurer as parties to a contract. However, case law shows clearly that there is no single legal definition of insurance. Tests that are often applied to the business or transaction in question include the following:

1. Is there a risk of economic loss to the beneficiary or insured
   a. independent of the contract itself?
   b. outside the control of either party?
   c. that may be distributed among those who are subject to loss?
2. Is this risk assumed by the insurer or promisor?
3. Does the contract incorporate a plan to distribute the costs of the loss among a group exposed to risk?

Case law and commentary on the subject contain the following sometimes contradictory examples of what the courts have held to be or not to be insurance.[2]

Insurance	*Not Insurance*
Indemnity for loss by theft	Lightning-rod salesman's guarantee
Indemnity for loss by death of cattle	Bicycle repair contract issued by a bicycle association
Contracts guaranteeing the performance of, or indemnifying against the nonperformance of, other contracts	Agreement to protect employer from striking employees
Contracts for replacement of plate glass, if broken	Tire warranty promising indemnity against defects in the tire
Newspaper promise to pay a stated amount to a person killed in an accident if at the time he or she had a copy of the newspaper on his or her person	Provision in the lease making the lessor responsible for replacement of a chattel injured by fire
	Contract entitling members of groups to medical services free or at reduced rates

For the purposes of this text, the following legal description of insurance will be accepted as a viable definition:

> An agreement by which one party, for a consideration usually known as a premium, promises to pay money or its equivalent, or to do an act valuable to the insured, upon the destruction, loss, or injury of something or someone in which the insured party held an interest.[3]

The discussion throughout this chapter and this text integrates both the economic and legal definitions of insurance.

Benefits and Costs of Insurance

Insurance, like most institutions, presents organizations and individuals with benefits and costs. The benefits will be discussed first.

Benefits. The benefits of insurance include indemnification, reduction of uncertainty, funds for investment, loss control, and aid to small businesses.

Indemnification. The direct advantage of insurance is indemnification for those who suffer unexpected losses. These unfortunate businesses and persons are restored or at least moved closer to their former economic position. The advantage to insured entities is obvious. Society also gains because these insureds are restored to production, tax revenues are increased, and welfare payments are reduced.

Reduction of Uncertainty. The pre-loss advantages of insurance are that (1) it eliminates the insured's risk, uncertainty, and adverse reaction to risk, and (2) it reduces the total risk, uncertainty, and adverse reaction to this risk in society. Before purchasing insurance, each potential insured is subject to considerable risk, each knows that this risk exists (consequently, its uncertainty is high), and each is worried about whether it will suffer any financial losses. Through the purchase of insurance, each insured transfers its risk to an insurer. The uncertainty is thus lessened and the insured is no longer as concerned about the financial loss. The insurer is subject to some uncertainty, but because the insurer pools the experience of many insureds, the insured losses are likely to be close to the expected losses. Consequently, the risk, uncertainty, and adverse reaction to risk in society are substantially reduced through insurance.

The insured's uncertainty is not eliminated if the insured has doubt concerning the insurer's ability to perform. Furthermore, if the insurer reserves the right to levy an assessment or promises to return a dividend if premiums exceed its needs, the insured assumes some risk concerning the dividend or an assessment. This risk should be small, however, because it depends upon the combined experience of the insurer. Finally, if the premium depends partly on the insured's own loss experience, the insured faces added uncertainty.

The insurer's uncertainty about future insured losses, though much smaller than the insured's uncertainty, is still significant in practice. The insurer must estimate what insured losses will be in future policy periods in order to compute the premium rates it should currently charge its insureds. Insurers typically estimate future insured losses by assuming that the future will be much like the past and by using the law of large numbers to project future losses based on past loss experience.

The law of large numbers is a statistical relationship that, loosely speaking, indicates that averages based on large amounts of data from past experience tend to be the averages of future events, provided underlying conditions do not change. More precisely, as applied to accidental losses that strike a group of similar insureds, the law of large numbers implies that as the number of future losses increases, the actual number and aggregate dollar amount of these losses approaches the average number and aggregate dollar amount of past losses. The law of large numbers is also known as the "law of averages."

As actual loss experience increases and more nearly approaches past average experience, the *difference between actual experience and past average, or expected, experience becomes a smaller percentage of the expected experience* for numbers of losses in a given time period, amounts of individual losses, and aggregate amounts of losses in a given time period.

Even with large amounts of data on many past losses, however, an insurer cannot predict future insured losses perfectly. The law of large numbers has two significant limitations. First, no matter how many past losses have occurred and have been used to compute expected losses for a current insurance policy period, there is some chance that actual losses for that period will differ significantly from the average or expected losses for that period. Second, and more important, underlying conditions affecting loss experience may change so that the future no longer comes close to repeating the past. For example, the probable frequency and severity of fire damage losses to buildings, of products liability claims, and of medical expense claims have changed markedly in past years. Thus, while the insurance mechanism has reduced insureds', insurers', and society's risk uncertainty and adverse reactions to risk, accidental losses are still not fully predictable on average or in the aggregate.

Several benefits result from this reduction of risk for insureds and for society. First, by eliminating the insured's uncertainty with respect to the risk insured, insurance eliminates the physical and mental strain caused by the fear and worry associated with that risk. Second, because industry purchases insurance to reduce its uncertainty, insurance also reduces uncertainty and inefficiency in the use of existing capital and labor, making more of these uses potentially more rewarding.

The reduction of uncertainty will also encourage the accumulation of new capital because potential investors are less likely to hesitate, their planning periods are lengthened, credit is more generally extended, and fewer resources are hoarded. Insurance, therefore, results in more nearly optimal production, price levels, and price structures. The price structures are further improved because the insurer's estimate of the expected loss for each insured is generally superior to that of the individual insured. Peter F. Drucker, a noted management authority, has emphasized the importance of insurance in this regard: "One of the greatest achievements of the mercantile age was the conversion of many of these physical risks into something that could be predicted and provided against. It is no exaggeration to say that without insurance an industrial economy could not function at all."[4]

Funds for Investment. Insurers can make more funds available for investment than insureds who "save for a rainy day" not only because their risk is small, but also because a constant inflow of new money makes it generally unnecessary for them to liquidate existing assets to pay insureds' claims. Life insurers normally provide about 10 percent of long-term funds raised in markets for investable funds. Property and liability insurers play a less important role than life insurers in these markets, mainly because their insurance policies cover shorter periods. As a result, property and liability accumulate fewer premium dollars in advance of loss payments. Nevertheless, their contribution is considerable. Self-insured private pension plans, which are insurance from the viewpoint of the covered employees and which closely resemble insured pension plans in their objective and operation, also provide a substantial proportion of the funds available in investment markets. The same is true of public pension plans covering the employees of state and local governments.

Loss Control. Although loss control is a somewhat tangential part of the insurance concept, the insurance industry is a leader in loss control. Both individual insurers and trade associations are involved in various loss control activities. Although recognizing the present contributions of insurers in this area, some observers believe that they should do much more.

Aid to Small Businesses. Insurance encourages competition, because without insurance, small businesses would be less effective competitors against big businesses. Big businesses may safely retain some of the risks that, if they resulted in loss, would destroy most small businesses. Without insurance, small firms would involve more risks and would be a less attractive outlet for funds.

Costs. Although the benefits of insurance are numerous, insurance is not without its costs.

Insurer's Operating Expenses. Insurers incur expenses such as marketing expenses, loss control costs, loss adjustment expenses, expenses involved in acquiring insureds, state premium taxes, and general administrative expenses. These expenses, plus a reasonable amount for profit and contingencies, must be covered by the premium charged. Employees and other resources that might have been committed to other uses are required by the insurance industry. (A contrasting benefit of insurance is that the industry is a creator of jobs.)

Moral Hazards. A second cost of the insurance industry is the creation of moral hazards. A moral hazard is a condition that increases the chance that some insureds or other persons will *intentionally* cause a loss or increase its severity. Some unscrupulous persons can make, or believe that they can make, a profit by bringing about an insured loss. For example, arson inspired by the possibility of an insurance recovery is a major cause of fires. Others abuse insurance protection by (1) making claims that are not warranted, thus spreading through the insurance system losses that they should bear themselves (for example, claiming automobile liability when there is no negligence on the part of the defendant), (2) using services dishonestly (for example, staying in a hospital beyond the period required for treatment), (3) charging excessive fees for services rendered insureds, as is done by some doctors and garages, and (4) granting larger awards in liability cases merely because the defendant is insured. Some of these abuses are fraudulent; others indicate a different (and indefensible) code of ethics where insurance is involved.

Morale Hazards. Another related cost is the creation of morale hazards. A morale hazard is a condition that causes persons to be *less careful* than they would otherwise be. Some persons do not consciously seek to bring about a loss, but because they have insurance they take more chances than they would if they had no insurance.

Together, moral and morale hazards describe the defects or weaknesses in human character that lead people to exaggerate losses or to cause them intentionally as a means of collecting insurance proceeds. Opinions differ on the degree to which moral and morale hazards are created by insurance, but all agree that some persons are vulnerable to these hazards and that morale hazards are more common than moral hazards.

Reduction of These Costs. The costs created by the existence of the insurance industry are far outweighed by the sizable advantages. The proper course of action is to reduce these costs. Insurers are constantly trying to reduce their costs through innovations in administrative procedures and marketing methods. Selling insurance to groups of persons instead of to individual persons is a prime example. The creation of moral hazard and morale hazard is offset, at least in part, by the loss control activities of insurers. Moral hazard is specifically attacked through such measures as reporting services on suspicious fires, a systematic index of automobile personal injury claims against all member insurers (which helps to reveal fraudulent claims), and close investigations of suicide claims. Morale hazard is most effectively handled by pointing out the direct relationship between premiums and losses and the sizable indirect losses and inconveniences that are not covered by insurance.

Limitations of Insurance

Some exposures to loss cannot be managed effectively through insurance. The following discussion focuses principally on private insurance, but some references will be made to the greater potential scope of public insurance.

Limitation to "Pure Risk" Exposures to Loss. Insurance has almost always been applied only to "pure risks," not speculative risks. In risk management and insurance, a pure risk arises from a situation that has only two possible outcomes: a loss or no loss. A speculative risk arises from a situation that has three possible outcomes: a loss, no loss, or a gain. For example, fires, floods, wars, and technological obsolescence create pure risks for most business firms that experience them because these perils can only bring losses to the firms. In contrast, new technologies, changes in consumer preferences, shifts in government policies, and the introduction of new products introduce new possibilities for gain in many organizations and are therefore considered speculative risks.

In general, households and business organizations welcome opportunities that generate speculative risks because of the potential gain they offer while also trying to reduce or contain the pure risks that these opportunities inevitably bring. In theory, pure risks are different from speculative risks. In practice, because they arise from the same business opportunities, activities, or other situations, pure risks and speculative risks must often be managed together, each with due attention to the other. With rare exceptions, speculative risks have not been insured, either because they do not sufficiently meet the characteristics of an ideally insurable exposure or because there is no reason for applying insurance to the challenges posed by speculative risks. For example, insuring against a speculative risk may involve a premium that would offset any advantages associated with the chance of gain. The best known example of speculative risk insurance permits purchasers of mutual fund shares to protect themselves against the shares being worth less than the purchase price a stated number of years later. This insurance has thus far met with limited success. A second example is provided by property or life insurance policies under which the face amount is adjusted upward as the Consumer Price Index increases in order to safeguard these policies' purchasing power.[5] Because insurance is not static, it may, however, be extended in the future to cover more speculative risks.

Characteristics of an Ideally Insurable Exposure. Among pure risks, the four following conditions should be satisfied before the risk is *ideally* insurable.

1. *A large number of independent units should be exposed to the risk and controlled by persons interested in insurance protection.* This requirement follows from the law of large numbers, since an insurance operation is safe only when the insurer is able to predict fairly accurately its expected losses. Enough units must have been exposed in the past to provide some reasonable estimate of the expected losses in the past that, when adjusted for changes in the environment, are used to estimate the losses expected underlying hazards of the future. Exposures insured in the future must be sufficiently numerous and similar to those insured in the past in order to make past loss experience useful in predicting future losses.

For insurance to operate properly, a large number of insured units should be exposed to similar hazards because fluctuations in loss experience vary inversely in size with the square root of the number of separate units exposed. The units should be exposed independently because, otherwise, what happens to one unit will determine what happens to other units, and the effect will be the same as if there were many fewer units. If an insurer intends to write more than one type of insurance, the requirement of large numbers (but not of independence) can be somewhat relaxed for any one type of exposure. Although the insurer would prefer to be able to predict accurately its loss experience with respect to each type of exposure, it can operate safely as long as it can predict fairly well its composite loss experience. The law of large numbers works in the same way for this composite exposure as it does for each type of exposure. Hence, an insurer need not have a large number of exposure units of just one type to satisfy the law of large numbers. It is sufficient if it has a large number of independent exposure units included among all its insureds. Indeed, an insurer may for this reason consider a certain type of exposure to be insurable even if it expects to insure only one unit. On the other hand, the smaller the number of exposure units of a given type an insurer covers, the less able it will be to predict losses accurately for that type of exposure. The exposure units insured should ideally be bascially similar or homogeneous. They should face about the same probability of an occurrence and the same potential loss severity. This need for homogeneity for each type or class of insureds holds whether the insurer intends to insure only one type of exposure or several different types.

The greater the variation among exposure units in the probabilities of loss and the magnitudes of the potential dollar losses, the more exposure units the insurer must have to achieve any specified degree of accuracy in predicting its loss experience. For example, if an insurer insures 100 dwellings, 90 of which are worth $50,000 and 10 of which are worth $200,000, the relative variation in the potential losses will be greater than if the insurer insures 100 dwellings, all of which are worth $65,000, even though the total insured values are the same ($6.5 million) in each case. The problem of heterogeneity would be even more evident if 99 of the dwellings were worth $10,000 and one were worth $5.51 million instead of 100 being worth $65,000 each. The loss of the $5.51 million dwelling would be equivalent to losing 551 $10,000 dwellings.

In order to interest enough individuals or organizations that together own a large number of units in insurance protection, two requirements must be satisfied. First, the potential loss must be serious enough in terms of its probability and its severity to cause many people to seek protection through insurance. Second, the expected loss must not be so great that the size of the premium will discourage the purchase of insurance.

2. *The loss—and, thus, the insurer's liability—should be definite or determinate in time, place, cause, and amount; otherwise, loss adjustment problems are created.* Another problem related to the next desirable characteristic is that the accumulation of loss experience becomes much more difficult when the loss is indefinite.

3. *The aggregate insured loss expected over some reasonable operating period should be calculable.* This condition is necessary if the premiums are to be set at the level necessary to produce with some certainty a reasonable, but not excessive, profit or operating margin for the insurer. Conditions 1 and 2 must exist before this condition can be satisfied, but, in addition, the expected loss should either be fairly stable over time or be otherwise reasonably predictable.

4. *The loss should be accidental from the viewpoint of the insured.* Good business judgment makes it clearly unwise to insure persons or organizations against losses they may intentionally cause. It is also unwise to insure against losses that are certain to occur, such as wear and tear, or losses that are easily preventable.

Departures From the Ideal. Ideal insurable exposures should meet all four requirements, but few (if any) currently insured exposures actually do. Most exposures that are considered insurable, however, come close to being ideal risks either inherently or because certain safeguards have been introduced. Some exposures whose insurability is questionable have been insured because of the importance to the public of providing protection against a given peril, because of social pressures, because the exposure is expected to become insurable in the near future, or for some other reason. Insurers differ widely in their appraisal of insureds and their exposures. Some insurers are eager to insure risks that others flatly reject. Some insure risks to which only a few units are exposed because they seek predictability only for their total writings, not for each type of coverage. The following illustrations clarify these points.

The risk of fire loss is typically insurable. A large number of units owned by persons or organizations interested in insurance protection are exposed to fire. Although many units may be adjacent to one another, a satisfactory degree of independence can be achieved by insuring only widely scattered units or by reinsuring adjacent units with other insurers. The loss is fairly definite in time, place, and amount. The expected loss is calculable, and the insured loss is accidental from the viewpoint of the insured since the insurance protection does not cover intentional losses.

The threat of death affects a large number of persons who are independently exposed and interested in insurance protection. The loss is normally definite in time and place, and since the amount payable is specified in the life policy, the loss—actually, the amount of the insurer's liability for a loss—is definite in amount. The insurer's expected loss is calculable. If suicide is excluded, the loss is accidental from the viewpoint of the insured. Suicide is excluded during the early (often first two) years of the contract, but state laws usually require that suicide be covered after that time on the grounds that (1) society benefits from payments to the beneficiaries and (2) life insurance contracts are not likely to be purchased by someone contemplating suicide within one or two years. This is an instance of a justifiable departure from ideal practice.

Another, more complex example is health insurance. Sickness is not definite in time and place, and some insurers question whether the sickness risk is insurable. On the other hand, insurance covering the costs of sickness is one of the most rapidly growing forms of insurance. At least four reasons can be advanced for this growth in spite of the questionable insurability. First, the loss of good health is one of the most important risks facing humankind, and if at all possible, protection should be made available. Second, the health insurance market is great, and if underwriting safeguards can be successfully introduced, health insurance can contribute a great deal to the growth of an insurer. Third, an insurer may be able to sell more life or other kinds of insurance because it also sells health insurance. Fourth, if private enterprise does not make health insurance available, the government almost certainly will, and private insurers are opposed to government activity in areas that they believe they can service.

Aviation in its early days presented many risks that insurers hesitated to insure largely because they had no basis for determining the premium. But the infant aviation industry needed the protection, and so insurance was written. Since loss experience has now been accumulated, the situation of aviation insurers has improved, although aviation insurance is still risky, particularly with respect to jumbo jets and hijacking. This example illustrates the writing of a questionable exposure that was expected to become insurable and did. Many new kinds of insurance originate in the same way.

Institutional Constraints. Although an insurer may decide that a particular type of exposure is commercially insurable, it may be unable to write that type of insurance because of several institutional constraints.

Regulatory Constraints. Most state laws prohibit the writing of life insurance by property and liability insurers, and vice versa. This constraint, however, can be bypassed in various ways, including writing some types of insurance through a subsidiary.

Many state laws also list the kinds of insurance that can be written by any one insurer. Many lists include "any line approved by the state insurance commissioner." Under this wording, any lines not specifically mentioned may be approved, but only after an extensive administrative process that most insurers may decide is not worth the effort.

State laws prescribe the minimum capital and surplus that an insurer must have to be authorized to transact business. These minimum requirements vary with the kinds of insurance the insurer intends to write. Some requirements may be so high that an insurer will forgo writing a line it would otherwise prefer to include in its portfolio.

Another factor that may deter entry into a new line is how state insurance departments regulate rates for the field the insurer is about to enter. Certain lines sometimes involve substantial red tape, making entrance into those lines much less attractive. The effect of regulation on the profitability of insurers in that line must also be considered.

Other Constraints. An insurer may wish to enter a certain line but may conclude that its present personnel—such as actuaries, underwriters, and claims adjusters—are not capable of writing and servicing this new line at a reasonable cost. Hiring new personnel may not be easy, and the reactions of present personnel to new people, especially if they command higher salaries, may cause serious problems.

Reinsurance facilities for the new line may also be needed. The interest of the insurer in writing the new exposure may depend on its ability to protect itself against catastrophic losses (which may occur even among exposures that are independent) and against substantial losses on single exposures.

Custom and tradition cannot be ignored. Most insurers hesitate to become involved in areas that have not been successfully tested by other insurers. Even if the exposure under consideration appears to meet all the requirements established for a commercially insurable exposure, insurers may be understandably reluctant to enter a new area.

Exposures Insurable by Public, Not Private, Insurers. Examples of pure risks that are generally considered to be uninsurable by private insurers through normal channels are those associated with flood losses to real estate (except under very special circumstances), bank insolvencies, and unemployment. The major problem associated with flood insurance is that those who would be interested in the protection would no doubt find the actuarially proper price to be too high. Nevertheless, because flood threatens many families and businesses, and because private insurance was not generally available, Congress passed the National Flood Insurance Act of 1968, under which the federal government provides subsidized protection. Bank insolvencies are largely unpredictable and present catastrophic possibilities. The same is true of unemployment. The expected loss is not calculable in the short run. These exposures are therefore insured by the government.

Government can insure risks that insurers cannot because it can make the insurance compulsory. This spreads the cost of the program over exposures of varying quality. It also allows premium rates to be varied over time as needs dictate without regard to losing any insureds. In this way, through higher premiums or general tax revenues, the government can even make up losses suffered in the past. For these reasons government insurance is available to protect bank depositors against bank failures and to protect persons against unemployment. Further, instead of or in addition to raising premiums, the government can in many cases reduce the benefits by amending a law—an option not available to private commercial insurers bound by legal contracts. Through its taxing power, the government may also subsidize voluntary public or joint public-private programs. Even government insurers, however, would prefer the more stable operations made possible when covered loss exposures approximate the insurable ideal.

Evolution of Insurability. A loss exposure that is generally uninsurable today may be considered insurable at some future date because of some change in the exposure itself, because of improvements in the knowledge or abilities of insurers, or because more compelling reasons are introduced for insuring the risk.

Two recently introduced types of insurance illustrate how the concept of an insurable risk is continually being expanded. The first type of coverage, sold to individual investors, guarantees prompt and full payment of interest and principal on specified municipal bonds. (A related coverage, sold to the issuer of the municipal bond, guarantees the payment of interest and principal to the purchasers of bonds issued by the insured municipality. This coverage is closely related to surety bonding.) A second type of insurance that has expanded the concept of insurability is a home warranty program sold to real estate agents for free distribution to buyers of used homes. The insurer promises to pay the buyer, during the first six months or year of home ownership, the cost of repairing any major structural defects and mechanical failures of heating, plumbing, and electrical systems that appear during this time. The real estate agent is responsible for seeing that prospective used homes are inspected and that sellers have made necessary repairs before the houses are listed for sale.

A third example illustrates how an expansion of the insurability concept is sometimes regretted. In 1974 Lloyd's of London marketed a computer leasing insurance policy under which Lloyd's promised to continue the payments to the lessor under a computer lease if the lessee terminated the lease prior to the nominal maturity date. Losses far exceeded expectations because IBM made some dramatic changes in their products that made many existing computers technologically obsolete. Many leases were canceled with unexpectedly high losses for Lloyd's. The major problem was Lloyd's' failure to anticipate the rapid technological obsolescence of computers.

A fourth example is *back-dated liability insurance.* In late 1980 the MGM Grand Hotel in Las Vegas had a serious fire. Eighty-four people died in the fire; more than 700 were injured. Suits were filed against MGM Grand Hotels, Inc., that far exceeded the limits of the corporation's liability insurance policies. Shortly after the fire, however, the corporation was able to secure special "back-dated" protection against these existing lawsuits plus others still to be filed as a result of the fire. Liability insurance normally applies only to future insured events—an insured's acts or the filing of a lawsuit against an insured—that occur after a policy is issued. However, in this case, the insurers reasoned that although some loss was almost certain, the amount of that loss was highly uncertain. In their opinion, the premium that was paid was sufficient to cover the present value of future claim payments from the fire plus their expenses and a reasonable underwriting profit. Some observers argue that back-dated liability insurance is simply an extension of the practice whereby one insurer sometimes sells to another insurer the liabilities it has established for claims that are known but have not yet been settled. Others point out that in the insurer situation the cases are older and the final outcome more predictable. Some deny that this new coverage is insurance. Only a few insurers write this coverage.[6]

Retroactive liability insurance, a closely related product that preceded back-dated liability insurance, also provides back-dated coverage, but retroactive insurance does not cover losses that are known to have already occurred. Situations that may create a demand for retroactive liability insurance include (1) policies written with limits now considered inadequate to cover past events that may produce claims in the future and (2) the total lack of coverage of such events that now seems highly desirable. These two conditions may arise, for example, because the legal climate has changed, increasing the potential loss; a merger or acquisition joins two firms with different insurance coverages; or a risk manager simply decides that the wrong decision was made. This type of insurance is much more commonly available than back-dated liability insurance, but most insurers still do not write this coverage.[7]

INSURANCE CONTRACT ANALYSIS

An insurer's commitments must ultimately be expressed in a contract. This contract is usually written and is typically called an insurance policy. All insurance policies have certain common features, which can be described in terms of (1) their structure or (2) the framework for analyzing the extent of the coverage they provide.

Policy Structure

A written insurance contract is a physical document containing policy provisions that perform certain functions. Risk management professionals need to understand the structure of a policy so that they may intelligently read and analyze that policy.[8] Sometimes risk management professionals need to suggest or draft modifications to an insurance policy so that it embodies the coverages that the risk management professional and an insurer's representative (usually the agent, broker, or underwriter) negotiate.

As a Physical Document. An insurance policy may be assembled in a variety of ways. This section deals with an insurance policy as a physical document, explaining the function of each of the written instruments that is likely to be found in, attached to, or incorporated by reference into any insurance policy. For the most part, insurance policies are *self-contained preprinted policies* that are one of the following:

- Assembled through adding a "form" or "coverage part" to a preprinted document containing *common provisions or*

- Specially composed in a so-called *manuscript* (typewritten) policy

This classification illustrates the major alternatives in insurance policy physical structure.

Self-Contained Policies. Some insurance policies are made up of a single document that contains all the agreements between the applicant and the insurer. A single, relatively standard document identifies the insurer and insured, the property or other subject matter of insurance, and the amounts, terms, and conditions of the coverage provided by the policy. Tailoring coverage to the needs of individual insureds is achieved through the declarations and the use of endorsements.

A self-contained policy is appropriate when a large number of insureds face a loss exposure or set of related exposures that are essentially similar from insured to insured. Insurance written to cover losses arising out of the ownership or use of private passenger autos is typically written in a self-contained policy that can be used nationwide. In those states where no-fault auto insurance laws require the use of provisions suited to insureds in a particular jurisdiction, the policy is tailored through the use of endorsements. Most life insurance and health insurance policies are also self-contained.

Common Provisions Approach. Many property and liability insurance policies are assembled by combining some document containing provisions applicable to a variety of coverages with one or more other documents providing a specific type of coverage and designated as *forms* or *coverage parts.* Historically, the best known common provisions document has been the standard fire policy. Though referred to as a "policy," this document is not really a complete contract until one or more forms have been attached. The term *jacket* has been used to represent a document containing common provisions and often serving as a wrapper or cover page for one or more coverage parts. This nomenclature can be used to refer to documents in a number of widely used types of insurance, particularly for business organizations.

Many inland marine and crime insurance contracts also use the common provisions approach. Although labels vary among insurers, many use a document called the "inland marine policy" in writing a wide variety of inland marine coverages, with the form(s) attached containing those provisions geared to meet a particular type of coverage need. Several crime insurance policies for business firms also follow the standard provisions approach.

Common provisions vary in length and complexity. In general, they contain provisions intended to be applicable to all or most insuring situations in which they are used, regardless of differences among insureds that may be recognized by the variety of forms used to complete the policy. In a few such policies, space for the declarations is an integral part of the document. In most cases, however, such as in general liability policies, a separate declarations page is used.

Manuscript Policies. The two approaches just described involve the use of preprinted material. In contrast, a manuscript policy, usually individually typewritten, is the product of negotiation between an insurer and an applicant (or the applicant's representative, such as a broker). Each provision in a manuscript policy is specifically drafted or selected for that one contract. Although some provisions may be taken verbatim from printed or standardized policies, each manuscript policy as a whole is a unique document. The use of manuscript policies is largely restricted to insureds of substantial size whose uniqueness of exposures and substantial bargaining power put them in a position of both needing and being able to demand individual treatment.

Because the wording of manuscript policies is developed through the joint effort of insurer and applicant, the two parties are more likely to be on equal footing in the event of a court's need to interpret ambiguities in the contract. In contrast, policies that the insurer framed with terms of its own choosing are likely to be interpreted against the insurer if a court finds the policy wording to be at all ambiguous.

Collateral Documents. In addition to the basic formats of insurance policies, several other documents—such as a written application, the insurer's bylaws, the terms of relevant statutes, or various miscellaneous documents—may be incorporated into a policy either by physical attachment or by appropriate reference. Any of these documents may become part of any insurance policy regardless of its physical format.

Written Application. Although insurer practices vary widely, for some types of insurance a written application is rarely or never required. For these coverages an applicant may orally request coverage in person or by telephone, and a representative of the insurer may create an oral insurance contract by immediately "binding" the requested coverage. However, for those lines of insurance that are relatively complicated or involve particularly complex underwriting or rating, the insurer typically requires a written application. Jewelers' block coverage almost always requires a written application, as do virtually all types of life and health insurance coverage. Even in some lines for which the insurer's representative has authority to bind coverage, a written application is required at a later date to substantiate the binder, and the submission is underwritten and rated by insurer personnel *after* coverage has been put into force through the representative's binder.

Beyond its underwriting importance, a written application is legally significant because it contains the statements or representations the applicant makes to secure coverage. The truth of these statements may be critical to the validity of any insurance contract. False information on the written application is often the insurer's only basis for demonstrating a lack of good faith. However, to be able to rely on the application as a basis for having the policy declared void, the application must often be part of the policy. This requirement stems from statutes and court decisions that stipulate that a written insurance policy must incorporate all the agreements between an insurer and an insured. In some jurisdictions, statutes explicitly require that any written application be made part of some specified types of insurance, especially life insurance policies. If a written application is not attached to the insurance policy, the policy remains valid; however, in such jurisdictions, failure to attach the application denies the insurer the right to have the policy declared void on the basis of false statements in the application.

Endorsements. An endorsement, once known as a "rider" in life and health insurance, is a provision that adds to, deletes, or modifies another document that is part of an insurance policy. Sometimes an endorsement is called a "policy change" or an "amendment." An endorsement is usually a printed paragraph or series of paragraphs on a separate sheet of paper attached to the other document(s) making up the policy, but occasionally an endorsement is typewritten or handwritten and attached to the other policy documents. An endorsement may even take the form of a handwritten note written in the margin of a policy, form, or coverage part, with the insurer's and insured's acceptance of this handwritten note being indicated by initialing and dating it.

There are thousands of standard pre-printed endorsements available to meet the needs of particular insureds. There are also "all-purpose" endorsements, which are little more than blanks on which special agreements between the insurer and the insured are recorded in typewritten or handwritten form. Depending on the provision that an endorsement extends, deletes, or modifies, any particular endorsement may serve as (1) a declaration (by identifying an additional named insured); (2) an insuring agreement (by identifying additional properties, loss exposures, or perils for which the insurer is willing to provide coverage); (3) an exclusion or deletion of an existing exclusion (an endorsement that deletes or narrows an exclusion has the net effect of broadening coverage and has often been labeled an "exception"); (4) a condition (an endorsement liberalizing the notice of loss requirement under certain circumstances); or (5) a miscellaneous provision.

In general, an endorsement takes precedence over any conflicting terms in the policy to which the endorsement is attached. Furthermore, a handwritten endorsement supersedes a preprinted or typewritten one. Both of these rules are based on the reasoning that alterations of the agreements between an insured and an insurer—especially alterations that they have indicated in handwriting—more accurately reflect their true intent than do the other terms of the policy.

An exception to this general rule arises in situations in which a statute or ruling requires that a particular policy be fully standardized, that it contain particular provisions whose wording or substance is specified, or that the policy not contain certain provisions whose wording or substance has been prohibited. In these situations an endorsement cannot be used to subvert the purpose of law or regulation by modifying the terms of an entirely standardized policy, changing the wording or substance of a required provision, or inserting a provision whose wording or substance had been prohibited. Any portion of an endorsement that attempts to override decisions of a duly constituted public authority regarding the proper content of an insurance policy is void. The policy is read and applied as if those portions of the endorsement did not exist.

Insurer's Bylaws and Relevant Statutes. In certain circumstances it is important that the bylaws of the insurer or the provisions of pertinent statutes be incorporated into an insurance policy. For example, when an insurer's organization structure gives insureds some rights or duties associated with the management of the insurer's operations—as is the case with mutual and reciprocal insurers as well as captives and pools—it is important that these rights and duties be made part of each insurance contract. Similarly, if an insurance policy provides protection against potential liability growing out of a specific statute—such as a workers compensation law or an auto insurance no-fault law—the provisions and amendments of these statutes actually define the insurer's obligation and must, at least by reference or implication, be made part of each insurance policy that is governed by such a statute. Furthermore, statutes in some states require that a particular type of policy contain provisions that differ slightly from the policies used in the majority of jurisdictions. These slight variations are often incorporated into the body of the policy through special provisions under the heading of "State Exceptions" to the standard policy. These state exceptions are effective only with respect to insureds whose losses come under the jurisdiction of a state in which the laws require such an exception.

The incorporation of relevant statutes is normally achieved by a general reference to them. For example, the usual workers compensation policy defines the insurer's primary obligation to be the following: "to pay promptly when due all compensation and other benefits required of the insured by the workers compensation law." Where pertinent, an insurer's bylaws may be incorporated by reference, even though a copy of the bylaws may also be physically attached to the policy. Most state exceptions are recited explicitly in the policy, and many policies contain provisions indicating that any of their clauses that violate any applicable statute are hereby deemed to be amended to conform to that statute. Such a provision, along with the statement of state exceptions, recognizes explicitly the interpretation a court will probably give to the policy to make it conform to the legal requirements of any particular jurisdiction. When a policy incorporates a particular set of bylaws or applicable statutes, the policy is interpreted to change automatically when these bylaws or statutes change, rather than being frozen by the bylaws or statutes that pertained when the policy first became effective.

Miscellaneous Documents. Subject to statutory and regulatory restrictions intended to standardize policies or otherwise govern policy content, an insurer and an insured may incorporate into an insurance policy virtually any documents they wish. Although these miscellaneous documents may be quite diverse, some of those more frequently incorporated include rating manuals, lists of covered locations, inspection reports, and specification sheets or operating manuals pertaining to safety equipment or procedures to be followed while the policy is in effect.

An insurer and an insured may agree that the coverage provided by a particular property or liability insurance policy depends upon the use of certain procedures or equipment in order to minimize losses. In such situations a set of operating instructions or a manual of specifications may be incorporated by reference and used to define the loss prevention measures that must exist as a condition of the coverage promised in the policy.

Functional Provisions. Some types of clauses in insurance policies are called *functional provisions* because, as a group, they perform certain functions that meet particular needs of many insureds or insurers. Some functional provisions are common to virtually all insurance policies; others are found only in some types of policies. In either case, closely related provisions of a policy are normally grouped together in sections identified by headings.

Despite the sometimes sharp differences among insurance policies, the contents of all property and liability insurance policies can be broken down into the following component parts or categories:

- Declarations
- Insuring agreements
- Exclusions
- Conditions
- Miscellaneous provisions

Every policy provision can logically be placed into one of these five categories. However, these five categories may not have precise counterparts in the language or structure of a given policy. Many policies do not group their provisions into sections with headings corresponding to these five categories. Other policies use some or all of these categories as section headings, but this does not mean that a provision that effectively serves the function of an exclusion will always be found in an "Exclusions" section. A single provision might simultaneously function as a condition or an exclusion, as well as an insuring agreement, and the provision itself might be found almost anywhere in the several documents that together constitute the entire contract, especially when the basic policy has several forms and endorsements attached.

The five customary categories are preserved here because they provide convenient headings for summarizing the general kinds of provisions contained in most property and liability policies.

Declarations. The *declarations* of an insurance policy are the typewritten statements that are entered into what are otherwise blank spaces in the printed policy form or on a separate "Declarations Page" attached to the policy form. Declarations personalize the policy by identifying the named insured(s) and describing each property or other exposure to be insured. In addition, the declarations typically specify the following:

- The policy number
- The numbers of all forms that are attached
- Applicable policy limit(s)
- Deductible(s)
- Inception and termination dates of the policy
- Premium and the basis for its determination
- Additional interests covered (such as the interests of a mortgagee or loss payee)

The declarations page may also contain information used by the insurer to rate the policy, issue it, and set up the necessary internal records.

Insuring Agreements. The *insuring agreements* are printed statements that summarize the insurer's obligation(s) by setting forth in broad terms what the insurer agrees to do under the contract. For example, one insuring agreement obligates the insurer to "pay for damage during the policy period to the glass described in the declaration. . . ." Another agreement obligates the insurer to "pay on behalf of the insured all sums which the insured shall become legally obligated to pay as damages because of *(A)* bodily injury or *(B)* property damage . . . arising out of the ownership, maintenance or use of the insured premises and all operations necessary or incidental thereto. . . ." These two excerpts happen to be fairly concise; however, some insuring agreements are long and contain numerous clarifications and definitions.

Whether lengthy or concise, insuring agreements merely state the basic thrust or general nature of the insurer's obligation(s). The full scope of the coverage cannot be determined without examining the rest of the policy, because the insuring agreements are invariably explained or modified by exclusions, conditions, and other policy provisions—including those contained in forms and endorsements attached to the basic policy.

Exclusions. In the jargon of property and liability insurance, the term *exclusion* usually refers to a policy provision, clearly identified as an exclusion, that eliminates coverage the insurer does not intend to provide. However, the term is broad enough to embrace *any* policy provision that serves the function of eliminating unintended coverages, whether or not the provision is labeled as an exclusion. Both definitions imply that the primary function of exclusions is to clarify the coverages granted by the insurer, not to take away coverage from the insured. This point may seem academic and insincere to any person who does not become aware of an exclusion until after a loss. It is natural for such a person to feel that coverage has, in effect, been "taken away," especially when the applicable exclusion is difficult to find in the policy. Even so, the drafters of insurance contracts are painfully aware how difficult it is to express an insurer's underwriting intentions in language that will not be misinterpreted by the courts. Specifying what an insurer does *not* intend to cover has proven to be one of several effective ways of clarifying what the insurer *does* intend to cover under an insurance policy.

What are the underlying purposes of policy exclusions? Collectively, exclusions serve at least six legitimate purposes:

1. Eliminate coverage for uninsurable loss exposures
2. Assist in the management of moral and morale hazards
3. Reduce the likelihood of coverage duplications
4. Eliminate coverages that are not needed by the typical purchaser
5. Eliminate coverages requiring special treatment
6. Assist in keeping premiums at a reasonable level

A particular exclusion often serves more than one purpose. Hence, in the explanations that follow, some of the examples used to illustrate one purpose could also have been used to illustrate other purposes.

Uninsurable Losses. One purpose of exclusions is to eliminate coverage for exposures that are considered uninsurable by private insurers. All exclusions of this type serve the basic purpose of eliminating coverage for loss exposures that do not adequately meet one or more of the various insurability conditions. For example, virtually all property and liability insurance contracts exclude as uninsurable any losses arising out of war. Although the exclusions in any particular contract depend on the nature and purpose of that contract, other common exclusions in this category involve losses caused by intentional acts by the insured, nuclear radiation, earthquake, flood damage to fixed-location, marring or scratching of furniture, normal wear and tear, mechanical breakdown, and *inherent vice.* (Inherent vice is a quality within an object that tends to destroy it, as when iron rusts, wood rots, or rubber deteriorates.) These exposures all fail to meet adequately at least one of the tests or characteristics of an insurable loss exposure. War and nuclear losses involve an incalculable catastrophe potential. Mechanical breakdown, intentional acts of the insured, inherent vice, and similar losses are not accidental or fortuitous in nature, but are controllable by the insured or highly predictable. Although some of these losses may theoretically be insured, the required premium is often so large that they remain uninsurable, as a practical matter, and are therefore excluded from the coverages offered by most private insurers.

Moral and Morale Hazards. A second purpose of exclusions is to assist in the management of moral and morale hazards, both defined earlier in this chapter. Exclusions can help manage moral hazards to the extent that they eliminate coverage for intentional acts of the insured. One example can be found in crime insurance policies that exclude coverage for any fraudulent, dishonest, or criminal act by any insured. Similarly, nearly all health insurance policies exclude coverage for losses arising out of self-inflicted injuries.

Morale hazards refer generally to the tendency of people to be less careful about preventing losses when they are insured. Exclusions can assist in managing morale hazards by eliminating coverages and making insureds themselves bear a financial penalty for their own carelessness. For example, under some contracts providing broad coverage on personal property, breakage of fragile articles is excluded unless caused by some specified peril such as fire, wind, or explosion. The intent is to eliminate coverage for breakage caused by careless handling or misuse. Some policies exclude coverage for theft from unattended and unlocked vehicles. Exclusions like these do not entirely eliminate moral and morale hazards. However, they can assist in their management.

Coverage Duplications. A third purpose of exclusions is to reduce the likelihood of unnecessary and wasteful coverage duplications. Coverage is eliminated from one kind of policy because it is likely to be provided by another kind of policy that is better suited to the task. For example, consider the following:

- Personal liability policies usually exclude losses arising from professional activities and business pursuits.
- Glass insurance policies routinely exclude losses caused by fire

because such losses are typically covered under the property insurance on the building.

- Commercial property insurance policies eliminate autos from the description of covered property, because auto physical damage insurance is readily available and widely purchased.

These are just a few of the many exclusions designed to avoid coverage overlaps among several different policies. Though exclusions alone do not entirely prevent coverage duplications, they do help reduce them, as do various other policy provisions.

Coverages Typically Not Needed. A fourth purpose of exclusions is to eliminate coverages that are not needed by the typical purchaser of that type of insurance, thus enabling insurers to charge more equitable premiums to all their insureds. For example, the typical insured does not own or operate private aircraft, use his or her personal auto as a taxicab for hire, or use his or her home as a storage warehouse for business property. Therefore, homeowners policies do not provide property insurance coverage for aircraft or business property in storage. Personal auto policies do not cover losses that occur while an otherwise insured vehicle is being used to carry people or property for a fee. People who need these coverages should obtain them separately by paying additional premiums. It would be unfair to reflect in the premiums for all insureds the cost of losses for these exposures not at all common to the usual insurance buyer. A significant degree of inequity is also likely to violate state rating laws and regulations, according to which insurance rates cannot be unfairly discriminatory. Exclusions are sometimes necessary, therefore, to achieve a reasonable degree of rating and premium equity.

Coverages Requiring Special Treatment. A fifth purpose of exclusions is to eliminate coverages requiring special treatment. As used here, the term "special" means rating, underwriting, or reinsurance treatment that is substantially different from what is normally applied to the contract containing the exclusion. Following are three examples:

- Policies covering valuable personal property frequently exclude coverage for losses that occur while the property is on exhibit at a convention or trade fair. Paintings, stamps, coins, and other collectors' items are often on display for members of the public or other collectors to enjoy, during which time they are considered highly vulnerable to theft and other perils.
- The typical policy covering products liability excludes coverage of the insured's liability for the expense of recalling products that are or may be defective.
- General liability policies for individuals usually exclude professional liability exposures.

These exclusions pertain to coverages that require special rating, underwriting, or reinsurance arrangements. These same exclusions might also serve the purposes of eliminating coverages not needed by the typical purchaser and reducing coverage duplications. Yet, excluding coverages requiring special treatment can be thought of as a somewhat different purpose of exclusions. It may be the primary or only reason a given insurer uses a particular exclusion. An insurer may exclude products recall coverage, for example, though it is needed by many insurance buyers and is not likely to result in duplicate coverage, simply because it is a highly specialized line the insurer does not wish to write. In fact, there are comparatively few insurers willing to write most specialty coverages. Further, some insurers would not be able to write highly specialized coverages even if they wanted to because of their inability to secure appropriate reinsurance protection.

Keeping Premiums Reasonable. A sixth purpose of exclusions is to assist in keeping premiums at a level that a sufficiently large number of insureds (and prospective insureds) will consider reasonable. Keeping the premiums reasonable is an objective shared by insurers, rate regulators, and consumers. All exclusions serve this purpose to some extent. However, it is the only or primary reason for using some exclusions. For example, there is really no other compelling reason under property insurance contracts for eliminating the coverage of marring and scratching, wear and tear, mechanical breakdown, or other highly predictable losses. Theoretically, such losses are not uninsurable. But in practice, covering them would require a higher premium than most people are willing to pay. They are uninsurable as a practical matter, therefore, because an insurer who automatically covered them under standard property insurance policies would probably price itself out of the market. The premiums for routine dental expense coverage are also more than most individuals are willing to pay out of their own pockets; yet, this coverage has been marketed very successfully in recent years. The primary difference between the two examples is that the vast bulk of routine dental expense coverage is written on a group basis and is paid for by employers as a tax-deductible expense for employers and an untaxed benefit to employees.

Once it is acknowledged that the broader concept of an exclusion refers to any policy provision that functions as an exclusion, it becomes apparent that keeping the premiums reasonable in the minds of insureds is a primary purpose of many exclusionary features of policy design. In both property and liability insurance (including multiple-line policies), the insured is given a fairly wide range of choice in terms of the breadth of coverage available from the same or different insurers. Generally, the fewer the exclusionary policy provisions, the higher the premium will be. That the reverse is also true reaffirms the point—one key purpose of exclusions is to keep the premium reasonable in the minds of a large number of buyers. Only when a sufficiently large number of insureds purchase a given coverage will the law of large numbers operate to make its sale a successful venture for the insurer. Exclusions may help achieve this goal while simultaneously giving the consumer a choice of coverages and premium levels.

Conditions. Depending on the type of policy, the insurer agrees to pay the insured, to pay on behalf of the insured, or to provide various legal defense or other services to or on behalf of the insured. The insurer's promises are invariably subject to a number of conditions. Conditions may be thought of as the various qualifications an insurer attaches to the promises it makes. They create actions that the insured must take or have others take if the insured is to have the legal power to hold the insurer to its duties under the insurance policy. The insurer's promises are contingent upon both the happening of an insured event *and* the performance of various acts by the insured person(s). Examples of common policy conditions include the insured's obligation to pay premiums, report losses promptly, provide appropriate documentation for losses, cooperate with the insurer in any legal proceedings, and refrain from jeopardizing an insurer's rights to recover from responsible third parties (under "subrogation" actions) amounts equal to the payments it has made to or on behalf of its insured. If the insured does not do these things, the insurer may be released from its obligation to perform some or all of the otherwise enforceable promises in the contract.

Miscellaneous Provisions. In addition to declarations, insuring agreements, exclusions, and conditions, insurance policies contain various provisions that generally deal with the relationship between the insured and the insurer. Although these provisions help to establish working procedures for carrying out the terms of an insurance contract, they seldom have the force of conditions. Thus, actions that depart from the procedures specified in the miscellaneous provisions normally do not affect the insurer's basic duty to provide insurance protection.

A sampling of miscellaneous provisions might include the following:

- A cancellation provision explaining the rights and obligations of each party in cancelling the policy and notifying the other party(ies)
- Options for the insured or insurer in receiving loss payments or discharging an obligation under the contract
- Valuation provisions setting forth standards for how losses under the policy will be measured (this is part of the insuring agreement in some policies)

- "Other insurance" provisions explaining the extent of the insurer's liability if other insurance covers the same loss
- A mortgage or loss payable clause specifying the rights and duties of the insurer and a mortgagee or other creditor of the insured

Some miscellaneous provisions are unique to particular types of insurers and may include the following:

- A policy issued by a mutual insurance company is very likely to describe the right of each insured to participate in the divisible surplus, if any, and to vote in the election of the board of directors.
- A policy issued by an assessment mutual typically describes the nature and limits of an insured's potential liability for assessments. (Insureds may be required to make extra payments to the assessment mutual based on its loss experience.)
- A policy issued by a reciprocal insurer is likely to specify the authority of the attorney-in-fact to carry out its powers on behalf of the insured.

Standard Policies and Some Exceptions. Fortunately, for many insureds, insurance contracts are highly standardized as a result of statutory or administrative directives, voluntary agreement, or customary practice.

In those states where, for example, some specific automobile liability insurance is mandated for all or some classes of vehicle owners or operators, the coverage is often prescribed, word for word, in a statute or in administrative regulations. All insurers writing such required coverage must issue policies that contain the entire mandated policy, with nothing more and nothing less. Any policy deviating from the required wording is interpreted by regulators and the courts as if it were worded in accordance with the law.

The advantages of a statutory standard policy prescribed word for word are that (1) the insured need not consider differences in policy language when selecting an insurer, (2) all insureds are subject to the same treatment, (3) policy conflicts do not arise when two or more insurers are required to provide the necessary protection or become involved in the same loss, (4) court interpretations of the contract become more meaningful, (5) insureds and insurance agents save time and energy in contract analysis, and (6) loss experience can be pooled for rate-making purposes. On the other hand, (1) desirable changes may be delayed because they can be accomplished only by revising a statute, (2) a contract that survives the legislative process may not properly balance the interests of all the affected groups, (3) the policy designed to meet the needs of the average insured may not meet the needs of many insureds, and (4) the advantages of experimentation and competition are lost.

A less restrictive statutory approach is the use of statutory standard provisions under which the state prescribes certain important provisions, but insurers can change the wording so long as the revised provision is at least as liberal as the statutory provision. This approach is best illustrated by standard life insurance and health insurance provisions. For example, all state laws prescribe clauses dealing with such matters as the period following the effective date within which any misstatements by the insured can be contested, the grace period following premium due dates within which premiums must be paid, and the minimum values to which the insured is entitled if he or she stops paying premiums. However, some important provisions, such as those describing the ways in which the insurers will pay out the proceeds, are not included among the standard provisions. State laws also prohibit certain types of provisions. For example, life insurers can only exclude certain causes of death, such as suicide, during the first two years or military service during wartime. A similar situation exists in health insurance, since most states have adopted the 1950 Uniform Individual Accident and Sickness Policy Provisions Law, which prescribes twelve required provisions (covering such matters as the entire contract, the time limit on certain defenses, reinstatement, and claims notices and proofs of loss) and eleven optional provisions (such as those regarding a change of occupation, other insurance, and cancellation). In 1974 the National Association of Insurance Commissioners, whose recommendations have no legal effect but strongly influence the actions of individual states, adopted a model regulation that sets minimum standards for individual health insurance policies.

In most states, insurance contracts must be approved by the state insurance department before they can be used. In the other states, contracts can be used without prior approval but they are subject to subsequent disapproval.

Voluntary standardization is common in many property and liability insurance lines. To some extent, such as in workers compensation insurance and automobile insurance, one of the original incentives for voluntary agreement was to make statutory or administrative action unnecessary. The voluntary products are generally known as "standard-provisions" contracts. All insurers using these contracts provide the same basic protection, but they have some flexibility with respect to the exact language and the arrangement of the provisions. These contract provisions are usually developed by rating bureaus, which may also develop a common price for the product. In only one instance—workers compensation—has this method produced complete standardization. In the past, there was a high degree of standardization in automobile insurance, but increased competition in recent years has resulted in a more diversified set of products.

Other forces favoring standardization are the tendency of businesses to produce a product that is not too different from that of their competitors and a hesitancy to experiment with new phraseology that may expose them to new risks of interpretation. On the other hand, competition also favors some product differentiation, and insurance contracts are seldom completely standardized. The degree of standardization varies among lines, with workers compensation insurance being a highly standardized field and marine insurance among the least standardized. Normally, the insurance buyer can expect some product differentiation, but understanding the contract issued by one insurer will have a high transfer value in understanding the contracts issued by other insurers.

Framework for Coverage Analysis

In performing their respective functions, the declarations, insuring agreements, exclusions, conditions, and miscellaneous provisions of an insurance policy (1) define the events for which that policy provides coverage, (2) limit the amounts the insurer will pay to finance recovery from an insured loss, and (3) specify actions that must be taken by or on behalf of an insured in order to legally bind the insurer to pay the insured.

In analyzing an insurance contract, one should first read the entire contract to gain some understanding of the format and the content. During the second reading the analyst should slowly and carefully seek answers to the following questions from all portions of the policy:[9]

1. Under what circumstances would the insurer be responsible for the loss? What events are covered?
   - What perils are covered?
   - What property or source of liability, or whose life or health, is covered?
   - What persons are covered?
   - What losses are covered?
   - What locations are covered?
   - What time period is covered?
   - Are there any special conditions that do not fall into any of the other six categories that may suspend or terminate the coverage?
2. If the insurer is responsible for the loss, how much will it pay?
3. What steps must the insured take following a loss to fulfill conditions that make the insurer's promises of protection legally enforceable?

This section focuses on analyzing the events that are covered, the amounts and limits on the amounts of recovery, and the actions to fulfill legal conditions and secure recovery after a loss has occurred. With respect to covered events and amounts and limits of recovery, an insured often has a number of basic choices regarding each of the questions marked above with a bullet. The following sections briefly describe each of these choices and the likely costs and benefits of each alternative to an insured (organization). In each case, the insured should select or negotiate for the alternative that, at a given time, generates for the insured the greatest net benefits or ratio of benefits to cost. The relevant benefits and costs are, in each case, likely to include effects on the following:

- The organization's total risk financing costs (for both retention and transfer)
- The reliability, or financial security, of the organization's overall risk financing program in generating necessary amounts of funds at appropriate times to pay for all foreseeable losses
- The ease of understanding and administering the organization's risk financing program, both by its own managers and personnel and by the insurance company personnel, marketing representatives, and regulators who implement and oversee the organization's risk financing activities
- The organization's relationships with its own personnel, customers, and potential claimants, and with its insurers, their representatives, and regulators

Some of these costs and benefits can be expressed with some precision. Among those that are reliably measurable in dollars are the risk financing costs and financial security considerations listed above as the first two bulleted items. Less directly quantifiable are the effects that a particular insurance coverage alternative may have on the simplicity of the organization's risk financing program and on its relationships with others whose cooperation is essential to proper risk financing for the organization. Nonetheless, all relevant benefits and costs—quantifiable and nonquantifiable—need to be considered when making each choice. The choices actually available may in some cases be restricted by legal requirements imposed by statutes, by the organization's own bylaws, or by the contracts (especially agreements with bondholders or other creditors) into which it has entered.

Events Covered. A particular event is covered only if it is included among the answers to all seven of the bulleted questions. For example, if the peril, property, loss, time, and location are covered under a property insurance policy but the person seeking payment is not, the insurer is not liable. As a result, a clear understanding of the information sought through each of the seven questions is extremely important.

Perils. Relevant considerations in determining what perils are covered are (1) whether the policy is a named perils or an "all-risks" policy, (2) how the covered or excluded perils are defined, (3) the excluded perils, and (4) the chain-of-causation concept.

Named-Perils Versus "All-Risks" Policies. Named-perils policies specify the perils covered. Loss by any peril not included in the list is not covered. The exclusions may except losses caused by the named peril on some occasions (for example, a fire caused by war).

"All-risks" policies cover all perils not otherwise excluded. In other words, a named-perils policy lists the included perils; an "all-risks" policy names the excluded perils. "All-risks" policies sometimes cover losses beyond one's wildest imagination because the insurer has not excluded the particular cause of loss. For example, more than one insurer has paid a claim because a police officer's horse licked paint off a car.

"All-risks" policies (1) generally provide broader coverage than named-perils policies and (2) permit the insured to consider explicitly all the perils that still exist if the policy is purchased. In some instances, the all-risks policy replaces two or more named-perils policies that would require more effort to administer and that might provide overlapping coverage. On the other hand, the "all-risks" policies may cost more than the insured is willing to pay. Furthermore, the insured may not want or need protection against some of the perils, known or unknown, included in the "all-risks" policy.

In some situations, broadly phrased named-peril coverage can be more favorable to the insured than is "all-risks" coverage that is subject to many exclusions. For example, comprehensive automobile insurance coverage provides "all-risks" coverage, but it excludes collision—the most common cause of damage to automobiles.

Life insurance policies and many of the newer property insurance policies are "all-risks" policies. Fire insurance and theft insurance policies illustrate the named-perils approach.

Perils Defined. A few policies define the covered perils. For example, burglary is commonly defined as "the felonious abstraction of insured property from within the premises by a person making felonious entry therein by actual force and violence, of which force and violence there are visible marks" on the exterior of the premises. Sometimes the peril is defined in a statute. For example, most states have statutes that define a riot as a violent or tumultuous act against the person or property of another by three or more persons. The first part of this definition is important in distinguishing between a riot and an act of vandalism, which applies only to property.

Most policies leave the interpretation of the covered perils to the courts. Courts, for example, have defined the perils of windstorm, explosion, accident, collision, and fires. Their interpretation of fire is particularly important because it adds so much meaning to the statutory policy and because fires are experienced by so many insureds. According to the courts, a fire has not occurred unless there has been a visible flame or glow. Scorching and consequent blackening, for example, may not have involved any fire. The courts have also held that the fire must be a "hostile" fire, not a "friendly" fire. A hostile fire is one that has escaped from its proper container. If an object is accidentally thrown into a furnace oven, the loss is not a fire loss because there has been no hostile fire. Some courts, however, also consider a fire raging out of control to be a hostile fire even if the fire remains in the proper container.[10]

The courts' interpretation of an accident as a sudden, unexpected event is also important because some liability policies cover accidents for which the named insured is legally responsible. Others are written on an occurrence rather than on an accident basis. Some courts have argued that an event is not an accident unless it is sudden. An occurrence, on the other hand, need not meet this requirement. As a result of this distinction, the gradual pollution of a stream with industrial wastes *might* not be covered under an accident policy but would be covered under an occurrence policy unless specifically excluded. Some courts also argue that deliberate acts that have unintentional and unexpected results are not accidents, but they would be occurrences.

Excluded Perils. Whether the policy is written on a named-perils or an "all-risks" basis, the exclusions in the policy pertaining to perils affect what perils are covered. The courts sometimes add exclusions not mentioned in the policy. For example, fires are excluded under the fire policy if they are caused by war or are intentionally set by public authorities (except to prevent the spread of fire). The policy does not exclude fires set intentionally by the insured, but the courts have held that to cover them would be contrary to public policy. Automobile comprehensive insurance covers all perils except collision, wear and tear, mechanical or electrical breakdowns, freezing, war, and confiscation by duly constituted public authorities. Losses caused intentionally by the insured are excluded by the courts. Liability policies written on an occurrence basis specifically exclude losses intentionally caused by the insured. Life insurance policies may exclude deaths caused by suicide for the first two years of the policy.

Concurrent Causation. In general, "all-risks" property insurance policies cover loss by any cause except certain excluded perils that are considered uninsurable or difficult to insure. The typical "all-risks" policy covers "all risks of direct physical loss" subject to exclusions and other policy conditions. "All-risks" policies typically contain exclusions for war, nuclear reaction, flood, earthquake, and a variety of maintenance-type items such as wear and tear. For many years this approach worked satisfactorily. In the early 1980s, however, the *concept of doctrine of concurrent causation* raised some serious issues that resulted in widespread changes to what had been known as "all-risks" insurance.

The concept of concurrent causation evolved, in part, from a lawsuit[11] growing out of property losses that occurred when record rains broke through flood-control facilities and inundated parts of a city. As far as insurers were concerned, this "flood" loss was clearly excluded. However, the holders of "all-risks" homeowners policies alleged that the proximate cause of the loss was "negligence of the water district"—a cause of loss drawn from liability insurance that was not excluded by the property insurance provisions of these policies. The court supported the policyholders' position on the basis that (1) the flood and (2) the negligent act of constructing flood-control structures were independent, concurrent causes that interacted with each other to produce the loss. Similar decisions were reached in other cases. In a case involving a landslide, the policyholder successfully argued that a "faulty installation of a drain by a third party" was the cause of the landslide, and such negligent actions by third parties were not excluded. A significant number of other courts[12] have disagreed, holding that each exclusion in an "all-risks" property insurance policy should be interpreted independently and that an insurer's failure to exclude the liability-related peril (or hazard) of negligence does not make negligence a cause of loss covered by an "all-risks" property insurance policy.

The effect of the concurrent causation concept is that the insurer with a so-called "all-risks" policy must pay if *any one* of the direct causes of loss is not specifically excluded. Stated differently, if a loss to property can be attributed to two causes—one excluded by the policy and one covered—the policy covers the loss. In short, the concept implies that none of the perils exclusions of an "all-risks" policy can bar coverage if it is possible to identify another, nonexcluded peril that somehow contributed directly to the loss.

In response to these decisions, most "all-risks" policies have been revised to delete the "all" from "all-risks"—a change intended to de-emphasize the breadth or presumably comprehensive nature of coverage. In addition, exclusions have been restructured to clarify insurers' intent. For example, some of the policy language makes it clear that certain losses are ". . . excluded regardless of any other causes or event contributing concurrently or in any sequence to the loss."

A further response to the concurrent causation doctrine has been the preparation of a so-called "special named perils" causes-of-loss form. This form is intended to replace the "all-risks" type of form if future court decisions do not uphold the exclusions of those revised forms. From the perspective of insurers, one remaining solution might be to return to named-perils type coverage with the broadest practical list of named perils. Another solution for insurers would be for a majority of courts to rule that negligence or other civil (not criminal) wrongdoing of a third party is not a peril that is even implicitly covered by an "all-risks" property insurance policy.

Chain of Causation. Courts have also contributed to the interpretation of the covered perils through the proximate-cause and chain-of-causation doctrines. According to the proximate-cause doctrine, a policy covering a named peril covers not only losses caused directly by that peril, but also losses caused by other perils set in motion by that named peril. To illustrate, a fire insurance policy covers not only hostile fire losses, but also losses caused by smoke and water damage resulting from the fire. In fact, a business can collect under its fire insurance policy for damage from smoke or water occasioned by a hostile fire next door even if there is no hostile fire on the insured premises. The fire insurer may be able to recover its payment from the owner or tenant of the building next door if it can prove negligence on that person's part. A health insurer is held responsible under a policy covering accidental injuries not only for disability income losses or medical expenses caused by an accidental injury, but also for losses caused by a disease contracted as a result of the accident.

Decisions about a specified peril being the proximate cause of some other peril depend upon how much space or time elapses between the two perils and whether there was some intervening cause. For example, the walls of a building left standing after a fire many collapse many days later and damage an adjoining building. To determine whether the fire was the proximate cause of the collapse of the walls, the court will consider the elapsed time and the presence of any strong winds.

A sound way to analyze perils covered is the chain-of-causation concept, which works as follows:

1. Construct a chronological scheme of the perils involved. In the illustration just cited, this chain is as follows:

   Windstorm → Fire → Smoke

2. Identify the peril (or perils) covered under the policy. In this illustration, the peril is fire.
3. Remember that the losses caused by all perils to the right of the specified perils are covered so long as they are a consequence of that specific peril and are not specifically excluded. In the illustration this means that the policy covers the losses caused by fire and by smoke. A problem may arise when a peril that is

specifically excluded interrupts the chain. For example, the fire insurance policy specifically excludes loss by theft. Suppose property is stolen as a result of the confusion surrounding the fire. Is the loss covered because the chain is fire → confusion → theft? A definite answer does not yet exist.

Property, Sources of Liability, or Lives. The *property* covered under a property insurance policy may be either personal property or real property. Personal property may consist of a specific item (for example, a machine, an automobile, or a watch), a specific type of property (machinery, equipment, or jewelry), or simply all personal property or contents not specifically excluded. The last description (1) provides broader coverage, (2) enables the insured to check explicitly the property that is not covered, and (3) may include new types of property acquired while the policy is in effect. On the other hand, for a given amount of insurance, insurers usually charge higher premiums for this broad coverage than for more specific insurance.

If the policy covers a business building, the building item typically includes machinery used for the service of the building, such as plumbing, air conditioning, heating apparatus, and elevators. Under most conditions, it also includes ovens, kilns, furnaces, and other equipment. Awnings, screens, storm doors, window shades, and the like, if owned by the building owner, are considered part of the building. Finally, personal property such as janitors' supplies, fuel, and any other property that is used solely in the service of the building is covered under the building item. Commonly excluded under the building item are excavations, underground flues and drains, and foundations below the ground.

Policies covering all personal property or contents commonly exclude automobiles, airplanes, animals, money, and securities. Policies covering specific types of property may exclude specific subtypes of items (for example, a policy may cover a contractor's equipment but not the trucks).

Liability insurance may be written on a selective or a comprehensive basis. Selective liability insurance policies cover named *sources of liability* such as the ownership, maintenance, or use of premises; the manufacture or distribution of products or services; the practice of accounting; or the ownership, maintenance, or use of an owned automobile. These stated sources may be further limited through exclusions. For example, automobile liability insurance may exclude situations in which the automobile is used as a taxi or a bus.

Comprehensive liability insurance covers all sources of liability not specifically excluded. For example, a comprehensive general liability insurance policy covers all sources other than the ownership, maintenance, or use of an automobile or an airplane and some other specified sources. The advantages and disadvantages of comprehensive liability insurance compared with selective liability insurance are basically the same as those stated above in the comparison of broad personal property coverage and more specific coverage.

The *person whose life or health is insured* is named in a personal insurance policy. Life insurance policies usually insure one person; health insurance policies commonly cover medical expenses occasioned by the poor health of the named insured or the named insured's family.

Persons. Property insurance policies may protect only the named insured against losses to property in which there is some financial interest. The insured may be a sole or part owner, a bailee with a liability interest in the property that is cared for or controlled, or a secured creditor. Other persons whose property interests may be covered include such varied groups as the named insured's family, guests, legal representatives, secured creditors, customers, or employees. These other persons may be protected against losses to their own property or their liability to the named insured for damage to that property. They may be covered automatically or only at the option of the named insured.

Secured creditors, such as a bank mortgagee or an automobile finance company, may receive special treatment under the policy. The usual procedure is to include in the owner's policy a standard mortgagee clause or a standard loss-payable clause in automobile insurance under which the insurer obligates itself to pay the mortgagee even if the owner violates the contract, so long as the breach was not within the control or knowledge of the mortgagee. Under these clauses, the insurer must also give the mortgagee separate notice of cancellation. The mortgagee can also sue the insurer in the mortgagee's own name. If the owner has violated the contract, the insurer has no obligation to the owner but must pay the mortgagee. In return for this payment the mortgagee must surrender to the insurer an equivalent amount of the claim against the owner. The insurer may, if it wishes, avoid sharing a claim against the owner by paying the mortgagee the total amount of the mortgage. If the insurer and the mortgagee share the claim, the mortgagee recovers the uninsured loss first if a foreclosure becomes necessary. If the owner has not violated the contract, the insurer usually makes the check payable jointly to the owner and the mortgagee. The mortgagee usually releases the money to the owner for repairs. The mortgagee could, however, claim this money and reduce the mortgage by an equivalent amount.

A property or liability insurance policy can be assigned by the named insured to some other party, such as a secured creditor, but the insurer must consent to the assignment. The insurer's consent is necessary because the hazard may be changed by the assignment. Life and health insurance contracts are assignable without the consent of the insurer, but the insurer is not bound to recognize the assignment until it has been filed with the insurer. In either case the assignee does not become a party to the contract and can collect only what the named insured would have collected except for the assignment. Following a loss, an insured can assign any claim against the insurer to some other person.

Liability insurance policies, like property insurance policies, may be limited to the named insured or extended to include other persons. Other possibilities are the insured's family, legal representatives, employees, friends permitted to drive the car, tenants who occupy a building owned by the insured, and distributors who market an insured's product.

The beneficiaries of a life insurance policy are named in the policy. Health insurance policies usually provide benefits for the person whose health is insured.

In choosing the persons (more precisely, the legal entities, including both organizations and the natural persons) to cover under the policies it purchases, an organization should be guided not only by its overall risk financing costs but also by concern for its relationships with its employees, customers, and others with whom it does business. If an organization is likely to be held legally responsible for the property or liability losses of others, such as its employees who may become involved in automobile accidents while acting for the organization or customers whose property the organization's activities may damage, it may be cost effective for the organization to include these entities as persons covered by its own insurance. Protecting such persons with the organization's own coverage is likely to be less expensive than resisting the legal claims these parties may bring against the organization after a loss. Insuring these interests is also likely to improve the organization's relationships with its employees, customers, and others whose interests the organization's insurance protects.

Losses Covered. Property insurance policies cover direct losses, indirect losses, and net income losses. Most property insurance policies cover only physical damage losses unless they are endorsed to cover other losses resulting from the same insured event.

In addition to paying settlements or court or statutory awards to the claimant, liability insurance policies provide certain supplementary services, such as investigation of the claim; negotiation and, it is hoped, settlement with the claimant; defense of the suit if this proves necessary; payment of premiums on bonds and of court costs that may be incurred in connection with the claim; and payment of expenses incurred by the insured in cooperating with the insurer. Some policies include a medical payments section under which medical expenses incurred by certain persons are paid without regard to the insured's liability.

Health insurance policies cover either a loss of income caused by the insured's disability or medical expenses. Policies may limit the types of medical expenses covered. Life insurance policies simply pay a specified amount upon the death of the insured.

In deciding which of its losses from a given event to try to cover by insurance rather than to retain or transfer to others, an organization's risk management professional must first recognize that, as discussed in the ARM 54 text (*Essentials of Risk Management*), any specific event may cause a wide range of property, net income, liability, and personnel losses. Most commercial liability policies, as well as most health insurance policies, cover many types of losses related to an insured organization's legal wrongdoing or an individual's loss of good health. Property insurance policies, in contrast, typically do not automatically cover losses of net income (decreased revenues or increased expenses) that may result from damage to the insured's property. Similarly, most liability insurance policies do not cover damage to an insured's own property that may be harmed in the same occurrence for which the insured organization may be found legally liable to others.

Concurrent net income losses following property damage or property lawsuits flowing from events for which the organization is held liable must usually be specifically insured if they are covered at all. To decide whether to insure these concurrent losses rather than to retain them (usually by default resulting from inaction), an organization's risk manager needs to consider all the losses that may flow from a given event. He or she should then estimate whether the organization's total risk financing costs will be increased or decreased by insuring these losses. Insuring these losses may also enhance the reliability or financial security underlying an organization's overall risk financing program. Failure to recognize and insure such concurrent losses may dramatically increase an organization's unintended retentions, thereby jeopardizing its financial ability to survive a major accident or a rapid series of large losses.

Time Period. The starting and expiration times of the coverage are almost always stated in the policy. Some policies state no expiration date; they are effective until canceled. So long as the peril begins to cause the insured to suffer loss or to incur liability before the expiration time, the entire loss resulting from that peril is covered.

Of particular interest are the hours at which the coverage begins and terminates (for example, noon or midnight) and the basis for determining the time of the loss (for example, standard time or daylight saving time and the time of an event at the address of the named insured or the time at the place of loss). Sometimes the coverage does not begin until some event occurs, such as the departure of a ship or the award of a contract to a successful bidder.

The policy term for most property and liability insurance policies is one year, but it may be some fraction of a year (for example, six months) or some multiple of a year (for example, three years). Some surety bonds run until canceled. Life and health insurance policies may be written for a specified number of years, until the insured reaches a specified age, or for the lifetime of the insured.

Insurance policies may be canceled only by mutual agreement, based upon a new consideration, of the parties to the policy unless the policy contains a provision to the contrary. Most property and liability insurance policies contain a cancellation provision that gives both the insured and the insurer the right to cancel the policy prior to the expiration date. Neither need give any reason for requesting the cancellation. If the insurer cancels the policy, the cancellation is effective a stated number of days after the insurer notifies the insured, and the insurer must return a pro rata portion of the premium to the insured. The required period of advance notice runs from midnight of the day on which notice is given. In many policies "notice by the insurer" means mailing of the notice, in which case the insured may receive less advance notice than the number of days stated in the policy.

If the insured cancels the policy, the cancellation is effective as soon as the insurer is notified. The insurer must return a short-rate portion of the premium. The short-rate return is less than a pro rata return because the insurer is permitted to recognize that most of the expenses other than losses have already been incurred. For example, the short-rate return after 180 days on a one-year policy is 40 percent. The short-rate cancellation also discourages the purchase of insurance to cover only the more hazardous parts of the policy period.

Automobile liability insurance policies covering the owners of private passenger automobiles usually prohibit the insurer from canceling the policy except for a few specified reasons such as nonpayment of premiums or revocation of the insured's driver's license or motor vehicle registration. Such a restricted cancellation provision is required by law in most states. Most states also restrict the right of insurers to cancel homeowners and other residence policies. Some of these statutes pertain to policies written for businesses as well as for families.

Life insurance policies cannot be canceled by the insurer; the insured can stop paying premiums but cannot recover premiums already paid. Health insurance policies include a wide variety of cancellation provisions. At one extreme, which has become much less common, the insurer may cancel the policy at any time after a stated number of days' notice. Noncancelable contracts, the other extreme, require the insurer to continue the coverage until the insured reaches some advanced age.

Standardized forms of most property and liability contracts expire at a particular hour and minute of a given day that an insured organization cannot change without a special endorsement or perhaps even a manuscript policy. Therefore, an insured does not have a wide range of choices about the inception and termination date and time of a particular policy. The most a risk management professional typically can do to strengthen the reliability of an organization's insurance coverage or to ease the administration of its insurance program is to try to avoid unintended coverage termination. This entails monitoring inception and termination dates, advising and assisting the affected managers in maintaining desired coverage, and securing any needed time extensions of coverage in unusual situations when coverage may be about to lapse while protection is still needed.

Locations. Insurance policies may be written on a specified locations basis or as floaters or floating insurance, in which case they cover losses anywhere within a specified area that is not excluded. In other words, some policies provide protection only if the loss occurs at one specified location; others cover all locations anywhere in the world that are not specifically excluded. Between these two extreme treatments of the locations covered are numerous other possibilities. For example, policies may cover losses at any one of a number of specified locations, at specified locations plus any new locations acquired by the insured, or anywhere within the United States and Canada that is not specifically excluded. Sometimes the coverage is more restricted as to perils, property, persons, or other features at certain locations.

Decisions regarding locations to which property or liability insurance should apply are typically difficult only when the operations of an organization (or of others whose interests the organization has chosen to protect through its own insurance coverage) change rapidly or frequently. The essence of these difficulties may be either (1) the failure to provide coverage at a location where protection is desired (thus reducing the reliability of the organization's risk financing program) or (2) maintaining coverage at a location where the organization no longer faces any significant loss exposures (thus raising its overall risk financing costs). One solution may be to purchase blanket or worldwide coverage, but this also tends to raise risk financing costs. A better solution is for the risk management professional to work closely with the operating managers of the organization's various departments or divisions—and the managers of other entities whose interests the organization wishes to protect through its own insurance—so that the risk management professional has current information on all the locations where the organization faces significant loss exposures. Although this solution is in principle the best, it may also complicate the administration of any large organization's risk financing program.

Special Conditions Suspending or Terminating Coverage. After analyzing the six features of an insurance contract described above, one may find some conditions that do not fit easily into any of these categories. Such conditions may be considered "special." For example, a property insurance policy may suspend coverage whenever there is any increase in the hazard within the knowledge or control of the insured, such as a change in occupancy from a retail store to paper manufacturing, without notification to the insurer. An automobile insurance policy normally covers anyone driving a covered car with the permission of the named insured; however, it does not cover any such person who uses the car while working in the business of selling, servicing, repairing, or parking automobiles. Instead of being considered a special condition, this automobile example might be considered a restriction on persons covered. Either analysis is equally acceptable.

Limitations on Amount of Recovery for Covered Events. Having defined covered events, or the circumstances under which a particular loss is covered, an insurance policy then usually specifies how much the insurer will pay for that loss. In insurance policies not subject to the principle of indemnity discussed earlier in this chapter (such as life insurance policies and some health insurance policies), the insurer agrees to pay a predetermined sum or a series of payments established in the insurance policy. For insurance policies that are subject to the principle of indemnity, the insurance policy typically does not mention any particular dollar amount that *will* be paid but, instead, imposes limitations on what *may* be paid. Many of these limitations—such as the amount of the loss, the amount of the applicable insurance, coinsurance provisions, and deductibles—stipulate that the insurer shall pay "no more than. . . ." This method of specifying the extent of the insurer's obligation to pay for losses has the effect of committing the insurer to pay no more than the *least* of these various limitations on its liability.

Amount of Loss. The essence of the principle of indemnity is that one who has suffered loss should recover no more—from insurance and any other source—than the amount of the loss. The amount recovered should be just enough to restore the indemnitee's pre-loss financial position. Therefore, most insurance policies specify that they will pay no more than the amount of the loss sustained.

Most insurance policies provide financial indemnity (although some provide services or replace items of property to return the insured to pre-loss condition). Therefore, most policies must specify how the amount of the loss is to be determined in dollars. Property insurance policies normally stipulate a valuation standard (such as actual cash value or replacement cost), with the same valuation standard being used as a measure of both the insurer's liability for loss and the insured's commitment to maintain insurance equal to at least a specified percentage of the value of the property (see the discussion that follows in the section "Coinsurance Requirements"). Similarly, policies covering net income losses limit recovery to "the actual loss sustained" as measured by the reduction in the gross earnings or some other gauge of the covered net income stream. Liability policies implicitly define and agree to reimburse covered losses as measured by court verdicts and settlements as well as defense costs incurred by or on behalf of an insured.

Policy Limits. Insurance policies also contain limits that state the maximum amount the insurer will pay for any given insured event. These limits may reduce the insured's recovery below the amounts indicated by the provisions and concepts just discussed. An insured organization may generally choose an amount of coverage (or a policy limit for any given type of loss) that the organization's management and risk management professional consider appropriate, provided the insurer is willing to offer the desired amount of coverage. In many cases, the insurer will need to draw upon its reinsurance resources to meet an insured's requests for coverage.

Many organizations choose policy limits that approximate their maximum foreseeable losses from any event as foreseen by their senior management or risk management professional. In some cases, however, insuring up to these maximum foreseeable losses may increase the organization's total risk financing costs to unacceptable levels or may require greater amounts of insurance than primary insurers and their reinsurers are collectively willing to offer as protection against one or more potentially catastrophic events. To increase the insurability of such exposures, an organization may agree to retain small losses up to a predetermined retention limit, or it may ask several insurers to accept one or more specified layers of excess coverage above the organization's own "self-insured retention" (SIR). Agreeing to retain acceptable amounts of smaller losses is generally preferable to doing without adequate coverage for extremely large losses.

In determining both retention levels and appropriate upper limits of coverage, an organization and its risk management professional should consider the factors of cost, premium savings, retention capacity, and tolerance for uncertainty described in the deductible decision models set forth in Chapter 3. The organization and its executives should also recognize that failing to insure up to the limits of maximum foreseeable losses from any single event or rapid series of events may jeopardize the overall reliability of the organization's risk financing program and complicate the administration of that program. Insufficient insurance may also create conflicts in the organization's relationships with its insurers, employees, customers, owners, and others who may look to the organization for compensation for those losses that they may suffer as indirect consequences of inadequately insured accidents that strike the organization. Only the financially strongest organizations should choose to retain the uppermost limits of potentially catastrophic losses.

Property Insurance. Property insurance policy limits may be stated in a variety of ways. These limits may be classified according to (1) whether there is an explicit dollar limit, (2) whether the limits provide specific coverage or blanket coverage, (3) whether the limits are subject to special internal limits, (4) whether the limits differ depending upon the perils, persons, types of loss, or locations covered, and (5) whether the limits are responsive to changes in the values of the property covered.

Most policies cover losses up to a stated number of dollars, but some policies, including most automobile physical damage insurance policies, do not include a dollar limit. In these policies the limit is, in effect, the maximum possible loss to the property.

If a single policy limit applies to many types of property at one location or property at two or more locations, this insurance is called *blanket* coverage. If different limits apply to narrowly defined types of property or to the same type of property at different locations, the insurance is called *divided* or *specific* coverage. For example, one limit may apply to a building, another to machinery, and still another to contents; or one limit may apply to contents at one location with a different limit applying to contents at another location. The effect is the same as if a separate policy had been written on each division of property, each having its own limit. A distinction might also be made between limits applying separately to a scheduled property item, such as Machine A, and limits applying to a fairly specific type of property. The major advantage of blanket coverage over specific coverage is the flexibility it provides by making the face amount of insurance available to cover losses to any item covered under the policy. On the other hand, blanket insurance may cost more and be subject to more severe coinsurance and other restrictive provisions.

Another approach places a limit on a certain type of property, but some subclass is subject to a lower *internal* limit. For example, one limit may apply to personal property, but losses of currency or coins may be limited to $500 or $1,000. This approach differs from the preceding case in that the internal limits are not separate, independent limits. In this example, a $1,000 recovery against a currency loss is charged against the overall policy limit.

The limits may differ depending upon the peril causing the loss, the persons insured, the type of loss, and the location.

Most property insurance limits are fixed at the beginning of the policy period, but some limits vary according to actual or expected changes in the value of the property covered. For example, automobile physical damage insurance is seldom written with stated dollar limits. Instead, the maximum payment under this insurance is the value of the car, which may vary during the policy period. Fixing dollar limits at the beginning of the period can cause problems when the value exposed fluctuates widely during the term of the policy.

The case of insurance on the contents of mercantile or manufacturing premises where the stock fluctuates in quantity and value is a good illustration. The fixed-amount approach would make it necessary for the insured to carry continuously an amount of insurance equal to the maximum value of the stock and to pay premiums for more insurance than is needed at other times, or to take less and run the chance of a loss exceeding the insurance, or continuously to watch the stock and the insurance and add or cancel insurance (at the higher short rates) to keep it in step with the stock. These alternatives entail excessive expense, risk, or labor, or all of them. Hence, *reporting forms* have been developed. These forms provide for a provisional amount of insurance or a stated percentage of the total concurrent insurance with maximum limits set for property in each location. Provisional values and a provisional premium are agreed upon. The insured makes monthly reports of values exposed to loss at each location. At the expiration of the policy term, the values in excess of those covered by specific insurance are averaged, appropriate rates are applied, and the premium is adjusted by the insurer. The insured either pays an additional premium on coverage in excess of the provisional amounts or receives a refund on amounts by which the provisional amounts exceed the actual. The principal advantage of these forms is that the insured is never overinsured or underinsured. For a large insured with multiple locations, the price is also usually more attractive than for equivalent nonreporting insurance. The principal disadvantage is the effort involved in making the periodic reports. A different example of variable limits is a provision under which the policy limit increases as a stated percentage per month reflecting a specified assumed rate of increase in property values.

Most property insurance policies provide for reinstatement of the limits to their original amount following a loss. A pro rata additional premium that covers the cost of the restored amount is sometimes payable.

Liability Insurance. Liability insurance policies usually contain separate limits applicable to awards or settlements for bodily injuries and for property damage. Until 1973 most bodily injury limits stated first the maximum amount payable on account of the injuries sustained by one person, and second the maximum amount payable per occurrence. For example, under a $25,000/$50,000 contract, the insurer would pay no more than $25,000 for claims arising out of injuries to one person. If two or more persons were injured in the occurrence, the insurer was not responsible for more than $50,000 of their combined claims, each individual claim being subject first to the per person limit. If two injured persons had claims of $40,000 and $20,000, the insurer would pay $25,000 plus $20,000, or $45,000. If three injured persons each had claims of $20,000, the insurer would pay $50,000. The property damage limit was usually a stated amount per occurrence. A major revision of an important group of liability insurance policies in 1973 abolished the per person limit but maintained separate per occurrence limits for the bodily injury and property damage coverages.

Single-limit liability insurance policies are becoming more common. A maximum amount is payable per occurrence regardless of the number of persons involved and the mix of bodily injuries and property damage. Because of this flexibility, a $25,000 single-limit policy is more liberal than a policy with $10,000/$20,000 bodily injury limits and a $5,000 property damage limit or than a $20,000 bodily injury limit and a $5,000 property damage limit.

Most liability insurance policies provide the same protection for each occurrence during the policy period, but with an aggregate limit stating the insurer's maximum liability for all such events during the policy period.

The defense and investigation costs and other supplementary benefits are not subject to any limits (except for some internal limits on some items) and are provided in addition to the limits applicable to awards or settlements.

Medical payments coverage, often written in conjunction with liability insurance, is usually subject to a specified dollar limit per person. The medical expenses must also be incurred within a specified period of time following the accident. Sometimes there is also a limit per accident.

Workers compensation policies do not place any dollar limit on compensation benefits other than those prescribed by statute.

Life and Health Insurance. Life insurance policies pay a stated amount upon death. This stated amount may increase or decrease during the lifetime of the insured. If death is caused by accidental means and the policy contains a multiple-indemnity rider, the insurer may pay some multiple—usually double—of the amount otherwise paid.

Health insurance policies limit the amount paid in various ways. Disability income policies usually state the amount paid per week or per month and the maximum number of weeks or months the benefit will be paid. Medical expense benefits of all types may be subject to a single amount or time limit, or separate limits may apply to each type of medical expense, such as hospital bills or doctors' fees. Internal limits may apply to such items as daily room-and-board charges and surgical fees. The limits may be doubled if the person is injured in certain specified types of accidents.

Coinsurance Requirements. An important concept affecting the amount of recovery under many business insurance policies is coinsurance.

Operation. The usual coinsurance clause states that if the insured fails to carry insurance equal to some specified percentage of the value of the property at the time of the loss, the insurer is responsible only for that portion of the loss that the amount of insurance bears to the amount required to escape any penalty. For example, assume that six months ago an insured purchased $100,000 of insurance on property with an actual cash value of $150,000. Assume further that the insurance policy contained an 80 percent coinsurance clause. If the property is worth $200,000 today, the amount the insurer would pay toward a loss today would be computed as follows:

$$\frac{\text{Amount of insurance}}{(\text{Coinsurance }\%)\left(\begin{array}{c}\text{Value at}\\ \text{time of loss}\end{array}\right)} \times \text{Loss}$$

but not to exceed the loss or the amount of insurance, or

$$\frac{\$\ 100{,}000}{0.80(\$200{,}000)} \times \text{Loss} = \tfrac{5}{8} \text{ of loss}$$

If the loss were $80,000, the insurer would pay $50,000. If the loss were $170,000, the insurer would pay $100,000, the amount of insurance. The insurer's liability will always be the amount of insurance when the loss exceeds the required insurance. The insurer's liability will be the loss only when the amount of insurance exceeds the required insurance and equals or exceeds the value of the loss.

If the insured purchases insurance from two or more insurers, each of which issues a policy containing the same coinsurance clause, each insurer will follow the same procedure in determining its liability. For example, if the insured whose situation was analyzed in the preceding paragraph had also purchased $60,000 from some other insurer, and the loss was $80,000, that insurer would pay ⅜ of $80,000, or $30,000. The insured would suffer no coinsurance penalty because the total amount of insurance would equal the amount required. If the total amount of insurance from all insurers exceeds the amount required, the liability of each insurer usually depends only on a pro rata liability clause. For example, if the same insured carried $100,000 with the first insurer and $80,000 with the second, the first insurer would be responsible for 5/9 of the loss, or $44,444, and the second insurer for 4/9, or $35,556.

Some types of property insurance always contain a coinsurance clause. For example, blanket forms and reporting forms are available only if the insured accepts some coinsurance condition. In other instances the insured can elect to buy insurance on a "flat" (no coinsurance) or some coinsurance basis. The incentive for accepting a coinsurance clause is a reduced rate. The reasons for the different discounts will be explained shortly, but sizable discounts are available under certain circumstances. For example, by having an 80 percent coinsurance clause included in fire insurance coverage, the owner of a fire-resistant building in a highly protected community can reduce the fire insurance rate by 70 percent.

Rationale. The purpose of coinsurance is to achieve indirectly large amounts of insurance relative to the value of the property. Because most property losses are small relative to the value exposed, the cost of providing insurance protection without any coinsurance on property of a specified value does not increase proportionately with the amount of insurance. For example, it does not cost twice as much to provide $80,000 of insurance on a $100,000 building as to provide $40,000 of protection. For the same reason, if all insureds with $100,000 buildings purchased $80,000 insurance policies, the insurance premium rate (price per $100 of insurance) could be considerably less than if they all purchased $40,000 of protection. Consequently, it would be unfair to charge the same premium rate per $100 for $40,000 and $80,000 policies. In other words, the premium rate should depend upon the relation between the insurance and the value of the property.

One solution would be to prepare a table of graded rates that decrease as the ratio of insurance-to-value increases. Each property to be insured would have to be appraised and the ratio of the desired amount of insurance to the value calculated. The proper rate could then be obtained from the table. This solution has usually been rejected because the insurer would incur considerable expense in appraising each property presented for insurance. The solution would also be inadequate from the insurer's viewpoint if the property values fluctuated widely during the policy period.

An alternative solution is the coinsurance clause. Each of the coinsurance discounts should produce a rate corresponding to the graded rate for the corresponding percentage relation between the insurance and the property value. For example, the discount for an 80 percent coinsurance clause should be related to the graded rate for insurance equal to 80 percent of the property value. The coinsurance discounts should vary with the type of property and the grade of community protection because smaller percentage losses are relatively more important with respect to high-grade properties in well-protected communities. The insureds who carry insurance equal to 80 percent or more of the value can select an 80 percent coinsurance clause, get the rate discount that will reduce the rate to the graded rate for 80 percent insurance to value, and yet avoid any coinsurance penalty. If a loss occurs, the insurer will pay the entire loss up to the insurance amount. Insureds who carry less insurance but elect the 80 percent clause will find that when a loss occurs, the insurer will assume that the insured has total insurance equal to 80 percent of the property value and determine its own liability on a pro rata basis. If, for example, the insurance amount is 40 percent of the property value, the insurer will pay only half the loss but never more than 40 percent of the property value. This approach to coinsurance is less costly for the insurer to administer because it needs only to check carefully the value of the relatively few properties involved in a loss.

Difficulties in Application. Basing the coinsurance calculation on the value at the time of the loss can be troublesome for the insured because the insured may wonder if enough insurance has been purchased to avoid a coinsurance penalty. This difficulty is especially evident with respect to personal property that fluctuates widely in value. One solution available to many insureds is an *agreed amount endorsement* under which the insured and the insurer agree in advance upon the valuation for coinsurance purposes. Another solution with respect to personal property is the reporting form described in the previous section, "Property Insurance," which is always written on a full-reporting (100 percent coinsurance) basis, but in which the insurance always equals the amount exposed.

If a loss is small, the cost of appraising the entire property following a loss in order to determine its value for coinsurance purposes may exceed or almost equal the loss. Under a *waiver of inventory clause,* the insurer agrees to waive the requirement of a separate inventory if the loss is less than, say, 2 percent of the insurance amount. The coinsurance clause, however, still applies.

An interesting variant of the typical coinsurance clause is used in burglary insurance covering merchandise, furniture, and fixtures. Under this clause, the insurer states that it shall not be liable for a greater proportion of the loss on merchandise than the policy limit bears to the *lesser* of two values: (1) a coinsurance percentage times the actual cash value of the merchandise or (2) a coinsurance limit. All policies contain coinsurance percentages and coinsurance limits. The coinsurance percentage varies by territory; it is higher in those territories where burglaries are more common. The coinsurance limit varies by trade group; it is higher for those trades with high-value, lightweight items. The coinsurance limit approximates the maximum probable burglary for each trade group regardless of the value exposed.

Deductibles. The following examples of deductibles are taken primarily from property insurance and health insurance, where they are most common, but deductibles are also found in liability insurance.

The first way to classify deductibles is according to whether they apply to each item damaged; each person insured; each occurrence, accident, or illness; or the total losses in a stated period. Deductibles applicable to the total losses in a year are usually called "aggregate deductibles." Both the frequency and the severity of the losses determine whether an insured will have a claim in excess of an aggregate deductible.

Second, the deductible may be a specified amount, a percentage of the loss, a percentage of the face amount of insurance, or a waiting period before disability income losses are paid, or it may be determined in some other way.

When the deductible is a stated dollar amount per loss, the amount of the deductible is first subtracted from the loss when calculating the insurer's loss payment. Thus, with a $50,000 policy subject to a $5,000 per-loss deductible, the insurer pays $35,000 for a $40,000 loss; the $50,000 policy face value amount of insurance becomes payable only for losses of $55,000 or more. When the deductible is a percentage of the policy's face value, the deductible is, again, a fixed amount. For example, a $50,000 policy subject to a 2 percent deductible would provide, in effect, a $1,000 per-loss deductible. For a $40,000 loss, the policy would pay $39,000; the policy face value of $50,000 would not be payable for losses less than 102 percent of the policy face value, or $51,000.

Expressing the deductible as a percentage of the loss differs from the other practices described above in that the deductible amount in dollars increases as the size of the loss increases. Sometimes a percentage deductible applies to losses after first subtracting a stated deductible amount; in other cases a percentage deductible is not permitted to exceed a stated dollar amount. Sometimes the deductible amount decreases as the loss size increases—for example, the insurer may agree to pay 125 percent of the losses in excess of $100 or more until the deductible amount is reduced to zero, after which the entire loss is paid. The result is a $100 deductible for losses of $100 or less, a $75 deductible for a $200 loss, a $25 deductible for a $400 loss, and no deductible for losses of $500 or more. A related concept in some disability income insurance policies (mainly workers compensation insurance) is a retroactive waiting period under which the waiting period is waived if the disability extends beyond a certain period. Still another type of deductible is a flat amount that decreases as the number of claim-free years increases.

A third type of deductible may apply to all losses covered under the policy or only to certain losses. For example, under an "all-risks" policy the deductible may not apply to losses caused by fire and several other specified perils.

A fourth type of deductible may be a franchise, in which case the insurer pays all losses that are larger than the franchise amount. For example, if the franchise is 3 percent of the amount of insurance, the insurer under a $10,000 policy would pay nothing on losses of less than $300 but would pay the total amount of larger losses. This approach is used primarily in marine insurance.

Actions After a Loss To Secure Recovery. The one remaining major aspect of an insurance policy—perhaps the most important—is a description of the procedures by which the insured actually goes about collecting funds from the insurer. These procedures are designed to fulfill the post-loss legal conditions to which the insurer's obligation to pay for losses is subject. An organization's risk management professional must be sure that senior management has specified the personnel responsible for working with insurers and their representatives in handling claims. The insurer has a right to hold the insured to specified procedures before it actually pays for or provides services or materials to restore an otherwise insured loss. Therefore, complying with this loss-adjustment procedure is a *condition precedent* to the insured's right to recover from the insurer for a covered loss.

It is often incorrectly said that an insured has a "duty" to follow the loss adjustment procedures in an insurance policy. The steps in the loss-adjustment procedure are technically not duties because an insured is not subject to any liability or other legal sanctions for failing to carry out these procedures. An insured willing to forgo the recovery that would otherwise be payable for a covered loss is free to disregard the loss-adjustment procedure. Presumably, it is because there are few such insureds that the loss-adjustment procedures are wrongly called "duties" rather than "conditions precedent" to the insured's right to recovery.

Although loss-adjustment principles and procedures in property and liability insurance policies have much in common, appropriate post-loss procedures for these two major types of policies can pose significantly different problems for an organization and its risk management professionals. Therefore, loss adjustment in the two policies will be discussed separately.

Property Insurance. In property insurance policies the insured is usually instructed to (1) notify the insurer, (2) protect the property from further damage, and (3) assist the insurer in its investigation of the loss.

Notice of Loss. The insured must usually notify the insurer or, in most instances, a duly authorized agent "immediately" or "as soon as practicable." The courts interpret both terms to mean as soon as is reasonably possible. Furthermore, notice to the agent is always sufficient. A few policies require that the notice be given within a specified period following the loss.

The policy usually requires that the notice be given in writing. Actually, however, oral notice to the insurer is usually sufficient unless the insurer or its agent objects. Even if the insurer objects, the policy requirement is ineffective if the insurer then proceeds to adjust the claim. Despite these liberal interpretations, however, the insured will be wise to give the notice in writing because it could be required as evidence in case the notice is questioned. Some policies, such as those covering theft losses, where prompt action may substantially reduce the amount of the loss, require a telegram or some other special, rapid form of communication.

The insured may also be expected to notify someone other than the insurer. Under a theft insurance policy, for example, the insured must tell the police as well as the insurer about the loss.

Protection of Property From Further Damage. All property insurance policies require the insured to protect the property from further damage. Failure to meet this requirement will release the insurer from any responsibility for further damage. Although not all policies specifically state that the insurer will reimburse the insured for any reasonable expenses incurred in protecting the property, such reimbursement is usually made. Only in marine insurance policies, however, is this reimbursement in addition to the face value of the policy. In some policies, such as business interruption insurance, the reimbursement is specifically limited to the reduction in the loss.

Ideally, the adjuster will arrive promptly on the scene and suggest the types of protective measures that should be adopted. The degree of supervision exercised by the loss adjuster over the insured's protective work depends upon the loss situation and the adjuster's evaluation of the insured. Sometimes the adjuster completely assumes the insured's responsibility. The insured should not hesitate, however, to take any action that appears reasonable and necessary before the arrival of the adjuster.

Examples of protective measures that have proved beneficial in some instances are the following: nailing of tar paper over holes in a roof; draining of plumbing in cold weather; separation of wet debris from woodwork; removal of contents from a building threatened by further damage; drying and greasing of wet machinery; prompt distribution of perishables to retailers or consumers or to cold storage plants;

separation and drying of wet merchandise; and coverage of exposed equipment with tarpaulins.

Assistance in the Investigation. The third procedure for the insured to follow is to assist the loss adjuster in the investigation. The adjuster must determine (1) whether the loss actually occurred, (2) whether it is covered under the contract, and (3) the extent of the loss. The burden of proof is upon the insured, and the better prepared the insured is to aid in these determinations, the more satisfactory and prompt the final loss adjustment is likely to be. If the adjuster has some doubt concerning whether the loss is covered, the insured may be asked to sign a nonwaiver agreement that states that the insurer is not admitting its liability by its investigation. Despite the nonwaiver agreement, however, the insurer may be held liable if it causes the insured undue expense or inconvenience. Sometimes in a doubtful situation the insurer does not request a nonwaiver agreement but sends the insured a *reservation of rights letter* in which it reserves the right to deny the claim later.

It is usually simple to determine whether the loss occurred, and the insured usually has no difficulty in proving the case. In some instances, however, particularly with respect to theft and mysterious disappearance, the adjuster may have to rely heavily upon the reputation of the insured.

To determine whether the loss is covered, the adjuster must be thoroughly acquainted with the property insured, the circumstances surrounding the loss, and the insurance policy. He or she must know whether the policy was in effect at the time of the loss and whether it covers the peril, the person(s), the property, the location, and the type of loss (direct or net income) involved in the claim. The policy may also specify some conditions not falling into any of these categories that, if they exist, suspend or terminate the coverage. The insurer can supply policy information, but the adjuster must rely upon the insured to provide information concerning the property and the circumstances of the loss. The insured can do this by exhibiting the remains of the property and the space it occupied and by offering testimony, fire department or police department records, plans and specifications, deeds, bills of sale, or other evidence.

The most difficult task in adjusting property losses is the valuation of the loss. For direct property losses the usual basis of recovery is the actual cash value of the loss. This measure is usually the cost of repair or replacement with new property less depreciation (including obsolescence) or alternatively the decrease in market value, but other measures are possible. Even after a measure has been agreed upon, disagreement may arise concerning such concepts as depreciation and market value.

Replacement cost coverage eliminates the problem of attempting to measure depreciation.

The insured and the adjuster may use one or more of several methods to establish the value of the property and the loss. For example, they may look at the property together and agree on the loss; they may make or have made separate estimates and reconcile their differences; they may prepare specifications for repair or replacement and submit these to be bid upon; they may accept the valuation of a single expert; or they may accept the amounts shown in accounting records.[13]

Property insurance policies generally require the insured to produce upon request at reasonable times and places all records pertinent to the valuation procedure. If the records have been destroyed or if they are otherwise unavailable, the insured does not usually lose the right to press the claim, but the adjustment process may be slower and the settlement less equitable. Under some policies the insured is required to keep records of the insured property that will enable the insurer to determine accurately the amount of the loss.

Net income losses are even more difficult to evaluate than direct property losses. The time required to restore premises to a tenantable condition, the net profit and continuing expenses that would have been covered by sales during the period a store must be out of operation, and the profits that a manufacturer would have made on the sale of some finished goods are examples of losses in this category. Often the losses must be estimated from sketchy accounting data.

The difficulties in measuring losses are compounded when the policy contains a coinsurance clause, because this clause may make necessary a valuation of the undamaged as well as of the damaged property. Except when the loss is small, the insurer is likely to require a detailed inventory of the damaged and undamaged property, and the insured is well-advised to keep adequate, up-to-date records for this purpose. The fire insurance policy specifically charges the insured with the preparation of such inventory records after any loss, but this provision is seldom enforced with respect to the undamaged property unless there is a coinsurance clause.

Within some specified period following the loss, such as thirty or ninety days, the insured must file a sworn detailed proof of loss with the insurer. The *proof of loss form* describes the time and cause of the loss, the persons who have interests in the property, the amount of the claim, and other facets of the loss. The insurer usually furnishes a blank proof-of-loss form, which the insured completes and signs. Most claims are adjusted swiftly and without difficulty, and in such cases the adjuster commonly completes the proof-of-loss form for the insured's signature after the adjustment has been completed. In situations where the insured's story may change or where a dispute has arisen, the adjuster may refuse to proceed with the adjustment until the insured has executed a proof of loss. Failure of the insurer to act within a reasonable time after the filing of a proof of loss may cause the insurer to lose its right to object to any features of the claim.

Several legal interpretations and statutes soften the impact of the proof-of-loss requirement upon the insured. Although policies specify the number of days within which the proof of loss must be filed, several states by statute or by court interpretation have either made it unnecessary for insureds to comply with this period or require the insurer to give additional notice of its intention to enforce this provision. Courts have also held that a material misstatement by the insured in the proof of loss shall not affect the insured's right of recovery unless the misstatement was intentional. The insurer or its representatives may be held to have waived the proof-of-loss requirement if they deny liability, if they promise to prepare the proof-of-loss statement for the insured, or if they begin to adjust the loss without notifying the insured that proof of loss will be required. The insured cannot be accused of failure to comply with the proof-of-loss provisions because of some defect that the insurer does not promptly point out. The insured can change the filed proof-of-loss form if it believes that the initial loss estimates were in error. Despite these favorable interpretations, the insured should make every attempt to comply with the policy provisions. The insured's case may be the exception that proves the rule. The insurer will usually pay the claim shortly after the insured files the proof of loss. Some contracts specify a period within which the claim must be paid.

Special Problems. In some property-loss adjustments, certain problems can create additional steps in the loss-adjustment procedure. For example, the procedure may be more lengthy and complex when there is (1) other insurance, (2) a third party who is responsible for the loss, or (3) some dispute over the valuation of the loss.

If two or more policies cover the loss, it is usually clear from policy provisions how the loss is to be apportioned among the various insurers, but sometimes the situation is ambiguous. For example, there may be two policies, each of which claims to provide excess insurance over any other insurance covering the loss. The courts usually resolve such situations in a way that is beneficial to the insured. In the case cited, they would probably require the insurers to share the loss on a pro rata basis. Most cases of this sort, however, are handled without going to court. Most insurers abide by the publication titled *Guiding Principles* (1963), which prescribes certain rules to be followed in settling disputes because of overlapping coverages.

The second special problem to be discussed arises when the insured has a legal right to recover his or her loss from some third party. The third party may be responsible as a result of negligence, a contract, or a statute. Common law and the subrogation clause in the insurance policy provide that the insurer, upon payment of the loss, may take over the right of the insured to collect from the responsible third party to the extent of the insurance payment. The insured, therefore, must be careful after (and before) a loss not to prejudice this right of the insurer. The right is particularly important in transportation insurance because of common carrier liability and in automobile collision insurance because another party is often at fault. In no event should the insured release the party responsible without the consent of the insurer simply because that party is willing to pay the part of the loss that is not insured.

The insurer may seek to recover from the third party in the name of the insured or in its own name. If the loss exceeds the insurance payment, the insured may join in the suit, sue in his or her own name for the entire amount of his or her interest only, or rely on the insurer to sue for the entire loss.

The third special problem occurs when the insured and the adjuster cannot reach an agreement concerning the valuation of the property or the loss. In this case, two policy provisions are pertinent. Under the first, either the insurer or the insured has the right to demand in writing that the differences be resolved by an appraisal. Each party names an appraiser, and the appraisers then select a competent and disinterested umpire. If the appraisers cannot agree on an umpire, provision is made for selection by the courts. The appraisers then value each property item and the loss to that item. Only their differences are submitted to the umpire. In the absence of fraud, collusion, or mutual mistake, an award signed by any two of the three persons is binding. The insured must pay the appraiser's fee plus one-half of the bill of the umpire and other appraisal charges. The insured must submit to the demand of the insurer for an appraisal, but in most instances, if the insurer refuses to submit to a similar demand of the insured, the insured's only remedy is to sue.

The second provision that becomes pertinent in a valuation dispute gives the insurer the right instead of paying the loss in cash to buy all or any part of the property at the agreed or appraised value or to repair, rebuild, or replace the property. Although this provision gives the insurer an out if it disagrees with either the insured's or the appraiser's estimate of the loss, in most property lines the insurer seldom exercises this option because of the difficulties involved in disposing of property or in repairing, rebuilding, or replacing to the insured's satisfaction.

These options are used, however, in settling personal property claims when the insurer can better dispose of the property than can the insured. For example, some merchandise damaged by smoke can often be reclaimed and sold by salvors employed by the insurer more advantageously than they could be sold by the insured. In other instances, the insured conducts the sale under the supervision of the insurer.

Replacement in kind instead of a cash payment is the usual rule when the insurer can replace the property more promptly or more economically than can the insured. Two illustrations of losses of this type are damage to or loss of glass and jewelry.

Liability Insurance. Liability insurance claims present some responsibilities and problems for the insured that differ from those associated with property insurance claims. Whereas property insurance claims are termed *first-party claims* because the insured has suffered the loss, liability losses are called *third-party claims* because the insured is legally obligated to pay some injured third party.

Common Principles and Procedures. Whenever an accident occurs, the insured should notify the insurer as soon as possible. The procedures related to notices of property losses also apply here, but there are three differences. First, the insured should notify the insurer of any accident that might result in a claim from a third party. The notice must contain any reasonably obtainable information concerning the time, place, and circumstances of the accident and the names and addresses of injured persons and witnesses. The insured should not wait for an injured party to file a claim but should notify the insurer whenever the possibility of a claim arises. Even if the injured party maintains that he or she was not injured, the insured should notify the insurer. Second, the courts will interpret the notice requirement in liability insurance policies more strictly because prompt investigation of the circumstances surrounding the accident is essential to protect the insurer's interest. The major problem in investigating liability claims is gathering the facts and interpreting them in the light of the law, the judge, the jury, and the plaintiff's attorney. Witnesses and evidence can quickly disappear, or witnesses can change their stories, and with the passage of time minor injuries can assume major proportions in the mind of the claimant. Third, the policy demands that insureds forward *immediately* to the insurers every notice of a claim or suit, summons, or other process delivered to insureds or their representatives.

During the adjustment process, the insured must cooperate with the insurer. The insurer provides the lawyers and is responsible for and in charge of the defense of the claim, but if the insurer requests the insured to do so, the insured must attend hearings and trials and assist in the general conduct of the suit by such means as securing and giving evidence, obtaining witnesses, and effecting settlements if the insurer believes that this process offers the best solution. For this assistance the insurer reimburses the insured for all reasonable expenses incurred at the insurer's request, usually including actual loss of earnings not to exceed a specified amount per day.

The insured must be careful both at the time of the accident and after it not to volunteer any payment, assume any obligation, or incur any expense other than the cost of essential immediate medical treatment of others. Paying these medical expenses is not regarded as an admission of liability but as the mark of a decent person and is a wise precautionary measure because it may substantially reduce the ultimate loss. The other actions, however, can interfere with the insurer's ability to defend the claim.

The insured need not submit a proof of loss in connection with liability losses. Such proof is unnecessary because the amount of the loss is fixed either by the judgment awarded by the courts or in an out-of-court settlement between the insurer and the claimant.

Special Problems. Special problems sometimes arise in connection with liability insurance claims. They may occur when (1) some third party is primarily responsible for the loss, (2) the suit or the judgment is in excess of the policy limits, or (3) the insured and the insurer cannot resolve their differences without resorting to a suit.

If some third party is primarily responsible for the accident for which the insurer pays a judgment in behalf of the insured, the insurer takes over any right the insured may have to sue the third party. This right may arise, for example, under a hold-harmless agreement or because some other party, such as an agent, is primarily responsible. Although insurers seldom exercise this right with respect to liability losses, the insured must be careful to preserve whatever right exists.

Often the injured party will sue for an amount far in excess of the policy limits. In such a case, the insurer is immediately expected to notify the insured so that the insured may participate in the defense.

A related problem arises when the claimant agrees to settle for an amount within the policy limits but threatens to sue for a much larger amount. If the insurer refuses and the claimant sues for and is awarded an amount in excess of the policy limits, the insurer is responsible for this excess only if a court decides that the adjuster was negligent or did not act in good faith in behalf of the insured.

Liability insurance policies do not specify any interval during which the insured must commence suit against the insurer in case of a disagreement, but they do assert that no one has a right of action against the insurer (1) unless the insured has complied with all the policy provisions and (2) until the insured's liability has been established either by a judgment awarded by a court or by a written agreement among the insured, the insurer, and the claimant. These conditions affect both insureds and claimants. If the insurer claims that the insured has violated the contract, the insured must defend himself or herself in court against the claimant before suing the insurer. The claimant has no rights under the policy if it is void with respect to the insured. Except in a few states with direct-action statutes that supersede these policy provisions, the claimant can never proceed directly against the insurer until the insured's liability has been established by the courts.

The Shared Objective: A Fair Settlement. The objective of the loss adjustment is a fair and prompt settlement of the claim. Insureds should realize that it is as wrong for an insurer to overpay its claims as to underpay them. Overpayments will usually be reflected in increased insurance costs or in a weakened financial condition of the insurer.

Small losses that, strictly speaking, are not covered under the policy are paid by some insurers as nuisance claims. The loss of goodwill and the expenses of an extensive investigation are considered more costly than the claim itself. Other equally reputable insurers argue that this practice leads to a misunderstanding of the insurance coverage and could prove very costly if all insureds submit such claims.

Many insureds are disappointed by loss adjustments because they have not read their policies. A loss the insured thought was covered may be excluded or not specifically included, or the policy may limit the amount recovered to less than expected. These disappointments are best averted at the time the risk management program is designed and not at the time of the loss adjustment.

Other insureds will be disappointed because of honest disagreements concerning the circumstances of the losses and the interpretations of the policies. If an insured feels correct after continued discussions with the insurer, and if this conviction is confirmed by some informed, objective third party, the insured should contact the state insurance department. If the department agrees with the insured, it may be able to force the insurer to act more favorably by moral suasion or by a threat to cancel its license to operate in the state. The insured may also resort to the legal remedies provided under the policy.

Still other insureds may exaggerate their claims either (1) because they consider it smart and socially acceptable to collect excess amounts from the impersonal insurers (which, they point out, have been collecting much more in premiums from insureds than they have paid in losses), or (2) because they consider it necessary to ask for too much initially in order to receive fair settlements. The first attitude would be disastrous if it were adopted by everyone, and yet it is true that society does to a certain degree condone such procedures. The second attitude is unnecessary so far as most (but unfortunately not all) adjusters are concerned.

Some risk managers whose firms are experience-rated or retrospectively-rated have accused insurance adjusters of loose and indifferent handling of claims because they have no incentive to keep costs down. Some insurers, on the other hand, point out that they are sometimes pressured to pay product liability and workers compensation claims that they would have preferred to fight. Neither practice is in the long run in the best interest of the insurer or of the risk manager.

Often the insured is dissatisfied not with the final settlement, but with the work required and the treatment by the adjuster. Some adjusters—but not most—are discourteous and overly demanding. In defense of those adjusters, it should be noted that they deal with some insureds who are misinformed, uncooperative, or dishonest even to the point of purposely causing the loss to make a profit on the insurance.[14] If the insured can erase at an early date any doubt the adjuster may have concerning the insured's motivations, the stage should be set for a more amicable and fair adjustment. If the insured and the insurer cannot reach an agreement, the courts will also look with more favor on the insured who has proceeded openly, fairly, and intelligently.

SUMMARY

The risk financing technique of insurance can be defined in an economic and managerial context as a device for pooling loss exposures to reduce uncertainty and for shifting to an insurer the financial burden of financing restoration of losses by drawing on the pool of resources thus created. In a legal setting insurance can be defined as a contract by which one party (insurer/transferee), in exchange for insurance premiums, provides the other party (the insured/indemnitee) with funds or services to restore defined losses. In both contexts insurance offers such benefits as indemnification for insured losses, reduction of uncertainty with respect to those losses, accumulations of capital available for investment throughout the economy, improved loss control for insureds, and greater financial security for insureds, especially small firms. Insurance simultaneously imposes such social and economic costs as moral and morale hazards and the administrative expenses associated with operating insurance organizations. Moreover, the benefits of insurance are principally available only for those loss exposures that possess sufficient characteristics of commercial or social insurability.

An insurance policy may be written as a self-contained policy, a series of common provisions prepared in advance to provide coverage for exposures confronting many insureds, or as a manuscript policy for a particular insured. Regardless of format, each policy provision performs one or more of several functions, including declarations to identify the contracting parties and to specify the particular exposures insured, insuring agreements to provide a broad foundation for the intended coverage, exclusions to remove coverage for specific exposures the insurer and the insured do not intend to cover, policy conditions to specify the activities for the insurer and the insured to carry out their contract, and various miscellaneous provisions.

The coverage provided by a given insurance policy may be analyzed by reading the policy to determine (1) what events are covered, (2) the amounts the insurer will pay upon the occurrence of an insured event, and (3) the procedures the insured must follow (conditions or legal prerequisites to the insurer's duty to pay) to recover compensation for a loss. An event is covered if the (1) peril, (2) property or source of liability (or lives), (3) persons, (4) losses, (5) time period, and (6) location of the event all are covered, provided that no special conditions that would have suspended or terminated the coverage were in existence at the time of the event, and if a sufficient amount of coverage applies to each of the various losses that may arise from any particular insured event. The risk management professional of an organization that is considering buying insurance may have a number of options with respect to each of these seven coverage variables. The best choice among the available options is likely to be the one that maximizes the benefits to the organization relative to the costs. Benefits and costs can generally be categorized in terms of the organization's total risk financing costs, the reliability of the organization's overall risk financing program, the ease of administering that program, and the organization's relationships with its managers and other employees, its insurers and their representatives, its customers, and its owners.

Given that an insured event has occurred, the insurer may pay a predetermined amount for the loss (as in a life insurance policy), but more often will pay the amount of the loss sustained provided that this amount does not exceed the least of the applicable policy limits or the limitations imposed by any coinsurance requirements or deductibles in the policy. To protect the right to recover compensation for an insured loss, the insured must follow specified loss adjustment procedures in the pertinent property insurance policy (pertaining to notifying the insurer, protecting the property from further damage, and assisting the insurer in any investigation of the loss) or liability policy (whose loss adjustment provisions typically relate to protecting the insurer's subrogation rights and cooperating with the insurer in its management of any claim against the insured).

Chapter Notes

1. Allan H. Willett, *The Economic Theory of Risk and Insurance* (Philadelphia: University of Pennsylvania Press, 1951), p. 72.
2. See *American Jurisprudence,* vol. 29 (Rochester, NY: Lawyers' Cooperative Publishing Co., 1960), pp. 430-445.
3. William R. Vance, *Handbook on the Law of Insurance,* 3rd ed. by Buist M. Anderson (St. Paul, MN: West Publishing Co., 1951), pp. 81-82. For a comprehensive study of legal definitions of insurance, see Herbert S. Denenberg, "The Legal Definition of Insurance," *Journal of Insurance,* vol. 30, no. 3 (September 1963), pp. 319-348.
4. Peter F. Drucker, *The New Society* (New York: Harper & Row Publishers, Inc., 1950), p. 57.
5. Mark Greene and Oscar Serbein, *Risk Management: Text and Cases,* 2nd ed. (Reston, VA: Reston Publishing Company, 1983), pp. 295-296.
6. "MGM Buys Back-Dated Cover," *Business Insurance* (9 February 1981), pp. 1, 22. "Back Dating: Issue Splits Risk Managers," *Business Insurance* (20 April 1981), pp. 1, 46.
7. Charles A. McAlear, "Retroactive Insurance: Turning Back the Clock for 300 Years," *Risk Management,* vol. 29, no. 9 (August 1982), pp. 30-32. McAlear observes that ocean marine insurers wrote retroactive insurance in ancient times, and still do, to insure vessels "lost or not lost" at the date the insurance commenced.
8. The analysis presented here is adapted from C. Arthur Williams, Jr., George L. Head, Ronald C. Horn, and G. William Glendenning, *Principles of Risk Management and Insurance,* 2nd ed. (Malvern, PA: American Institute for Property and Liability Underwriters, 1981), pp. 49-63.
9. This method of analysis is adapted from the method presented in Robert I. Mehr, *Fundamentals of Insurance,* 2nd ed. (Homewood, IL: Richard D. Irwin, Inc., 1986), pp. 127-147.
10. Robert E. Keeton and Alan I. Widiss, *Insurance Law,* Practitioner's Edition (St. Paul, MN: West Publishing Co., 1988), pp. 486-491.
11. Safeco Insurance Co. v. Guyton, 692 Fed. 2d 551 (9th Cir., 1982).
12. E. B. Metal and Rubber Industries, Inc. v. Federal Insurance Co., 444 NYS 2d 321 (1981) is a leading example of these rulings.
13. P. I. Thomas and P. H. Reed, *Adjustment of Property Losses,* 4th ed. (New York: McGraw-Hill Book Company, 1977), pp. 9-12. Thomas and Reed list eleven different methods.
14. For example, see "Insurance Companies, Cheated for Centuries, Are Still Being Taken," *The Wall Street Journal* (23 December 1974), p. 1.

CHAPTER 6

Excess Insurance and Reinsurance

In the risk financing programs of many organizations, primary coverage from only one insurer has its limitations as a risk transfer technique. For commercially insurable exposures, the protection available from a single primary insurer is thus restricted:

1. To the limit of the primary insurer's liability for each loss
2. To losses caused directly by perils covered by the primary insurance policy
3. By the primary insurer's financial ability to meet its policy obligations

Excess insurance, which helps to reduce the first two limitations mentioned above, is purchased directly by the insured organization and provides a policy that "sits above" that of the primary insurer. (Excess insurance can be written above a sizable self-insured retention as well.) If the insured desires extremely high limits of insurance, then excess insurance may be purchased in layers, with a different insurer on each layer. Although the primary insurer may provide limits of only \$1 or \$2 million, excess insurers provide higher limits that may range from \$1 million to hundreds of millions of dollars.

There are two forms of excess insurance: straight excess and umbrella. Straight excess only provides coverage above the primary insurer's limits of liability, usually for the same perils and on the same terms as the primary insurer. An umbrella also provides coverage above the primary insurer's limits of liability, but in addition provides coverage for some perils not covered by the primary insurer, subject to a modest retention by the insured for these additional perils. For example, a primary insurer may provide liability coverage with an exclusion for personal injury caused by discrimination. An umbrella policy that sits above this primary coverage may not contain a discrimination exclusion, thereby "dropping down" and providing discrimination coverage that the primary insurer does not provide. The umbrella usually specifies a modest self-insured retention, such as $10,000, when it drops down to cover perils not covered by the primary policy. Thus, a straight excess policy helps to overcome the first limitation mentioned above, and an umbrella policy helps to overcome the first two limitations.

The third limitation, the possible inability of the primary insurer to meet its financial obligations, is reduced through reinsurance. Unlike primary and excess insurance, which are purchased directly by the insured organization, reinsurance is purchased by an insurer. Reinsurance is a means by which an insurer transfers a portion of its risk to another organization, called the reinsurer. By sharing risk with one or more reinsurers, an insurer may underwrite a larger volume of risks and offer higher limits of liability while maintaining stability of its underwriting results. Reinsurance is purchased by primary insurers, excess insurers, and even reinsurers in order to protect their book of reinsurance business.

This chapter discusses those aspects of excess insurance and reinsurance that are important for a risk management professional to understand. Included is the role of excess insurance and reinsurance in risk financing, as well as the specific terms of excess insurance and reinsurance contracts.

BASIC DEFINITIONS AND INTERRELATIONSHIPS

An organization may purchase some form of excess insurance in order to provide financial security against extremely severe single losses or unexpectedly rapid accumulations of smaller losses that exceed its planned retention levels or primary insurance limits. To ensure that an organization's primary and excess insurers are able to fulfill their policy obligations, a risk management professional must inquire as to the adequacy of the insurers' reinsurance coverage.

Definitions

The fields of excess insurance and reinsurance include many terms devised by insurers to differentiate between often subtle differences in insurance protection that extends to higher limits or more perils than does primary insurance. Therefore, it is wise to define excess insurance and reinsurance in detail.

As previously mentioned, *excess insurance* provides limits of coverage above the limits provided by any applicable underlying risk financing plan (which may be primary insurance, a lower layer of excess insurance, or some planned level of retention). Most, but not all, forms of excess insurance written to overlay primary insurance incorporate, by reference or physical attachment, the coverage provisions of that underlying policy. They are, therefore, said to *follow form.*

Reinsurance is a contractual arrangement under which one insurer, known as the reinsured, transfers or cedes to another insurer, called the *reinsurer,* some or all of the reinsured's obligations under primary or excess insurance policies (including umbrella). (The reinsured is sometimes referred to as the *primary insurer* or *cedent,* depending on the circumstances.) Following this initial transaction, reinsurers may also further reinsure some of the loss exposures they assume under reinsurance contracts. Such transactions are known as *retrocessions,* and the insurer or reinsurer to which the exposure is transferred is known as the *retrocessionnaire.* The ceding reinsurer is called the *retrocedent.*

The original insured is usually not a party to the reinsurance or retrocessions into which a cedent or retrocedent may enter. Therefore, in most situations, the insured under a primary, excess, or umbrella policy has no rights against a reinsurer or retrocessionaire, who, in like manner, has no duties to the insured. Nonetheless, an insured should take interest in its insurer's reinsurance as well as any retrocession arrangements because they greatly influence an insurer's ability to meet its obligations to policyholders. Reinsurance also strengthens and smooths the operation of primary and excess insurance markets by making it more likely that an organization seeking insurance will be able to obtain adequate limits of coverage from one (or a few) insurers rather than buying bits and pieces of insurance from many companies. It also allows smaller insurers to compete more effectively with larger ones, thus increasing the number of options available to insurance buyers.

There is one major exception to the general rule that an insured has no direct right of legal action against a reinsurer. This exception arises when a reinsurer authorizes a reinsured to attach to its policies an endorsement, called an *assumption certificate* or, more coloquially, a *cut-through clause* or *cut-through endorsement.* This endorsement provides that, if the reinsured becomes insolvent, its obligations under a policy to which the endorsement is attached become the direct obligations of the reinsurer. (Statutes in a few states also give insureds limited rights in some situations to make legal claims directly against reinsurers, even in the absence of a cut-through endorsement, provided the reinsured is insolvent.) Assumption certificates are difficult to obtain, and there is some controversy regarding their effectiveness. Some states only allow a cut-through to third parties such as mortgagees, and only then if there is a new or revised reinsurance contract. A risk management professional should attempt to obtain assumption certificates for insurance policies purchased from insurers of questionable financial stability.

Insurer/Insured Relationships

Exhibit 6-1 shows how planned levels of retention, primary insurance, straight excess insurance, and umbrella insurance can form a "wall" of financial protection against specified losses. (The analogy to a "wall" seems apt because any white "hole" in the shaded area may point to some unanticipated and undesirable retentions by an organization whose management considers itself fully protected against all accidental losses.) The vertical axis of Exhibit 6-1 is dollars of exposure, loss, and/or insurance in $1,000 units. Insurance coverages for five groups of perils (arbitrarily labeled A through E along the horizontal axis) consist of (1) two primary insurance policies, P1 and P2; (2) one straight excess policy, E1, which provides an additional $200,000 of coverage above each primary coverage, (3) a second straight excess policy, E2, which provides $400,000 in coverage for any losses, except those in peril group D, that exceed the excess coverage in policy E1; and (4) an umbrella policy, which provides $600,000 of coverage above any other insurance and drops down to provide the same $600,000 of insurance for peril group C, to which no other insurance applies. The insured has chosen a $50,000 per-loss deductible or other self-insured retention (SIR) for peril groups A through E. The combination of these two primary, two excess, and one umbrella policies provides, for losses that exceed the $50,000 SIR, coverage up to $1,700,000 for peril group A, $1,400,000 for peril group B, $600,000 for peril group C, $1,100,000 for peril group D, and $1,600,000 for peril group E.

Notice the white area above the sixth peril group, F. This group represents perils that the organization's risk financing program has not recognized. The organization has provided for neither insurance nor a self-insured retention for these perils. If any losses occur that fall under peril group F, the organization's only "alternative" is unplanned retention. Sometimes, the organization may have a planned but undesirable retention because insurance may not be available. Good examples would be the perils of war, flood, and pollution.

The amount of insurance protection that should be purchased is much easier to determine for property exposures than for liability exposures. The upper bounds—the maximum possible loss from property or net income exposures—are easier to calculate with reasonable certainty than are the upper bounds for liability coverage. For property and net income exposures it is reasonably possible to determine how much insurance is "enough," but there are few, if any, limits to an organization's potential liability losses, and it is therefore difficult to determine the

Exhibit 6-1
Structuring Retention with Primary, Excess, and Umbrella Policies

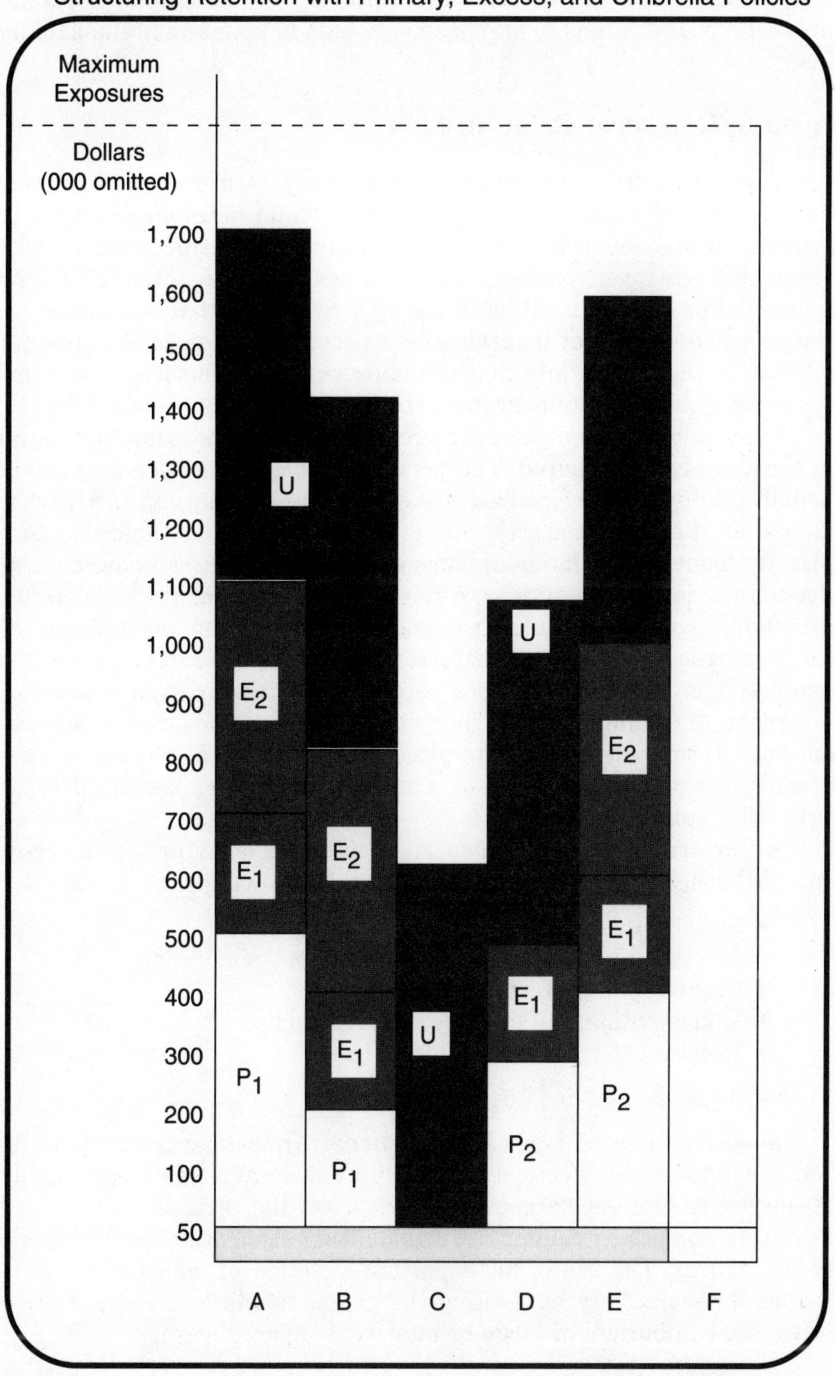

amount of liability insurance to purchase. Many times, the limit purchased depends on current market conditions. When umbrella prices are low, organizations tend to purchase very high limits of umbrella liability insurance.

Insurer/Reinsurer Relationships

Appropriate reinsurance enables a primary insurer to offer insureds higher limits of reliable coverage than it would otherwise be able to provide.[1] Moreover, it is through reinsurance and retrocession that insurers and reinsurers pool exposures. In this way, they often achieve on a national or international basis the *spread of risk* that is essential to the proper operation of insurance as an economic and social device for alleviating the uncertainty that would prevent many insureds (or insurers lacking adequate reinsurance) from taking advantageous risks.

In most cases, a reinsurer (or a retrocessionaire) does not assume all of the risk of the reinsured. The reinsurance or retrocession agreement usually requires the reinsured to keep a part of the risk; this part is known as the reinsured's retention. In concept it is comparable to a primary insured's retention of some of its loss exposures under deductibles or self-insured retentions. A reinsured's retention, like an insured's retention, gives it a continuing financial interest in the management of the loss exposures it has transferred. A reinsured's retention may be expressed as a dollar amount, a percentage of the original amount of insurance, or a combination of the two. (Like primary insurance, reinsurance and retrocession contracts place an upper limit on the reinsurer's or retrocessionaire's liability for a single loss or for a series of losses within a given period.)

An insurer may seek reinsurance arrangements for a number of specific, closely related reasons such as the following:

- Stabilization of loss experience
- Increased underwriting capacity and surplus relief
- Catastrophe protection
- Underwriting and management assistance
- Retirement from a class of business

Each of these is described below.

Stabilization of Loss Experience. An insurer can attract and retain capital more effectively if it can promise investors a reasonably steady income for each accounting period. Yet the variability of insured losses is a potentially dangerous, destabilizing element to the net income of an insurer. Therefore, an important function of reinsurance is to reduce this variability by limiting the extent to which any one insurer bears the full burden of large or numerous insured losses.

Increased Underwriting Capacity and Surplus Relief. *Capacity* refers to the amount of coverage an insurer can provide; that is, the size of an individual loss exposure and the aggregate volume of loss exposures it can reasonably undertake. There are two kinds of underwriting capacities in property-liability insurance, *large line capacity* and *premium capacity.*

Large Line Capacity. Large line capacity refers to an insurer's ability to provide a large amount of insurance in a single primary or excess policy on a single loss exposure. Few insurers would independently have enough resources to write the several hundred million dollars of coverage that many organizations now seek in property insurance on large building complexes or in liability insurance for hazardous activities such as airplane flights or large spectator events. In many cases, such as earthquake insurance, line capacity depends on aggregations of losses among policies as well as the amount insured in any one policy. Reinsurance allows any one insurer to underwrite and distribute portions of massive exposures, with each party to the reinsurance transaction retaining only that portion of the risk that it can safely bear.

Reinsurance arrangements also allow a primary insurer to comply with state insurance regulations that prohibit a property or liability insurer from writing, after subtracting approved reinsurance, an amount of insurance under any one policy that would be in excess of 10 percent of its *policyholders' surplus.* The policyholders' surplus of an insurer is, in general terms, its net worth—its assets minus its liabilities (the latter consisting primarily of reserves for losses and for unearned premiums). This net worth is called "surplus as regards policyholders" or "policyholders' surplus" because, if necessary, the full amount of this net worth is, in principle, available to pay insured losses.

Premium Capacity. The second kind of underwriting capacity, premium capacity, is the aggregate premium volume for any number of exposures an insurer can safely write in a given accounting period. This capacity is also limited by state regulations and the generally accepted principles of property-liability insurance finance. Although the exact theoretical relationship between premium volume and policyholders' surplus is debatable, property-liability insurance financial analysts generally consider an insurer to be dangerously overextended if its written premium, exceeds its policyholders' surplus by more than some specified ratio. Although a ratio of three to one once was considered safe, various current authorities often advocate lower ratios.

Reinsurance offers a solution to this limitation on an insurer's underwriting capacity. Insurance accounting practices related to reinsurance lower the reinsured's reported ratio of written premiums to policyholders' surplus in two ways. First, written premiums are stated in terms of

Exhibit 6-2
Typical Effects of Reinsurance on a Primary Insurer's Financial Statement

Effect of Reinsurance on Net Written Premiums		
	Without Reinsurance	With Reinsurance
Gross Written Premiums	$15,000	$15,000
Reinsurance Ceded	0	10,000
Net Written Premiums	$15,000	$ 5,000

Effect of Reinsurance on Policyholders' Surplus		
	Without Reinsurance	With Reinsurance
Assets	$20,000	$13,000
Liabilities & Policyholders' Surplus		
Unearned premiums	$ 7,500	$ 2,500
Loss & loss adjustment reserves	7,500	2,500
Total Liabilities	15,000	5,000
Policyholders' Surplus	5,000	8,000
Total Liabilities & Policyholders' Surplus	$20,000	$13,000

net premiums, which are premiums for the portion of the insured exposure retained by the reinsured. Thus, if the reinsured reinsures two-thirds of the exposure, it needs to recognize only one-third of the total premium for this coverage as having been "written." Without reinsurance, the insurer whose financial position is shown in the upper portion of Exhibit 6-2 has net written premiums of $15,000; however, with two-thirds of its exposure reinsured, the insurer has only $5,000 of net written premiums. Second, reinsurance provides *surplus relief.* Under statutory insurance accounting, an insurer writing new policies must immediately write off all the expenses of issuing these policies. However, the insurer cannot report as current income any of the premium collected for the new business. Premiums must be earned gradually over the term of each policy. This statutory accounting requirement creates a drain on the funds the insurer holds as surplus for policyholders.

Because premiums collected cannot be used immediately to offset the front-end expenses associated with acquiring the new business, these expenses must be paid from the surplus. To compensate a primary insurer for at least some of these expenses, most reinsurers pay a ceding commission to the primary insurer to cover the acquisition costs associated with the ceded policies. For example, the lower portion of Exhibit 6-2 shows the balance sheet of a primary insurer who has ceded two-thirds of its exposures on a particular set of policies to a reinsurer. Without reinsurance, the primary insurer has a surplus of $5,000. After the primary insurer cedes two-thirds of these exposures to a reinsurer, the primary insurer's assets, liabilities, and surplus change as follows:

- Assets decrease by the $10,000 of the ceded exposure and increase by the ceding commission (in this case 30 percent of the policies ceded, or $3,000) so that the primary insurer's assets fall to $13,000.
- Liabilities decrease by two-thirds (the amount of insurance ceded).
- Surplus increases by $3,000, the amount of the ceding commission, making the primary insurer's total liabilities and surplus balance with its total assets. This $3,000 is surplus relief—the ceding commission offsets the reduction in the primary insurer's surplus posed by statutory accountng requirements.

Thus, reinsurance increases a primary insurer's underwriting capacity as its net written premiums decrease and its surplus held for policyholders increases. This decrease in written premiums and increase in policyholders' surplus reduces the primary insurer's ratio of net written premiums to policyholders' surplus. Reducing this ratio enables the primary insurer to write additional insurance.

Catastrophe Protection. Earthquakes, hurricanes, tornadoes, industrial explosions, plane crashes, and similar disasters can suddenly obligate insurers to pay millions, even billions, of dollars to help insureds finance recovery from such losses. If the bulk of the liability for these insured losses fell solely on one or a few insurers, their financial viability could be endangered. Through risk spreading, reinsurance and retrocession allow most potentially catastrophic exposures to be distributed among many insurers, reinsurers, and retrocessionaires. Therefore, when a disaster does occur, numerous insurers may directly or indirectly absorb some of the resulting losses. If reinsurance and retrocessions have been properly arranged, no insurer will become insolvent as a consequence. Thus, the mechanism by which reinsurance stabilizes a reinsured's underwriting results also protects it from bankruptcy that could otherwise occur as the result of an insured catastrophic event.

Underwriting and Management Assistance. Reinsurers do business with a variety of commercial and captive insurers in many different circumstances. In doing so, they accumulate a great deal of information about the experience of insurers and insureds in dealing with particular loss exposures, loss control, insurance coverages, and other risk financing techniques. This experience can be helpful to many reinsureds, particularly those who are relatively small or inexperienced. A major reason many commercial insurers and captives heavily reinsure a particular type of business with one principal reinsurer is that they can rely on that reinsurer's expertise in the management of that particular line of coverage. Because reinsurers properly consider their relationships with each of their reinsureds and retrocessionaires to be confidential, a reinsurer must be careful when offering advisory services to ensure that it does not reveal proprietary information obtained through confidential relationships with others. Those who benefit from these services must similarly respect confidentiality.

Retirement From a Class of Business. A commercial or captive insurer may occasionally decide for sound business reasons to withdraw from a particular class (or all) of its insurance activities. It may wish not only to stop writing new policies but also to relieve itself of liabilities under existing insurance contracts. Rather than incurring the ill will of insureds and third parties, as well as adverse publicity and perhaps lawsuits by simply canceling it policies, an insurer will often seek a reinsurer to whom it can shift its obligations.

The process of insuring an entire class, territory, or book of policies is known as *portfolio reinsurance.* This kind of reinsurance establishes another exception to the general rule that reinsurers do not assume any direct liability to the insureds of an insurer. Under portfolio reinsurance the reinsurer essentially takes over for the retiring primary company. In the absence of fraud by the primary company, the portfolio reinsurer does not have any recourse against that company if the experience on the ceded business is not as favorable as expected.

EXCESS INSURANCE

This section deals with straight excess insurance. (Umbrella insurance is covered later in this chapter.) The policies described here are intended to provide coverage that is no broader, but sometimes more restricted, than underlying primary policies.

Purposes of Excess Insurance

Straight excess insurance policies can strengthen an organization's risk financing program in at least three significant ways:

- Taking the place of broader (and consequently more expensive) umbrella insurance when only higher limits are required.

- Filling the gaps between the upper limit of liability of a primary policy and the dollar amount at which the coverage of an umbrella or other excess policy begins. (This is sometimes referred to as a "buffer layer.")
- Building several "layers" of additional insurance above either primary or umbrella insurance in order to obtain needed coverage when no one insurer is willing to provide adequate amounts of insurance at a price acceptable to the insured.

A straight excess insurance policy can sit above the limits provided by a risk financing plan, such as a retrospective rating plan or a captive. For example, a captive may issue a primary policy with a limit of $1 million. The straight excess policy could sit directly above this policy and provide much higher limits of protection.

Types of Excess Insurance. As mentioned, because excess insurance policies are usually written to follow the form of any underlying insurance, they can be as diverse and difficult to classify as many primary insurance contracts. This difficulty is increased because there are few, if any, standard excess insurance policies. Nonetheless, straight excess insurance arrangements can be broadly grouped in terms of how the policy defines the minimum loss to which it will respond, that is, the nature (but not the dollar amount) of that straight excess policy's *attachment point.* Straight excess insurance policies can therefore be classified as (1) specific (per-loss occurrence or claim) excess insurance, (2) annual aggregate excess insurance, and (3) combined specific/aggregate excess insurance.

Specific Excess Insurance. Specific excess insurance covers otherwise insured losses that exceed a specified dollar amount per loss, per occurrence, or per claim. Specific excess insurance then covers only that portion of such losses that exceeds this specified dollar attachment point. The attachment point is usually equal to the upper limit of any stipulated underlying primary insurance or a self-insured retention. In effect, the upper limit of this underlying insurance or SIR is a per-loss "deductible" for the excess insurance coverage.

Because this specifically insured or retained "deductible" applies separately to each loss, occurrence, or claim, it is important that the excess insurance policy state, and that the excess insurer and the insured agree on, the meaning of loss, occurrence, or claim so that there are no post-loss disputes as to when or how often the deductible to that excess coverage must be absorbed by the insured. For example, assume that a manufacturer faces several hundred products liability claims because several separately produced batches of its products were defective as a result of one design error. It is vital that the insured manufacturer, the excess products liability insurers, and any primary insurers understand whether the insured must bear the self-insured retention—or whether the primary insurer must pay its limited liability—only once (because of the one design error), several times (once for each defective batch of product), or many times (once for each claimant bringing suit).

Annual Aggregate Excess Insurance. An annual aggregate excess policy does not pay any losses (does not "attach") until the total amount of otherwise insured losses from one or several insured events in a given year reaches, or aggregates to, a specified dollar amount. When that point is reached, the aggregate excess policy pays all insured losses (perhaps subject to a relatively small per-loss deductible to be borne by the insured) that occur during the remainder of the year. In contrast to specific excess insurance, which offers protection principally against individual losses that are unusually large, aggregate excess insurance is designed primarily to protect against a series of losses that, although individually small, may accumulate to a total that exceeds the insured's retention capacity.

For example, Exhibit 6-3 portrays the financial position of Instant Photos, which has an insurance policy with Ultimate Insurance that contains a $2,500 per-loss deductible. Instant Photos must retain the first $2,500 of each loss, whether there are two covered losses of $10,000 each or twenty covered losses of $10,000 each. In the first case, Instant Photos must retain a total of $5,000 of losses, and in the latter case, $50,000 of losses. If the risk management professional or senior management of Instant Photos determines that the most the firm can safely retain during any twelve consecutive months is $25,000 of losses, this firm should purchase annual aggregate excess coverage from an excess lines insurer, such as A. A. Excess Insurance, with an attachment point of $25,000. If the two $10,000 losses were to occur now, Instant Photos would still pay $5,000; but, for twenty losses of $10,000 each occurring during any twelve consecutive months, Instant Photos would have to retain only $25,000.

Annual aggregate excess insurance is also known as stop-loss excess insurance because once the attachment point has been reached, the insured (or the primary insurer) is not responsible for paying any losses that occur for the rest of the year. Once Instant Photos has retained a total of $25,000 of losses during twelve consecutive months, the excess insurance in the previous example attaches (becomes effective) so that A. A. Excess Insurance is responsible for any further covered losses as long as those losses during any twelve consecutive months continue to exceed $25,000. For the twenty claims shown in the lower portion of Exhibit 6-3, Instant Photos would be responsible for $25,000 of the losses, Ultimate Insurance, the primary insurer, would be obligated to pay $75,000 of the losses, and A. A. Excess Insurance would be responsi-

Exhibit 6-3
Financial Impact of Annual Aggregate Excess Insurance on Insured

	Without Annual Aggregate Excess		With Annual Aggregate Excess		
	Instant Photos	Ultimate Insurance	Instant Photos	Ultimate Ins.	A.A. Excess Ins.
Two claims					
1	$2,500	$ 7,500	$2,500	$ 7,500	$0
2	2,500	7,500	2,500	7,500	0
Total	$5,000	$15,000	$5,000	$15,000	$0
Twenty Claims					
1–10	$ 2,500 each	$ 7,500 each	$ 2,500 each	$ 7,500 each	$ 0
11–20	2,500 each	7,500 each	0	0	10,000 each
Total	$50,000	$150,000	$25,000	$75,000	$100,000

ble for $100,000 of the losses. However, there is usually a limit placed on the annual aggregate or stop-loss excess insurance policy, above which the insured must purchase additional insurance or start paying the losses again.

Although annual aggregate excess insurance may apply over primary insurance, it is more commonly used with self-insured retentions (SIRs). This is because most primary property and some liability insurance policies are written without an annual aggregate limit of liability; the face amount or other limit of such primary insurance is normally automatically restored after each loss and remains fully available to pay any further losses that occur during the year. However, some primary policies, such as the ISO Commercial General Liability policy, do have annual or policy-term aggregate limits, in which case it is important to coordinate these aggregate primary limits with the attachment points of any annual aggregate excess coverage. An organization retaining its own losses, however, often cannot easily restore its ability to pay additional losses. Therefore, annual aggregate excess coverage is often essential to the viability of a retention program whose stability could just as easily be threatened by an extraordinary accumulation of smaller losses as by a single unusually large loss.

Combined Specific/Aggregate Excess Insurance. Excess insurance can be written so that it attaches either when any individual loss exceeds the particular dollar amount of the attachment point or when the total amount of several losses occurring within a given year aggregates to another, higher attachment point. Notice, however, that the attachment point for the annual aggregate must be a larger dollar amount than the attachment point for the specific excess insurance. This combined type of excess coverage provides more protection (can be expected to pay more losses, and, thus, also to be more expensive) than either specific excess or annual aggregate excess coverage with the same dollar attachment points. It would, however, be particularly appropriate to use such combined excess coverage in conjunction with the SIR of an organization that could retain a moderate number of average-sized losses, but that would have difficulty absorbing either one very large loss or an unusually large number of smaller losses.

For example, assume that Shoes 'R Less has purchased combined specific/aggregate excess coverage with A. A. Excess Insurance with a per-loss SIR of $10,000 followed by the specific excess coverage attaching at $10,000 for each loss. Assume further that Shoes 'R Less can afford to retain no more than $70,000 during any consecutive twelve months and that the company has purchased annual aggregate excess coverage that attaches at $70,000. If Shoes 'R Less has four $25,000 covered losses during a twelve-month period, Exhibit 6-4 shows that

Exhibit 6-4
Impact of Combined Specific/Annual Aggregate Excess Insurance

	Shoes	Specific	Aggregate
Four Losses			
1	$10,000	$15,000	
2	10,000	15,000	
3	10,000	15,000	
4	10,000	15,000	
Total	$40,000	$60,000	
Ten Losses			
1–7	$10,000 each	$ 15,000 each	$ 0
8–10	0	0	25,000 each
Total	$70,000	$105,000	$75,000

the firm retains $40,000, and the specific coverage pays the remaining $60,000. In contrast, if Shoes 'R Less has ten $25,000 losses during this period, the annual aggregate coverage attaches with the seventh loss. This coverage pays the remaining three losses that occur during these twelve months.

Basket Retentions. The preceding discussions of specific, annual aggregate, and combined forms of excess insurance have implied that any given form of excess coverage applies solely to a particular policy or line of property or liability coverage. This does not have to be the case. Any of these forms of excess insurance can be structured to attach once the overall retained losses (or losses covered by primary insurance) amount to a specified *combined total for several lines* of property or liability coverage. An excess insurance arrangement under which the insured retains a variety of losses from different lines of insurance is said to be characterized as a "basket retention." This type of excess insurance—particularly when applied on an annual aggregate basis over many loss exposures—provides the insured with complete financial protection for a retention program that involves several lines of insurance. Insurance companies are reluctant to underwrite excess insurance over a basket retention, and thus it is very difficult to obtain.

To illustrate, suppose Shoes 'R Less carries a $3,000 per-loss deductible on its business property damage insurance, a $7,500 per-claim deductible on its products liability policy, and a $5,000 per-accident deductible on its automobile physical damage coverage. Assume also that Shoes

'R Less can safely retain only $50,000 of accidental losses during any twelve months, regardless of the type of loss. This $50,000 of retained losses could arise from ten automobile accidents or from five business property losses, two products liability claims, and four automobile accidents, or any combination of lesser numbers of any of these types of losses. Therefore, Shoes 'R Less may wish to purchase a basket retention excess policy rather than separate excess policies for each type of loss exposure. If this basket coverage can be arranged, this excess policy will attach, and any future losses will be paid by this excess coverage up to its limits, once Shoes 'R Less has paid a total of $50,000 for any or all of these types of losses during any twelve consecutive months.

Provisions of Excess Insurance Contracts

Excess insurance policies covering property and liability exposures follow no uniform format and contain few uniform provisions. Nonetheless, as stated, most straight excess insurance policies (that is, excluding umbrella policies) are written to follow the form of any underlying insurance. Most straight excess insurance contracts are consequently read and applied as if they were "vertical" extensions of their underlying policies. Thus, straight excess insurance policies are best analyzed not in terms of the details of the underlying coverages but in terms of how the straight excess policies in general differ from primary insurance policies. Notable differences may occur in the declarations, insuring agreements, exclusions, conditions, and coverage period of the straight excess policy.

Declarations. For an excess policy to follow form over an underlying primary policy, its declarations section must parallel that of the primary policy. For example, if any insured, location, coverage part, or endorsement is described differently in the declarations section of the excess policy than it is in the primary policy, the excess contract is very likely to provide coverage that is narrower than that of the primary contract. Perhaps the insured under both policies wants the excess policy to be narrower than the primary policy. For example, the excess insurance could be written to apply to only particular (but not all) insureds, locations, types of losses, or designated perils. In this case, the declarations section of the excess policy may correctly omit the undesired coverage; otherwise, any such differences in the declarations sections of the two policies are likely to signal potentially serious oversights or gaps in securing intended coverages.

Insuring Agreement. Much as in a primary insurance policy, the insuring agreement of an excess policy is usually worded to provide a broad grant of coverage that is then restricted by exclusions, limits of liability, definitions, and other provisions in the excess policy.

Coverage. If the excess policy incorporates, by physical attachment or by reference, the broad grant(s) of coverage in the underlying insurance, few fundamental coverage problems are likely to arise. However, an excess policy that contains its own listing or description of perils and types of losses covered creates potential difficulties; for example, a loss covered by the primary policy may not be covered by the excess, or vice versa. Therefore, the coverage grants and the insuring agreements of both policies should be carefully compared, and any differences should be removed or discussed with the insurer's representative to resolve any potential misunderstandings before losses occur.

In coordinating primary and excess coverages for liability exposures, it is important that both contracts define the insured events in parallel language. Most primary liability insurance policies define the insured event as either (1) an occurrence that causes injury during the policy period or (2) the filing, during the policy period, of a claim against the insured alleging harm (regardless of when the harm occurred). The first definition provides what is known as *occurrence coverage.* The second definition provides *claims-made coverage.* A primary occurrence liability insurance policy typically states the insurer's policy obligation as a maximum dollar sum *per occurrence.* A claims-made liability policy also states the insurer's limit as a maximum number of dollars *per occurrence* regardless of the number of claims that relate to each occurrence. Moreover, both occurrence and claims-made coverages may be subject to limits on the aggregate number of claims or occurrences for which coverage is provided during any twelve consecutive months or over the life of the policy. Both occurrence and claims-made liability policies also generally offer coverage subject to overall annual or policy-term aggregate limits on the insurer's liability.

If the primary and the excess liability insurance policies do not similarly define insured events as an occurrence or a claim, any differences are likely to generate gaps in coverage that the insured and the insurer do not intend. For instance, if one policy is written (or can be interpreted) to provide occurrence coverage and the other provides claims-made coverage, then disputes are likely to turn on the question of whether the attachment point of the excess coverage has been reached when the primary policy has paid its limit.

Limits of Liability. As stated, the primary and excess insurer's limits of liability should be expressed similarly. In addition, the dollar amounts of the primary insurer's upper limits of liability and the excess insurer's attachment point should dovetail to meet the insured's objec-

Exhibit 6-5
Excess—Primary Coordination Problems

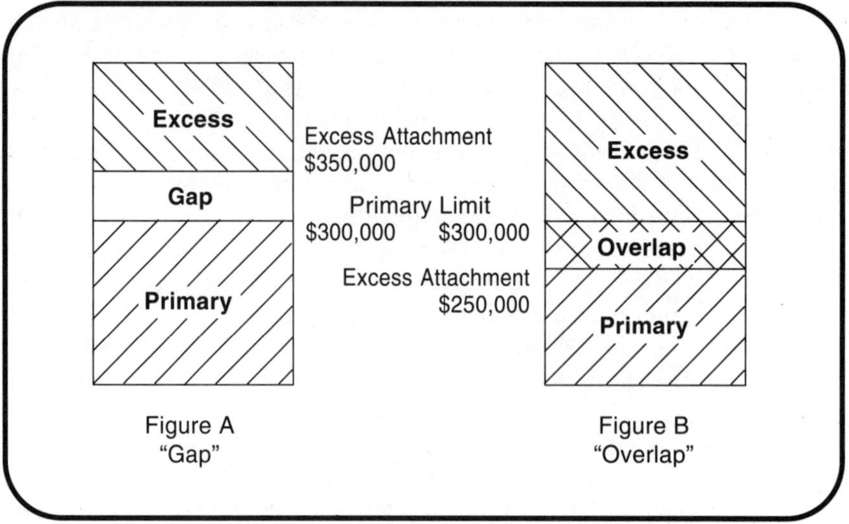

tive. This will normally mean that the excess coverage begins when the primary coverage (or planned self-insured retention) ends.

As a basic example, if a primary insurance policy covers up to $200,000 per occurrence, then excess insurance written to protect against the same loss should attach when losses exceed $200,000 per occurrence. If several layers of excess insurance have been obtained, each should attach when the layer directly "beneath" it has reached its limit of liability. The failure to coordinate these limits is likely to cause two major problems, each of which costs the insured money. The first problem would be unintended gaps in coverage. For example, if the applicable primary coverage for liability claims is $300,000 but the intended excess coverage attaches only to claims that exceed $350,000, then the insured is left with an unplanned retention of $50,000, as shown on the left side of Exhibit 6-5. The second problem would be the payment of unnecessary premiums. For example, as shown on the right side of Exhibit 6-5, the insured may have $50,000 of overlapping coverage because the excess insurance has been written to attach for any claim that exceeds $250,000, even though the primary insurance covers up to $300,000 per claim.

Definitions. The definitions of perils, losses, interests insured, and similar items should be essentially identical in a primary policy and the excess contract.

Coordinating the primary and excess coverages calls for careful attention to the definition of loss, which can include or exclude adjustment expenses. When a primary and an excess policy pay portions of an insured loss, the primary and excess insurers must apportion between themselves not only the loss paid but also the *allocable loss adjustment expenses* attributable to the loss. For all types of insurance—and especially for many types of liability coverage in which these allocable expenses often reach 30 or 40 percent of the insured loss payment—these expenses can be considerable. Therefore, effective cooperation between a primary and an excess insurer requires that they agree on the extent to which each is responsible for allocable loss adjustment expenses.

There are two ways of sharing allocable loss adjustment expenses between the primary insurer and excess insurers, depending on whether the expenses are within or outside of the limits of the primary policy. If included within the primary limits, the allocable loss adjustment expenses are usually also included within the excess limits. If outside the primary limits, the allocable loss adjustment expenses are usually prorated between the primary and excess insurers in proportion to the amount of the loss paid by each. When an excess policy defines loss in language that does not include allocable loss adjustment expenses, the amount of primary insurance must be adequate to pay for allocable loss adjustment expenses for the entire actual loss.

Exclusions. Primary and excess insurance contracts normally include an exclusions section that clearly specifies the exposures each insurer does not intend to cover. In an excess policy written precisely to follow form, this section may simply refer to the exclusions in the underlying insurance. If the excess coverage does not strictly follow form, or if it is excess over a self-insured retention, its exclusions section should be similar to that normally found in a primary policy. These exclusions will usually be tailored to the basic nature of the property, net income, or liability exposures to which the excess insurance applies.

Conditions. The conditions section of any insurance policy specifies the actions required by each party of the contract that make the contractual obligations of the other parties legally binding. The actions required by the policy are, in effect, conditions precedent to each party's right to require other parties to that contract to perform according to its terms.

In an excess policy, the conditions section usually contains provisions dealing with the same topics as the corresponding section of a primary policy, such as notice of loss or claim, assistance and cooperation, subrogation, policy changes, cancellation, and premium audit (if applicable). In addition, excess insurance contracts typically contain conditions excusing the excess insurer from any liability if the insured fails either to maintain the primary insurance specified in the declarations or to notify the excess insurer of a loss for which that insurer may be responsible.

To enforce its rights under a primary insurance policy, an insured organization must act as specified according to the conditions section of the policy. In addition, the respective rights of the insured and of the *excess* insurer may be governed by provisions in the conditions section of an excess policy. Therefore, in order to maintain the applicable insurance and to enhance the working relationships of the insured, the primary, and the excess insurers, an organization's risk management professional should confirm that the actions specified by any contract are clear, reasonably feasible for all parties, and internally consistent. For example, the insured's fulfilling a condition precedent to its rights to recover from one insurer does not breach a condition precedent to its right to recover from the other. Developing this mutual understanding may require extensive communication among the parties before any major loss occurs. Such an understanding saves money, delay, and aggravation for all parties.

Policy Period. An excess insurance policy is usually written for one or three years, but it can be written for any length of time. Because excess insurance usually follows the form of the underlying insurance, it is normal for primary and excess coverages to begin and expire at the same hour of the same day. This prevents confusion that can stem from policy periods that do not run concurrently. Excess insurance is often written to be effective only if the insured maintains specified primary insurance. Therefore, the expiration of the primary coverage before the end of the term of the excess coverage would also effectively terminate the excess coverage (or at least suspend it until new primary coverage acceptable to the excess insurer is secured). This problem would arise if the insured expected the excess coverage to be independently effective.

UMBRELLA INSURANCE

As previously stated, straight excess and umbrella insurance provide coverage that extends to limits of liability that are higher than underlying primary insurance. They can also be written to overlay a self-insured retention (SIR). An important difference between straight excess and umbrella coverage is that umbrella insurance can be, and normally is, written to cover a broader range of perils.

Before exploring umbrella coverages, one other crucial difference between straight excess and umbrella insurance should be explained. Umbrella insurance typically applies only to liability exposures, and not to property or net income losses. Straight excess insurance can be written to cover liability, property, or net income exposures. Although there is, in theory, no reason why umbrella coverage could not also apply to property and net income losses, some practical and historical factors account for its exclusive application to liability coverage.

The history of property and net income policies has been characterized by a trend toward broadening insurance. This trend makes protection available for consistently more types of losses from more perils. Having begun as named-peril coverages, many property and net income insurance contracts are now available on an *"all-risks" basis.* "All-risks" insurance contracts typically cover all property or net income losses caused by any peril, *except* for losses and perils that the policy explicitly excludes. In contrast, liability insurance policies have historically contained some very important exclusions that create gaps in coverage. As a result, drop-down features of umbrella liability insurance have helped to fill these gaps. The following discussion shows how umbrella insurance applies to liability coverages.

As in straight excess insurance contracts, there are several different umbrella contracts, and no one policy is standard. Nonetheless, different umbrella policies share many characteristics, provisions, and approaches to providing coverage. For instance, most umbrella policies overlay primary insurance for some liability exposures and provide primary coverage subject to a modest retention for other liability exposures. In the first case, the umbrella functions much as a straight excess policy, with the contract following the form of the primary insurance. In the second case, where there is no underlying insurance, an umbrella contract must be much more detailed than when it acts as straight excess insurance so that it completely identifies the exposures that will be covered. The following discussion more closely examines umbrella coverage by examining declarations, insuring agreements, exclusions, conditions, and the policy period.

Declarations

The declarations section of an umbrella policy is much like that of an excess insurance contract. It identifies the entity or entities insured, the attachment points and upper limits of liability of the various coverages, the beginning and end of the policy period, and the underlying insurance or insured retentions. The underlying coverages are normally scheduled in this section or in an attachment to the umbrella policy. Maintaining these coverages (or substitutes approved by the umbrella insurer) is usually a condition precedent to the umbrella insurer's obligation to provide coverage.

Insuring Agreement

The protection umbrella insurance provides on an excess basis is expressed in different, more general terms than the protection it provides for otherwise uninsured perils. Umbrella coverage on an excess basis specifies that there will be continuing, specific amounts of coverage for lines such as general liability, automobile, employers liability (not workers compensation), and any other liability normally covered by primary insurance. The details of the excess coverage provided by the umbrella for these liabilities are similar to those of the primary policy. The umbrella sometimes incorporates the primary insuring agreement by reference.

Specific Coverages. Among liability exposures covered only by the umbrella, an insured can often choose the ones to be covered. However, so that an insured will not select only coverages to which it faces an extraordinarily high exposure and to achieve a reasonable spread of risk, many umbrella insurers group optional coverages into several packages, limiting the insured's choice to one or more packages. By packaging less popular coverages with the one or two an insured may particularly want, the insurer increases the sale of those less popular coverages, thus enabling the law of large numbers to operate.

The normally uninsured liability exposures umbrella policies most frequently cover are described below. They are personal injury; blanket contractual liability; damage to property in the insured's care, custody, or control; liability resulting from the use of nonowned aircraft or watercraft; and advertisers' liability.

Personal Injury. Primary liability insurance policies normally cover only the insured's liability for *bodily injury* to others. Bodily injury in this sense means a visible injury or illness that usually results from some external force or disease-causing agent. The personal injury coverage provisions of an umbrella extend to liability for specified torts to others that cause no bodily injury—torts such as assault, infliction of mental distress, false arrest, false imprisonment, malicious prosecution, defamation, and invasion of privacy. These torts are not typically defined in the policy; instead, the umbrella insurer agrees to pay money damages that may be levied against the insured for these torts as each is defined in the state or federal statute. Like all umbrella coverages, the personal injury provision excludes some liability—notably for discrimination or infringement on civil rights.

Blanket Contractual Liability. In terms of any liability that an insured may assume under contract (such as a hold-harmless or other indemnity agreement), primary liability insurance policies normally cover only liability assumed under *incidental contracts.* These contracts include easement agreements (except railroad grade crossing agreements), agreements required by municipal ordinance, elevator or escalator agreements, and leases of insured premises. Primary liability policies that are specifically written to cover the liability assumed by the insured under contract usually require that the contract is specifically referred to in, or even physically attached to, this explicit contractual liability coverage.

An umbrella policy, however, is often written to provide *blanket contractual liability coverage* of any liability the insured may assume under any of several broad classes of contracts, such as for the sale or service of a product, purchase agreements, construction contracts, or leases of real property. Because of the unpredictable, extremely large, and widely varied liabilities an insured may intentionally or inadvertently assume under a contract, blanket contractual liability coverage is carefully underwritten. (Some insurers may also provide blanket contractual liability coverage to some insureds in a primary policy outside the umbrella framework.)

Care, Custody, or Control. Typical primary liability policies exclude the insured's liability for damage to others' property that may be in the insured's care, custody, or control. Such property includes the personal property (and often the vehicles) of the insured's employees or business visitors, leased machinery and equipment, and merchandise held on consignment. A tenant leasing part of a building, or a subcontractor working on a portion of a building under construction, has occasionally been held to be in the care, custody, or control of the entire structure. The care, custody, or control coverage of an umbrella policy essentially drops down to cover many of the care, custody, or control liability exposures that are excluded in the primary policy.

Nonowned Aircraft or Watercraft. Primary insurance policies normally exclude liability for bodily injury or property damage arising from the use of large watercraft or any aircraft. Insureds who own and operate such craft normally buy specific coverage for the accompanying liability exposures; however, organizations that lease or otherwise control the use of craft they do not own are likely to overlook completely the related liability exposures. Umbrella policies cover these incidental exposures, usually in a way that is similar to how a primary policy writes coverage for an organization that owns and regularly operates such craft.

Advertisers' Liability. Advertisers' liability is a general term referring to liability for defamation, copyright infringement, invasion of privacy, wrongful interference with economic rights, and similar torts arising from any publication, broadcast, telecast, or similar transmittal of any oral or written material (including, of course, actual advertisements). Organizations that normally engage in publishing, broadcasting, or other similar activities often purchase specific, primary advertisers' liability coverage for these exposures. However, for organizations that only sometimes engage in such activities, an umbrella policy provides comparable coverage for their incidental exposures.

Limits of Liability. The limits of liability of an umbrella policy extend from the attachment point to the umbrella insurer's upper limit of liability per claim or per occurrence for any exposure. An umbrella policy, like an excess policy, typically provides the same dollar amount of coverage for each claim or occurrence to which it applies. This amount is also the same for each type of loss. For example, in Exhibit 6-1 the umbrella provides $600,000 of coverage for every insured claim in each peril group. So even though an umbrella insurer's upper limits of liability vary with each different attachment point, the umbrella still provides $600,000 of coverage. (Compare coverage U in peril group A to coverage U in peril group D in Exhibit 6-1.)

When the umbrella policy acts as excess coverage, the attachment point is usually the upper limit of the primary insurer's liability. Therefore, as with excess coverage, it is important that the primary insurer's limit of liability and the umbrella insurer's attachment point be expressed in the same terms so that it is clear where one ends and the other begins. For example, both should be stated as dollar amounts per occurrence, per claim, or "per person." Moreover, unless the insured specifically wants to retain part of the loss, the attachment point of the umbrella policy should equal the limit of the primary or excess insurance.

Underwriting considerations or insurance market availabilities may create a gap in coverage between the upper limit of liability of the underlying insurance and the attachment point of the umbrella coverage. An alert risk financing professional should be aware of such gaps, should work to minimize them, and should inform the organization's senior management of the gaps, the reasons for them, and how to deal with them.

Definitions. The insuring agreement of most umbrella policies states that the insurer will indemnify the insured for, or pay on the insured's behalf, the ultimate net loss covered by the umbrella policy in excess of the retained limit. The *retained limit* is the applicable upper limit of liability in the specified underlying insurance or of the SIR. The definition of *ultimate net loss* is, however, somewhat more complex, in part because it may or may not include defense cost or other allocable loss adjustment expenses. In all cases, however, ultimate net loss means at least the amount actually paid or payable for the settlement of a covered claim *minus* deductions for salvage and subrogation recoveries due the insurer.

When ultimate net loss is defined to *include* defense costs or other allocable adjustment expenses, these expenditures reduce the amount of protection the insured has within the policy limit. For example, assume that a court imposes an $800,000 judgment on an insured with a $1 million umbrella policy. If defense costs are $300,000 and there is no other applicable insurance or self-insured retention, then the $800,000 claim plus the first $200,000 of defense costs exhaust this liability policy. The insured must pay the remaining $100,000 of defense costs. If, in this example, the ultimate net loss were defined to *exclude* defense costs, and if (as is usual) the umbrella policy were written to obligate the insurer to pay defense costs in addition to the ultimate net loss, then the umbrella policy would pay the entire loss.

Although defining ultimate net loss to exclude defense and other allocable loss adjustment expenses is normally advantageous to the insured, just because defense costs are treated separately does not necessarily mean that the insured will receive coverage for these costs as additions to the limit of the umbrella liability policy. Defense costs may be handled in a variety of ways; only the study of each umbrella policy clarifies the extent to which that policy covers these costs. For example, given the wording of some umbrella policies, there is no coverage for defense costs even for otherwise covered claims. Another possibility designed to encourage an insured to defend all claims vigorously is for the umbrella insurer to pay all defense costs for insured claims that fall within a self-insured retention.

When a claim is covered under the underlying and umbrella policies, some umbrella policies exclude coverage of defense costs until the primary insurer's share of liability is determined. The umbrella insurer then pays (or reimburses the insured or primary insurers) for its proportion of the total defense costs. Other umbrella policies excuse the insurer from paying any defense costs for claims that do not reach the attachment point, but they authorize the umbrella insurer to pay all such costs incurred after that point has been reached. Such an arrangement may give the excess insurer greater control over the defense of claims it covers.

Exclusions

Because umbrella liability coverage is usually very broad, the exclusions section is usually the longest in an umbrella policy. In analyzing exclusions, it is important to distinguish between umbrella coverages that are excess and the other, broader, umbrella coverages for which there is no other insurance. When the umbrella is excess coverage and is written strictly to follow form, then the umbrella policy merely incorporates (physically or by reference) the exclusions in the underlying policy. These exclusions therefore apply to the umbrella coverage—to those losses where the umbrella is excess. Any other exclusions in the umbrella policy will apply to losses for which only the umbrella provides insurance.

If the umbrella is not written to follow the form of the underlying insurance, then only the exclusions delineated in the umbrella policy apply to the umbrella coverage. These exclusions can then apply to all types of coverage in the umbrella policy, regardless of whether there is any underlying insurance.

As in primary and excess liability coverages, some exclusions apply to all coverages under an umbrella, and other exclusions are specific to particular umbrella coverages. For all coverages, an umbrella policy normally excludes liability arising from the following:

- Bodily injury or property damage expected or intended by the insured (except for the use of reasonable force to protect persons or property)
- Any obligation of the insured under a workers compensation, disability benefit, or similar statute (unless assumed by the insured under contract)
- Pollution of the environment (because of many lawsuits attempting to override this and similar exclusions, the pollution exclusion in many umbrella and other liability policies is often extensive and varies widely among insurers)
- Ownership, maintenance, use, loading, or unloading of all aircraft or watercraft over a certain length (size) unless aircraft or watercraft umbrella liability coverage has been purchased
- Nuclear energy (this exclusion also tends to be extensive and to vary materially among insurers)
- Recall of the insured's products when they are known or suspected to be defective

Other exclusions apply only to particular optional coverages for which the umbrella policy may have been written. For example, if the policy covers advertisers' liability, no coverage applies to breaches of contract; failure of the insured's goods or services to conform to advertised quality or performance; mistaken description of goods or services; or any "advertising" (broadly defined to include most forms of mass communication) by an insured that is in the advertising, broadcasting, telecasting, or publishing business (unless the umbrella coverage is excess over primary insurance also covering such an insured).

The preceding exclusions are merely illustrative. They do not include all the exclusions that might be in an umbrella policy. A risk management professional must carefully read the exclusions of each umbrella policy for differences in wording and structure from one insurer to the next, and for any one insurer over time. To counter court decisions they regard as unfavorable and to overcome many insureds' impression that an umbrella policy provides "all-risks" legal protection, many umbrella insurers have gradually narrowed the scope of typical umbrella liability coverage. For example, some years ago, a few umbrella policies did not exclude liability arising from war and similar hostile activities. Today, virtually all umbrella contracts contain such an exclusion, and newer policies contain especially broad war risk exclusions.

Another illustration of the current trend toward narrower umbrella coverage is the growing number of insurers who are making such contracts contingent on a greater number of specific forms of underlying coverages than generally were previously required. For example, most umbrella policies historically have not, and still do not, exclude liquor liability for any insured. However, for insureds whose businesses relate directly to manufacturing, distributing, or vending alcoholic beverages, most umbrella insurers now require underlying liquor liability insurance (rather than the insured's self-insured retention) as a condition for obtaining umbrella coverage of this liability.

This trend may or may not continue. As with all lines of insurance, the scope of protection provided by an umbrella policy can be expected to shift somewhat in response to both long-term legal trends and short-term fluctuations in the insurance market. Thus, although the risk management professional should not assume that any insurance contract is "standard," caution is especially necessary when dealing with umbrella coverages. As with all types of insurance, whenever there is doubt about the exposures a particular policy covers, a risk management professional should confer with a representative of the insurer to reach a mutual understanding of the protection each expects a particular insurance policy to provide.

Conditions

The procedures in the conditions section for carrying out the terms of an umbrella policy largely parallel those found in primary and excess contracts. As always, risk management professionals should be certain that the procedures for insureds and others are consistent—that fulfilling the conditions under one contract will not jeopardize coverage under another.

The insured and the risk management professional should clearly understand not only the procedures for reporting claims or incidents to umbrella, excess, and primary insurers, but also the basis on which the insurance is written. Like primary liability contracts, umbrella insurance may be written either on an occurrence or a claims-made basis. Because the nature of the insured event triggering coverage differs from one basis to the other, questions about coverage are almost certain to arise unless the primary, excess, and umbrella policies initially have been written in precisely parallel occurrence or claims-made language.

For example, coverage under most current primary liability policies written on a claims-made basis is triggered when oral or written notice is first received by the insured or insurer. However, umbrella liability coverage may be triggered by a variety of circumstances. Some umbrella policies, for example, state that coverage is not triggered until the insurer receives written notice of a claim. This seemingly minor difference in claim-reporting procedures can place an insured in a difficult position when, for example, the insured is orally notified of the claim (thus automatically triggering the primary coverage) just before the primary (and probably umbrella) policy expires. The required written notice to the umbrella insurer has not yet been given, and it probably cannot be sent to or received by this insurer during the policy period. If the umbrella coverage is being terminated, no umbrella coverage would apply. If the umbrella coverage is being renewed, the claim would probably fall within the new policy period. The mechanics, legal implications, and insurance-pricing consequences of such situations should be agreed upon in advance by an insured organization and its primary, excess, and umbrella insurers.

Policy Period

As with excess insurance, umbrella insurance should be written so that the period corresponds with that of any underlying coverage. This practice helps to avoid difficulties that can arise when, because of a difference in coverage periods, an insured expects to be covered by umbrella insurance on the basis of the underlying insurance contract, but is not. Concurrent policy periods are a special concern in umbrella coverage of liability exposures because, unlike most excess insurance covering liability exposures, umbrella policies need not be written to follow the form of the underlying coverage. It is more likely, therefore, that the umbrella policy would not necessarily "follow" the policy period of the underlying coverage. This can create a problem when an umbrella policy is expected to drop down and pick up the aggregates of the underlying policy. If the policy dates are not concurrent, the umbrella may not recognize the exhaustion of the underlying aggregate limits. The same problem can occur with excess insurance.

Such difficulties can be avoided by the judicious use of extended reporting periods for claims-made umbrella coverages involving lines of insurance where claims are reported late. Arranging primary, excess, and umbrella policies to avoid difficulties with incurred-but-not-reported occurrences and claims is an important and complex task for any risk management professional.

REINSURANCE

Just as an insured organization must turn to primary, straight excess, and umbrella insurers for financing recovery from losses that exceed their retention ability, so do these insurers need to rely on reinsurers and retrocessionaires for protection against losses to insured policyholders that exceed these insurers' retention capacities. If a risk management program is to depend on insurance, the risk management professional must, in turn, be able to ensure the financial soundness of the reinsurance arrangements upon which the insurer and, ultimately, its insureds rely. To do so, the risk management professional must recognize the importance of reinsurance in risk financing, distinguish among the types of reinsurance, and understand the provisions that typically appear in reinsurance contracts. These subjects are discussed in this portion of the chapter.

Importance of Reinsurance in Risk Financing

Reinsurance performs two basic functions in an organization's risk financing program. First, it enhances the reliability and indirectly lowers the cost of commercial insurance. In implementing its risk financing program, an organization may deal directly with a reinsurer who is (1) acting as a primary insurer under a portfolio reinsurance arrangement or *assumption endorsement* (cut-through clause); (2) reinsuring, according to the insured organization's specifications, coverage "fronted" through a commercial or captive originating insurer of the insured's choice; or (3) providing reinsurance for a "pool" in which the insured organization participates. Second, by purchasing (or even selling) reinsurance directly, an organization can gain direct access to the reinsurance market, negotiating with reinsurers without having to rely on any marketing intermediaries.

Improved Cost-Effectiveness of Commercial Insurance. Because every insured organization depends on the financial reliability of its commercial insurance, the risk management professional must be certain of the soundness of its insurers' reinsurance. Virtually every commercial insurer reinsures a significant portion of most lines of coverage it writes and such insurance can be said to be "only as good as" its reinsurance.

For some exposures, a risk management professional will only need to confirm the existence and financial ratings of its insurers' reinsurance.

In other cases, especially those involving high limits of primary or excess coverage, a risk management professional will want to inquire more specifically into the types and limits of reinsurance that have been obtained and from whom it has been purchased. The purpose is to be sure that this reinsurance is appropriate for the coverage the insured organization wishes. In unusual situations a risk management professional may further specify the types and amounts of reinsurance to be purchased as a condition precedent to dealing with that primary insurer.

As insurers and reinsurers cede and retrocede coverages to develop a better spread of risk, they may become quite interdependent. A reinsured for one exposure or type of insurance may become a reinsurer of at least part of another insurer's exposures. Both of these companies may, in turn, become retrocessionaires of the coverage on a third set of exposures or other line of insurance. As a result, through reinsurance, the "fortunes" of many insurers or reinsurers may become mutually dependent as each relies on the good faith and financial strength of the other.

Although these interdependent relationships are normally appropriate and even desirable, any truly catastrophic reinsured loss, any scandal in reinsurance markets, or any bankruptcy of a major insurer or reinsurer that calls into question the integrity or financial strength of the overall reinsurance network can also raise questions about the soundness of a risk financing program. Although there may be little that a risk management professional can do to avert such "systemic disturbances" in the insurance/reinsurance market, every professional should be familiar enough with the reinsurance arrangements of the organization's insurers to be able to (1) investigate reinsurance-related issues with insurers' and reinsurers' representatives, (2) supply information about reinsurance to the organization's managers and owners, and (3) renegotiate key elements of the organization's insurance and risk financing program if and when this program is threatened by weaknesses in reinsurance markets.

Direct Dealings With Reinsurers. As mentioned, an insured is normally not a party to any contracts with a reinsurer; only insurers and reinsurers typically enter into reinsurance contracts. However, an insured organization may deal with one or more reinsurers that (1) have taken the place of primary insurers through portfolio reinsurance or assumption endorsements, (2) are reinsuring fronted coverage arranged by or at the request of the insured organization, or (3) are reinsuring a captive insuring arrangement or a pool of which the insured organization is a member.

Acting as a Primary Insurer. As previously mentioned, when a primary insurer retires from an entire type of insurance or a territory, and reinsures this entire block or "book" of outstanding business on a portfolio basis, the reinsurer effectively becomes the primary insurer of this part of the cedent's business. The reinsurer then deals with the policyholders as if it were the original primary insurer.

The risk management professional whose organization's insurance has been reinsured through a portfolio arrangement will want to learn the details of this transfer. However, the transfer itself does not have to be difficult. It is likely that the coverage from the reinsurer will be at least as financially reliable and competitively priced as that of the retiring insurer. In fact, the transition may be so well managed that many insureds may not realize that a transfer has occurred. They will just continue to work with the same agents or brokers, who will now be representing the reinsurer who has become the primary insurer.

An organization's risk management professional will be more concerned when the organization is dealing with a reinsurer under an assumption certificate or cut-through clause or endorsement. Cut-through dealings signal that the reinsured is having financial difficulties. This endorsement is usually attached to the organization's primary insurer.

An *assumption certificate* attached to a primary policy obligates the reinsurer to assume all the obligations of the reinsured if it becomes bankrupt or unable to fulfill its obligations. Thereafter, the organization will need to purchase new primary coverage, presumably with insurers having greater financial strength. The direct protection by the reinsurer under an assumption certificate may be extremely important to an insured organization. Even more significant, the triggering of the endorsement should prompt a complete reexamination of the organization's insurance program. The reinsurer's obligation under the assumption certificate does not extend beyond the coverage period of the original insurance; therefore, unless the original primary insurer regains its financial reliability almost immediately, the organization's complete insurance program may need to be restructured before the cut-through protection expires.

A typical assumption endorsement appears in Exhibit 6-6, but the wording of this particular endorsement is only representative; there is no standard form for this or many other reinsurance contract provisions.

Reinsuring Fronted Coverage. An organization may decide to retain losses through its captive insurance company or may want a particular insurer to provide coverage. If the captive or chosen insurer is not licensed to provide the type of insurance sought, the organization may have to arrange for a licensed insurance company to "front" the coverage. *Fronting* means that a licensed insurance company issues a policy but does not retain the risk, which is reinsured through another company chosen by the insured, often the insured's captive.

Exhibit 6-6

Typical Assumption ("Cut-through") Endorsement to a Reinsurance Contract

> In the event that ________ (ceding insurer) fails to pay any amount due under its policy no. ________ for any reason, including by reason of insolvency, receivership, or reorganization of the ceding company, it is understood that the reinsurer will be liable for its portion of such covered loss and will make payment thereof directly to the policyholder and the policyholder will have a direct right of action against the reinsurer for such amount payable under the policy, in each case in accordance with the terms of the policy without diminution because of the insolvency, receivership, or reorganization of the ceding insurer.

Reprinted with permission from V. M. Stephens, William S. McIntyre, and Jack P. Gibson, *Risk Financing* (Dallas: International Risk Management Institute), P.V.D.I., June 1986.

For example, Apex Company seeks to finance its products liability losses through an affiliated captive, but the captive is not licensed to issue products liability policies. Therefore, in order to utilize its captive as a risk financing vehicle, Apex Company purchases products liability coverage through Betterman's Insurance Company, which is licensed as a products liability insurer. Betterman's Insurance Company issues a policy naming the Apex Company as the insured and immediately reinsures this policy through Apex's captive. The net result is that Apex Company has its products liability losses insured through its affiliated captive.

In effect, the insured is "renting the license" of the fronting company in order to direct the insurance to its captive or a specific reinsurer. The insured organization is actually doing business with a reinsurer. For practical or legal reasons a primary insurer is issuing the policies in its own name, but it is really fronting as the *de facto* "agent" of the reinsurer.

The fronting insurer is normally paid for this service. This fee is often a percentage of the insurance premium involved in the transactions, but it can also be a flat amount. Because the security of a risk financing program that is built on such arrangements depends on the reinsurance backing, the risk management professional for the insured should regularly confirm that the fronting company has purchased the required reinsurance. In addition, the effectiveness of the reinsurer's working relationship with the primary insurer that fronts for it is an integral part of the insuring arrangement. It should not be inferred from this description that there is any deception, illegality, or other impropriety in fronted insurance arrangements. Thoughtfully structured, they can be as financially secure, legal, and creatively productive as any other insuring arrangement.

Recent proposals to ban fronting arrangements have met resistance from the insurance buying community. Regulators fear that irresponsible use of fronting arrangements adds to insurer insolvency and general instability of the insurance industry because financially weak reinsurers may be used. However, in most cases fronting is an accepted industry practice that is used for responsible insurance transactions.

Reinsuring a Captive or Pool. The risk management professional often plays many roles. Two of these are as (1) the buyer of insurance for an organization and (2) an official of or an informal adviser to the management of the affiliated (captive) insurer or the pool from which the organization buys insurance. Thus, much like a senior executive of a commercial insurer that may be a reinsured in some transactions and a reinsurer in others, an organization's risk management professional may represent both the buyer and the provider of insurance. (As explained in Chapter 10, the federal tax code encourages a minimum of overlap between an organization's own management and the management of its captive. Nevertheless, without contravening this code, a risk management professional—especially one who serves a client rather than a principal employer—may often legitimately act for both the insured organization and its captive insurer.)

Captives and pools purchase reinsurance directly. Therefore, as a manager in a captive or pool, a risk management professional may be part of decisions that directly affect one or more insurers, insureds, and reinsurers. In this position, the risk management professional must again be concerned with the financial strength, integrity, and operating efficiency of the reinsurer. It is on these qualities that the reliability of the captive or pool (and, therefore, the solidity and the effectiveness of the organization's own risk financing program) rely.

Exhibit 6-7 shows the way in which fronting and reinsurance are used for a typical captive insurance company.

Notice the direct involvement between the insured and the front company, and through ownership, between the insured and the captive insurer. The insured is also involved with the reinsurer indirectly through the captive.

For a group captive such as a risk retention group, the quality of the group's reinsurance is very important for its financial viability. Group captives many times insure ultrahazardous exposures for which it is difficult to obtain good quality reinsurance, so the risk management

Exhibit 6-7
Premium and Loss Flows for a Typical Captive Insurance Company

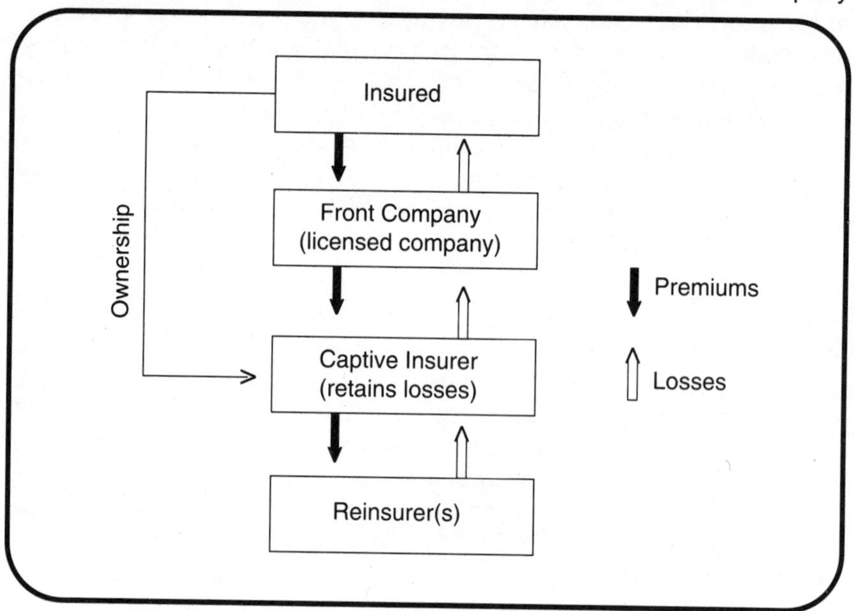

professional should examine the group's reinsurance program very carefully before joining such a group.

Types of Reinsurance

Reinsurance contracts can also be classified according to two characteristics: (1) how these contracts specify the manner in which insurance is to be placed and (2) how they apportion between the reinsurer and the reinsured the obligations to (and the premiums received from) primary insureds.[2] In terms of the first characteristic, reinsurance contracts are identified as either *treaty reinsurance,* which deals uniformly with substantial groups of reinsured policies, or *facultative reinsurance,* which deals separately with individual reinsured primary policies. In terms of the second characteristic, reinsurance contracts are either pro rata (proportional) or excess of loss (nonproportional). In pro rata reinsurance the reinsurer and cedent divide all premiums and losses according to some fixed percentage. In excess of loss reinsurance the reinsurer bears only the upper portion of larger losses as these may be defined in the reinsurance contract, and receives some part of the premium that is appropriate for the losses the reinsurer pays.

Thus, reinsurance contracts are either treaty or facultative reinsurance and either pro rata or excess of loss. (The only exception is finite risk reinsurance, which is discussed later.) As shown in Exhibit 6-8, both facultative and treaty reinsurance contracts can be either pro rata or excess of loss. In principle, whether a reinsurance contract uses a treaty approach or a facultative approach to identify its insurance obligations has nothing to do with whether the reinsurance contract describes the respective obligations of the reinsured and reinsurer on a pro rata or an excess of loss basis. However, in practice, more treaty than facultative arrangements may be classified as pro rata. The various types of treaty and facultative reinsurance, which are shown in Exhibit 6-8, are discussed throughout this section.

Reinsurance in practice may not be as consistent with its principles as Exhibit 6-8 may imply for two reasons. First, the terminology for describing reinsurance contracts is not as standardized or consistent as Exhibit 6-8 suggests. A number of seemingly distinct terms may be used by different reinsurers to describe what is essentially the same reinsurance arrangement. Second, a single reinsurance contract may treat some policies on a treaty basis and others on a facultative basis. The same contract may also describe the reinsurer's obligations in pro rata terms for some types of ceded insurance and in excess of loss terms for others. In both cases, what appears to be one reinsurance contract can logically be analyzed as several separate reinsurance arrangements that happen to be stated in a single document. Nonetheless, for ease of explanation and understanding, the following discussion of reinsurance contracts adheres as closely as possible to the framework in Exhibit 6-8.

Classifying Reinsurance by Method of Ceding Insurance. The two basic groups into which all reinsurance contracts fall are treaty reinsurance and facultative reinsurance. There are also some reinsurance arrangements that are called facultative treaties, which are discussed later. These exist because reinsurance contracts occasionally need to be tailored to the needs of individual ceding insurers and the capabilities of particular reinsurers; such contracts have both facultative and treaty characteristics.

Treaty Reinsurance. "Treaty" can be a somewhat ambiguous term. In some reinsurance contexts, it is simply a synonym for contract. Any ongoing arrangement between a reinsurer and a reinsured (or between a retrocedent and retrocessionaire) can be properly labeled as a treaty. In a more precise sense, however, *treaty reinsurance* applies to any reinsurance contract under which the reinsurer agrees to accept all policies of a certain class (line of insurance, limit of liability, or type of insured) for which a reinsured writes insurance. In effect, the reinsured makes an advance agreement with a reinsurer to cede all policies within

Exhibit 6-8
Categories of Reinsurance

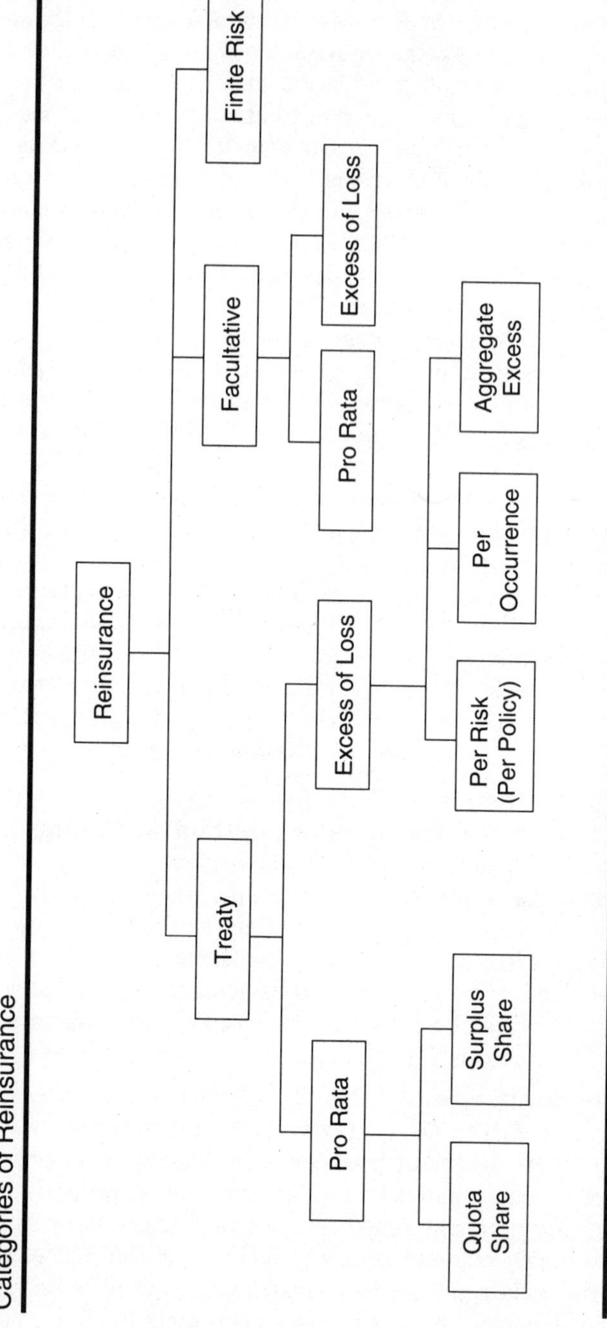

certain classes of business as outlined in the reinsurance contract, and the reinsurer agrees to accept all insured exposures in these classes. A few treaty reinsurance arrangements modify the reinsured's obligations by allowing it to cede only certain policies.

Traditional treaty reinsurance has advantages and disadvantages. One advantage is that the reinsured is assured of the reinsurer's acceptance of all policies, or *cessions,* that come within the terms of the treaty, and the reinsured knows the portion of the premium or other costs that constitute the reinsurance premium for this protection. A second advantage, promoting the efficiency of reinsurance transactions, is that the reinsured and the reinsurer need not negotiate every cession. This automatic acceptance reduces handling expenses.

One disadvantage in traditional treaty reinsurance is that a treaty obligates the reinsured to cede and the reinsurer to accept cessions at a fixed reinsurance premium rate. This is determined when the treaty is negotiated and cannot be adjusted during the life of the treaty even if loss experience indicates that the reinsurance protection is overpriced or underpriced. An important limitation is that it is hard for treaties to meet all the underwriting needs of the cedent. For example, certain especially hazardous operations may be excluded from a treaty, or a treaty's coverage limits may not be sufficiently high for some exposures.

Facultative Reinsurance. When making *facultative reinsurance* arrangements, the reinsured selects the policies it wishes to reinsure and offers each one to the reinsurer as a distinct transaction. The reinsurer is free to accept or reject each submission, and both parties can negotiate the price (reinsurance premium) at which any cession is made. A facultative reinsurance arrangement essentially establishes the broad boundaries of the area in which the reinsured and the reinsurer can negotiate separate agreements. The boundaries pertain to the general type of insurance or insured and how they will apportion the exposure and the premium.

Like treaty reinsurance, facultative reinsurance has advantages and disadvantages. One of the advantages is that both parties to the contract can be extremely flexible; neither is required to participate in a particular cession. Second, facultative reinsurance gives the reinsured a wide range of opportunities to reinsure unusual or extrahazardous exposures, especially those a reinsurer might be reluctant to accept automatically on a treaty basis without the power to accept or reject individual cessions. Third, facultative reinsurance gives the reinsured a way to obtain reinsurance without jeopardizing favorable treaty reinsurance relationships intended for more standard exposures. Consequently, facultative reinsurance can be said to protect a treaty arrangement from adverse underwriting results and, therefore, higher future reinsurance costs. Finally, facultative reinsurance allows a reinsured to reinsure, one at a time, exposures that are larger than the normal, less flexible treaty reinsurance limits would permit. Therefore, facultative reinsurance can be an elastic source of additional underwriting capacity.

One disadvantage of facultative reinsurance is that each submission must be negotiated separately. This adds to the time and expense of obtaining reinsurance. A second disadvantage is that the reinsured cannot be assured of the availability of appropriate reinsurance at what it believes is a reasonable cost for any given exposure it insures on a primary basis.

Facultative Treaty Reinsurance. The distinctions between traditional treaty and facultative reinsurance are based partly on the extent of flexibility or freedom the reinsured and the reinsurer have in any reinsurance transaction. Because the degree of flexibility or freedom on the part of either party can vary, there are some gray areas in reinsurance arrangements. Under a *facultative treaty,* the cedent can choose the risks it would like to cede, and the reinsurer has the option to reject these risks. A facultative treaty is merely a statement of intention by the parties, which are not obligated to cede or accept risks. However, these contracts stipulate the particular premium rate and terms of the reinsurance arrangement, as does treaty reinsurance, if the parties agree to the cession. A *facultative obligatory treaty* is different in that, even though the reinsured can choose the risks it wishes to cede, the reinsurer must accept the ceded risks. A facultative obligatory treaty must be carefully underwritten by the reinsurer because of the possibility of adverse selection.

Classifying Reinsurance by Apportionment of Insured Obligation. Reinsurance arrangements are often classified by the reinsurer's and the primary insurer's respective duties to pay for insured losses and by their rights to share premiums paid by primary insureds.

Pro Rata Reinsurance. Pro rata reinsurance arrangements are ones in which the cedent and the reinsurer share insurance, premiums, and losses proportionally on the basis of predetermined percentages or dollar amounts of retention by the cedent. There are two main forms of pro rata reinsurance: quota share and surplus share. In quota share, the cedent cedes a proportional part of every exposure, beginning with the first dollar of loss and the first dollar of premium. In surplus share, the cedent cedes a proportional part of every exposure and premium above a given dollar amount of retention of both exposure and premium.

Quota Share. Under a *quota share contract,* the reinsured cedes a part of every exposure it insures within the class or classes subject to the treaty. Even the smallest loss exposures are reinsured. The insured's retention is stated as a percentage of the amount of insurance, so that

Exhibit 6-9
Division of Insurance, Premium, and Losses Under Quota Share Treaty With 25 Percent Retention and $250,000 Limit

	Matchless Fire	Solid Re	Total
Policy A			
Insurance	$2,500	$7,500	$10,000
Premium	25	75	100
Loss	2,000	6,000	8,000
Policy B			
Insurance	$25,000	$75,000	$100,000
Premium	250	750	1,000
Loss	2,500	7,500	10,000
Policy C			
Insurance	$37,500	$112,500	$150,000
Premium	375	1,125	1,500
Loss	15,000	45,000	60,000

the dollar amount of its retention varies with the amount of insurance. The reinsurer assumes all of the amount of insurance except for the reinsured's retention up to the reinsurance limit. The reinsurer receives the same percentage of the premium (less the ceding commission) as it does of the amount of insurance and pays the same percentage of each loss.

To illustrate the application of a quota share contract to different situations, assume that Matchless Fire Insurance Company has purchased from Solid Re a quota share arrangement with a retention of 25 percent. Matchless Fire has written three policies. Policy A insures Building A for $10,000 for a premium of $100, with one loss of $8,000. Policy B insures Building B for $100,000 for a premium of $1,000, with one loss of $10,000. Policy C insures Building C for $150,000 for a premium of $1,500, with one loss of $60,000. Exhibit 6-9 shows how the insurance, premiums, and losses under these policies would be split between the ceding company and the reinsurer. Notice that in each case the ceding company retains 25 percent of the insurance and the premium and pays 25 percent of the losses. However, the dollar amount of its retention increases as the amount of insurance increases.

Compared to other types of reinsurance, quota share agreements have the advantage of being simple to rate and simple to administer, since the reinsurer receives the agreed percentage of all covered premiums. The principal disadvantage is that a quota share contract results in ceding a large share of presumably profitable business on the smaller risks that the reinsured could otherwise retain. Because of this disadvantage, quota share reinsurance has been declining in popularity. However, it is still widely used, primarily in property insurance, and principally by small insurers and insurers that need to increase surplus by receiving a ceding commission that is credited to the reinsured's expenses. Quota share is the most effective treaty for that purpose.

Quota share contracts are not very effective in stabilizing loss experience and in coping with catastrophes since they do not affect the ceding company's loss ratio. Of course, a favorable ceding commission may have an effect on the ceding company's combined ratio since reinsurance commissions received are credited against expenses in the ceding company's annual statement. Over a period of years, one company showed a negative expense ratio on its annual statement because its ceding commissions on its reinsurance contracts were greater than all of its expenses paid. Of course, a reinsurer must anticipate an extremely low loss ratio in order to pay such a high ceding commission.

A quota share contract can be reasonably effective in improving the ceding company's large line capacity, depending upon the percentage retention required. However, it is not as effective in that regard as surplus share and per risk excess arrangements. (Per risk arrangements are part of excess of loss reinsurance and are described later in this chapter.)

Quota share contracts are effective in risk sharing, and they can be effective in reciprocity. For example, an automobile insurer active only in the United States recently negotiated a reciprocal quota share arrangement with another automobile insurer active only in Canada. The U.S. insurer reinsures on a quota share basis 30 percent of the direct business written by the Canadian company, and the Canadian company reinsures 80 percent of the direct business written by the U.S. company. Because of the difference in the size of the companies, the dollar amounts of insurance exchanged are approximately equal. However, each insurer has increased both the number and the geographic spread of the cars insured. Such an arrangement should help to stabilize the loss experience of both insurers.

Surplus Share. Surplus share contracts, like quota share contracts, are proportional reinsurance; that is, the reinsured and the reinsurers share the insurance, the premiums, and the losses in the same percentage. The difference between them is in the way the retention is stated. The retention under a quota share contract is stated as a *percentage* of the amount insured, and the retention under a surplus share contract is stated as a *dollar amount.* However, the reinsured may elect to retain more than the minimum retention stated in the contract. If the amount of insurance under a given policy is less than the retention amount, no coverage under the policy is reinsured. If the amount of insurance under a policy exceeds the retention amount, the amount of insurance over and above the retention is ceded to the reinsurer on a proportional basis, subject to the reinsurance limit and possibly other limitations of the contract. The reinsurer receives the same percentage of the premium as it does of the insurance and pays the same percentage of each loss regardless of size. Therefore, the major difference between quota share and surplus share is that although the same *percentage* of reinsurance applies to all eligible policies under quota share, the percentage *varies* from policy to policy in a surplus share contract, depending on policy size and other conditions in the reinsurance agreement.

To illustrate a surplus share arrangement, assume that Matchless Fire Insurance Company has purchased from Solid Re a surplus contract with a retention of $25,000 and a limit of $250,000. This would be referred to as a "ten-line" surplus arrangement since the reinsurer will accept coverage up to ten times the retention amount. Exhibit 6-10 shows how this arrangement would apply to the same three policies used in Exhibit 6-9. Notice that under a quota share contract (Exhibit 6-9) the percentage retention remains constant while the dollar amount of retention increases as the amount of insurance increases. Under a surplus share arrangement (Exhibit 6-10), the dollar amount of retention remains constant while the percentage decreases as the amount of insurance increases. This is the major difference between quota share and surplus share contracts.

Surplus share contracts are sometimes built up in layers, with a different reinsurer for each layer. For example, if Solid Re had been unwilling to provide the full $250,000 of coverage that Matchless Fire wanted, Matchless might have built up the required coverage in the following three surplus share arrangements:

Reinsurer	*Retention*	*Reinsurance Limit*
Solid Re	$215,000	$100,000
Super Re	125,000	100,000
Jumbo Re	225,000	50,000

For Policy B in Exhibit 6-10, the coverage would have been split $25,000 for Matchless Fire and $75,000 for Solid Re. Policy C would have been split $25,000 for Matchless Fire, $100,000 for Solid Re, and $25,000 for Super Re. Jumbo Re would not become involved until the amount of insurance on one loss exposure exceeded $225,000. Losses and premiums would still be shared pro rata between Matchless Fire and all reinsurers

Exhibit 6-10
Division of Insurance, Premium, and Losses Under Surplus Share Contract With $25,000 Retention and $250,000 Limit*

	Matchless Fire	Solid Re	Total
Policy A			
Insurance	$10,000	$ 0	$10,000
Premium	100	0	100
Loss	8,000	0	8,000
Policy B			
Insurance	$25,000	$75,000	$100,000
Premium	250	750	1,000
Loss	2,500	7,500	10,000
Policy C			
Insurance	$25,000	$125,000	$150,000
Premium	250	1,250	1,500
Loss	10,000	50,000	60,000

* This example assumes that MFIC always retains its maximum net line. This is common, but most treaties permit smaller retention as long as the line limit is not violated.

that provided coverage on the particular loss exposure that sustained loss. Jumbo Re would not contribute to any of the losses in Exhibit 6-10 because none of the amounts of insurance exceeded the retention under its contract. Super Re would be involved only with respect to Policy C.

In the preceding example, Solid Re's contract would be referred to as the first surplus because it would come into play at the lowest amount of insurance. Super Re's contract would be the second surplus, and Jumbo Re's contract would be the third surplus. As in Exhibit 6-10, it is assumed that policy limits are spread so as to fill the ceding company's retention first, then its first surplus, and so on. This is not usually a contract requirement, and in the interest of providing better balance (relation of contract capacity to premium volume), the ceding company may decide to place part of each ceded policy in all its surplus share arrangements or any combination of them.

Surplus share reinsurance has been a common form of reinsurance for property insurers, though it has been losing ground to excess reinsurance in recent years. It has seldom, if ever, been used for liability insurance.

Quota Share and Surplus Share: Advantages and Disadvantages. The principal advantage of surplus share contracts over quota share contracts is that surplus share arrangements, because of their minimum dollar retentions, avoid ceding loss exposures that are so small that the reinsured can afford to retain them. This retention helps to save in reinsurance premiums and reduces the processing of reinsurance claims. It also provides a more logical approach to reinsurance because no reinsurance is purchased unless the loss exposure is beyond the capacity of the reinsured.

The principal disadvantage of surplus share arrangements in comparison with quota share is the increased administrative expense. Since not all loss exposures are reinsured, the reinsured must maintain a record of those that are reinsured and furnish a report of them to the reinsurer each month or at another agreed frequency. This listing of reinsured exposures, which usually includes premium and loss information, is known as a *bordereau.* Only a loss bordereau would be necessary under a quota share contract since the reinsurer receives a fixed percentage of all covered premiums.

Like the quota share contract, the surplus share is not designed to protect the ceding company from catastrophic losses. This function of reinsurance is satisfied by excess of loss arrangements (described below). Pro rata reinsurance contracts generally have no occurrence limit. For example, a regional insurer may write primarily large property exposures within a one- or two-state territory and use surplus share as its major form of reinsurance. A severe earthquake might damage or destroy many of the ceded exposures, resulting in a very large loss to the reinsurer.

Excess of Loss Reinsurance. As previously mentioned, *excess of loss reinsurance* differs from pro rata reinsurance in that the cedent and reinsurer do not share insurance, premiums, or losses in any given proportion. In fact, only losses are ceded. The reinsurance premium is usually stated as a percentage of the ceding company's premium income for the covered lines of business. This percentage is subject to negotiation and will vary by line and from one reinsurer to another. Commissions are not generally paid to the ceding company under excess of loss contracts, although there are exceptions.

There are three general classes of excess of loss reinsurance: *per-risk excess, per-occurrence excess* (also known as per-loss excess), and *aggregate excess.*

Per-Risk Excess. The retention under a per-risk excess contract is stated as a dollar amount of *loss* (not an amount of insurance), and the reinsurer is liable for all or a part of the loss to any one exposure in excess of the retention and up to the agreed reinsurance limit. In some cases, the reinsurer may agree to pay only a stated percentage, such as 90 percent or 95 percent, of the loss in excess of the retention, though this provision is more common to per-occurrence excess and aggregate excess contracts.

The retention amount under a per-risk excess of loss contract is usually set at a level to exclude a large majority, by number, of expected claims. This practice is consistent with the theory that excess of loss contracts are intended to protect the reinsured against unusual loss situations. However, the retention is sometimes set low enough so that reinsurance claims occur frequently. Reinsurance arrangements with such low retentions are frequently referred to as *working covers* or *working excess contracts.*

The retention under a per-risk excess contract applies separately to each subject of insurance. For example, if Matchless Fire Insurance Company insured the Sheer Hosiery Company at 1110 Main Street and the Desiccated Sprinkler Company next door at 1112 Main Street and they both burned, the retention under a per-risk excess contract would apply separately to each. As will be shown, this is quite different from the other forms of excess reinsurance.

In contrast to pro rata reinsurance, reinsurers under excess of loss reinsurance do not participate in all losses. They participate only in those that exceed the reinsured's retention, and then only in the part in excess of the retention. This difference is emphasized here because it is a frequent source of confusion among persons who are not familiar with reinsurance practices. Exhibit 6-11 shows how Matchless Fire and Solid Reinsurance would split the losses of $8,000, $10,000, and $60,000 under a per-risk excess contract with a retention of $25,000. The amount of insurance and the premium for each policy are not mentioned in Exhibit 6-11 because they are not material to the division of losses under an excess contract.

The principal advantage of a per-risk excess contract over proportional contracts is that, in general, less premium is paid to the reinsurer. This permits the reinsured to earn income on the investment of these funds. Administration costs are also lower since fewer reinsurance claims are processed. Also, it is not necessary to keep track of the loss exposures reinsured in the same manner as under a surplus share contract. The excess of loss treaty is concerned only with losses.

Per-risk excess contracts are very effective in providing large line capacity since they absorb the large losses that make large lines hazardous to the direct insurer. They are much more effective in this regard than quota share contracts and somewhat more effective than surplus share arrangements, particularly if the reinsurance premium cost is considered.

Per-risk excess contracts are very effective in stabilizing loss experience because they lessen the impact of large losses, which contribute disproportionately to fluctuations of loss experience. The loss experience

Exhibit 6-11
Division of Losses under Per-Risk Excess Contract with $25,000 Retention

	Total Loss	Matchless Fire	Solid Reinsurance
Policy A Loss	$ 8,000	$ 8,000	$ 0
Policy B Loss	$10,000	$10,000	$ 0
Policy C Loss	$60,000	$25,000	$35,000

of the reinsurer need not be the same as that of the reinsured in any given year, and it normally would not be. However, over the long run, each reinsured should expect to pay its own reinsurance losses plus the reinsurer's operating expenses. That is, the reinsured gives up a part of its profits in the good years in order to transfer unprofitable business to the reinsurer in the bad years, thus stabilizing its loss experience over time.

Per-risk excess arrangements are helpful in catastrophes since they pay the amount in excess of the ceding company's retention on each individual claim. However, they are far less effective in this regard than per-occurrence excess contracts, especially since many per-risk excess arrangements contain a limitation on losses recoverable for any one loss occurrence such as a hurricane, tornado, or earthquake.

Per-Occurrence Excess. Under per-occurrence excess reinsurance a reinsured is covered for all insured losses arising from any one occurrence regardless of the number of insured exposures or insured interests that may be harmed. Therefore, in discussing this type of excess reinsurance, it is important to distinguish between property insurance and liability insurance exposure.

In property insurance the number of separate items and parties suffering loss and the total potential loss are reasonably determinable in advance. In liability insurance policies the total potential losses are highly unpredictable. Another difference between property and liability coverage is the length of time required for the full development and settlement of all losses. In a liability claim, the time between the date of loss and notice to excess reinsurers may be several years. Final settlement of known losses may require many more years. In some cases, there may be questions about the time of the occurrence, as in the case of carcinogenic exposures that may not manifest themselves for decades. The total amount of a property loss is usually known within a short time after the loss.

Property insurers are especially prone to large accumulations of losses arising from a single occurrence, such as a hurricane, that damages many insured properties. Most of the individual claims are relatively small, but the accumulated amount can be staggering. Per-occurrence excess contracts, sometimes called catastrophe contracts, are especially designed to cope with this problem, though some catastrophe excess contracts may also be applicable to a large loss arising from damage to a single subject of insurance or a single large liability claim.

Like the per-risk excess reinsurance, the retention per occurrence is stated as a dollar amount. However, unlike the per-risk excess, all of the losses arising from a single occurrence are totaled to determine when the retention has been satisfied. For example, assume the three losses in Exhibit 6-11 are due to one occurrence. The per-occurrence excess contract with a $25,000 retention limit covers the total of the three losses, minus the $25,000 of retained losses. Therefore, the excess insurer pays a total of $53,000 for the three losses, rather than $35,000 payable in the per-loss example. The catastrophe reinsurance limit also applies to the total of all losses from one occurrence. Consequently, the definition of "occurrence" becomes an issue.

The definition of occurrence is very important because it controls the application of the retention and the reinsurance limit. The retention and the reinsurance limit apply separately, but only once, to each occurrence. For, example, if a hurricane travels up the East Coast and causes wind damage over a period of three days, all of the damage would be from a single occurrence as defined in most catastrophe reinsurance policies. Consequently, the reinsured would be required to absorb only one retention, and the reinsurer's liability could not exceed the amount stated in the contract. However, if the storm lasted longer than seventy-two hours, it would be two occurrences. Therefore, the reinsured would be required to absorb up to twice the stated retention, and the reinsurer would pay up to twice its treaty limit since catastrophe contracts typically restore the full original coverage following a loss—but only once—for damage resulting from one storm.

If the same hurricane brought heavy rains that caused the flooding of one river that drained into the Atlantic Ocean and of another that drained into the Gulf of Mexico (a common occurrence), the floods in the two rivers would be two separate occurrences under most reinsurance contracts. Consequently, the retention and the contract limit would apply separately to each river, even though both floods originated from the same storm system. (These definitions are merely illustrative; different definitions might be used by different reinsurers, or even by the same reinsurer in different reinsurance contracts.)

Per-occurrence excess reinsurance contracts are very effective for the purpose for which they were designed, which is smoothing the fluctuations in loss experience to the extent that such fluctuations result from an accumulation of losses from catastrophes. Such arrangements do not contribute significantly to the ceding company's premium capacity (except to the extent that they stabilize loss experience) since they are not designed to cover individual losses; nor do they contribute to large line capacity unless written to cover for a single large loss as well as for an accumulation of losses. Per-occurrence excess reinsurance does not provide significant surplus relief since the reinsurance premium is a relatively small percentage of the direct premiums, and the reinsurer usually does not pay a ceding commission.

Per-occurrence excess reinsurance arrangements usually provide that the reinsurers will pay up to a stated percentage, such as 90 or 95 percent, of the loss in excess of the retention. Therefore, not only does the reinsured pay the losses up to the retention, but it also participates in the loss above the retention. There are two reasons for this: (1) reinsurers do not maintain large claim departments and therefore are not equipped to handle a large number of losses; and (2) it encourages the reinsured to settle losses economically since they will be participating in the loss even though the retention is exhausted.

Per-occurrence excess reinsurance also differs from per-risk excess contracts in that the per-occurrence coverage, although written for a specific period of time (generally twelve months), is usually noncancelable by either party.

Aggregate Excess. Under aggregate excess reinsurance, the reinsurer begins to pay when the reinsured's claims for some stated period of time, usually one year, exceed the retention stated in the contract. The retention may be stated in dollars, as a loss ratio percentage, or as a combination of the two. The size of the retention is subject to negotiation between the reinsured and the reinsurer, but it would not usually be set so low that the reinsured would be guaranteed a profit on its premium. Also, the reinsurer normally does not pay all losses in excess of the reinsured's retention, but only a percentage of the excess, usually 90 or 95 percent. This feature is intended to discourage the reinsured from relaxing its underwriting or loss adjustment standards after its retention has been reached.

As might be expected, the reinsurance premium for an aggregate excess contract is likely to be larger than that for a per-risk or per-occurrence excess coverage. (Of course, this depends on the specific attachment points of the various types of reinsurance.) Aggregate excess contracts are much easier to obtain for property exposures than liability exposures, because of the greater stability of property losses over time. Consequently, such arrangements are used only if the potential loss fluctuations are sufficiently large in relation to the reinsured's surplus to policyholders to pose a threat of insolvency. Aggregate excess contracts are purchased most often by small property insurers.

Since the aggregate excess contract puts a cap on the reinsured's losses (or loss ratio), it would appear that no other reinsurance would be needed. In fact, both of the clauses just quoted prohibit reinsurance on the reinsured's retention. However, it is common to have other arrangements, either pro rata or excess of loss, in conjunction with aggregate excess contracts. In some cases, the reinsurer may insist on other arrangements as a condition of providing the aggregate excess coverage. In those cases, the other contracts would be written for the benefit of both the reinsured and the aggregate excess reinsurer. That is, the reinsured's retention and the aggregate excess reinsurer's liability would both relate to the net loss after the proceeds of all other reinsurance had been deducted.

The aggregate excess contract is the most effective of all forms of reinsurance in stabilizing the underwriting results of the reinsured, particularly if the cost of reinsurance is ignored. It is also effective in coping with catastrophes since the cap it puts on losses would apply to an accumulation of claims from a catastrophe.

However, an aggregate excess contract does not usually involve a ceding commission. Therefore, it does not provide significant surplus relief or premium capacity. It should logically increase premium capacity because the reinsured would need less surplus to absorb the remaining fluctuation in loss experience. However, current regulatory techniques are not sophisticated enough to adjust premium-to-surplus ratio requirements to reflect the greater loss stability provided by aggregate excess coverage.

A summary of the functions or purposes of reinsurance and how well each type of reinsurance serves those purposes is shown in Exhibit 6-12.

Finite Risk Financing Programs. Finite risk reinsurance, which is mentioned as a major category of reinsurance in Exhibit 6-8 is a type of reinsurance whereby the objective is to increase the stated policyholders' surplus of the reinsured. It involves transactions whereby a combination of underwriting, timing, and credit risk is transferred to the reinsurer, with the transfer of underwriting risk limited to a finite amount.

The same concept can also provide risk financing for an organization that is willing to retain a share of the underwriting risk. Thus, finite risk

Exhibit 6-12
Functions of Reinsurance by Type of Reinsurance

	Premium Capacity	Large Line Capacity	Catastrophe Protection
Quota Share	Yes	No	Yes, reduces the amount of catastrophe cover needed
Surplus Share	Yes	Yes	Probably some, but not purchased for this purpose
Per Risk Excess	No	Yes	Possibly, to some extent, but not purchased for this purpose
Catastrophe	No	No	Yes, sole purpose

reinsurance protects a *primary insurer*; finite risk insurance protects a *primary insured*. Under a risk financing insurance program, a primary insurer is the indemnitor, and the noninsurance organization is the indemnitee. In a finite risk reinsurance program, the reinsurer is the indemnitor of a primary insurer who is the indemnitee. In either case, the finite risk financing program enables the entity to gradually stabilize its costs of the accidental losses covered by the program. Finite risk financing allows the indemnitee, in essence, to borrow funds to pay for losses as they occur and then to repay some or all of these funds over several subsequent accounting or policy periods.

Finite risk financing programs typically possess three elements: (1) a finite risk financing contract limit, (2) an exposure fund, and (3) a sharing of the costs of losses between the indemnitor and the indemnitee.[3]

The first element of a finite risk financing program is an overall aggregate contract limit (that is, a "finite risk"). As with any contract of insurance where a premium is paid for a limit of coverage, a contract term must also be stated. A finite risk financing program contract term can be either single- or multi-year, and payment of the contract premium can be arranged to suit the parties. A multi-year premium payment plan reduces fluctuations in the annual costs of risk financing, which is often a significant financial benefit to the indemnitee. The flexibility of this arrangement effectively enables the indemnitor to provide the indemnitee with funds to pay for the indemnitee's losses, but those funds are eventually restored to the indemnitor under an adjustable schedule.

In exchange for providing this limit of coverage, the indemnitor receives from the indemnitee a contract premium, which includes a contracting fee. The net premium, the contract premium less the fee, composes the bulk of the second element of the program, the exposure fund. At any given time, the *exposure fund* consists of the net premium, less any losses that have been paid under the contract, plus any interest income credited to the exposure fund. In contrast to many traditional insurance programs, the interest credited under a finite risk financing program becomes a part of the indemnitee's exposure fund and is therefore available to pay covered losses.

Covered losses reduce the exposure fund only when they are paid. Thus the time value of money is a key factor in any finite risk financing program. The time value of money is the ability of funds to earn interest when invested over time. This time value of money, or earned investment credit, is an integral feature of the exposure fund. Losses may be reported quickly, but the pay out, especially for long-tailed claims, may take years. Only paid losses deplete the exposure fund. Therefore, the longer it takes for losses to be paid, the more interest the exposure fund earns.

The third element common to finite risk financing is the indemnitee's ability to share in favorable underwriting experience under the contract. The indemnitee retains the right to regain possession of any positive exposure fund balance. Both the indemnitor and the indemnitee anticipate that the exposure fund balance will grow over time with the accumulation of interest and with favorable loss experience. If losses paid during the contract period do not exhaust the exposure fund, the indemnitee is entitled to a return of any positive fund balance remaining at the end of the contract. At this time, the indemnitee must also assume all remaining liabilities under the contract.

However, if the indemnitee decides that its best financial decision is not to receive a direct return of the exposure fund balance, other options are available. Because of the flexible nature of finite risk financing programs, the contract can usually be endorsed at almost any time to extend the policy period, to provide additional limits, to reduce or expand the indemnitee's retention if one exists, or to provide coverage not originally included. The indemnitor and the indemnitee can thus agree to rewrite their contract to reflect past experience and current conditions, essentially renegotiating the indemnitor's loan of funds to the indemnitee to finance recovery from the indemnitee's losses.

If the exposure fund balance is exhausted, the indemnitor pays any future covered losses out of its own funds, subject to a maximum equal to the remaining contract limit. These possible payments represent an underwriting loss to the indemnitor resulting from the exposures assumed by the indemnitor when the contract was written. The possibility of such additional loss payments gives finite risk financing programs an essential element of insurance.

Reinsurance Contract Provisions

Because primary insurers and reinsurers are familiar with the procedures for implementing their reinsurance program, detailed reinsurance contract provisions are usually not necessary. In addition, individuals in the business of insurance and reinsurance adhere to a tradition that disputes between primary insurers and reinsurers should, if possible, be settled by arbitration rather than courtroom proceedings. The arbiters are usually insurance and reinsurance professionals experienced in interpreting contracts. As a result, reinsurance contracts are typically rather short in comparison to most other insurance agreements.

Although reinsurance contracts are by no means standardized, most of them contain provisions for essentially the same subjects as primary, excess, and umbrella policies—reinsuring clauses, exclusions, conditions, and coverage periods. The following sections briefly describe the most important provisions.[4]

Reinsuring Provisions. Like any insurance policy, a reinsurance contract must express the intent to shift the financial burden of some losses from the reinsured to the reinsurer. The wording that describes this transfer is usually quite brief in reinsurance contracts. It is often included in a preamble or an opening statement of general intent known as a *business covered or reinsurance clause.* This part of the contract would essentially include a description of the underlying insurance policies being reinsured, a statement about how they are being reinsured (on a pro rata or excess of loss basis), and a citation of the requisite exchange or legal consideration binding the parties.

The intent of the basic reinsuring clause is reinforced by a *retained obligations clause* and by an assumption clause (or cut-through clause or endorsement) if it is chosen. The former provision describes the types and amounts of policyholders' losses the reinsured intends to continue to pay without reinsurance. It is essentially equivalent to a deductible or self-insured retention provision in a primary or excess insurance policy. Only when a loss under a reinsured policy exceeds the reinsured's retained obligations does the reinsurance attach to protect the reinsured against more severe losses.

As mentioned, an assumption endorsement attached to a primary reinsured policy extends the reinsurer's obligations directly to the reinsured's policyholders if the reinsured is financially unable to meet its obligations to the primary policyholders. (Prudent insureds may have more faith in the financial strength of an insurer's reinsurer than in the insurer itself and may be willing to do business only if the primary policy is endorsed with such an assumption clause.) Without this endorsement, any reinsurance proceeds receivable are considered among the insolvent insurer's assets made available to the general pool of the insolvent insurer's creditors. The assumption endorsement thus allows reinsurance proceeds to bypass the liquidation process and to be paid to the insured for covered losses. The reinsurance contract may therefore contain a provision reiterating or summarizing the general requirement of the assumption clause.

The courts have not tested the validity of the assumption clause. Therefore, there is a chance that the liquidator would not allow the payment of funds by the reinsurer to bypass the liquidation process.

Exclusions. Like exclusions in all types of insurance policies, the exclusions in reinsurance contracts delineate the exposures that are not intended to be reinsured. Reinsurance coverage for a reinsured does not have to be as broad as the coverage for a primary insured. Therefore, to the extent that a risk financing program depends on the financial strength of a reinsurer, the risk management professional should confirm the extent of reinsurance coverage.

The selection and wording of the exclusions in a reinsurance contract are negotiated by the reinsured and the reinsurer. The choice and drafting of exclusionary clauses are often part of the reinsurer's underwriting process. Some typical reinsurance contract exclusions deal with the following:

- Classes of insurance that are not included in the reinsurance contract, such as boiler/machinery losses from a reinsurance contract that covers fire and the extended coverage perils.
- Extrahazardous exposures that the premiums paid to the reinsurer (and probably the rate paid by the primary insured) do not cover, such as flood in a property reinsurance contract or, when reinsuring employers' liability, injuries from underground construction work.
- Losses under policies the reinsured has erroneously classified into a class that falls within the scope of the reinsurance contract but, if the policies had been correctly classified, would not be within the scope of the reinsurance.
- Losses that are deemed uninsurable and, therefore, are usually explicitly excluded from the underlying coverage, such as nuclear or war damage or harm intended by the insured. Reinsurance coverage naturally does not apply to any loss the reinsured's policy does not cover. However, if some error or other unusual event negated an exclusion in the reinsured's policy, the reinsurer could still rely on the exclusion in the reinsurance contract.

Conditions. In any insurance or reinsurance contract, the conditions describe the actions one party must take to bind the other party to its obligations under that contract. One party's failure to fulfill a condition relieves the other from its contractual obligations. The principal conditions in most reinsurance contracts relate to premiums and commissions for ceded insurance and losses, to the reporting and adjusting of reinsured losses and claims, to correction of errors and omissions in the reinsurance transaction, to arbitration between the reinsured and the reinsurer, and to cancellation of the reinsurance contract.

Premium/Commission Payments. Just as an insured must regularly pay premiums to an insurer, so must a reinsured make payments to a reinsurer for its coverage. This reinsurance premium, or an initial deposit premium, is normally payable before the reinsurance becomes effective, although the final premium may be adjusted to reflect the reinsurer's loss experience on the coverage. For pro rata reinsurance, the reinsurance premium is usually a predetermined percentage (perhaps varying with the type of exposure) of the original premium paid by the cedent's policyholder. For excess of loss reinsurance, this premium is negotiated by the reinsured and the reinsurer.

With pro rata reinsurance, to offset its reinsurance premiums, a cedent normally receives or is credited with a *ceding commission.* This is intended to reimburse the cedent for its expenses in initially underwriting and issuing insurance to its policyholder. These are expenses that the reinsurer neither faces nor incurs in obtaining business from the cedent. In addition, the cedent may receive or be credited with an additional *contingent commission,* which is, in effect, a reduction of the reinsurance premium, if the reinsurer's loss experience on the ceded insurance is more favorable than anticipated.

Claim/Loss Reporting and Adjustments. As an insurer requires prompt notification of a loss or situation that may cause a loss, so does a reinsurer require prompt notification in order to cover the reinsured portion of a loss. For an excess of loss reinsurer, notification may be required when the loss exceeds a certain percentage of the underlying amount. Prompt notice allows the reinsurer to protect its interests in the loss or claim and to establish appropriate reserves.

Most reinsurance contracts also give the reinsurer the right to participate in adjusting the insured loss, or at least that portion of the loss that is reinsured. Under these circumstances, the reinsurer can often demand a role in managing an insured's loss or claim. However, this right aside, the loss adjustment provisions of a reinsurance contract usually require the reinsurer to abide by the reinsured's loss or claim settlements.

Correction of Errors/Omissions. Reinsurance contracts normally provide that errors, omissions, and inadvertent delays in providing information or paying claims do not relieve the reinsurer or reinsured of commitments under the contract. Such a provision is consistent with the ultimate objective of providing the promised financial protection to insureds. If the reinsurer and reinsured cannot readily rectify any errors, omissions, or delays, either may invoke the arbitration provisions of the reinsurance contract.

Arbitration. For speed and consistency in resolving disputes among themselves, reinsurers and reinsureds usually agree that both have the right to initiate arbitration procedures and that neither may resort to court action before such arbitration has been completed.

Cancellation. Although some reinsurance contracts have a definite policy term, most treaties are written on a *good-until-canceled basis,* giving the reinsured or the reinsurer the power to cancel. Because reinsurance is a particularly complex transaction built on trust, ninety days' written notice by the canceling party is usually required. This notice should give the reinsured enough time to arrange replacement reinsurance.

The most obvious consequence of cancellation is that it relieves the reinsurer of its obligations for losses incurred under policies issued after the reinsurance has been canceled. The issue of cancellation becomes more ambiguous with respect to losses stemming from events covered by policies reinsured before the reinsurance contract was canceled. For instance, is the reinsurer obliged for losses that were incurred before, but not reported to the insurer or reinsurer until after, cancellation?

Because of these problems, the reinsurance contract should detail any remaining coverage obligations of the reinsurer. It should also specify the extent of the reinsurer's duties to return to the reinsured any unearned reinsurance premiums on policies for which the reinsurer's continuing obligations have been reduced or terminated.

SUMMARY

To obtain higher or broader limits of insurance protection than primary insurance can provide, many risk financing programs use excess insurance. This can be straight excess coverage or umbrella coverage. Moreover, a risk financing plan may require more underwriting capacity than any one insurer can provide on its own. Therefore, both a strong risk financing program and the ability of an insurer to provide protection rely on the reinsurance arrangements that distribute policyholders' loss exposures throughout the insurance and reinsurance markets. A risk management professional must not only build a "wall" of financial protection for an organization by using self-insured retentions, primary insurance, straight excess coverages, and umbrella policies, but must also be aware of the reinsurance arrangements that back these coverages.

The two basic types of excess insurance described in this text are straight excess insurance and umbrella insurance. Straight excess insurance applies only over primary insurance and provides coverage that is never broader, but can be more restrictive, than this primary insurance. Umbrella insurance applies as excess over primary insurance and as primary or "drop-down" insurance for exposures not covered by the first layer of primary insurance. Umbrella insurance is more suited to high limits of broad coverage for liability exposures than to property exposures, which can be adequately covered by straight excess insurance.

The coverage provided by primary, straight excess, and umbrella insurance can be described in terms of the provisions in a policy, which include declarations, insuring agreements, exclusions, conditions, and specifications of policy periods. To avoid gaps and overlaps in coverage, a risk management professional must be sure that the policies dovetail with one another in terms of interests, exposures, perils, losses, and amounts.

Primary, straight excess, and umbrella insurance arrangements are directly made between an organization and its insurers; but as mentioned, the strength of these arrangements will likely depend on the insurers' reinsurance contracts. In addition, the risk management professional may deal directly with a reinsurer when the reinsurer takes the place of any insolvent ceding insurer as allowed by an assumption endorsement; when the reinsurer provides protection that is fronted by a commercial or captive insurer; or when the reinsurer provides coverage for a captive insurer or pool in which the insured organization participates.

To ensure that reinsurance arrangements fit an organization's needs, the risk management professional should know what type of reinsurance is provided. It may be treaty reinsurance, which applies to all policies that fall within the scope of the treaty, or facultative reinsurance, which only applies to a single policy. The risk management professional should also know the extent to which reinsurance is provided. This can be through pro rata reinsurance of all covered losses or excess of loss reinsurance of extremely large losses on a per-risk, per-occurrence, or aggregate-excess basis. An understanding of these arrangements allows the risk management professional to determine if the insurer can be counted on to finance the organization's recovery from extremely large losses.

Chapter Notes

1. Bernard L. Webb, J. J. Launie, Willis Park Rokes, Norman A. Baglini, *Insurance Company Operations,* 3rd ed. (Malvern, PA: American Institute for Property and Liability Underwriters, 1984), vol. 1, pp. 322-331.
2. Bernard L. Webb, Howard N. Anderson, John A. Cookman, and Peter R. Kensicki, *Principles of Reinsurance* (Malvern, PA: American Institute for Property and Liability Underwriters, 1990), vol. 1, pp. 147-174.
3. Joseph Sarosi, "Finite Risk—A Risk Financing Alternative," *Public Risk,* vol. 6, no. 1, January 1992, pp. 9-12.
4. Robert W. Strain, *Reinsurance* (New York: The College of Insurance, 1980), pp. 79-116.

CHAPTER 7

Using Noninsurance Transfers

The law of contracts gives contracting parties many opportunities to decide how to deal with losses that may affect one or more of them as they carry out their agreement. They may agree, for example, that one party will reimburse another for its loss. Alternatively, they may agree that one party will undertake an activity (and with it the resulting loss exposures) that another party would normally perform. Another possible arrangement is that one or more of the parties involved will waive rights to sue the other(s) for either breach of contract or some tort related to the activity covered by the contract. This chapter analyzes such contracts—contractual transfers in which no party acts as an insurer, and in which the parties shift exposures to potential loss or the financial burden of paying for actual losses.

A brief hypothetical scenario illustrates the various categories of these contractual transfers. The remainder of the chapter then uses some of the details in this scenario to illustrate the relevant principles.

The transferees in the risk-shifting contracts in this chapter do not act as insurers. Instead, the transferees agree to perform actions that either shift some of the transferors' (1) *exposures* to loss that *may* occur in the future or (2) cost of financing recovery from *losses* that *have* already occurred. From a transferor's perspective, the first noninsurance transfer is a means of risk control because it rids the transferor of a loss exposure, or some *possibility* of loss. The second transfer is risk financing because it provides the transferor with a source of funds to finance recovery from an *actual* loss. When the transfer changes neither the frequency nor the severity of potential losses, but only who pays for losses when they occur, then the transfer involves only risk financing, not risk control.

AN ILLUSTRATIVE SCENARIO

Peter Builder, who for twenty years has bought land near urban areas to develop as shopping centers and shopping malls, is considering purchasing a sixty-acre tract from Ms. Cellar, a widow. Peter is aware that a major aquifer that provides water for a nearby town lies beneath Ms. Cellar's land. Constructing a mall on this property may disrupt the aquifer and interfere with the townspeople's common law water rights. Peter, realizing that any interference with the natural flow of this water may subject him to personal liability, is reluctant to purchase the tract as an individual. He creates Terra Corporation, which he, his wife and children, and several close business associates own, and to which Ms. Cellar sells the tract at a favorable price. Terra mortgages the land, its principal asset, to raise funds, and then lends the money to Peter Builder to finance the development of another "Peterbuilt" mall on the land.

Peter Builder is not sure how or if any excavation and landscaping activities will change the natural flow of the aquifer. He decides to subcontract the excavation and landscaping to Digger Phelps, Inc., an earth-moving contractor, specifying that only Digger's employees will perform this work. Their contract also provides that Digger Phelps will reimburse Terra for the cost of replacing or repairing any Terra structures damaged by Digger's equipment or personnel during the landscaping and excavating. Peter Builder is less than fully confident of Digger's reliability and ability to do the work and asks Digger's father, an old friend of Peter's who preceded Digger in the business, for a guarantee that the elder Phelps will complete the excavation if Digger does not.

As the shopping mall is developed, the newly constructed buildings become Terra's property. Terra leases them to various business people, including Lester E. Hassle, principal stockholder of Less Hassle Bank, which has seven state-chartered branches. Many merchants are eager to become tenants in Peterbuilt Mall and willingly agree to pay premium rents. They also agree in their leases not to sue Terra or any of its stockholders for any harm they may suffer because of any change in the natural condition of the land on which the mall is built or because of any change in the surface or subsurface condition of the land. They further commit themselves to hold harmless both Terra and the Builder family from any similar claims by customers, employees, occupants, or other users of their leased premises. Peter Builder also leases an office for himself and his staff, but he does not agree explicitly to hold Terra, himself, and his family harmless from others' claims. No individual or organization can hold itself harmless.

Each tenant also agrees to have a *waiver of subrogation* clause in each of its insurance contracts, wherever possible, for the benefit of Terra and the Builder family. Because of these waivers, no tenant's insurer is likely to sue Terra or the family to recover funds that the insurer may pay as indemnity for losses for which Terra or the family may be responsible.

Illustrations in the Scenario

The Peterbuilt Mall scenario introduces a number of risk control and risk financing contractual transfers, not involving insurance, that this chapter will analyze.

Examples of Risk Control Transfers. Risk control transfers shift an exposure from the transferor to transferee before the loss occurs. Any loss from such an exposure is then the transferee's responsibility. The scenario described above illustrates the following contractual transfers for risk control:

- *Incorporation.* Legally, a corporation is a person distinct from its shareholders and is, in the absence of fraud or overriding concerns for justice, solely responsible for its own wrongs (including those of its agents). As a result, by acting through Terra rather than as an individual, Peter Builder has shifted to Terra many of the liabilities that would otherwise fall upon him. There is also a transfer to the corporation's creditors of losses incurred when the company's assets are insufficient to pay debts and claims. Furthermore, acting through Terra insulates the family's assets from claims arising from any wrongs for which the corporation may be liable. This insulation is effective unless a court later determines that Terra is merely an *alter ego* for Builder; that is, a court could find that the corporation is really nothing more than Builder himself operating in the guise of a corporation.
- *Leases.* The owner of real property may be liable for any harm done to others because of the unsafe general condition of that property. A lessee, however, usually cannot be held liable to those harmed unless the harm arises from a condition the lessee has introduced to the leased property or unless the lessee has assumed liability under an *exculpatory agreement* excusing the lessor from liability. Thus, the owner of property can shift loss exposures inherent in that ownership, such as potential liability for altering an aquifer's course, by first selling the property to another and then leasing it back from the new "owner."

In the preceding scenario, Peter Builder probably has avoided personal liability as an owner of the tract by (1) having Terra buy the ground and (2) renting office space in the mall. Similarly, Lester E. Hassle and the other business occupants of the mall are only lessees and are, therefore, insulated from the common law liability that attaches to ownership of real property. Just as "ownership has its special rewards," so does it carry its special loss exposures. Many, but not all, of these exposures can be shifted by shifting ownership.

- *Subcontracts.* All activities present loss exposures for those who perform those activities. Peter Builder, recognizing that the initial landscaping and excavation work could be hazardous, contracted with Digger Phelps to do this work. Consequently, Digger's employees (not Peter's) are exposed to injury, and Digger (not Peter) may be liable for any changes the excavation makes in the natural flow of the aquifer. Unless Peter was somehow negligent or otherwise at fault in selecting Digger or supervising his work, he would incur no liability from the excavating.
- *Surety and Guaranty Agreements.* A surety is a person or organization that guarantees to one party to a contract that another party to that contract will perform as promised. *Personal suretyship* has a long history, dating back to ancient times, and often involves relatives and friends helping each other. *Corporate suretyship,* on the other hand, arose to meet the demands of growing modern economies and is a business in itself. Corporate sureties are much more common today than personal sureties. The surety is typically not a party to the contract.

In the scenario, Digger Phelps' father acted as a surety in guaranteeing to Peter Builder that Digger would complete the excavation work as promised in the contract. In the language of suretyship Digger is the *principal* or ***obligor*** (the party obligated) and Peter Builder is the ***obligee*** (the beneficiary or party to whom the contractual obligation guaranteed by the surety is owed).

The surety promises to fulfill the principal's promise if the principal is not able or willing to do so. The surety, by taking some action other than just paying the obligee, can protect the obligee by assuming the burden for potential loss. For this reason, suretyship and guaranty agreements are, in principle, contractual transfers for risk control. In practice, however, the surety usually carries out its guarantee by paying another party to perform the principal's promise. For example, Digger's father, who is now retired, would probably hire a landscaper who is active in the business to finish Digger's work rather than finish it himself. Even if Digger's father acts as a surety by paying someone else to do the work, completion of the work still benefits the surety. It is not a payment to or on behalf of the obligee and thus is not risk financing for the obligee.

The father's right, as surety, to complete Digger's unfinished work does not violate the contract provision that only Digger's employees work on the land. The major purpose of the original limitation was to preclude Digger from subcontracting to someone even less competent—a limit designed to protect Terra. However, if Digger breaches his promise to perform, the only real protection for Terra is to have someone equally competent complete the work.

- *Waiver Agreements.* A waiver is an informed relinquishment of a known legal right. Through the waivers in Les Hassle's and the other mall tenants' contracts, these people relinquished their rights to sue the Builder family and Terra. Waivers remove a potential liability from those who could be held responsible for harm. Via their waivers, the mall tenants have excused Peter Builder and the others from potential liability for harm to them.

Examples of Risk Financing Transfers. Risk financing contractual transfers shift to the transferee the financial burden of restoring losses that have already struck the transferor. If the transferee fails to provide the compensation the contract calls for, the burden of the loss remains with the transferor and has not been effectively transferred. The scenario illustrates the following contractual transfers for risk financing:

- *Indemnity Agreements.* Under an indemnity agreement, one party to a contract, the *indemnitor,* agrees to pay another, the *indemnitee,* if the latter suffers a specified type of loss. For example, Digger Phelps, in his contract with Terra, agreed to pay the corporation the cost of replacing or repairing any structures damaged by his equipment or employees while landscaping or excavating.
- *Hold Harmless Agreements.* A hold harmless agreement is a commitment made by one party to a second party to assume responsibility for legal claims that may be brought against the second party because of activities covered by the contract. For example, as part of their leases, the mall tenants agreed to hold Terra and the Builder family harmless from suits that might be brought against them by persons using each tenant's leased premises. In this context, holding harmless usually entails both providing legal defense for and paying any settlement or verdicts on behalf of the transferor—here, Terra or the Builders. Hold harmless agreements are a special type of indemnity agreement and deal only with specified activities.

Risk Control Versus Risk Financing. Through the four contractual transfers for risk control—incorporation, leases, subcontracts, and waiver agreements—the shifting of a loss exposure from a transferor to a transferee (1) rids the transferor of most of the possibility of suffering any loss from the transferred exposure and (2) creates a duty for the transferee to protect the transferor from loss by doing something other than paying money to (or on behalf of) the transferor.

In contrast, in the two contractual transfers for risk financing—indemnity agreements and hold harmless agreements—the loss exposure is not shifted from the transferor to the transferee. Only the financial burden of losses is shifted. Moreover, the transferee's duty is to pay money to (or on behalf of) the transferor after the transferor has suffered some loss. Thus, although a contractual transfer for risk control makes it very unlikely that the transferor will suffer any loss, a contractual transfer for risk financing becomes operative only after the transferee has suffered loss. The transferor is then entitled to receive, or have paid on its behalf, money that indemnifies the transferor for the loss. If the transferee is unable or unwilling to provide the required funds, the financial burden of the loss remains with the transferor.

Generalizing From the Scenario

The Peterbuilt Mall scenario illustrates the general truth that activity implies risk. Even a seemingly passive activity such as owning the properties on which Terra builds exposes the mall owner to possible loss. An organization's choice of activity or asset results in its assumption of the exposures to accidental loss that accompany that activity or asset. How an organization deals with loss exposures so that it (or those it serves) can benefit is a challenge to risk management.

One obvious option is to avoid assets or activities that are so risky that the associated accidental or business losses appear to outweigh the benefits. There are, however, two significant difficulties in this approach. First, losses and benefits from untried projects can be extremely difficult to forecast. Second, some exposures (such as those associated with natural disasters, hiring employees, or using motor vehicles) may be very difficult to avoid completely.

When avoiding assets or activities is either inadvisable or unfeasible, the creative use of contracts provides an organization with many options for coping with the loss exposures inherent in the activities and assets. The following two sections describe different types of contracts and how they are used.

Insurance Versus Noninsurance Transfers. Insurance contracts allow an organization to transfer many of the financial consequences of accidental losses. Under an insurance transfer, the insurer/

transferee is the indemnitor (the provider of indemnity or other benefits) and the insured/transferor is the indemnitee (the recipient of the benefits). An insurance contract thus obligates an insurer to pay money or other benefits to (or on behalf of) an insured under circumstances specified in the contract. These circumstances generally relate to the occurrence of an accidental loss that qualifies as an insured event and fulfills the policy's pertinent conditions.

Corresponding to the insurer's contractual obligation or duty, the insured has the contractual right to receive (or to have provided on its behalf) indemnity or other benefits under the same circumstances that the insurer has the duty to provide them.

The typical insurance policy, therefore, creates certain conditional duties for one contracting party and correlative conditional rights for the other. Because these duties and rights pertain to financing recovery from accidental losses, and because exercising these rights and duties usually transfers the financial burden of loss, an insurance policy can be called a contractual transfer for risk financing. Because the transferee is an insurer, this transfer could also be called a contractual insurance transfer. The last term, however, is redundant, and "insurance" is more convenient and adequately descriptive.

Noninsurance transfers differ from insurance in that the transferee under a noninsurance transfer does not act as an insurer. The transferee does not have the objective of pooling others' loss exposures and becoming a transferee in order to make a profit. Under a noninsurance transfer the transferee accepts the exposure to loss or the financial burden of the transferor's actual losses as an incidental aspect of another business transaction. The transferee expects to profit from this transaction, and not from the risk transfer. Insurers, however, can be parties to noninsurance contractual transfers. For example, an insurer could be managing the construction of the malls that Peter Builder is erecting, and this insurer could be a transferor just as Peter is in the preceding scenario. In this situation, however, the fact that the building owner is an insurer would be only coincidental to the owner's status as a transferor.

Risk Control Transfers Versus Risk Financing Transfers. As shown by the various agreements in the Peter Builder scenario, a contract can effectively (1) create rights and duties that relate to risk control and risk financing and (2) establish transferees other than insurers. Because of (1) the common law right to make contracts, (2) the contract-drafting skill of risk management professionals, lawyers, and other business executives, and (3) constant changes in business practices, there can be no permanent catalog of all types of noninsurance contracts and contract provisions. It is possible, however, to classify

Exhibit 7-1
Families of Contractual Transfers: Risk Control and Risk Financing

Characteristic	Risk Control Transfer	Risk Financing Transfer
Subject of transfer	Exposure to loss (possibility of loss)	Financial burden of actual loss
Timing of transfer	Before transferor's loss	After transferor's loss
Effect of transferee's nonperformance	Loss falls on transferee	Loss falls on transferor (never truly transferred)
Frequent examples	Incorporation Lease Subcontract waivers Exculpatory agreements Surety agreements	Indemnity agreements (including insurance) Hold harmless agreements

these agreements into two large categories, risk control transfers and risk financing transfers. *Risk control transfers* include incorporations, leases, subcontracts, surety agreements, and waivers. *Risk financing transfers* include indemnity and hold harmless agreements. Exhibit 7-1 summarizes the significant differences between these two categories of contractual transfers.

In noninsurance contractual transfers for risk control and risk financing, the contract is generally formed before any loss occurs. However, because risk control transfers shift exposures to loss rather than the financial burdens of an actual loss, a risk control transfer becomes effective only when the transferee actually performs the action that rids the transferor of a loss exposure. For example, in the Peterbuilt Mall case, Peter Builder may choose to have the elder Phelps guarantee that, if Digger cannot complete the excavation, the elder Phelps will. However, Peter Builder cannot be certain that this guarantee effectively transfers the risk of noncompletion until the elder Phelps has actually completed the work.

In contrast, risk financing transfers provide the transferor with protection only after the funds to restore a loss are paid over. Until a loss has occurred, the transferor cannot be certain that the transferee will pay. If the transferee fails to provide the expected funds, the transferor receives no protection and has never truly transferred the financial burden of the loss to the transferee. For example, Peter Builder and Terra have Digger Phelps' promise of reimbursement for any damage Phelps' activities may do to Terra's structures, but they cannot be sure of this protection until Phelps' employees have damaged a Terra building and Phelps has actually paid for the damage.

Another critical difference between a risk control and a risk financing transfer becomes apparent when a transferee becomes bankrupt or otherwise unable to perform the terms of the contractual transfer. In a risk financing transfer, a bankrupt transferee provides no protection to the transferor, who must therefore pay for its own accidental loss. In a risk control transfer, however, a bankrupt or uncooperative transferee remains responsible for its own accidental losses, leaving the transferor's protection intact.

TYPES OF CONTRACTUAL TRANSFERS

This section examines the more frequent examples of each of the risk control and risk financing contractual transfers listed at the bottom of Exhibit 7-1. (This chapter treats commercial insurance only in passing to clarify how other transfer mechanisms differ from it.) In the absence of transfers for risk control or risk financing, common law and state and federal statutes apportion risks of loss among the parties to a business transaction. In very broad terms, an organization or individual that owns property must bear the losses that arise from that ownership. Similarly, an organization or individual that engages in an activity must bear the losses generated by that activity for which it is legally responsible. However, common law and many state and federal statutes also permit the parties to a business agreement to make different contractual arrangements for dealing with exposures to loss or the financial burden of actual losses. These agreements change the otherwise applicable apportionments of loss exposures or actual losses.

As stated previously, the two general types, or families, of contractual transfers are risk control transfers and risk financing trans fers. Risk control transfers include incorporation, leasing, subcontracting, suretyship, and waivers. Risk financing transfers include insurance, indemnity agreements among noninsurers, and hold harmless agreements.

Risk Control Transfers

Many risk management professionals are experienced in insurance or financial management and they are accustomed to dealing with contracts for restoring actual losses. These risk management professionals may also find that risk control transfer contracts are new to them because most of these documents traditionally have been handled by departments other than risk management. For example, some of these professionals may not have handled leases and written agreements. In these contracts parties shift exposures to possible losses by committing themselves to actions rather than by committing money to rectify a potential loss. Noninsurance contractual transfers for risk control have long been important, if not fully recognized, risk management tools.

Incorporation. The business corporation originated in fourteenth and fifteenth century Europe, when various countries enacted statutes permitting individuals to establish private businesses.[1] The corporation enabled business leaders to accumulate capital by taking small amounts from many individuals or firms in exchange for proportional shares in the corporation. Incorporation permitted a group of individuals to start a business that would otherwise have required more capital or entailed more risk than any individual or small group would have been willing or able to venture. Examples of activities that incorporation facilitated included exploring unknown territories, developing new technologies, and founding very large financial institutions. To encourage individuals and small businesses to participate in corporate activities, the statutes authorizing private corporations included a crucial provision limiting each stockholder's potential loss: no stockholder could lose more than the value of the shares that the stockholder owned. Thus, each stockholder's personal assets or holdings in other businesses were insulated from any possible losses in the corporate venture.

Modern incorporation statutes in the United States, as well as most western countries, provide similar stockholder protection. In the absence of fraud or other intentional wrongs by the founding stockholders, the most a corporation can lose in either a business venture or because of an accident or lawsuit is the value of that corporation's assets. Consequently, any one stockholder's maximum financial loss is the value of that stockholder's shares. If the corporation has relatively little capital, the amount the corporation (and thus any one of its stockholders) can lose is correspondingly limited.

The principle of incorporation thus allows an entrepreneur to organize various business enterprises so that a separate corporation conducts each one of them. In doing so, the risk control technique of *segregation* is applied; that is, the "divisions" between exposure units become the legal boundaries of separate corporations. In this way, the founder(s) of a business can limit loss potentials arising from business risks, accidental losses, or liability claims. Limiting potential liability losses is an important reason why, for instance, an owner of several taxicabs or trucks often forms a separate corporation according to the activities of each vehicle. The individual entrepreneur thus shifts to the corporation exposures that would otherwise threaten personal finances, while the corporation itself is exposed to loss no greater than its assets. Similarly, stockholders can largely control the total value of a corporation's assets by contributing or withdrawing capital to or from the enterprise. The corporation, as legally separate from any of its stockholders, can serve as a transferee for exposures that individual stockholders might otherwise face. As a transferee, and in exchange for the capital contributed by one or more stockholders, every corporation agrees to carry out the business activities for which it has been organized.

The protective legal barrier between a corporation's assets and activities and those of each of its stockholders is particularly clear with respect to accidental physical damage to the corporation's assets or net income losses from interruption of its business. This barrier, however, can sometimes be penetrated. For example, courts may seek to "pierce the corporate veil" by attacking a major managing stockholder's personal assets. This can be done in cases involving liability claims against the corporation where (1) corporate assets appear to have been manipulated in order to frustrate creditors of a corporation seeking bankruptcy protection or (2) the corporate form appears to mask the personal wrongs of a predominant stockholder or major executive. In these cases, the courts often place more importance on compensating those harmed by the corporation than on maintaining the usual separation between corporate property and stockholders' personal assets.

Those who do business with small corporations, and thus regularly become their creditors, are aware of the limited personal liability of a corporation's owners. Therefore, to preserve their access to the personal assets of these stockholders, creditors frequently require that the corporate owners personally cosign with the corporation all contracts, notes, and other credit obligations. In effect, this action "desegregates" corporate and personal finances and liability. In doing so, it undercuts the usual protection an owner acquires by the risk transfer mechanism of incorporation. It also undercuts the usual protection a corporation acquires by statutes providing that the most the owners of a corporation can lose is the value of their investments in that corporation.

The corporation thus becomes equivalent to a partner or proprietor with respect to owners' personal liability. However, these types of arrangements with creditors do not defeat the advantages of corporate liability with respect to obligations arising out of tort claims. It should also be noted that there are several forms of organization other than the joint stock, limited liability corporation, presenting a wide range of options with regard to limitation or nonlimitation of liability.

Leasing. The law separates ownership of property—that collection of rights and duties of those who are said to "own" property—into many separate "bundles," or groups of rights and duties. One important bundle is the right to occupy or use real or personal property for a period between two specified points in time. This right is only a portion of an owner's (*lessor's*) right to occupy and use this property without a time limit. This more limited right is known as a *leasehold,* under which the *lessee* may occupy or use the real or personal property for the period specified in the contract establishing the leasehold. This contract is commonly called a *lease.* Before and after a leasehold is in effect, the right to occupy or use the property remains with the owner.

Certain obligations and exposures to loss accompany the ownership of property, but do not accompany its use or occupancy. Some of these obligations are taxes, loss from physical destruction of the property or its obsolescence, and liability for dangerous conditions of or on the property. A *tenant* (or lessee) does not suffer any of these losses unless (1) the lease obligates the lessee to return the property to the lessor in the same condition at the end of the lease as at its beginning or (2) the lessee alone has caused a dangerous condition that has harmed others. If the property occupied or used by a lessee is damaged or destroyed during the term of a lease, the lessee's only loss may be the use of the property for the remaining term of the lease. The lessee can often recover this loss simply by leasing other substitute property. The lessor, however, loses the rental value of the property.

By leasing property rather than owning it, a lessee eliminates the exposure to loss of the value of the entire property, as well as much of the potential liability for harm to others resulting from dangerous property conditions. By only leasing rather than owning a particular item of property, an organization usually can leave these exposures with the owner. If an organization already owns some property, it can shift the associated exposures by selling the property while retaining the right to occupy or use it under a lease with the new owner. This transaction is known as a sale-and-lease-back arrangement, which also allows the former owner of property to convert its equity into cash. The new owner is often a corporation or other organization created or selected by the former property owner primarily for these risk-shifting and financing purposes. The new owner may even be a real estate management firm, more able than the former owner to control or retain losses related to property ownership. If fraud is not involved, courts will usually uphold such a transfer (except when there were dangerous conditions on the property that were apparent before the property was sold and leased back).

Because the basic law of leaseholds leaves the lessor, and permanent property owner, with obligations and loss exposures related to property ownership, the lease agreement need not specify that the lessee is relieved of these obligations and exposures. This arrangement is implicit in common law. Thus, many leases are silent with respect to exposures to accidental loss. In fact, most lease provisions that mention loss exposures refer to obligations the lessee would not otherwise have with respect to preventing or paying for accidental losses. For example, lease agreements for real property often specify that the lessee will return the property to the lessor in its pre-lease condition with only "fire, flood, and ordinary wear and tear excepted." This wording transfers to the lessee the exposure to and financial responsibility for damage or destruction of the property by all perils other than those excepted. The lessor therefore retains or agrees to otherwise finance losses from fire, flood, and ordinary wear and tear.

A lease of all or part of a building may give the tenant the right to alter the leased space for personal or business purposes, such as conducting a manufacturing operation or displaying merchandise for retail sale. The lease should specify whether the alterations made by the tenant, often called *improvements and betterments,* become the property of the lessor or remain the property of the lessee. If the lease agreement does not stipulate otherwise, permanently attached improvements and betterments made by the lessee, or "irremovable" improvements such as display windows or wide doorways, become the lessor's property.

Improvements and betterments not permanently attached, or "removable" improvements such as display cases, carpets, and many lighting fixtures, remain the property of the lessee, who may remove them at any time. A lease often obligates a lessor to repair or replace permanently attached improvements and betterments if they are damaged or destroyed during the leasehold of the lessee who installed them. Otherwise, it is usual for the lessor and the lessee to bear any losses to those improvements and betterments that are their respective property.

The test for removability is not whether the improvements and betterments in question are attached to the structure, but whether they can be taken out of the structure without significantly and permanently damaging it. This test differs from the usual criterion in insurance that considers any property attached to a structure to be part of that structure and not part of its contents. For example, in insurance contract interpretation, wall-to-wall carpeting is part of a structure because it is usually attached to the structure at the carpet's edge. Under a lease, however, such carpeting would typically be a removable improvement because it can be taken up without damaging the underlying floor. In contrast, a solid stone mosaic floor would be a permanent part of a building for insurance and lease purposes because its removal would damage the building.

Contracting for Services. An individual or organization that performs a particular activity is generally held primarily responsible for any losses generated by that activity. Thus, an organization not wishing to undertake the loss exposures associated with any given activity can contract with another organization to perform it. For example, Peter Builder's contracting the excavation and landscaping work with Digger Phelps has the result that Digger's machinery and employees, not Terra's, are exposed to any damage and injury from this work. In general, any property, net income, or personnel loss exposure associated with an activity can be transferred successfully in this way, provided the transfer agreement meets the legal requirements for a fairly bargained, clearly stated shift of both the loss exposures and the actual losses associated with that activity. In this case, both the exposure to these losses and the burden of financing recovery from them rests on the subcontractor.

The situation is somewhat different with the *liability* exposures associated with a particular activity. They are not transferred so easily, especially with respect to harm to third parties. For example, if negligence on the part of Digger's employees created a hazard (perhaps a large, unguarded hole) that caused injury to a pedestrian, the employees and Digger would clearly be primarily liable. However, the injured person would probably sue Terra as the responsible party for the general condition of the land it owned.

Because the law seeks to provide compensation to those who are injured, courts tend to ignore contractual "side agreements" that would frustrate the otherwise valid claims brought by outside parties. For example, a pedestrian falling into a hole left by Digger's employees could probably obtain at least a court hearing, if not a trial, based on the contention that Terra was negligent in selecting Phelps as a subcontractor or in failing to supervise the subcontractor's work properly. Furthermore, aside from any contracts between Terra and Digger, the pedestrian could probably sue Terra for failure to maintain its land in safe condition.

Despite the difficulty of "subcontracting away" liability exposures, this method is frequently used to shift exposures to organizations better able to prevent or to finance recovery from losses generated by particular activities. Thus, many organizations normally contract with specialty firms not only for building construction projects, but also for maintenance activities and transportation of raw materials and finished products. Another use of subcontracting for shifting loss exposures is the currently widespread practice of contracting for temporary employees from agencies who are the direct employers of the temporary workers. This technique allows the contractor to leave with the agency the loss exposures associated with personnel, such as resignation and retirement. The contracting organization thus receives most of the benefits of temporary labor without assuming all the associated employee benefits exposures.

The performance of each of these contracted activities requires equipment or skills often unrelated to an organization's primary productive activities, equipment, and expertise. The organization may, therefore, obtain these services more cheaply and reliably through an outside source whose special skills and resources also help to perform specified tasks more safely. In addition, because these activities are the contractor's primary business, a competent contractor should be able to arrange more reliable and less expensive risk financing for the losses arising from the activities than other organizations that do not specialize in these activities.

Although this contractual transfer for risk control is often called subcontracting, it is not necessary for the transferor to be an independent contractor and the transferee to be technically a subcontractor. Any contract engaging another party to perform a service and, implicitly, to assume the loss exposures associated with that service can be a valid application of this technique. Historically, however, this shifting of exposures was pioneered principally by general construction contractors who, not wishing to assume the exposures involved in such activities as excavation or electrical wiring, hired subcontractors for this work. The general contractor thus became the transferor and the subcontractor became the transferee. Thus, by common practice, the transferee became known as a subcontractor.

Suretyship and Guaranty Agreements. A *surety* is a person or organization that guarantees to one party to a contract (the *obligee*) that another party (the *principal* or *obligor*) will perform as promised. The surety's commitment is to perform or to hire an outside party to perform in the principal's place as soon as the principal's failure or inability to perform becomes clear and the obligee demands performance from the surety. A *surety agreement* thus protects the obligee by providing a second source of performance. If the principal does not perform or pay as promised, the surety promises to do so.[2]

Similarly, under a *guaranty contract*, an obligee to whom a promise has been made can also look to a *guarantor* for performance. However, unlike a surety, a guarantor is obligated to perform only after the obligee has made every reasonable and legal effort to compel the principal's performance. A surety agreement, on the other hand, permits the obligee to demand performance of the surety as soon as the principal's first substantial failure to perform becomes apparent. Thus, a guarantee contract provides the obligee with an alternative to a surety agreement as a means of guaranteeing the performance of a promise.

Both agreements allow the obligee to practice a form of segregating exposures that is somewhat comparable to having standby replacement machinery. If the principal does not perform, the obligee may turn to the surety or guarantor for performance.

Another important difference between the two agreements is that a guaranty contract is a two-party agreement between the guarantor and the obligee. It is separate from the agreement between the obligee and the principal. Under a surety agreement, the original promise of the principal is also the promise of the surety. Under a guaranty agreement, the guarantor's promise should parallel, but may differ in some details from, the principal's promise to the obligee. As a consequence, a guarantor is not as precisely bound as a surety by the terms of the contract containing the principal's promise to the obligee.

Under suretyship law, if the principal may rightfully refuse to perform, the surety is also released from performance. This may occur if the underlying promise was secured through fraud or if the basic contract between the principal and obligee was otherwise defective. Whether a guarantor is released under similar circumstances depends on the wording of the separate guaranty contract. Thus, unlike a surety, a guarantor may not be released from its promise to the obligee by any rule of contract law that might release a principal or surety from a promise to the obligee. As mentioned below, the surety may have some further independent defenses relieving the surety of the obligation to perform.

Like other types of noninsurance contractual transfers, a surety agreement also differs from most insurance contracts in two ways:

1. The surety's primary obligation is to perform as promised for the obligee, not to pay money to compensate the obligee for the principal's breach of contract.
2. A surety agreement is a three-party contract; virtually all insurance policies are two-party contracts.

Some insurers routinely function as and even specialize in being sureties. These insurers are examples of corporate rather than personal suretyship, from which most of the laws of suretyship and guaranty originated. Insurers that issue performance bonds assuring performance of an obligation are acting as sureties, not as insurers. However, insurance written against employee dishonesty, though often termed *fidelity bonds,* is a two-party contract between the employer and the insurer. Dishonest employees of the insured are not direct parties to this insurance arrangement.

A surety has a number of rights to protect it against sustaining loss from the principal's misconduct or collusion between the principal and the obligee to the surety's detriment. These rights include exoneration, subrogation, indemnity, and contribution.

The doctrine of *exoneration* applies if the obligee does not protect its rights against the principal but passively relies upon the surety. For example, if the principal falls behind schedule or indicates an intention not to perform as promised, and if the obligee then fails to preserve its rights against the principal, the surety is released or exonerated from liability to the extent that the surety can show that the obligee's inaction increased the surety's loss or otherwise harmed the surety. As previously explained, an obligee is entitled to the surety's protection as soon as the principal is in breach, but the obligee must not then release the principal from the consequences of its nonperformance.

Under doctrines of *subrogation,* a surety that fulfills a principal's promise to an obligee is entitled to the same payment the principal would have received. Thus, if a surety completes construction of a building on which a principal has defaulted, then the obligee (the building owner) must pay the surety for the portion of the work completed on the same basis that it would have paid the defaulting contractor. The initial contractor's failure to carry out its promise does not relieve the obligee of paying for the work because this would be an undue benefit to the obligee. The obligee's payment to the surety at the contracted price thus promotes equity and provides a good example of a risk control transfer in that it involves a commitment to *act,* not to pay.

Indemnity applies when a surety expends effort or money to fulfill the principal's promise to the obligee. Under these circumstances the surety can proceed directly against the principal to recover the fair price of its effort or any funds it has paid to the obligee as compensation for the principal's inaction. The principal must then indemnify the surety for the costs of fulfilling the promise.

Contribution comes into play if there are two or more sureties. The basic law of suretyship obligates each surety to perform in full on the principal's behalf. If necessary, each must carry out the entire promise to the obligee. Among themselves, however, each surety is liable only for a proportionate share of the cost of carrying out the promise. Accordingly, any one surety is entitled to compensation from each of the others so that each surety ultimately shares a prorated portion of the total cost of fulfilling the principal's promise.

As mentioned, because a surety's contractual commitment is the same as the principal's, any justification (or legal defense) for nonperformance that releases the principal from the underlying contract also releases the surety. The surety can also be legally released under the following three circumstances:

1. If the suretyship agreement is invalid. This can occur, for example, if the surety's promise was obtained by fraud or if the surety did not receive adequate legal consideration (anything of value) in exchange for its promise.
2. If the obligee releases the principal from the contract. If this

happens, the surety is also released because holding the surety while excusing the obligee can clearly lead to collusion against the surety.

3. If the original contract is modified without the surety's consent. Because the surety's promise is the same as the principal's, any attempt by the obligee and principal to alter—and especially to make more demanding—the principal's commitments releases the surety from its original commitment.

The law of suretyship and guaranty agreements is much more complex than the summary explanation in this section. A comprehensive treatment of the subject is the Associate in Fidelity and Surety Bonding (AFSB) Program, intended for specialists in this field. Portions of the preceding discussion about suretyship also apply to guaranty contracts. Because many organizations become involved in surety and guaranty agreements, a risk management professional should be aware of the advantages these contracts provide for additional support for promises, thus reducing the likelihood that one party to a contract will suffer loss because of another's breach. Any organization should seek legal counsel regarding the choice or entry into surety or guaranty agreements.

Waivers. All individuals and organizations are subject to legal action (1) for breach of contract by any party with whom they have entered into contracts; (2) in tort by anyone against whom these individuals or organizations may have committed a civil noncontractual wrong; and (3) by the local, state, or federal government for having committed a crime. Conversely, every individual or organization has the right to sue (1) those with whom they have entered into a contract for breach of that contract and (2) those who may have committed torts against them. (Only government bodies that enforce the law have the power to seek a criminal indictment against an individual or organization.) This right to sue under contract or tort law does not guarantee that the plaintiff will win, but being subject to civil suits creates loss exposures for virtually every organization and individual. Even if a civil or criminal action is groundless, the defendant can incur costs of investigation and legal defense.

Any individual or organization having the power to sue in contract or in tort may also *waive,* or knowingly relinquish, that right. After a waiver has been given, the organization or individual subject to suit no longer faces a liability exposure to those who have waived this right. For example, common law gives a lessee of real property the right to sue a lessor for failing to maintain habitable premises. As long as the lessee maintains this right, the lessor is exposed to liability losses if the lessee should sue and win in court. If, however, a lessee waives its right to sue, the lessor no longer faces this liability exposure from the lessee. Consider, for example, a lease provision that reads as follows:

> Lessee, as a material part of the consideration to be rendered to the Lessor hereby, waives all claims against Lessor for damages to the goods, wares and merchandise in, upon or about said premises and for injuries to Lessee, his agents or invitees in or about said premises. . . .[3]

Unless improperly obtained or nullified by applicable state or local law, this provision relieves the landlord of any concern that the tenant will sue to collect for damage to any "goods, wares, and merchandise" or for any injuries to the tenant or persons who may be on the premises at the tenant's request. As worded, the clause is broad, apparently excusing the lessor from liability even for intentional harm to the lessee. The lessor is not exposed to, and does not face the possibility of loss from, liability to the lessee for claims falling within the scope of this provision. If the lessee should sue the lessor, the lessor should be able to defeat the claim because of the waiver.

When an organization obtains valid waivers, it rids itself of those liability loss exposures. Thus, waivers can function as effective risk control mechanisms. For example, the preceding lease provision severely limits the landlord's exposures to suits from the lessee. Such a provision does not, however, prevent others, such as the lessee's employees, other agents, guests, or other invitees, from directly suing the landlord. Further, the provision does not obligate the lessee to hold the lessor harmless from suits; that is, to provide the lessor with legal defense and to pay any verdicts or judgments levied against the lessor.

In order to be effective, however, a waiver must be bargained fairly, must not be obtained by coercion, deceit, or concealment, and may need to be supported by specific legal consideration paid to the lessee by the lessor. As long as a waiver does not seem unreasonable to a court and does not contravene applicable law, the waiver can be a most effective shield against potential liability. Although this example is drawn from a lease, any other kind of contract can contain waivers. Some contracts contain a single provision granting *mutual waivers,* but the courts do not generally require reciprocity as long as there is some evidence of fair bargaining and reasonable disclosure regarding the waiver.

Waivers are generally embodied in original contracts signed before the parties begin their contractual dealings and before any of them has suffered harm for which it might sue and for which a waiver might become relevant. It is possible, however, for an organization or individual to waive its rights to sue after it has suffered some harm for which it might have sued. When a retroactive waiver is made, it is sometimes referred to as an *exculpatory* or *excusing agreement.* In this context, an exculpatory agreement is a type of waiver. (In less precise usage "exculpatory agreement" is synonymous with waiver.)

Risk Financing Transfers—Commitments To Pay

A risk financing transfer is a contract, or provision of a contract, by which the transferee agrees to pay money to, or on behalf of, the transferor after the transferor has suffered some specified loss. If the transferee is an insurance company, this contractual transfer for risk financing is termed *commercial insurance,* or simply *insurance.* If the transferee is not an insurer, and if the losses paid relate to the transferor's liability losses, these contracts are called *indemnity agreements* or *hold harmless agreements.*

In all types of such contractual transfers, the transferor's protection is only as reliable as the transferee's ability and willingness to pay money when needed to restore the loss. In the Peter Builder scenario, Terra required each mall tenant to hold Terra and the Builder family harmless from claims for alteration of the aquifer's course. This achieved a noninsurance contractual transfer for risk financing from Terra to these tenants for this type of loss.

In some cases, however, a risk financing transfer to a noninsurer may be highly reliable. Such a transfer can provide dependable protection for a transferor when the following conditions exist:

- Some characteristic of the loss puts it outside the scope of typical insurance contracts. For example, the peril causing the loss may not be covered by the typical insuring agreement, or the standard for evaluating a loss may not give the insured/transferor an amount of money sufficient to restore the transferor's loss. Other examples are newspaper publishers and airlines, which are often unable to obtain insurance for their net income losses resulting from labor union strikes. They have developed elaborate contracts for combining these exposures and paying resulting losses among themselves.
- The transferee's degree of commitment to fulfilling all the terms of its general business contracts with the transferor motivates the transferee to provide full indemnity when an insurer might question the indemnitee's right to payment.
- The transferee has special ability to evaluate the transferred risk, as in maintenance agreements and guarantees for services.

Indemnity Agreements. In general, any party to a contract has the right by common law to agree to pay or indemnify the other party for any losses the latter may suffer in carrying out the terms of the contract. Thus, the range of transactions in which noninsurance contractual transfers appear is extremely broad. However, the common law of contracts and the statutes of some jurisdictions limit a given party's right to make another party pay for a loss. Indemnity agreements are therefore classified in terms of both (1) the types of transactions in which they are likely to appear and (2) the extent to which they create duties that the transferee would not have under common law.

Hold Harmless Agreements. Indemnity agreements may provide a transferor with funds for restoring any type of accidental loss to property, net income, liability claims, or the loss of the services of the transferor's key personnel. The group of indemnity agreements that cover the transferor's liability losses growing out of the activities under the contract between the transferor and transferee has become very large and diverse. Therefore, these indemnity agreements have been given the label of "hold harmless agreements."

Under a hold harmless provision the transferee agrees to hold the transferor harmless from specified classes of liability claims by providing the transferor with funds to pay (or by paying on the transferor's behalf) for legal defense, verdicts and settlements, court costs, and other expenses related to the types of claims encompassed by the agreement. Hold harmless agreements are classified in terms of the degree of responsibility the transferee assumes for claims against the transferor. The following section provides detailed examples of indemnity and hold harmless agreements.

NONINSURANCE CONTRACTUAL TRANSFERS FOR RISK FINANCING

The wording and use of noninsurance contractual transfers for risk financing are largely unregulated. Therefore, there are no standard forms for indemnity and hold harmless provisions and no uniform practices for their use or for identification of the parties as transferor and transferee. In general, one party transfers the financial burden of losses whenever one of the following is present:

1. That party has the bargaining power to require the other party to be its transferee.
2. Such a transfer is standard practice for the type of transaction or industry involved.
3. The transaction calls for a risk financing transfer under the criteria described in the section "Factors Affecting Appropriate Use of Risk Financing Transfers," later in this chapter.

The following discussion classifies indemnity and hold harmless provisions according to the types of transactions in which they appear and the extent to which they alter liabilities for losses as established by common law.

Agreements/Provisions Classified by Type of Transaction

Any written contract may contain a noninsurance contractual transfer for risk control or risk financing. For example, the ticket a garage owner normally gives those who park their cars contains a very broad waiver of the car owner's common law right to bring claims against the garage owner for damage to the vehicle and its contents. Automobile rental agreements require the lessee to purchase insurance or otherwise bear the financial burden for damage to the vehicle. Otherwise, the rental company, as the vehicle owner, would have that responsibility under common law in virtually all circumstances. Finally, two organizations agreeing to the sale, rental, or maintenance of a product or piece of equipment may each insert into its own document a provision that makes the other party an indemnitor.

These provisions may be so enmeshed in the documents exchanged that neither party realizes that there is a mutual promise to indemnify the other. This situation creates almost insoluble problems of contract interpretation. These conflicts can render both provisions, and each party's attempt to collect indemnity from the other, virtually meaningless. To avoid these difficulties, each organization's risk management professional, legal counsel, and key managers should recognize where to look for the more common forms of indemnity and hold harmless agreements.

Construction Agreements. A building contractor's work creates a number of loss exposures, principally liability exposures, for the owner of the land and the building under construction. For example, a contractor's activities may harm its own employees and those of any subcontractors, pedestrians, owners of adjoining properties, or even the entire community. As a landowner, the individual or organization for which the building is constructed is ultimately liable for all such harm. The owner is also liable for any breaches of building permit provisions or building codes that may result from the contractor's or architect's decisions and other efforts.

For protection against liability losses related to these exposures, landowners normally require that they be held harmless by the building contractor or the architect from certain claims related to the construction. Contractors and architects do not usually have enough bargaining power to remove hold harmless provisions from a contract because the landowner can often find another contractor or architect who will agree to the hold harmless provisions.

The exact extent of the claims against which the contractor or architect agrees to hold the landowner harmless can be determined only by a very careful reading of the indemnity or hold harmless provision. The provision may still leave some questions about the scope of the losses for which the contractor agrees to pay unanswered. The Appendix to this chapter, *American Institute of Architects Document 201*, shows, in Section 3.18, an example of a hold harmless agreement pertaining to liability claims against a building owner.

A hold harmless provision can be difficult to understand. Those familiar with insurance, however, should apply the framework for interpreting an insurance policy to the analysis of hold harmless provisions. For instance, careful reading of *Document 201* will reveal the following:

1. The contractor must pay only for claims against the owner (and persons affiliated with the owner), and not for any property damage, loss of income, or extra expenses the owner may incur.
2. The contractor's financial obligation to respond to claims is unlimited (only as to claims by employees of the contractor or any subcontractor). There is no gauge for measuring the maximum dollar value of the claims to which the contractor must respond, even though virtually all insurance policies specify a maximum.

In addition, this provision does not indicate whether the transferee/indemnitor is obligated to pay punitive damages for which the transferor/indemnitee may become liable or whether bankruptcy of the transferee/indemnitor will relieve it of any further liability. The effect of punitive damages and bankruptcy on both hold harmless and other indemnity agreements varies greatly among jurisdictions. In some, the payment of punitive damages by the transferee is included automatically within a hold harmless agreement. In others, punitive damages are included only if specified. In still others, contractual transfer of the obligation to pay punitive damages is illegal. Bankruptcy excuses a transferee/indemnitor in some jurisdictions, often depending on the nature of the harm suffered by the claimant who brings suit against the transferor/indemnitee.

Service Agreements. Constructing a building is a highly specialized type of service that results in a tangible product which, when finished, ends the contractor's services. Other services, however, frequently including maintenance and transportation, are purchased on a continuing basis. The providers of such services often agree to a generic type of hold harmless agreement, such as the following provision in a contract under which a college (Owner) purchases continuing bus transportation for its students:

> The Contractor shall be responsible from the time of the beginning of operations, for all injury or damage of any kind resulting from said operations, to persons or property regardless of who may be the owner of the property. In addition to the liability imposed upon the Contractor on account of personal injury (including death) or property damage suffered through the Contractor's negligence, which liability is not

> impaired or otherwise affected hereunder, the Contractor assumes the obligation to save the Owner harmless and to indemnify the Owner from every expense, liability or payment arising out of or through injury (including death) to any person or persons or damage to property (regardless of who may be the owner of the property) of any place in which work is located, arising out of or suffered through any act or omission of the Contractor or any Subcontractor, or anyone directly or indirectly employed by or under the supervision of any of them in the prosecution of the operations included in this contract.[4]

The contractor's obligation under this provision is markedly broad because (1) the contractor agrees to hold the owner harmless from virtually all property, liability, and other losses (except, most likely, revenue losses) that the owner may suffer because of the contractor's errors and (2) the contractor agrees to be responsible for even those claims brought against the owner because of the owner's sole negligence.

Purchase Order Agreements. The raw materials, components, and supplies purchased by manufacturer, wholesaler, or retailer from another person or organization (a vendor) for use in a product the purchaser sells to others may be the basis for a products liability claim against the purchaser. The items purchased from the vendor may prove defective, or they may be the wrong type or grade for use in the product. In such a situation, common law gives the ultimate buyer or other user of the product the right to sue everyone involved in the production or sale of that product, ranging from the supplier of the raw materials to the retailer. Any organization in this chain also has the right to ask any other party in the chain to provide it with protection against any products liability claims. The traditional practice is for each organization to seek hold harmless indemnity from its immediate supplier or vendor through a provision such as the following:

> The Vendor agrees to indemnify and save harmless the Purchaser and its agents, representatives, and employees from any and all charges, claims, and causes of action by third persons, including but not limited to agents, representatives, and employees of the Vendor and of the Purchaser based upon or arising out of any damages, losses, expenses, charges, costs, injuries, or illness sustained or incurred by such person or persons resulting from or in any way, directly or indirectly, connected with the performance or nonperformance of this Agreement, of the vending services provided for hereunder, or the performance of or failure to perform any work or other activity related to such vending services, provided, however, that notwithstanding the foregoing, the Vendor does not agree to indemnify and save harmless the Purchaser, its agents, representatives and employees from any charges, claims, or actions based upon or arising out of any damages, losses, claims, expenses, charges, costs, injuries, or illness sustained or incurred as the sole result of the negligence of the Purchaser, its agents, representatives, or employees. In the event a claim is filed against the Purchaser

> for which the Vendor is to be held liable under the terms of this agreement, the Purchaser will promptly notify the Vendor of such claim and will not settle such claim without the prior written consent of the Vendor.[5]

Like an insurance contract, this provision also has some "exclusions" and "conditions." For example, the provision exempts the indemnifying vendor from responding to claims brought against the purchaser based entirely on the purchaser's "sole negligence" without any fault of the vendor. This provision also makes the vendor's promise conditional upon the purchaser's immediately notifying the vendor of any claim. The vendor has authority to manage claims, while the purchaser is barred from making any separate settlement with a claimant. However, notice that, unlike an insurance contract, this provision does not obligate the purchaser/indemnitee to cooperate with the vendor/indemnitor in the vendor's management of any claim.

This provision also protects the purchaser, suggesting that the purchaser has enough bargaining power to obtain a promise of indemnity from the vendor and that the vendor's eagerness to contract with the purchaser made the agreement at least tolerable to the vendor. These relationships may be reversed. A vendor who is the exclusive national manufacturer of a very popular product may be able to require each wholesale or retail purchaser to agree to hold the manufacturer harmless from products liability or other claims, or even from losses not involving liability that the manufacturer may suffer. Marketers throughout the distribution chain may have no choice but to provide the manufacturer with this promise of protection if they wish to carry the product.

When several parties in the production-marketing chain enter into a series of indemnity or hold harmless agreements, considerable confusion can result. If all agreements shift the financial burden of losses one "link" back along the chain, then the original manufacturer (or even raw material supplier) may become obligated to finance the losses of all claims against other parties. In the opposite case, when the financial burden is shifted forward, then the retailer may become burdened with the losses of all the parties in the chain. In a yet more complicated situation in which the agreement provides for indemnity from purchasers and from vendors, the aggregate liability of all the producers and marketers may accumulate at various points along the chain. Even greater confusion can exist in construction situations, where the contractor and subcontractors all sign agreements holding each other as well as the owner harmless.

A need exists to guard against confusion and to ensure that financial responsibility is equitably and efficiently distributed. To meet this need, the agreements should be planned so that exposures fall on those who are most qualified to prevent losses or so that losses that do occur fall on those who are qualified to finance their recovery. This chapter addresses these concerns later in the section entitled "Management of Noninsurance Contractual Transfers."

Lease of Premises Agreements. Even though leases of real or personal property may contain no explicit risk transfer provisions, they are inherently contractual transfers for risk control. A lease by nature allows a lessee to enjoy the use of property for a specified period without having to assume many of the loss exposures that are inherent in property ownership. Although such *exposures* remain with the lessor, a lessor can attempt to shift the financial burden of some *actual losses* to the lessee, particularly if the lessor has superior bargaining power. In the Peterbuilt Mall example, Peter Builder's Terra Corporation was able to get merchants to sign leases in which they agreed not to sue Terra for any losses resulting from changing land conditions. If the merchants were not so eager to locate at the new mall, they may not have accepted this transfer of financial burden. Thus, a lease may also contain elements of risk financing transfers. This illustrates a frequent but little-noticed aspect of noninsurance contractual transfers: a single agreement, even a single contract provision, can embody transfers for both risk control and risk financing.

A lessee of all or part of another's premises must accept the entire lease agreement as prepared by the lessor. Many lease agreements are consequently written so that they substantially favor the lessor. Furthermore, unlike insurance contracts, which courts often interpret in an insured's favor, courts usually read leases as if the parties had roughly equal bargaining power. This is particularly true if the lessee is an organization renting business space rather than an individual or family renting "personal" space. Finally, a lessee wishing to do business in a particular location often has a limited choice regarding the number of properties that are available for rent. Therefore, a lessee may have to agree to a hold harmless provision such as the following, which is common in mall and shopping center properties:

> Lessee shall indemnify and save harmless Lessor from and against any and all loss, cost (including attorneys' fees), damages, expense and liability (including statutory liability and liability under workers compensation laws) in connection with claims for damages as a result of injury or death of any person or damage to any property sustained by . . . Lessee and . . . all other persons . . . which arise from or in any manner grow out of any act or neglect on or about the Shopping Center by Lessee, Lessee's partners, agents, employees, customers, invitees, contractors, and subcontractors.[6]

This provision obligates the lessee to respond only to liability claims that may be brought against the lessor, and not to the lessor's property damage, net income, or other losses. This clause is quite broad in the sense that the lessee's financial responsibility extends not only to the lessor's common law liabilities, but also to its statutory liabilities, including workers compensation claims. In numerous states an attempt to shift workers compensation and other statutory liability would be highly vulnerable to a court challenge by an injured employee of the lessor or by some third party injured in the shopping center. Both could claim that the financial security of their statutory protection had been jeopardized significantly by an attempted contractual shift from the lessor to the presumably less financially able lessee.

Equipment Lease Agreements. An individual or organization that obtains the use of major items of equipment by leasing them must usually promise to return the equipment in its original condition, often subject to certain exceptions. This promise protects the lessor against loss to the equipment, which is often out of the lessor's direct control or supervision for substantial periods. The promise is exemplified by the following indemnity provision in a lease agreement for machine tools:

> The Lessee covenants that it will, in respect of the Equipment,
>
> - pay the rentals promptly when due,
> - assume responsibility for them, at current values, against fire and loss or damage from whatever cause arising,
> - employ them only on work carried out on the Lessee's premises,
> - permit the Lessor to inspect them at all reasonable times, and
> - on termination of this agreement return them to the Lessor at the expense and risk of the Lessee.[7]

This clause is not burdensome for the lessee because (1) the lessee does not assume any financial responsibility for liability claims against the lessor that may arise from the lessee's possession or use of the equipment and (2) the lessee is responsible only for the property value of the leased equipment, and not for the revenue the lessor could have earned on the equipment had it remained undamaged and available for another rental.

Other equipment leases, however, obligate the lessee to hold the lessor harmless from liability claims related to the equipment while it is in the lessee's possession. The lessee may even be required to maintain insurance that provides the lessor with liability (and often other) protection. An example of such a broader commitment for the lessee is the following provision in a lease for trucks and trailers, referred to as equipment:

> Lessee shall maintain Public Liability and Property Damage Insurance as well as Workers Compensation Insurance and agrees to hold Lessor harmless from any such claim while said equipment is in the actual service of the Lessee; however, Lessor shall maintain at his or her own expense Public Liability and Property Damage Insurance which shall be effective while the equipment is parked, deadheading, bobtailing,

> or otherwise being operated in any manner other than under or pursuant to specific dispatch instructions from the Lessee; and the Lessor will save Lessee harmless from any loss, claim, or liability while the equipment, or either unit thereof, is so used or employed. This shall be construed to mean that the Lessee will not be responsible for Public Liability, Property Damage, Workers Compensation or Cargo Insurance when the equipment is being used other than in connection with the transportation of freight under the authority and with the authorization of the Lessee, or when the same is being used in any manner except under or pursuant to dispatch instructions of the Lessee.[8]

This provision attempts to distinguish sharply between the exposures to the equipment when in normal use by the lessee and exposures at all other times. It obligates the lessee to provide indemnity (through insurance) only when the equipment is in normal use. In the Peterbuilt Mall case, for example, the Terra Corporation may lease a tractor-trailer rig so that Peter Builder can haul some supplies for the mall from the supplier to the construction site. While Peter Builder has control of the rig, Terra's insurance covers it, but if the rig is stolen while parked and waiting to be picked up by Peter Builder, the rig owner's policy covers any losses resulting from the rig's theft.

Bailment Contracts. Many business transactions involve placing *personal property* (property other than real estate) in the custody of some other party, for such purposes as repair, transportation, or safekeeping. This temporary transfer of the custody of property is known as a bailment. The party having temporary custody is a *bailee,* and the owner to whom the property is to be returned is the *bailor.* For example, when one of Terra's vehicles is at the Goodridge Garage, where Peter Builder usually has the company's vehicles serviced and repaired, the garage is the bailee and Terra is the bailor. Similarly, when the quarry from which Terra purchases building stone places a shipment in the hands of an independent trucker for delivery to a Terra building site, the trucker is a bailee. The owner of the stone—which could be either the quarry or Terra, depending upon the terms of their contract of sale—is the bailor.

Like most bailments in business situations, both of these arrangements are known as *compensated bailments* rather than as *gratuitous bailments.* (The latter occurs when, say, one friend lends an umbrella or a book to another friend.) In a compensated bailment the bailor pays the bailee for work or service related to the bailed property. These bailments also are said to be *mutual benefit bailments* in the sense that both the bailee and bailor expect to benefit from their business transaction. For example, Goodridge Garage receives money for maintaining Terra's vehicles, and Terra gains repairs and maintenance in exchange.

Under the common law of compensated mutual benefit bailments, the bailee must exercise ordinary care for the safety of the bailor's property in contrast to the slight care required of a bailee in a gratuitous bailment or a bailment that benefits only the bailee (the friend who borrows a book). The common law requires, in most cases, that a compensated mutual benefit bailee return the property to the bailor in its original condition, excusing the bailee only for damage caused by acts of God and normal wear and tear.

A special class of compensated mutual benefit bailees consists of common carrier transporters of others' goods—that is, carriers who stand ready to transport anyone's cargo in accordance with an established schedule and set fees. A common carrier situation is a mutual benefit bailment; but, because of the public interest in safe, efficient, and effective transport of goods, the degree of care required of common carriers exceeds that of an ordinary bailee. Any loss that results from an accident, or even a third party's act, results in the carrier's liability. A common carrier is responsible for any damage to a bailor shipper's cargo except that caused by (1) acts of God, (2) warlike activities (usually described as involving acts of a public enemy, but not including rioting or terrorism), (3) exercise of public authority (as when police block the access to a particular neighborhood, thus depriving a business located there of its usual profits), (4) fault or neglect by the shipper (such as poor packaging or labeling), and (5) any *inherent vice* of the cargo (that is, any potential for the shipper's goods to destroy themselves, as when ice melts or explosives explode because of improper packaging or labeling).

A compensated mutual benefit bailee is usually held responsible for damage to a bailor's property and must not only replace it with comparable property, but must also compensate the bailor for any loss of profits, continuing expenses, and other financial harm that the bailor has suffered as a consequence of damaged property.

A bailor and bailee may alter the common law apportionment of their respective loss exposures by contract. For example, in many business situations bailees seek to limit their liability through posted notices or contract provisions stating that they are not responsible for damage to bailors' goods. They may also attempt to limit their liability to a specified amount per item or only to the value of the property (excluding any profits or loss of use the bailor would have earned from the property). In contrast, a bailor may seek to increase a bailee's liability by, for example, holding the bailee responsible for specified acts of God (such as windstorm).

Either party to a bailment contract may have business reasons for undertaking loss exposures that the common law usually places on the other party. Courts respect each party's freedom of contract to bargain fair apportionments of loss exposures. They have been, however, reluctant to enforce exposure-shifting bailment contract provisions that are contrary to practice within the particular industry, not equitably negotiated, or less than adequately disclosed.

For example, a "Not Responsible For Damage To Vehicles" statement on the back of tickets given to customers of a public parking garage is ignored by most courts as an inadequately disclosed and unbargained attempt to shift the garagekeeper's liability, contrary to the bailor's reasonable expectation.

Contracts of Sale and Supply. Contracts pertaining to marketing goods and services offer innumerable opportunities for transferring loss exposures between buyers and sellers. The transfer usually favors the party with the greater bargaining power. For example, in order to maintain firmer control of their products as they move through marketing channels, some manufacturers and processors sell their goods on consignment. This arrangement leaves title to the property in the hands of the manufacturer or processor until the distributor sells the goods to the retailer or ultimate consumer. This arrangement also means that the distributor, having never taken title to the goods, is never exposed to loss from their damage or destruction. Ownership, and thus the loss exposure, moves directly from the manufacturer or processor to the retailer or consumer, allowing the distributor to earn revenue only from its distribution.[9]

Another type of contract related to property ownership is a service or maintenance agreement under which a sales or maintenance organization promises to protect the buyer or other owner of substantial personal property against specified types of losses to or arising from that property. If the service or maintenance firm promises to provide services only but does not also agree to indemnify the property owner for losses, the agreement is one of risk control, not risk financing. If, in contrast, the maintenance or service firm agrees to "hold [the owner] harmless" from liability claims against the owner, then the agreement becomes a risk financing transfer. Service and maintenance agreements, under which a property owner is a transferor of some exposures, differ from lease agreements, under which the transferor never faces ownership-related exposures while having the right to use the leased property. They call for payment of money rather than simply provision of services.

Service and maintenance firms become transferees under the following types of sale and supply agreements:

- Agreements to deliver fuel to the customer so that the customer never runs out of fuel. The fuel dealer is obligated to pay for any frozen pipes and certain other losses if the customer is ever without fuel.
- Purchase agreements for data processing equipment, air condi-

tioners, vehicles, or similar items with guarantees of maintenance and replacement as necessary.

- Service contracts under which real estate agents undertake the maintenance of specified items of equipment, such as heating systems, in homes they sell.

Such service and supply contracts are very similar to insurance if they go beyond guarantees of the quality of the goods or the reliability of the supplier's performance and extend to other causes of loss. For example, courts have found sales and supply firms to be engaged in the business of insurance, thus making them subject to the provisions of the applicable state insurance code in the following situations:

- A tire dealer agrees to give an allowance for unused mileage if a tire that it sold is damaged by road hazards.
- A glazier promises to replace plate glass windows broken by any cause.
- A fuel oil dealer agrees to deliver oil for the next ten years at a lower price per BTU than any other energy firm serving the same area. (This exposes the dealer to a substantial business risk if, for example, hydroelectric or nuclear power becomes cost-effective in its area.)

Inadvertently becoming subject to an insurance code can be restrictive and costly for a sales or supply organization. In effect, the firm can be forced to withdraw from the ambitious service or maintenance agreements through which it sought to attract customers by becoming the transferee of exposures that customers usually bear.

Sales and service contracts may substantially modify the common law doctrines that distribute loss exposures between buyers and sellers of property. The fundamental common law is that risk of loss—both to property itself and from loss of use of that property—moves with the title to property, with the owner always bearing these exposures. Therefore, special risk transfer provisions aside, the time when ownership changes is important in identifying and managing an organization's loss exposures. For example, when Company S sells a product to Company B in another city, specifying when Company B acquires ownership is essential. (This is also good practice even if Company S and Company B are neighbors because accidents may occur even in apparently safe areas.)

Company S may provide in its standard sales contract that each sale is "F.O.B. Detroit," where Company S is located. The abbreviation *F.O.B.* stands for *free on board,* meaning that the seller is free of responsibility for the goods once they have reached the designated location. Regardless of whether Company S delivers its products in its own vehicles or by common or contract carrier, this provision means that Company B acquires the goods (and the related loss exposures) as soon as they are aboard a carrier in Detroit. If, however, the specification is "F.O.B. Des Moines," which may be the location of Company B's warehouse or perhaps some central distribution point, then Company B owns and is responsible for the loss of the goods when they reach Des Moines and are ready to be unloaded.

However, an alternative sales contract—particularly a contract of sale for permanently installed equipment—may provide that Company B does not become the owner until the property has been unloaded and installed and has passed a series of operational tests in the buyer's facility. Such an arrangement allows the seller to maintain control of the property and to ensure that it has been appropriately placed in service. If, in contrast, Company S wishes Company B to be responsible for damage to the property throughout its transport, Company S may require that Company B take title to the property at Company S's shipping dock. The bargaining power of the buyer and seller, as well as industry custom, is likely to influence these allocations of loss exposures.

Responsibilities for ownership exposures may be divided, with different responsibilities being transferred at different times. *C.I.F.* stands for *cost-insurance-freight*, and means that the price includes the cost of goods, insurance, and the freight charges to the destination. If the shipment between Company S and Company B is under C.I.F. terms, Company B acquires ownership as soon as the goods are on board a carrier. Company S, however, must purchase sufficient insurance and pay for the freight. If the insurance is less than the amount established by the custom of the trade or the specifications of the sales contract, Company S, because it has failed to fulfill the C.I.F. conditions, must compensate the buyer, Company B, for its loss. This arrangement illustrates how it is often possible to combine risk control transfers (pertaining to the shifting of title and consequent exposure to loss) with risk financing transfers, here obligating the seller to provide insurance for, or to indemnify directly, the buyer.

Another frequent allocation of exposures in sales of property occurs in *installment* or *conditional sales contracts*, under which the seller commonly reserves ownership rights until the buyer has met all the conditions of the contract, most notably the buyer's final installment payment. Although the seller usually retains title, exposure to loss because of damage to the property may be transferred by the sales contract immediately to the buyer. This transfer can be achieved by a contract provision obligating the buyer to complete the contract by continuing installment payments even though the property may be lost or damaged before the buyer has made the final payment. Such an arrangement preserves the seller's right under an installment contract either to receive the full purchase price or, if the buyer defaults, to repossess the property. Here the buyer may also secure insurance or other risk financing to protect its interests and obligations arising out of the property. During the time between the first and last installment payment, therefore, both the buyer and the seller are exposed to loss from damage and have an insurable interest in the property.

A common arrangement is that property that has been sold remains in the hands of the seller for later delivery to the buyer. Valuable items of personal property, as well as substantial quantities of fungible goods (commodities or bulk goods, all parts of which are presumed to be uniform), are often sold in this way. The contract of sale becomes effective as soon as the buyer and seller have agreed on the particular items or quantity to be sold, the price, and the delivery date. The sales contract commonly specifies that ownership of the property transfers to the buyer at that time. Although the ownership-related exposure to damage thus passes to the buyer, the seller having custody of it still has a bailee's responsibility for its safety. In such cases, therefore, both the bailor's ownership interest and the bailee's liability for damage may expose each to loss and support each party's purchase of appropriate insurance or other risk financing arrangements. These exposures may be altered by specific agreement.

Agreements Classified by Responsibility Transferred

The common law defines the transferor's and transferee's obligations in contractual transfers of exposures to loss or of the financial responsibility for loss unless the contracts provide otherwise in a legally permissible way. These agreements may also define these obligations in a way that modifies each party's responsibility under common law. Classified in terms of the extent to which these agreements modify common law, they can be grouped according to whether they achieve one of the following:

1. Restate existing common or statutory law
2. Shift responsibility for joint fault to one party based on stated conditions
3. Shift all responsibility to one party except for losses that are the transferor's sole fault
4. Shift all responsibility

Although these four types of provisions can be applied to any property, net income, liability, or personnel loss, most pertain to a transferor's potential or actual liability losses.

Restating Law. By embodying in their contract the essential provisions of the existing law as they understand it to govern their transactions, the parties to a contract may eliminate much uncertainty about how the law will apportion legal or financial responsibility for losses that either of them may suffer in carrying out their contract. Such contracts eliminate, or at least greatly reduce, any likelihood that (1) a court may misinterpret their intentions, (2) a court case or statute may affect their respective rights, or (3) an accident occurring in, or otherwise involving, some other jurisdiction may bring that jurisdiction's laws into play.

Each of these three sources of uncertainty is a cause of *juridical risk,* the possibility that a court will reach a decision that differs from the parties' expectations; that is, that the court will change what the parties thought they understood to be the law.[10] In applying a fairly bargained contract in which the parties have expressed their intent clearly, courts generally enforce the contract, allowing the parties to "make their own law" as far as equity allows. A clause that merely restates existing law may only name the appropriate provisions of an existing statute or cite relevant court cases, identify the jurisdiction by whose laws the parties intend to be bound, or recite the substance of their understanding of the current law. An example of the third alternative is the following provision for the sale and delivery of construction equipment from a seller to a buyer, both of which are business organizations:

> *Application of Law.* The buyer and seller agree that each shall bear any loss resulting from physical damage to the equipment that occurs during the time each party, respectively, holds title to the equipment. Title to the equipment shall pass in accordance with the customary trade interpretation of the conditions of sale specified at the top of this agreement. "Loss" here means any damage to the equipment, loss of income to the owner from its use, and liability for harm to others arising from the ownership, use of, or defects in the equipment. This provision shall be interpreted in accordance with the common law and statutes of the state in which both parties are situated, as enacted or interpreted as of the date of this agreement. Except as provided in these statutes or court rulings, neither the buyer nor the seller shall be responsible for indemnifying the other for any loss relating to the ownership, maintenance or use of, or defect in, this equipment.[11]

Shifting Responsibility for Joint Fault. Two or more individuals or organizations working together to carry out their contract may jointly harm some third party, or at least be joined as defendants in a civil suit charging them both with fault for a breach of contract or a tort. The facts of the situation may not be clear as to which party is at fault or as to their relative proportions of fault. Determining who is responsible and to what extent may be a very difficult, time-consuming, and contentious process.

These difficulties can be eliminated to a great extent, and one contracting party's common law responsibility for joint civil wrongs can be shifted to the other contracting party. The one to which such joint responsibility is shifted (the transferee) must agree to hold the other party (the transferor) harmless from claims arising from their joint fault. Such a transfer is embodied in the italicized portion of the following clause from a lease for an entire commercial building:

> Lessee shall repair partitions, all structural and window glass, electric and plumbing fixtures, and all machinery installed in the leased premises. Lessee shall be liable for, and shall hold the Lessor harmless with respect to, all claims relating to damage or injury to the property or persons of others alleged to have occurred on or to have been caused by the condition of the leased premises, if such injury or damage is alleged to have been caused by an act or neglect of the Lessee (including anyone in the Lessee's control or employ) *or the joint act or neglect of the Lessee and Lessor.* The Lessee shall at once report in writing to the Lessor any defective condition known which the Lessor is required to repair, and failure to so report shall make the Lessee responsible for damages resulting from such defective condition.[12]

This provision is noteworthy because the italicized words pertaining to joint responsibility are surrounded by many other provisions describing the lessee's responsibility not only for liability claims but also for damage to the premises. The eleven words are designed to shift the otherwise joint responsibilities for harm to others, making what once was joint the *sole* responsibility of the transferee. This responsibility could be overlooked easily by the lessee, especially if such a provision is typed or otherwise prepared individually for each agreement and not made a part of the preprinted form. In short, both the transferor and the transferee must be sure that the provisions express their shared intent.

Shifting Responsibility Except Transferor's Fault. The preceding provision would arguably not apply if the two contracting parties and some outside third party all were named defendants in a civil suit. The clause does not mention the third party's fault. Nor does it refer to claims arising from more complex chains of causation like suits for bodily injury or property damage involving the fault of the transferor, coupled with some slight fault of the plaintiff or the wrongful acts of a civil authority or other entity immune from suit. In these more complex cases a transferee (such as the above lessee) could maintain, with some reasonable chance of success, that it was not obligated to hold the transferor harmless from the claims of others.

A hold harmless provision that would protect the transferor in such cases would be phrased to apply to all claims except those arising from the transferor's sole fault. The following is an example of such a provision in a contract for the construction of a building:

> The Contractor shall indemnify and hold harmless the Owner from

> and against all claims attributable to bodily injury unless caused entirely by the Owner's act or omission.

Under this provision the contractor would not be obligated to respond to a suit against the owner if the contractor could show that, regardless of any allegations, the owner solely caused the injury to the plaintiff. If the concluding words of the above clause had read "... alleged to have been caused entirely by ..." the wording of the plaintiff's complaint, rather than the actual facts of the case, could determine whether the contractor was obliged to hold the owner harmless. To further illustrate the importance of carefully phrasing hold harmless provisions, assume the clause read as follows:

> The Contractor shall indemnify and hold harmless the Owner from and against all claims ... attributable to bodily injury ... whether or not caused in part by the Owner.

The words following "whether" do not limit the contractor's duty to respond—in fact, the provision seeks to make the contractor financially responsible for all claims regarding bodily injury against the owner. However, the reference to bodily injury is itself a limitation, excluding other sorts of claims.

Shifting All Responsibility. Beginning with a relatively simple restatement of common law, the three preceding indemnity and hold harmless provisions have sought to progressively improve the position of the transferor, shifting ever greater financial burdens to the transferee. A yet more extreme provision appears in a contract that a municipality requires of the owner of a building that was to be demolished by explosives. The parties to the contract are the municipality, the general contractor for the entire project, and the explosives subcontractor chosen by the general contractor.

Because work with explosives is inherently dangerous and imposes strict liability without fault on those who engage in or direct it, the municipality wants to hold the parties involved financially responsible for all claims that might be lodged against the city or its personnel because of this project. The permit for the demolition therefore includes the following provision:

> The undersigned owner, general contractor and subcontractor (hereinafter collectively referred to as "Indemnitors") for and in consideration of the undertaking of the municipality to provide regular police, fire and other assistance during the Activity, and for other good and valuable consideration, the receipt and sufficiency whereof is hereby acknowledged by Indemnitors, do hereby jointly and severally covenant, undertake and agree that they, and each of them, will indemnify and hold harmless (without limit as to amount) the municipality and its officials, officers, employes and servants in their official capacity (hereinafter collectively referred to as "Indemnitees"), and any of them,

> from and against all loss, all risk of loss and all damage (including expense) sustained or incurred because of or by reason of any and all claims, demands, suits, actions, judgments and executions for damages of any and every kind and by whomever and wherever made or obtained, alleged caused by, arising out of or relating in any manner to the Activity, and to protect and defend Indemnitees, and any of them, with respect thereto.[13]

The owner of the structure to be demolished, once made aware of the potential personal liability under the above provision, will be held harmless by the general contractor under the following provision:

> *Indemnification.* General Contractor warrants that it is an independent contractor and agrees to indemnify and save harmless the Owner from and against any loss or expense by reason of any liability imposed by law on the Owner and from and against claims against Owner for damages because of bodily injuries, including death, at any time resulting therefrom, accidents sustained by any person or persons on account of damage to property rising out of or in consequence of the performance of this Agreement, whether such injuries to persons or damage to property are due or claimed to be due to any negligence of general contractor, the Owner, their agents, servants, or employees, or of any other person.[14]

As a result of this provision, the general contractor demands to be indemnified by the subcontractor under the following very similar provision:

> *Indemnification.* Subcontractor warrants that it is an independent contractor and agrees to indemnify and save harmless the Owner and General Contractor from and against any loss or expense by reason of any liability imposed by law upon the Owner and General Contractor and from and against claims against Owner and General Contractor for damages because of bodily injuries, including death, at any time resulting therefrom, accidents sustained by any person or persons on account of damage to property rising out of or in consequence of the performance of the Agreement, whether such injuries to persons or damage to property are due or claimed to be due to any negligence of General Contractor, the Owner, their agents, servants, or employees, or any other person.[15]

These three provisions together would place the financial burden of all claims on the subcontractor. The municipality, once sued, could turn to the owner for protection, the owner could turn to the general contractor, and the general contractor could turn to the subcontractor. The city, the owner, and the primary contractor may not have considered fully (1) whether the subcontractor was financially able to provide the protection provided for in the hold harmless provisions, (2) whether placing the entire financial burden of potential losses on the subcontractor was the most efficient allocation of risk control and risk financing responsibilities for all the parties, or even (3) whether the courts would uphold each attempted transfer.

A court considering these matters could refuse to enforce the provisions against the subcontractor. Instead, the owner, the primary contractor, and even the city could be held liable if some of the subcontractor's blasting activities damaged nearby properties. A court could also find these provisions unenforceable for the following reasons:

- They were negotiated fairly, but resulted from inappropriate use of the transferor's economic power.
- They sought to transfer a legal duty (here, conducting blasting operations safely) that is so fundamental that the law will not recognize an attempted transfer without prior consent through legislation or court order.
- They improperly tried to deprive members of the public exposed to harm of the compensation (from both the owner and the primary contractor) to which the public was entitled, thus harming the public interest and violating public policy.

This section has examined noninsurance contractual transfers for risk financing by classifying agreements in terms of the (1) type of transaction and (2) extent of responsibility transferred. The next section will examine legal principles underlying noninsurance contractual transfers by discussing both the freedom to make contracts and limitations on that freedom.

LEGAL PRINCIPLES UNDERLYING NONINSURANCE CONTRACTUAL TRANSFERS

The following discussion focuses on noninsurance contractual transfers, especially for risk financing. These transfers constitute sound risk management only when the transfers properly apply legal and managerial principles determining when and to what extent to alter responsibilities for managing loss exposures and for financing recovery from actual losses under the law. Just as contracts can modify common law, the law can check noninsurance contractual transfers.

The great diversity in the wording and application of noninsurance contractual transfers for risk control and risk financing illustrates the importance of freedom of contract as a principle in English and American common law. There are, however, common law and statutory restrictions on this freedom. The limitations are important because they protect the public by preventing unconscionable behavior by parties to contracts.

Freedom of Contract

Under the legal doctrine of freedom of contract, legally competent parties are free to bargain as long as the bargaining does not unreasonably interfere with the rights of others. Contracting parties thus have the mutual powers to bind to one another to carry out the bargain, and the courts will enforce a contract against any contracting party who may later decide not to abide by its terms. Some of those terms may be the contract provisions assigning responsibility for risk control or risk financing to various parties. As part of enforcing the provisions of valid contracts, courts require compliance with these risk-shifting provisions.

Limitations on This Freedom

Despite the latitude historically enjoyed by the parties to a contract, courts now increasingly refuse to enforce noninsurance transfers that (1) manifestly have not been bargained fairly (that is, are "unconscionable" because they are so drastically unfair to the transferee) or (2) unreasonably interfere with the rights of others who are not parties to the contract, thus making the transfer against public policy or contrary to the public interest. Furthermore, statutes in many states attempt to preserve fairness and to foster economically appropriate allocations of loss exposures and actual losses that are consistent with public policy by such legislative strategies as (1) prohibiting certain types of transfers (particularly hold harmless agreements) in some contracts, (2) prohibiting certain wording in some types of contractual transfers, or (3) prescribing precisely the wording of transfer provisions.

Limitations Under Common Law. A fundamental objective of common law is to balance the interests of individuals and groups whose actions, if based only on self-interest, can create conflict, often infringing on others' rights. With respect to contractual transfers of loss exposures or of the cost of losses, this objective requires balancing (1) the potentially competing interests of contracting parties and (2) the collective rights of contracting parties as a group against those of society and the economy. Unconscionability is the key concept on which competing interests between contracting parties are balanced. Public policy or public interest is the key point of balance between contracting parties and the community as a whole.

Unconscionability. When enforcing contracts, the courts generally assume that, because they are carrying out the original intentions of the contracting parties, it is appropriate to hold each party to the original, freely made promises. As a result, the true consent of the parties is an essential prerequisite of any valid contract. Without it, the courts have little basis for requiring a party to fulfill a promise. At times, however, courts find that unconscionability exists in a contract.

In cases involving unconscionability, courts may infer from the terms of the contract itself an absence of true consent because no party would have agreed voluntarily to a contract so unfavorable to its interests. An *unconscionable contract or provision* is so intolerably offensive to the courts' sense of basic justice that the courts cannot in good conscience enforce it. Therefore, one party must have been physically, psychologically, or economically coerced into signing the contract, and it would now be unconscionable to hold that party to such an unfair bargain even though the contract appears to be valid. For example, assume that an employee were to waive all rights to workers compensation benefits shortly after suffering a seriously disabling injury and that the employee had not reclaimed the common law right to sue the employer for negligence or other cause for the injury. A court would probably refuse to enforce this waiver and would allow the employee to pursue statutory workers compensation benefits. A court may reason that the employee would have agreed to such a waiver only by being misled or coerced and, thus, that the waiver agreement did not rest on a true meeting of the minds of the employer and the employee. Having deduced the absence of mutual consent from the inequity of the waiver, a court would probably ignore it.

Public Policy. Questions about the unconscionability of a contract provision require a court to examine the bargaining relationships between the parties to that contract. In terms of public policy, the implications of a contract provision demand that a court consider the economic and social consequences of a particular contract provision if entire groups of people or organizations, situated similarly to the specific parties who bring their dispute to court, were to enter into contracts like the one the court happens to be considering. The *public policy* of a given country, state, or other jurisdiction is the set of assumptions and principles (often unstated) on which the laws and court decisions of that jurisdiction are based.

Many contracts considered by the courts to be unconscionable would also be found contrary to public policy. For example, the same injured employee's waiver of workers compensation benefits, described as unconscionable, could also be contrary to the public policy objectives of workers compensation statutes. One of the goals of these laws, and part of public policy as to how recovery from work injury losses should be financed, is to relieve the government, and ultimately the taxpayers, of the burden of financing medical care and living expenses for an employee disabled on the job. Given this objective, any agreement between an employer and an employee waiving the employee's statutory right to workers compensation benefits without receiving in return some alternative compensation would probably not be honored by the courts because it puts the burden of the loss on society rather than the employer. As such, the contract is contrary to public policy.

Another example of how an improper risk control transfer can be limited because of unconscionability or public policy reasons is an agreement between a common carrier and a cargo shipper who excuses the carrier from liability for damage to the cargo caused by the carrier's negligence. The Federal Interstate Commerce Act makes a common carrier liable for all damage to goods except for specified causes. Therefore, any dilution of this liability by a private risk transfer agreement would be contrary to the act's objective of protecting the public by encouraging common carriers to transport goods carefully. Moreover, because common law traditionally requires a very high standard of care on the part of a common carrier, a court would likely infer that a shipper would have excused a carrier from negligence only if coerced. This coercion would make the contract unconscionable, thus negating the shipper's waiver.

Statutory Limitations. Nearly half of the states have statutes that deal with indemnity and hold harmless agreements.[16] Various states may prohibit the agreements, forbid the use of certain wording in certain contracts, or specify precise wording of the agreements. These statutes reflect legislative questioning of one contracting party's attempt to limit its liability for negligence or other wrongdoing by compelling another party to waive its right to sue or to pay the transferor's losses. This legislation reflects public concerns for (1) preserving incentives for organizations to act carefully to prevent harm to others and (2) providing a source of adequate compensation for those harmed, especially compensation from financially strong organizations, who may likely be the ones to have the bargaining power to enforce an unconscionable indemnity or hold harmless agreement.

The current statutory limitations on indemnity and hold harmless agreements are noteworthy for their diversity, especially their variations with respect to the following:

- The types of noninsurance contractual transfers to which the statutes apply (generally for risk financing, not risk control)
- The parties the statutes regulate in terms of who can be a transferor or a transferee
- The scope of the exposures (particularly liability exposures) whose transfer the statutes seek to regulate

Each statute must therefore be read carefully to determine how it treats these variables. For example, consider the following Georgia statute:

> A covenant, promise, agreement, or understanding in, or in connection with, or collateral to, a contract or agreement relative to the construction, alteration, repair, or maintenance of a building structure, appurtenances, and appliances including moving, demolition, and excavating connected therewith, purporting to indemnify or hold harmless the

> promisee against liability for damage arising out of bodily injury to persons or damage to property caused by or resulting from the sole negligence of the promisee, his agents or employees, or the indemnitee, is against public policy and is void and unenforceable provided, that this section shall not affect the validity of any insurance contract, Workers Compensation agreement, or other agreement issued by an admitted insurer.[17]

This statute applies only to indemnity and hold harmless agreements that (1) relate to building construction/demolition, (2) seek to transfer the promisee/indemnitee's sole negligence, and (3) apply only if the transferee/indemnitor is not an insurance company admitted to Georgia. It is not explicit whether it excludes insurers only when conducting an insurance business or, more broadly, any noninsurance contract into which an insurer may enter as an ordinary indemnitor or indemnitee. Thus, this statute would not be relevant to any indemnity or hold harmless agreement in which any one or more of the following conditions prevailed:

- The agreement did not pertain to building construction/demolition.
- The agreement applied to losses other than those "caused by or resulting from the sole negligence of the promisee" (such as the joint negligence of the promisee/indemnitee and the promisor, or the joint fault of the promisee and some third party not involved in the contract, or even the willful misconduct of the promisee).
- The promisor/indemnitor is an insurer admitted in the jurisdiction.

There is a very broad range of circumstances for which executives and their legal counsel or risk management professionals draft creative indemnity or hold harmless agreements. It would be a legislative challenge to draft a statute that applied equitably and unambiguously to certain contracts and not to others. For example, with regard to the preceding provision, statutes in other states refer not only to the building structure, appurtenances, and appliances, but also to roads, highways, and bridges. It is not clear whether the statute in the example applies to contracts involving highway, road, or bridge construction—the term "building structure" is, arguably, vague.

Despite these difficulties, the statutes that apply to hold harmless and indemnity agreements can be classified into those that prohibit transfer, those that prohibit particular wording, and those that prescribe the exact wording in any clause the contracting parties choose to include in their agreement.

Prohibitive Statutes. A statute that attempts to prohibit virtually all indemnity and hold harmless agreements protecting certain classes of persons reads as follows:

> Indemnification Agreements Prohibited. Any agreement or provision whereby an architect, engineer, surveyor or his agents or employes is sought to be held harmless or indemnified for damages and claims arising out of circumstances giving rise to legal liability therefor on the part of any said persons shall be against public policy, void and wholly unenforceable.[18]

This New Hampshire statute is very broad and bars both hold harmless and indemnity agreements that might be applicable in "circumstances giving rise to legal liability," regardless of the nature of the wrongdoing or the sole or joint fault of any specified or unspecified party. Perhaps significantly, the statute is also very narrow in denying hold harmless or indemnity protection only to architects, engineers, surveyors, and their associates. Any hold harmless or indemnity agreement in which, for example, a building owner, contractor, or subcontractor is involved is presumably valid in this jurisdiction. This statute is similar to other statutes generally dealing with noninsurance contractual transfers or specifically with indemnity and hold harmless agreements. The scope of the statute is broad in some respects and narrow in others. It probably reflects the legislative concerns prevailing when the statute was enacted more than it represents a thorough attempt to protect the public interest.

Statutes Prohibiting Particular Wording. In a very important sense, statutes that prohibit a narrowly defined class of hold harmless or indemnity agreements—such as those defined in terms of the transferor's "sole negligence"—effectively forbid the use of this wording in these provisions. An alert business executive, attorney, or risk management professional concerned with contracts drafted or carried out in jurisdictions having these statutes must take care that these specific words do not appear. To validate their contracts, they will instead ensure that the hold harmless and indemnity agreements protecting them are phrased in terms of, say, the transferee/indemnitor's "joint fault," or "shared legal responsibility." In short, the key words of a statute prohibiting a certain type of risk transfer agreement are the very words that ought to be avoided in a risk-shifting provision that the drafter hopes will prove enforceable.

Other statutes more directly address the wording of risk control and risk financing transfers. For example, a Nevada statute provides as follows:

> No agency of this state nor any political subdivision, municipal corporation or district, nor any public officer or person charged with the letting

> of contracts for the construction, alteration or repair of public works shall draft or cause to be drafted specifications for bids, in connection with the construction, alteration or repair of public works:
>
> (a) In such a manner as to limit the bidding, directly or indirectly, to any one specific concern or . . .
>
> (c) In such a manner as to hold the bidder to whom such contract is awarded responsible for extra costs incurred as a result of errors or omissions by the public agency in the contract documents.[19]

This statute notably prohibits (1) only public entities and their officials and agents from drafting bids for contracts that hold the bidder "responsible for extra costs incurred as a result of errors or omissions by the public agency *in the contract documents,*" not other errors or omissions, and (2) then only in building/demolition contracts for public works. The statute appears to have been drafted in response to a legislative concern rather than as a general statement of public policy toward holding others "responsible for . . . errors and omissions" of another contracting party. The statute has no application to private organizations or individuals, public contracts unrelated to public works, or errors and omissions of the public agency that are not reflected in the contract documents.

Statutes prohibiting particular wording in risk transfer agreements generally have very narrow targets. Compliance with these statutes primarily involves avoiding the prohibited words and other related phrases. Creative draftsmanship and contract design can usually achieve the contracting parties' intentions almost as fully as if this kind of prohibitory statute did not exist.

Statutes Prescribing Certain Wording. In an attempt to prevent a transferee/indemnitor from undertaking burdensome commitments in an indemnity or hold harmless agreement, some states specify that if a particular type of contract does contain any such provision, the wording of the provision must incorporate certain phrases. The following Florida statute illustrates this limitation:

> Any portion of any agreement or contract for, or in connection with, any construction, alteration, repair, or demolition of a building, structure, appurtenance, or appliance, including moving and excavating connected with it, or any guarantee of, or in connection with, any of them, between an owner of real property and an architect, engineer, general contractor, subcontractor, materialman, or between any combination thereof, wherein any party referred to herein obtains indemnification from liability for damages to persons or property caused in whole or in part by any act, omission, or default of that party arising from the contract or its performance shall be void and unenforceable unless:
>
> (1) The contract contains a monetary limitation on the extent of the

indemnification and shall be a part of the project specifications or bid documents, if any, or

(2) The person indemnified by the contract gives a specific consideration to the indemnitor for the indemnification that shall be provided for in his contract and section of the project specifications or bid documents if any.[20]

The Florida legislature appears to have reasoned that an indemnity or hold harmless agreement for building construction/demolition has been fairly bargained if (1) the indemnitor's obligation has some monetary limit and (2) the transferor gives specific legal consideration to the transferee for the promise of protection. Again, this entire provision applies only to construction/demolition projects, not to any bailment, equipment lease, sales or service contract, or any other contractual transfers for risk financing or risk control. Nor does this statute require that every construction contract contain these provisions. The statute only demands that, if a hold harmless or indemnity agreement is included, it must contain the specified wording.

As another illustration, South Dakota enacted the following requirements with respect to all "construction contracts" that contain indemnity provisions:

> Section 1. Construction contracts, plans and specifications which contain indemnification provisions shall include the following provision:
>
> The obligations of the contractor shall not extend to the liability of the architect or engineer, his agents or employes arising out of (1) the preparation or approval of maps, drawings, opinions, reports, surveys, change orders, designs or specifications, or (2) the giving of or the failure to give directions or instructions by the architect, or engineer, his agents or employes, provided such giving or failure to give is the primary cause of the injury or damage.
>
> Section 2. Any indemnification provision in a construction contract in conflict with the above provision shall be unlawful and unenforceable.[21]

This statute does not require an indemnification provision in every construction contract. It does demand, however, that any party, public or private, excuse the contractor and its associates from indemnifying an architectural or engineering firm and its associates from claims arising out of specified situations. Notice that the precise wording of the required provision is specified for this type of contract but for no others.

MANAGEMENT OF NONINSURANCE CONTRACTUAL TRANSFERS

An organization's risk management professional faces a variety of uses for noninsurance contractual transfers for both risk control and risk financing, so he or she should be aware of the legal restrictions on their use. An organization's risk management professional must work to develop a consistent, feasible program for managing such contractual transfers and for becoming a transferee or transferor, where appropriate, but always with a clear understanding of the nature, scope, and direction of each transfer. In some situations the organization will not seek to be a transferor or a transferee, but will strive to let the common or statutory law work as intended to apportion exposures to, and the financial burden of, specified types of losses. Consistent and effective control of noninsurance contractual transfers requires (1) careful attention to factors affecting appropriate uses of such transfers from the standpoint of both the organization and society and (2) a clearly written and widely disseminated organizational policy with general administrative controls and specific control measures for managing noninsurance contractual transfers.

Factors Affecting Appropriate Use of Risk Transfers

Many executives, and even some risk management professionals, view noninsurance contractual transfers, and especially those for risk financing, as a contest between themselves and their counterparts in the opposing organization. They try to beat the opposition before they are beaten. The contest can be a serious and important one since the use and wording of contract provisions, especially liability-related hold harmless agreements not connected with construction contracts, are largely unregulated. Many organizations concerned about their rising liability insurance costs consider waivers and hold harmless agreements as clever ways to reduce their liability exposures and loss costs, often at others' expense, and the drafting of provisions for shifting exposures and risk financing obligations can be a means to this end.[22]

In the perspective of sound risk management, however, the goal is to employ noninsurance contractual transfers in ways that efficiently apportion loss exposures and the cost of losses for both the transferor, the transferee, as well as for the economy as a whole. *Efficiency* here refers to both organizational and economy-wide cost of risk. Therefore, the most efficient transfer lowers the cost of risk for each contracting organization.

Because the drafting and use of noninsurance contractual transfers can become a contest, a risk management professional should participate not as a contestant but as a referee, seeking fairness and mutual benefit for all participants. As such, this person should consider the following three factors that are relevant to the fairness of the contract and the mutual benefit of the contracting parties: (1) the legal enforceability of these provisions, (2) the relative abilities of the parties to manage risk (that is, to keep losses from happening and to pay for those that do), and (3) the price or other legal consideration the transferor has given explicitly or implicitly to the transferee.

Enforceability. Legal enforceability is one of the factors that determines the appropriate use of a contract. In fact, it can determine whether that contract can be used at all. A contract is not enforceable if it is found to be unconscionable or in violation of public policy or statutes. Second, it can be difficult to enforce a contract if the transfer provisions do not conform to the law. The result is that the transfer as interpreted by the courts will often differ from what the parties had in mind (see material under the heading "Restating Law"). Third, as discussed under the heading "Purchase Order Agreements," attempts by the parties to a contract to rid themselves of the same or related exposures or financial burdens can make it difficult to enforce the contract because risks have been transferred and retransferred to the extent that it can be almost impossible to tell who has agreed to accept what.

Ability To Manage Risk. Another factor to be considered is the ability of the transferee to pay major losses when they occur. Has the transferee accepted in this and other contracts more responsibility than it can handle? Construction companies, in particular, are a common target for hold harmless clauses. As a group they are also subject to sudden and severe financial strains in the ordinary conduct of their own business. It can be questioned whether there is always wisdom in such extensive pyramiding of responsibilities.

As a general practice, transferees must receive enough benefits from their contracts to cover the obligations assumed under them. However, what are fair benefits for the transferee may not always be reasonable for the transferor to offer. Noninsurance transfer, therefore, may not be the most efficient method for handling a given exposure. Moreover, transfers may render impracticable, or even preclude, handling of an exposure in a more efficient way. Not only may the transferee be unable to pay for large losses, but it may also be unable to do anything effective about reducing the losses.

These limitations on the efficacy of transfer apply particularly when the negligence exposure is transferred. This may violate the fundamental general management principle of keeping responsibility and authority in the same hands. That is, when liability for the negligence of one's own employees is transferred, the incentive to control negligence is divorced from the authority to do so. The transferor retains the authority, whereas the transferee acquires the responsibility and, thus, the incentive.

Consideration Paid. The third factor that is related to the fairness of a contract is the price or other consideration given by the transferor to the transferee. With respect to cost, the greatest efficiency will commonly be achieved when the responsibility for the financing of losses and the authority for the practical control of the hazards involved are lodged with the same party. This proposition requires such arrangements as having manufacturers rather than distributors assume the full financial responsibility for losses arising from faulty products and for defective materials used in the manufacturing process. It also calls for manufacturers to assume full responsibility for claims arising out of statements in their advertising. But distributors should have full financial responsibility for claims arising out of their own statements in selling and advertising and for their own acts of assembling, disassembling, mixing, storing, and packing of products. Similarly, contractors should have full financial responsibility for the activities of their employees and agents and the condition of the premises, equipment, and materials under their control or supervision, or to which their expertise applies. On the other hand, the building owner should have full responsibility for losses arising out of such items as specifications and from any use the owner makes of the premises on which the contractor is working. Since these dividing lines between responsibilities are not clear in all instances, the underlying contract, in the interests of economy and the ease of enforcement, should be specific and carefully worded.

In determining who can best manage exposures and pay for losses, it is important that the contractual transfer not be considered by itself. How one transfer relates to another should be considered. This sometimes leads to exceptions to the general rule of merging responsibility and authority. Consider the responsibility of a single tenant in a large office building for damage to the entire building. The general rule would require this tenant to assume liability for all damage arising from the small portion of the premises the tenant actively controls. But this rule would make it necessary for the tenant to buy insurance against its possible liability for severe fire damage to the building, duplicating the owner's insurance covering the same property.

Once a risk management professional or other executive has considered these factors in determining the fairness of a contract, risk management efforts should concentrate on establishing an effective program for controlling noninsurance transfers.

Elements of a Noninsurance Transfer Control Program

The first and most important step in establishing a sound program for controlling an organization's use of, and liability exposures under, the various noninsurance contractual transfers is to develop a consistent transfer strategy. This ensures that the organization is (1) a transferor when this role serves both the organization and the general economy, (2) a transferee when this role is similarly appropriate, and (3) neither a transferor nor transferee when neither role is appropriate.[23]

Much of the material in this chapter has been directed at protecting an organization from inadvertently becoming a transferee. This protective stance can be regarded as the *defensive strategy* toward noninsurance contractual transfers or trying to avoid becoming the "victim" of such a transfer. A defensive strategy should reflect an understanding of the conditions under which it is dangerous for an organization, and thus economically inefficient for society, to become a transferee. Such a strategy may also reflect a negative, distrustful attitude toward noninsurance transfers as a risk management technique. For some, this attitude may be justified by experience.

The opposite position, the *aggressive strategy* of trying to take advantage of other organizations by using economic power to impose transfers, is also frequently inappropriate for an organization and society. Indeed, unwavering pursuit of an aggressive strategy is regarded by many risk management professionals as unethical. It is possible that an unduly aggressive strategy has prompted others to follow a defensive strategy consistently and for legislatures and the courts to look with suspicion upon transfers that are handled under such circumstances.

A more balanced and productive strategy is neither consistently defensive nor consistently aggressive. Instead, it is developed out of an examination of the implications of alternative noninsurance transfer arrangements for the contracting organizations and the economy. As a result, transfers are used only when they benefit all the contracting parties without, at the very least, harming the general economy. Therefore, a sound policy rests both on a good general administrative program and on specific controls to secure appropriate transfers while avoiding inappropriate ones.

General Administrative Controls. Regardless of the size of the organization, it is important that there is an organized administrative program for controlling contractual transfers. The risk management professional needs to cultivate an understanding with everyone who is involved with contracts, including those who draw up as well as those who accept contracts. These people should also be encouraged to stay in close touch with the risk management department and to inform it of the status of all contracts.[24]

The initial objective of these controls should be to give all contract-related personnel a clear understanding of the exposure that may be hidden in the most "simple" contracts and the need to submit such documents for review by experienced personnel. In practically every organization a large number of the contracts are, for the most part, routine. Standard wording should be formalized, along with a policy statement about the use of it. The control system can be tailored readily to this situation. To illustrate, some weeks or months of careful scrutiny will probably indicate that purchase orders, service contracts, and various other more or less common contracts contain only a standard indemnity agreement. Once the responsible executives have discerned this pattern, appropriate decisions can be made about dealing with the liability involved. These contracts can then be left to periodic auditing.[25]

The more dangerous areas relate to contracts that cannot be classified as "routine." With these contracts effective education and training for all responsible personnel are of major importance. It cannot be emphasized enough that risk transfer agreements are not easy to spot, are not easy to evaluate, and can be hazardous. The risk manager or other official with responsibility for controlling these transfers must be given an adequate opportunity to perform the difficult function of reading and interpreting each contract. Unlike routine contracts, these types of agreements need more attention than periodic auditing.[26]

Even the most imaginative and thorough administrative program for controlling contractual transfers should be reviewed periodically. It is quite possible, for instance, that procedures that were "always used" can become unnecessarily cumbersome or insufficiently precise. Similarly, the cost of administering the program must be known and monitored. Control, which depends upon a knowledge of the facts, is the key objective.[27]

Specific Control Measures. Having identified and evaluated the exposure in the contractual transfer provisions, the person responsible for risk management must make decisions about the treatment of these exposures or must present recommendations to management. A risk manager who can establish the proper authority should be able to review all contracts before they are finally executed. This review is an opportunity to reject inappropriate contracts. A department head preoccupied with the benefits of a contract for that department may not be as sensitive to an indemnity provision as a professional risk manager.[28] Too often this apparently insignificant clause can adversely affect the financial stability of the entire organization.

Assuming that the risk manager reviews a contract and recommends endorsement, as is most often the case, important considerations are as follows:[29]

- To what extent can the assumption of exposure be reduced?
- What exposure can the organization afford to assume?
- To what extent should contractually assumed exposures be transferred by insurance?

- Can specific provisions of contracts be deleted, particularly those that involve exposures that can be neither safely retained nor transferred?
- Is it possible to negotiate clearer contract language, especially to clarify the intentions of the parties on all points that seem likely to present problems?

Reduction of Exposures Assumed. Reducing the exposures assumed is both a specific and a general matter. For example, both parties to a contract may wish to consider cutting the scope of the transfer clause in a *specific* contract to that which can be handled by the transferee's insurance effectively and economically. The contract drafters on both sides should understand insurance clearly, and especially its applications and shortcomings in contractual liability coverage. In addition, the drafters cannot overlook the uncertainty of a court's interpretation of this coverage and of the contractual transfer agreement itself.[30]

In general terms, risk management professionals should be cautious about the number of contractual transfers that are simultaneously in effect. Numerous transfers not only have complicated business relationships but raised costs as well. Wherever the use of a contractual transfer can be eliminated, the exposures must be assumed or otherwise managed.[31]

Retention of Exposures. A given agreement or group of agreements may present exposures that the organization is willing to assume without insurance. These will usually involve only minor and remote hazards, free of any element of catastrophe. However, if the risk management professional determines that exposures introduced by the contract are dangerously severe, retention may be unwise.[32]

Transfer Through Insurance. For exposures to be covered by insurance, the risk management professional must be as certain as possible of the available coverage. The risk management professional must also examine the other contracting party's insurance protection, if any. There are not only questions of arranging needed coverage but also of obtaining from the insurer a clear explanation of its coverage and legal defense obligations.[33]

Dealing With "Unmanageable" Provisions. Even the best use of loss reduction, retention, and insurance may fall short of helping to control contractual transfers. Rather than avoid such a contract, management can seek to remove some of the provisions. Examples include eliminating transfers of liability related to acts of God, contingencies for which no insurance can be obtained, and claims caused entirely by the transferor's alleged fault without any claimed wrongdoing by any other party (that is, the transferor's so-called "sole negligence"). The ability to make such changes depends on the bargaining strengths of the parties and the importance of their contractual relationship.[34]

Clarity of Contract Language. Wherever possible, the contract language should be clarified. Clarification may be possible more often than is at first supposed. Definitions are very important, yet often omitted.[35]

Fundamental Guidelines

The following are the basic guidelines for the proper use by all parties of noninsurance contractual transfers for risk control or risk financing:[36]

- *Make sure the indemnitor can stand behind its commitment financially.* In view of some court decisions, it is almost imperative that this commitment be backed by insurance of at least \$1,000,000 per occurrence. Department managers may complain that this coverage is excessive, but the risk management professional should explain that responsible organizations should carry at least this limit.
- *Require a certificate of insurance for contractual liability coverage before contract operations begin.* The certificate should state clearly that the *insurer* must provide at least thirty days' notice of cancellation or material change in coverage.
- *Be named as an additional insured in addition to obtaining a waiver of subrogation.* Although being added as an additional insured can pose some problems, such as an obligation to pay premiums or to comply with certain policy conditions after the loss, the advantages far outweigh the disadvantages. (In some circumstances, the additional insured status is not desirable.)
- *Avoid being too severe.* If a contractual transfer is too extreme, the courts may construe it as invalid because it is unconscionable or contrary to public policy. The further apart the two parties are in their bargaining power and knowledge of the terms of the contract, the more chance there is of an unenforceable agreement.
- *Avoid ambiguity.* The courts do not favor agreements that indemnify individuals or organizations against the consequences of their own negligence or intentional wrongdoing. If contract language is ambiguous, courts generally construe an indemnity agreement to make it consistent with common law doctrine and public policy. Generally, this will mean that a person or organization is indemnified for liability especially if it was only passively negligent in causing loss or injury.
- *Become more actively involved in legislation.* Many of the

present statutes limiting noninsurance indemnification are the products of lobbying efforts by special interest groups. Risk management professionals have an obligation to their organizations and the public to present compelling reasons for laws that can benefit an organization and the economy.

SUMMARY

Two or more individuals or organizations may contract with one another to shift either loss exposures or the financial burden of actual losses. A contract provision shifting loss exposures obligates the transferee to act instead of or on behalf of a transferor, and no payment is required. This arrangement achieves risk control for the transferor because there is no longer any possibility of loss from a transferred exposure, even if the transferee should become bankrupt. In contrast, a contract provision for risk financing obligates the transferee to pay losses to or on behalf of the transferor, thus providing the transferor with protection only when the transferee can and will provide the promised funds. For both transfers to be effective, they must be enforceable in the courts.

Contractual transfers for risk control are achieved through such mechanisms as incorporation, leases, subcontracts, surety or guaranty agreements, and waivers. All contractual transfers for risk financing can be described as indemnity agreements, but agreements that pertain to the transferor's liability claims are known as hold harmless agreements. One useful way of classifying indemnity agreements is in terms of the transactions with which they are associated, such as construction agreements, purchase order agreements, leases of premises and equipments, bailment contracts, and sale and service agreements. In addition, hold harmless agreements may be classified further as those that do the following:

1. Restate the law
2. Obligate the transferee to finance liability claims involving the joint fault of the transferor and the transferee
3. Require the transferee to respond even to claims alleging the transferor's sole fault
4. Require the transferee to pay all the transferor's liability losses of any sort

Organizations and individuals have a general right, frequently described as the freedom of contract, to transfer exposures and the financial burden of actual losses, provided that these transfers violate no rights of the contracting parties or of society. Freedom of contract, however, is limited by common law and statutes. Thus, on the basis of common law, any attempted risk control or risk financing transfer that is undisclosed to the transferee or is improperly obtained through coercion or deception will probably be rejected. Similarly, courts refuse to enforce contracts that are contrary to public policy. Statutes in about half the states further limit freedom of contract in the following ways:

1. Entirely prohibiting certain transfers
2. Prohibiting specified wording in particular types of transfers
3. Mandating a particular wording of any transfer agreement the parties may choose to include in their contract

The management of an organization should allocate exposures to loss and financial burdens of actual losses in ways that minimize the cost of risk for all concerned and that respect all parties' rights and responsibilities. To achieve this objective, management should draft, approve, and monitor all contracts with the following guidelines in mind:

- The transfer is fairly bargained and fully understood by all contracting parties; that is, the allocation of responsibilities between transferees and transferors should be as exhaustive and unambiguous as possible.
- The transfer agreement deals explicitly with all aspects of the loss exposure or of the actual losses (including all the property, net income, liability, and personnel losses that can stem from any particular accident).
- The agreement details or gives procedures for how it will be implemented.
- Exposures and losses should be transferred on a basis that is at least as efficient (that is, as inexpensive or as profitable) as other equally reliable risk management techniques.
- Transferees should be able and willing to meet their risk control and risk financing obligations.
- Each transferee should have significant ability and authority to apply risk control to the losses for which it is financially responsible.
- The price or other legal consideration a transferor gives a transferee should make the transfer financially attractive to both parties.
- The parties should anticipate and plan for any changes in their activities that might occur during the life of the contract, bearing in mind the effect those changes may have on the risk transfer agreement.

Chapter Notes

1. For documentation of the historical aspects of this discussion, see *Cambridge Economic History of Europe* (London: Cambridge University Press, 1977), vol. 5: *The Economic Organization of Early Modern Europe,* ed. E. E. Rich and C. H. Wilson, pp. 439–447.
2. G.W. Crist, Jr., *Corporate Suretyship,* 2nd ed. (New York: McGraw-Hill Book Company, 1950), pp. 3–8. Robert I. Mehr and Bob A. Hedges, *Risk Management: Concepts and Applications* (Homewood, IL: Richard D. Irwin, Inc., 1974), pp. 142–144.
3. *The Hold Harmless Agreement,* 3rd ed., Georgia Chapter of The Society of Chartered Property and Casualty Underwriters, The National Underwriter Company, Cincinnati, 1977, pp. 87–88.
4. *The Hold Harmless Agreement,* pp. 98–99.
5. Adapted from *The Hold Harmless Agreement,* 3rd ed., pp. 89–90.
6. Adapted from *The Hold Harmless Agreement,* 3rd ed., p. 97.
7. Adapted from *The Hold Harmless Agreement,* 3rd ed., p. 107.
8. Adapted from *The Hold Harmless Agreement,* 3rd ed., p. 109.
9. Mehr and Hedges, pp. 138–140.
10. The term "juridical risk" in a risk management context appears to have originated in print in Mehr and Hedges, *Risk Management in the Business Enterprise* (Homewood, IL: Richard D. Irwin, Inc., 1963), pp. 439-444.
11. A standard clause adapted from several sources.
12. Adapted from several provisions cited in *Insuring the Lease Exposure,* Cincinnati Chapter of The Society of Chartered Property and Casualty Underwriters, The National Underwriter Company, Cincinnati, 1981.
13. *The Hold Harmless Agreement,* 3rd ed., p. 101.
14. *The Hold Harmless Agreement,* 3rd ed., p. 102.
15. *The Hold Harmless Agreement,* 3rd ed., pp. 102–103.
16. See Alan M. Pearce, "Legal Prohibitions Against Use of Hold Harmless Agreements," *Risk Management,* April 1977, p. 30, for a good discussion of legal prohibitions.
17. Ga. Code Ann. § 20–504.
18. N.H. Rev. Stat. Ann. § 338A:1 (1975).
19. Nev. Rev. Stat. § 338.140 (1975).
20. Fla. Stat. Ann. § 725.06.
21. S.D. Codified Laws Ann. § 53.9 (1972).
22. Mehr and Hedges, pp. 147–150, 414–416.
23. Much of this section is adapted from *The Hold Harmless Agreement,* 3rd ed., p. 117–125.
24. *The Hold Harmless Agreement,* 3rd ed., pp. 117–118.
25. *The Hold Harmless Agreement,* 3rd ed., pp. 118–119.
26. *The Hold Harmless Agreement,* 3rd ed., p. 119.
27. *The Hold Harmless Agreement,* 3rd ed., p. 119.

28. *The Hold Harmless Agreement,* 3rd ed., pp. 119–120.
29. *The Hold Harmless Agreement,* 3rd ed., p. 120.
30. *The Hold Harmless Agreement,* 3rd ed., p. 121.
31. *The Hold Harmless Agreement,* 3rd ed., pp. 121–122.
32. *The Hold Harmless Agreement,* 3rd ed., p. 122.
33. *The Hold Harmless Agreement,* 3rd ed., p. 122.
34. *The Hold Harmless Agreement,* 3rd ed., pp. 122–123.
35. *The Hold Harmless Agreement,* 3rd ed., p. 124.
36. Adapted from Pearce, p. 38.

APPENDIX TO CHAPTER 7

General Conditions of the Contract for Construction

THE AMERICAN INSTITUTE OF ARCHITECTS

AIA Document A201

General Conditions of the Contract for Construction

THIS DOCUMENT HAS IMPORTANT LEGAL CONSEQUENCES; CONSULTATION WITH AN ATTORNEY IS ENCOURAGED WITH RESPECT TO ITS MODIFICATION

1987 EDITION

TABLE OF ARTICLES

This document has been approved and endorsed by the Associated General Contractors of America.

INDEX

GENERAL CONDITIONS OF THE CONTRACT FOR CONSTRUCTION

ARTICLE 1

GENERAL PROVISIONS

1.1 BASIC DEFINITIONS

1.1.1 THE CONTRACT DOCUMENTS

The Contract Documents consist of the Agreement between Owner and Contractor (hereinafter the Agreement), Conditions of the Contract (General, Supplementary and other Conditions), Drawings, Specifications, addenda issued prior to execution of the Contract, other documents listed in the Agreement and Modifications issued after execution of the Contract. A Modification is (1) a written amendment to the Contract signed by both parties, (2) a Change Order, (3) a Construction Change Directive or (4) a written order for a minor change in the Work issued by the Architect. Unless specifically enumerated in the Agreement, the Contract Documents do not include other documents such as bidding requirements (advertisement or invitation to bid, Instructions to Bidders, sample forms, the Contractor's bid or portions of addenda relating to bidding requirements).

1.1.2 THE CONTRACT

The Contract Documents form the Contract for Construction. The Contract represents the entire and integrated agreement between the parties hereto and supersedes prior negotiations, representations or agreements, either written or oral. The Contract may be amended or modified only by a Modification. The Contract Documents shall not be construed to create a contractual relationship of any kind (1) between the Architect and Contractor, (2) between the Owner and a Subcontractor or Sub-subcontractor or (3) between any persons or entities other than the Owner and Contractor. The Architect shall, however, be entitled to performance and enforcement of obligations under the Contract intended to facilitate performance of the Architect's duties.

1.1.3 THE WORK

The term "Work" means the construction and services required by the Contract Documents, whether completed or partially completed, and includes all other labor, materials, equipment and services provided or to be provided by the Contractor to fulfill the Contractor's obligations. The Work may constitute the whole or a part of the Project.

1.1.4 THE PROJECT

The Project is the total construction of which the Work performed under the Contract Documents may be the whole or a part and which may include construction by the Owner or by separate contractors.

1.1.5 THE DRAWINGS

The Drawings are the graphic and pictorial portions of the Contract Documents, wherever located and whenever issued, showing the design, location and dimensions of the Work, generally including plans, elevations, sections, details, schedules and diagrams.

1.1.6 THE SPECIFICATIONS

The Specifications are that portion of the Contract Documents consisting of the written requirements for materials, equipment, construction systems, standards and workmanship for the Work, and performance of related services.

1.1.7 THE PROJECT MANUAL

The Project Manual is the volume usually assembled for the Work which may include the bidding requirements, sample forms, Conditions of the Contract and Specifications.

1.2 EXECUTION, CORRELATION AND INTENT

1.2.1 The Contract Documents shall be signed by the Owner and Contractor as provided in the Agreement. If either the Owner or Contractor or both do not sign all the Contract Documents, the Architect shall identify such unsigned Documents upon request.

1.2.2 Execution of the Contract by the Contractor is a representation that the Contractor has visited the site, become familiar with local conditions under which the Work is to be performed and correlated personal observations with requirements of the Contract Documents.

1.2.3 The intent of the Contract Documents is to include all items necessary for the proper execution and completion of the Work by the Contractor. The Contract Documents are complementary, and what is required by one shall be as binding as if required by all; performance by the Contractor shall be required only to the extent consistent with the Contract Documents and reasonably inferable from them as being necessary to produce the intended results.

1.2.4 Organization of the Specifications into divisions, sections and articles, and arrangement of Drawings shall not control the Contractor in dividing the Work among Subcontractors or in establishing the extent of Work to be performed by any trade.

1.2.5 Unless otherwise stated in the Contract Documents, words which have well-known technical or construction industry meanings are used in the Contract Documents in accordance with such recognized meanings.

1.3 OWNERSHIP AND USE OF ARCHITECT'S DRAWINGS, SPECIFICATIONS AND OTHER DOCUMENTS

1.3.1 The Drawings, Specifications and other documents prepared by the Architect are instruments of the Architect's service through which the Work to be executed by the Contractor is described. The Contractor may retain one contract record set. Neither the Contractor nor any Subcontractor, Sub-subcontractor or material or equipment supplier shall own or claim a copyright in the Drawings, Specifications and other documents prepared by the Architect, and unless otherwise indicated the Architect shall be deemed the author of them and will retain all common law, statutory and other reserved rights, in addition to the copyright. All copies of them, except the Contractor's record set, shall be returned or suitably accounted for to the Architect, on request, upon completion of the Work. The Drawings, Specifications and other documents prepared by the Architect, and copies thereof furnished to the Contractor, are for use solely with respect to this Project. They are not to be used by the Contractor or any Subcontractor, Sub-subcontractor or material or equipment supplier on other projects or for additions to this Project outside the scope of the

Work without the specific written consent of the Owner and Architect. The Contractor, Subcontractors, Sub-subcontractors and material or equipment suppliers are granted a limited license to use and reproduce applicable portions of the Drawings, Specifications and other documents prepared by the Architect appropriate to and for use in the execution of their Work under the Contract Documents. All copies made under this license shall bear the statutory copyright notice, if any, shown on the Drawings, Specifications and other documents prepared by the Architect. Submittal or distribution to meet official regulatory requirements or for other purposes in connection with this Project is not to be construed as publication in derogation of the Architect's copyright or other reserved rights.

1.4 CAPITALIZATION

1.4.1 Terms capitalized in these General Conditions include those which are (1) specifically defined, (2) the titles of numbered articles and identified references to Paragraphs, Subparagraphs and Clauses in the document or (3) the titles of other documents published by the American Institute of Architects.

1.5 INTERPRETATION

1.5.1 In the interest of brevity the Contract Documents frequently omit modifying words such as "all" and "any" and articles such as "the" and "an," but the fact that a modifier or an article is absent from one statement and appears in another is not intended to affect the interpretation of either statement.

ARTICLE 2

OWNER

2.1 DEFINITION

2.1.1 The Owner is the person or entity identified as such in the Agreement and is referred to throughout the Contract Documents as if singular in number. The term "Owner" means the Owner or the Owner's authorized representative.

2.1.2 The Owner upon reasonable written request shall furnish to the Contractor in writing information which is necessary and relevant for the Contractor to evaluate, give notice of or enforce mechanic's lien rights. Such information shall include a correct statement of the record legal title to the property on which the Project is located, usually referred to as the site, and the Owner's interest therein at the time of execution of the Agreement and, within five days after any change, information of such change in title, recorded or unrecorded.

2.2 INFORMATION AND SERVICES REQUIRED OF THE OWNER

2.2.1 The Owner shall, at the request of the Contractor, prior to execution of the Agreement and promptly from time to time thereafter, furnish to the Contractor reasonable evidence that financial arrangements have been made to fulfill the Owner's obligations under the Contract. *[Note: Unless such reasonable evidence were furnished on request prior to the execution of the Agreement, the prospective contractor would not be required to execute the Agreement or to commence the Work.]*

2.2.2 The Owner shall furnish surveys describing physical characteristics, legal limitations and utility locations for the site of the Project, and a legal description of the site.

2.2.3 Except for permits and fees which are the responsibility of the Contractor under the Contract Documents, the Owner shall secure and pay for necessary approvals, easements, assessments and charges required for construction, use or occupancy of permanent structures or for permanent changes in existing facilities.

2.2.4 Information or services under the Owner's control shall be furnished by the Owner with reasonable promptness to avoid delay in orderly progress of the Work.

2.2.5 Unless otherwise provided in the Contract Documents, the Contractor will be furnished, free of charge, such copies of Drawings and Project Manuals as are reasonably necessary for execution of the Work.

2.2.6 The foregoing are in addition to other duties and responsibilities of the Owner enumerated herein and especially those in respect to Article 6 (Construction by Owner or by Separate Contractors), Article 9 (Payments and Completion) and Article 11 (Insurance and Bonds).

2.3 OWNER'S RIGHT TO STOP THE WORK

2.3.1 If the Contractor fails to correct Work which is not in accordance with the requirements of the Contract Documents as required by Paragraph 12.2 or persistently fails to carry out Work in accordance with the Contract Documents, the Owner, by written order signed personally or by an agent specifically so empowered by the Owner in writing, may order the Contractor to stop the Work, or any portion thereof, until the cause for such order has been eliminated; however, the right of the Owner to stop the Work shall not give rise to a duty on the part of the Owner to exercise this right for the benefit of the Contractor or any other person or entity, except to the extent required by Subparagraph 6.1.3.

2.4 OWNER'S RIGHT TO CARRY OUT THE WORK

2.4.1 If the Contractor defaults or neglects to carry out the Work in accordance with the Contract Documents and fails within a seven-day period after receipt of written notice from the Owner to commence and continue correction of such default or neglect with diligence and promptness, the Owner may after such seven-day period give the Contractor a second written notice to correct such deficiencies within a second seven-day period. If the Contractor within such second seven-day period after receipt of such second notice fails to commence and continue to correct any deficiencies, the Owner may, without prejudice to other remedies the Owner may have, correct such deficiencies. In such case an appropriate Change Order shall be issued deducting from payments then or thereafter due the Contractor the cost of correcting such deficiencies, including compensation for the Architect's additional services and expenses made necessary by such default, neglect or failure. Such action by the Owner and amounts charged to the Contractor are both subject to prior approval of the Architect. If payments then or thereafter due the Contractor are not sufficient to cover such amounts, the Contractor shall pay the difference to the Owner.

ARTICLE 3

CONTRACTOR

3.1 DEFINITION

3.1.1 The Contractor is the person or entity identified as such in the Agreement and is referred to throughout the Contract Documents as if singular in number. The term "Contractor" means the Contractor or the Contractor's authorized representative.

3.2 REVIEW OF CONTRACT DOCUMENTS AND FIELD CONDITIONS BY CONTRACTOR

3.2.1 The Contractor shall carefully study and compare the Contract Documents with each other and with information furnished by the Owner pursuant to Subparagraph 2.2.2 and shall at once report to the Architect errors, inconsistencies or omissions discovered. The Contractor shall not be liable to the Owner or Architect for damage resulting from errors, inconsistencies or omissions in the Contract Documents unless the Contractor recognized such error, inconsistency or omission and knowingly failed to report it to the Architect. If the Contractor performs any construction activity knowing it involves a recognized error, inconsistency or omission in the Contract Documents without such notice to the Architect, the Contractor shall assume appropriate responsibility for such performance and shall bear an appropriate amount of the attributable costs for correction.

3.2.2 The Contractor shall take field measurements and verify field conditions and shall carefully compare such field measurements and conditions and other information known to the Contractor with the Contract Documents before commencing activities. Errors, inconsistencies or omissions discovered shall be reported to the Architect at once.

3.2.3 The Contractor shall perform the Work in accordance with the Contract Documents and submittals approved pursuant to Paragraph 3.12.

3.3 SUPERVISION AND CONSTRUCTION PROCEDURES

3.3.1 The Contractor shall supervise and direct the Work, using the Contractor's best skill and attention. The Contractor shall be solely responsible for and have control over construction means, methods, techniques, sequences and procedures and for coordinating all portions of the Work under the Contract, unless Contract Documents give other specific instructions concerning these matters.

3.3.2 The Contractor shall be responsible to the Owner for acts and omissions of the Contractor's employees, Subcontractors and their agents and employees, and other persons performing portions of the Work under a contract with the Contractor.

3.3.3 The Contractor shall not be relieved of obligations to perform the Work in accordance with the Contract Documents either by activities or duties of the Architect in the Architect's administration of the Contract, or by tests, inspections or approvals required or performed by persons other than the Contractor.

3.3.4 The Contractor shall be responsible for inspection of portions of Work already performed under this Contract to determine that such portions are in proper condition to receive subsequent Work.

3.4 LABOR AND MATERIALS

3.4.1 Unless otherwise provided in the Contract Documents, the Contractor shall provide and pay for labor, materials, equipment, tools, construction equipment and machinery, water, heat, utilities, transportation, and other facilities and services necessary for proper execution and completion of the Work, whether temporary or permanent and whether or not incorporated or to be incorporated in the Work.

3.4.2 The Contractor shall enforce strict discipline and good order among the Contractor's employees and other persons carrying out the Contract. The Contractor shall not permit employment of unfit persons or persons not skilled in tasks assigned to them.

3.5 WARRANTY

3.5.1 The Contractor warrants to the Owner and Architect that materials and equipment furnished under the Contract will be of good quality and new unless otherwise required or permitted by the Contract Documents, that the Work will be free from defects not inherent in the quality required or permitted, and that the Work will conform with the requirements of the Contract Documents. Work not conforming to these requirements, including substitutions not properly approved and authorized, may be considered defective. The Contractor's warranty excludes remedy for damage or defect caused by abuse, modifications not executed by the Contractor, improper or insufficient maintenance, improper operation, or normal wear and tear under normal usage. If required by the Architect, the Contractor shall furnish satisfactory evidence as to the kind and quality of materials and equipment.

3.6 TAXES

3.6.1 The Contractor shall pay sales, consumer, use and similar taxes for the Work or portions thereof provided by the Contractor which are legally enacted when bids are received or negotiations concluded, whether or not yet effective or merely scheduled to go into effect.

3.7 PERMITS, FEES AND NOTICES

3.7.1 Unless otherwise provided in the Contract Documents, the Contractor shall secure and pay for the building permit and other permits and governmental fees, licenses and inspections necessary for proper execution and completion of the Work which are customarily secured after execution of the Contract and which are legally required when bids are received or negotiations concluded.

3.7.2 The Contractor shall comply with and give notices required by laws, ordinances, rules, regulations and lawful orders of public authorities bearing on performance of the Work.

3.7.3 It is not the Contractor's responsibility to ascertain that the Contract Documents are in accordance with applicable laws, statutes, ordinances, building codes, and rules and regulations. However, if the Contractor observes that portions of the Contract Documents are at variance therewith, the Contractor shall promptly notify the Architect and Owner in writing, and necessary changes shall be accomplished by appropriate Modification.

3.7.4 If the Contractor performs Work knowing it to be contrary to laws, statutes, ordinances, building codes, and rules and regulations without such notice to the Architect and Owner, the Contractor shall assume full responsibility for such Work and shall bear the attributable costs.

3.8 ALLOWANCES

3.8.1 The Contractor shall include in the Contract Sum all allowances stated in the Contract Documents. Items covered by allowances shall be supplied for such amounts and by such persons or entities as the Owner may direct, but the Contractor shall not be required to employ persons or entities against which the Contractor makes reasonable objection.

3.8.2 Unless otherwise provided in the Contract Documents:

.1 materials and equipment under an allowance shall be selected promptly by the Owner to avoid delay in the Work;

.2 allowances shall cover the cost to the Contractor of materials and equipment delivered at the site and all required taxes, less applicable trade discounts;

.3 Contractor's costs for unloading and handling at the site, labor, installation costs, overhead, profit and other expenses contemplated for stated allowance amounts shall be included in the Contract Sum and not in the allowances;

.4 whenever costs are more than or less than allowances, the Contract Sum shall be adjusted accordingly by Change Order. The amount of the Change Order shall reflect (1) the difference between actual costs and the allowances under Clause 3.8.2.2 and (2) changes in Contractor's costs under Clause 3.8.2.3.

3.9 SUPERINTENDENT

3.9.1 The Contractor shall employ a competent superintendent and necessary assistants who shall be in attendance at the Project site during performance of the Work. The superintendent shall represent the Contractor, and communications given to the superintendent shall be as binding as if given to the Contractor. Important communications shall be confirmed in writing. Other communications shall be similarly confirmed on written request in each case.

3.10 CONTRACTOR'S CONSTRUCTION SCHEDULES

3.10.1 The Contractor, promptly after being awarded the Contract, shall prepare and submit for the Owner's and Architect's information a Contractor's construction schedule for the Work. The schedule shall not exceed time limits current under the Contract Documents, shall be revised at appropriate intervals as required by the conditions of the Work and Project, shall be related to the entire Project to the extent required by the Contract Documents, and shall provide for expeditious and practicable execution of the Work.

3.10.2 The Contractor shall prepare and keep current, for the Architect's approval, a schedule of submittals which is coordinated with the Contractor's construction schedule and allows the Architect reasonable time to review submittals.

3.10.3 The Contractor shall conform to the most recent schedules.

3.11 DOCUMENTS AND SAMPLES AT THE SITE

3.11.1 The Contractor shall maintain at the site for the Owner one record copy of the Drawings, Specifications, addenda, Change Orders and other Modifications, in good order and marked currently to record changes and selections made during construction, and in addition approved Shop Drawings, Product Data, Samples and similar required submittals. These shall be available to the Architect and shall be delivered to the Architect for submittal to the Owner upon completion of the Work.

3.12 SHOP DRAWINGS, PRODUCT DATA AND SAMPLES

3.12.1 Shop Drawings are drawings, diagrams, schedules and other data specially prepared for the Work by the Contractor or a Subcontractor, Sub-subcontractor, manufacturer, supplier or distributor to illustrate some portion of the Work.

3.12.2 Product Data are illustrations, standard schedules, performance charts, instructions, brochures, diagrams and other information furnished by the Contractor to illustrate materials or equipment for some portion of the Work.

3.12.3 Samples are physical examples which illustrate materials, equipment or workmanship and establish standards by which the Work will be judged.

3.12.4 Shop Drawings, Product Data, Samples and similar submittals are not Contract Documents. The purpose of their submittal is to demonstrate for those portions of the Work for which submittals are required the way the Contractor proposes to conform to the information given and the design concept expressed in the Contract Documents. Review by the Architect is subject to the limitations of Subparagraph 4.2.7.

3.12.5 The Contractor shall review, approve and submit to the Architect Shop Drawings, Product Data, Samples and similar submittals required by the Contract Documents with reasonable promptness and in such sequence as to cause no delay in the Work or in the activities of the Owner or of separate contractors. Submittals made by the Contractor which are not required by the Contract Documents may be returned without action.

3.12.6 The Contractor shall perform no portion of the Work requiring submittal and review of Shop Drawings, Product Data, Samples or similar submittals until the respective submittal has been approved by the Architect. Such Work shall be in accordance with approved submittals.

3.12.7 By approving and submitting Shop Drawings, Product Data, Samples and similar submittals, the Contractor represents that the Contractor has determined and verified materials, field measurements and field construction criteria related thereto, or will do so, and has checked and coordinated the information contained within such submittals with the requirements of the Work and of the Contract Documents.

3.12.8 The Contractor shall not be relieved of responsibility for deviations from requirements of the Contract Documents by the Architect's approval of Shop Drawings, Product Data, Samples or similar submittals unless the Contractor has specifically informed the Architect in writing of such deviation at the time of submittal and the Architect has given written approval to the specific deviation. The Contractor shall not be relieved of responsibility for errors or omissions in Shop Drawings, Product Data, Samples or similar submittals by the Architect's approval thereof.

3.12.9 The Contractor shall direct specific attention, in writing or on resubmitted Shop Drawings, Product Data, Samples or similar submittals, to revisions other than those requested by the Architect on previous submittals.

3.12.10 Informational submittals upon which the Architect is not expected to take responsive action may be so identified in the Contract Documents.

3.12.11 When professional certification of performance criteria of materials, systems or equipment is required by the Contract Documents, the Architect shall be entitled to rely upon the accuracy and completeness of such calculations and certifications.

3.13 USE OF SITE

3.13.1 The Contractor shall confine operations at the site to areas permitted by law, ordinances, permits and the Contract Documents and shall not unreasonably encumber the site with materials or equipment.

3.14 CUTTING AND PATCHING

3.14.1 The Contractor shall be responsible for cutting, fitting or patching required to complete the Work or to make its parts fit together properly.

3.14.2 The Contractor shall not damage or endanger a portion of the Work or fully or partially completed construction of the Owner or separate contractors by cutting, patching or otherwise altering such construction, or by excavation. The Contractor shall not cut or otherwise alter such construction by the

Owner or a separate contractor except with written consent of the Owner and of such separate contractor; such consent shall not be unreasonably withheld. The Contractor shall not unreasonably withhold from the Owner or a separate contractor the Contractor's consent to cutting or otherwise altering the Work.

3.15 CLEANING UP

3.15.1 The Contractor shall keep the premises and surrounding area free from accumulation of waste materials or rubbish caused by operations under the Contract. At completion of the Work the Contractor shall remove from and about the Project waste materials, rubbish, the Contractor's tools, construction equipment, machinery and surplus materials.

3.15.2 If the Contractor fails to clean up as provided in the Contract Documents, the Owner may do so and the cost thereof shall be charged to the Contractor.

3.16 ACCESS TO WORK

3.16.1 The Contractor shall provide the Owner and Architect access to the Work in preparation and progress wherever located.

3.17 ROYALTIES AND PATENTS

3.17.1 The Contractor shall pay all royalties and license fees. The Contractor shall defend suits or claims for infringement of patent rights and shall hold the Owner and Architect harmless from loss on account thereof, but shall not be responsible for such defense or loss when a particular design, process or product of a particular manufacturer or manufacturers is required by the Contract Documents. However, if the Contractor has reason to believe that the required design, process or product is an infringement of a patent, the Contractor shall be responsible for such loss unless such information is promptly furnished to the Architect.

3.18 INDEMNIFICATION

3.18.1 To the fullest extent permitted by law, the Contractor shall indemnify and hold harmless the Owner, Architect, Architect's consultants, and agents and employees of any of them from and against claims, damages, losses and expenses, including but not limited to attorneys' fees, arising out of or resulting from performance of the Work, provided that such claim, damage, loss or expense is attributable to bodily injury, sickness, disease or death, or to injury to or destruction of tangible property (other than the Work itself) including loss of use resulting therefrom, but only to the extent caused in whole or in part by negligent acts or omissions of the Contractor, a Subcontractor, anyone directly or indirectly employed by them or anyone for whose acts they may be liable, regardless of whether or not such claim, damage, loss or expense is caused in part by a party indemnified hereunder. Such obligation shall not be construed to negate, abridge, or reduce other rights or obligations of indemnity which would otherwise exist as to a party or person described in this Paragraph 3.18.

3.18.2 In claims against any person or entity indemnified under this Paragraph 3.18 by an employee of the Contractor, a Subcontractor, anyone directly or indirectly employed by them or anyone for whose acts they may be liable, the indemnification obligation under this Paragraph 3.18 shall not be limited by a limitation on amount or type of damages, compensation or benefits payable by or for the Contractor or a Subcontractor under workers' or workmen's compensation acts, disability benefit acts or other employee benefit acts.

3.18.3 The obligations of the Contractor under this Paragraph 3.18 shall not extend to the liability of the Architect, the Architect's consultants, and agents and employees of any of them arising out of (1) the preparation or approval of maps, drawings, opinions, reports, surveys, Change Orders, designs or specifications, or (2) the giving of or the failure to give directions or instructions by the Architect, the Architect's consultants, and agents and employees of any of them provided such giving or failure to give is the primary cause of the injury or damage.

ARTICLE 4

ADMINISTRATION OF THE CONTRACT

4.1 ARCHITECT

4.1.1 The Architect is the person lawfully licensed to practice architecture or an entity lawfully practicing architecture identified as such in the Agreement and is referred to throughout the Contract Documents as if singular in number. The term "Architect" means the Architect or the Architect's authorized representative.

4.1.2 Duties, responsibilities and limitations of authority of the Architect as set forth in the Contract Documents shall not be restricted, modified or extended without written consent of the Owner, Contractor and Architect. Consent shall not be unreasonably withheld.

4.1.3 In case of termination of employment of the Architect, the Owner shall appoint an architect against whom the Contractor makes no reasonable objection and whose status under the Contract Documents shall be that of the former architect.

4.1.4 Disputes arising under Subparagraphs 4.1.2 and 4.1.3 shall be subject to arbitration.

4.2 ARCHITECT'S ADMINISTRATION OF THE CONTRACT

4.2.1 The Architect will provide administration of the Contract as described in the Contract Documents, and will be the Owner's representative (1) during construction, (2) until final payment is due and (3) with the Owner's concurrence, from time to time during the correction period described in Paragraph 12.2. The Architect will advise and consult with the Owner. The Architect will have authority to act on behalf of the Owner only to the extent provided in the Contract Documents, unless otherwise modified by written instrument in accordance with other provisions of the Contract.

4.2.2 The Architect will visit the site at intervals appropriate to the stage of construction to become generally familiar with the progress and quality of the completed Work and to determine in general if the Work is being performed in a manner indicating that the Work, when completed, will be in accordance with the Contract Documents. However, the Architect will not be required to make exhaustive or continuous on-site inspections to check quality or quantity of the Work. On the basis of on-site observations as an architect, the Architect will keep the Owner informed of progress of the Work, and will endeavor to guard the Owner against defects and deficiencies in the Work.

4.2.3 The Architect will not have control over or charge of and will not be responsible for construction means, methods, techniques, sequences or procedures, or for safety precautions and programs in connection with the Work, since these are solely the Contractor's responsibility as provided in Paragraph 3.3. The Architect will not be responsible for the Contractor's failure to carry out the Work in accordance with the Contract Documents. The Architect will not have control over or charge of and will not be responsible for acts or omissions of the Contractor, Subcontractors, or their agents or employees, or of any other persons performing portions of the Work.

4.2.4 Communications Facilitating Contract Administration. Except as otherwise provided in the Contract Documents or when direct communications have been specially authorized, the Owner and Contractor shall endeavor to communicate through the Architect. Communications by and with the Architect's consultants shall be through the Architect. Communications by and with Subcontractors and material suppliers shall be through the Contractor. Communications by and with separate contractors shall be through the Owner.

4.2.5 Based on the Architect's observations and evaluations of the Contractor's Applications for Payment, the Architect will review and certify the amounts due the Contractor and will issue Certificates for Payment in such amounts.

4.2.6 The Architect will have authority to reject Work which does not conform to the Contract Documents. Whenever the Architect considers it necessary or advisable for implementation of the intent of the Contract Documents, the Architect will have authority to require additional inspection or testing of the Work in accordance with Subparagraphs 13.5.2 and 13.5.3, whether or not such Work is fabricated, installed or completed. However, neither this authority of the Architect nor a decision made in good faith either to exercise or not to exercise such authority shall give rise to a duty or responsibility of the Architect to the Contractor, Subcontractors, material and equipment suppliers, their agents or employees, or other persons performing portions of the Work.

4.2.7 The Architect will review and approve or take other appropriate action upon the Contractor's submittals such as Shop Drawings, Product Data and Samples, but only for the limited purpose of checking for conformance with information given and the design concept expressed in the Contract Documents. The Architect's action will be taken with such reasonable promptness as to cause no delay in the Work or in the activities of the Owner, Contractor or separate contractors, while allowing sufficient time in the Architect's professional judgment to permit adequate review. Review of such submittals is not conducted for the purpose of determining the accuracy and completeness of other details such as dimensions and quantities, or for substantiating instructions for installation or performance of equipment or systems, all of which remain the responsibility of the Contractor as required by the Contract Documents. The Architect's review of the Contractor's submittals shall not relieve the Contractor of the obligations under Paragraphs 3.3, 3.5 and 3.12. The Architect's review shall not constitute approval of safety precautions or, unless otherwise specifically stated by the Architect, of any construction means, methods, techniques, sequences or procedures. The Architect's approval of a specific item shall not indicate approval of an assembly of which the item is a component.

4.2.8 The Architect will prepare Change Orders and Construction Change Directives, and may authorize minor changes in the Work as provided in Paragraph 7.4.

4.2.9 The Architect will conduct inspections to determine the date or dates of Substantial Completion and the date of final completion, will receive and forward to the Owner for the Owner's review and records written warranties and related documents required by the Contract and assembled by the Contractor, and will issue a final Certificate for Payment upon compliance with the requirements of the Contract Documents.

4.2.10 If the Owner and Architect agree, the Architect will provide one or more project representatives to assist in carrying out the Architect's responsibilities at the site. The duties, responsibilities and limitations of authority of such project representatives shall be as set forth in an exhibit to be incorporated in the Contract Documents.

4.2.11 The Architect will interpret and decide matters concerning performance under and requirements of the Contract Documents on written request of either the Owner or Contractor. The Architect's response to such requests will be made with reasonable promptness and within any time limits agreed upon. If no agreement is made concerning the time within which interpretations required of the Architect shall be furnished in compliance with this Paragraph 4.2, then delay shall not be recognized on account of failure by the Architect to furnish such interpretations until 15 days after written request is made for them.

4.2.12 Interpretations and decisions of the Architect will be consistent with the intent of and reasonably inferable from the Contract Documents and will be in writing or in the form of drawings. When making such interpretations and decisions, the Architect will endeavor to secure faithful performance by both Owner and Contractor, will not show partiality to either and will not be liable for results of interpretations or decisions so rendered in good faith.

4.2.13 The Architect's decisions on matters relating to aesthetic effect will be final if consistent with the intent expressed in the Contract Documents.

4.3 CLAIMS AND DISPUTES

4.3.1 Definition. A Claim is a demand or assertion by one of the parties seeking, as a matter of right, adjustment or interpretation of Contract terms, payment of money, extension of time or other relief with respect to the terms of the Contract. The term "Claim" also includes other disputes and matters in question between the Owner and Contractor arising out of or relating to the Contract. Claims must be made by written notice. The responsibility to substantiate Claims shall rest with the party making the Claim.

4.3.2 Decision of Architect. Claims, including those alleging an error or omission by the Architect, shall be referred initially to the Architect for action as provided in Paragraph 4.4. A decision by the Architect, as provided in Subparagraph 4.4.4, shall be required as a condition precedent to arbitration or litigation of a Claim between the Contractor and Owner as to all such matters arising prior to the date final payment is due, regardless of (1) whether such matters relate to execution and progress of the Work or (2) the extent to which the Work has been completed. The decision by the Architect in response to a Claim shall not be a condition precedent to arbitration or litigation in the event (1) the position of Architect is vacant, (2) the Architect has not received evidence or has failed to render a decision within agreed time limits, (3) the Architect has failed to take action required under Subparagraph 4.4.4 within 30 days after the Claim is made, (4) 45 days have passed after the Claim has been referred to the Architect or (5) the Claim relates to a mechanic's lien.

4.3.3 Time Limits on Claims. Claims by either party must be made within 21 days after occurrence of the event giving rise to such Claim or within 21 days after the claimant first recognizes the condition giving rise to the Claim, whichever is later. Claims must be made by written notice. An additional Claim made after the initial Claim has been implemented by Change Order will not be considered unless submitted in a timely manner.

4.3.4 Continuing Contract Performance. Pending final resolution of a Claim including arbitration, unless otherwise agreed in writing the Contractor shall proceed diligently with performance of the Contract and the Owner shall continue to make payments in accordance with the Contract Documents.

4.3.5 Waiver of Claims: Final Payment. The making of final payment shall constitute a waiver of Claims by the Owner except those arising from:

- **.1** liens, Claims, security interests or encumbrances arising out of the Contract and unsettled;
- **.2** failure of the Work to comply with the requirements of the Contract Documents; or
- **.3** terms of special warranties required by the Contract Documents.

4.3.6 Claims for Concealed or Unknown Conditions. If conditions are encountered at the site which are (1) subsurface or otherwise concealed physical conditions which differ materially from those indicated in the Contract Documents or (2) unknown physical conditions of an unusual nature, which differ materially from those ordinarily found to exist and generally recognized as inherent in construction activities of the character provided for in the Contract Documents, then notice by the observing party shall be given to the other party promptly before conditions are disturbed and in no event later than 21 days after first observance of the conditions. The Architect will promptly investigate such conditions and, if they differ materially and cause an increase or decrease in the Contractor's cost of, or time required for, performance of any part of the Work, will recommend an equitable adjustment in the Contract Sum or Contract Time, or both. If the Architect determines that the conditions at the site are not materially different from those indicated in the Contract Documents and that no change in the terms of the Contract is justified, the Architect shall so notify the Owner and Contractor in writing, stating the reasons. Claims by either party in opposition to such determination must be made within 21 days after the Architect has given notice of the decision. If the Owner and Contractor cannot agree on an adjustment in the Contract Sum or Contract Time, the adjustment shall be referred to the Architect for initial determination, subject to further proceedings pursuant to Paragraph 4.4.

4.3.7 Claims for Additional Cost. If the Contractor wishes to make Claim for an increase in the Contract Sum, written notice as provided herein shall be given before proceeding to execute the Work. Prior notice is not required for Claims relating to an emergency endangering life or property arising under Paragraph 10.3. If the Contractor believes additional cost is involved for reasons including but not limited to (1) a written interpretation from the Architect, (2) an order by the Owner to stop the Work where the Contractor was not at fault, (3) a written order for a minor change in the Work issued by the Architect, (4) failure of payment by the Owner, (5) termination of the Contract by the Owner, (6) Owner's suspension or (7) other reasonable grounds, Claim shall be filed in accordance with the procedure established herein.

4.3.8 Claims for Additional Time

4.3.8.1 If the Contractor wishes to make Claim for an increase in the Contract Time, written notice as provided herein shall be given. The Contractor's Claim shall include an estimate of cost and of probable effect of delay on progress of the Work. In the case of a continuing delay only one Claim is necessary.

4.3.8.2 If adverse weather conditions are the basis for a Claim for additional time, such Claim shall be documented by data substantiating that weather conditions were abnormal for the period of time and could not have been reasonably anticipated, and that weather conditions had an adverse effect on the scheduled construction.

4.3.9 Injury or Damage to Person or Property. If either party to the Contract suffers injury or damage to person or property because of an act or omission of the other party, of any of the other party's employees or agents, or of others for whose acts such party is legally liable, written notice of such injury or damage, whether or not insured, shall be given to the other party within a reasonable time not exceeding 21 days after first observance. The notice shall provide sufficient detail to enable the other party to investigate the matter. If a Claim for additional cost or time related to this Claim is to be asserted, it shall be filed as provided in Subparagraphs 4.3.7 or 4.3.8.

4.4 RESOLUTION OF CLAIMS AND DISPUTES

4.4.1 The Architect will review Claims and take one or more of the following preliminary actions within ten days of receipt of a Claim: (1) request additional supporting data from the claimant, (2) submit a schedule to the parties indicating when the Architect expects to take action, (3) reject the Claim in whole or in part, stating reasons for rejection, (4) recommend approval of the Claim by the other party or (5) suggest a compromise. The Architect may also, but is not obligated to, notify the surety, if any, of the nature and amount of the Claim.

4.4.2 If a Claim has been resolved, the Architect will prepare or obtain appropriate documentation.

4.4.3 If a Claim has not been resolved, the party making the Claim shall, within ten days after the Architect's preliminary response, take one or more of the following actions: (1) submit additional supporting data requested by the Architect, (2) modify the initial Claim or (3) notify the Architect that the initial Claim stands.

4.4.4 If a Claim has not been resolved after consideration of the foregoing and of further evidence presented by the parties or requested by the Architect, the Architect will notify the parties in writing that the Architect's decision will be made within seven days, which decision shall be final and binding on the parties but subject to arbitration. Upon expiration of such time period, the Architect will render to the parties the Architect's written decision relative to the Claim, including any change in the Contract Sum or Contract Time or both. If there is a surety and there appears to be a possibility of a Contractor's default, the Architect may, but is not obligated to, notify the surety and request the surety's assistance in resolving the controversy.

4.5 ARBITRATION

4.5.1 Controversies and Claims Subject to Arbitration. Any controversy or Claim arising out of or related to the Contract, or the breach thereof, shall be settled by arbitration in accordance with the Construction Industry Arbitration Rules of the American Arbitration Association, and judgment upon the award rendered by the arbitrator or arbitrators may be entered in any court having jurisdiction thereof, except controversies or Claims relating to aesthetic effect and except those waived as provided for in Subparagraph 4.3.5. Such controversies or Claims upon which the Architect has given notice and rendered a decision as provided in Subparagraph 4.4.4 shall be subject to arbitration upon written demand of either party. Arbitration may be commenced when 45 days have passed after a Claim has been referred to the Architect as provided in Paragraph 4.3 and no decision has been rendered.

4.5.2 Rules and Notices for Arbitration. Claims between the Owner and Contractor not resolved under Paragraph 4.4 shall, if subject to arbitration under Subparagraph 4.5.1, be decided by arbitration in accordance with the Construction Industry Arbitration Rules of the American Arbitration Association currently in effect, unless the parties mutually agree otherwise. Notice of demand for arbitration shall be filed in writing with the other party to the Agreement between the Owner and Contractor and with the American Arbitration Association, and a copy shall be filed with the Architect.

4.5.3 Contract Performance During Arbitration. During arbitration proceedings, the Owner and Contractor shall comply with Subparagraph 4.3.4.

4.5.4 When Arbitration May Be Demanded. Demand for arbitration of any Claim may not be made until the earlier of (1) the date on which the Architect has rendered a final written decision on the Claim, (2) the tenth day after the parties have presented evidence to the Architect or have been given reasonable opportunity to do so, if the Architect has not rendered a final written decision by that date, or (3) any of the five events described in Subparagraph 4.3.2.

4.5.4.1 When a written decision of the Architect states that (1) the decision is final but subject to arbitration and (2) a demand for arbitration of a Claim covered by such decision must be made within 30 days after the date on which the party making the demand receives the final written decision, then failure to demand arbitration within said 30 days' period shall result in the Architect's decision becoming final and binding upon the Owner and Contractor. If the Architect renders a decision after arbitration proceedings have been initiated, such decision may be entered as evidence, but shall not supersede arbitration proceedings unless the decision is acceptable to all parties concerned.

4.5.4.2 A demand for arbitration shall be made within the time limits specified in Subparagraphs 4.5.1 and 4.5.4 and Clause 4.5.4.1 as applicable, and in other cases within a reasonable time after the Claim has arisen, and in no event shall it be made after the date when institution of legal or equitable proceedings based on such Claim would be barred by the applicable statute of limitations as determined pursuant to Paragraph 13.7.

4.5.5 Limitation on Consolidation or Joinder. No arbitration arising out of or relating to the Contract Documents shall include, by consolidation or joinder or in any other manner, the Architect, the Architect's employees or consultants, except by written consent containing specific reference to the Agreement and signed by the Architect, Owner, Contractor and any other person or entity sought to be joined. No arbitration shall include, by consolidation or joinder or in any other manner, parties other than the Owner, Contractor, a separate contractor as described in Article 6 and other persons substantially involved in a common question of fact or law whose presence is required if complete relief is to be accorded in arbitration. No person or entity other than the Owner, Contractor or a separate contractor as described in Article 6 shall be included as an original third party or additional third party to an arbitration whose interest or responsibility is insubstantial. Consent to arbitration involving an additional person or entity shall not constitute consent to arbitration of a dispute not described therein or with a person or entity not named or described therein. The foregoing agreement to arbitrate and other agreements to arbitrate with an additional person or entity duly consented to by parties to the Agreement shall be specifically enforceable under applicable law in any court having jurisdiction thereof.

4.5.6 Claims and Timely Assertion of Claims. A party who files a notice of demand for arbitration must assert in the demand all Claims then known to that party on which arbitration is permitted to be demanded. When a party fails to include a Claim through oversight, inadvertence or excusable neglect, or when a Claim has matured or been acquired subsequently, the arbitrator or arbitrators may permit amendment.

4.5.7 Judgment on Final Award. The award rendered by the arbitrator or arbitrators shall be final, and judgment may be entered upon it in accordance with applicable law in any court having jurisdiction thereof.

ARTICLE 5

SUBCONTRACTORS

5.1 DEFINITIONS

5.1.1 A Subcontractor is a person or entity who has a direct contract with the Contractor to perform a portion of the Work at the site. The term "Subcontractor" is referred to throughout the Contract Documents as if singular in number and means a Subcontractor or an authorized representative of the Subcontractor. The term "Subcontractor" does not include a separate contractor or subcontractors of a separate contractor.

5.1.2 A Sub-subcontractor is a person or entity who has a direct or indirect contract with a Subcontractor to perform a portion of the Work at the site. The term "Sub-subcontractor" is referred to throughout the Contract Documents as if singular in number and means a Sub-subcontractor or an authorized representative of the Sub-subcontractor.

5.2 AWARD OF SUBCONTRACTS AND OTHER CONTRACTS FOR PORTIONS OF THE WORK

5.2.1 Unless otherwise stated in the Contract Documents or the bidding requirements, the Contractor, as soon as practicable after award of the Contract, shall furnish in writing to the Owner through the Architect the names of persons or entities (including those who are to furnish materials or equipment fabricated to a special design) proposed for each principal portion of the Work. The Architect will promptly reply to the Contractor in writing stating whether or not the Owner or the Architect, after due investigation, has reasonable objection to any such proposed person or entity. Failure of the Owner or Architect to reply promptly shall constitute notice of no reasonable objection.

5.2.2 The Contractor shall not contract with a proposed person or entity to whom the Owner or Architect has made reasonable and timely objection. The Contractor shall not be required to contract with anyone to whom the Contractor has made reasonable objection.

5.2.3 If the Owner or Architect has reasonable objection to a person or entity proposed by the Contractor, the Contractor shall propose another to whom the Owner or Architect has no reasonable objection. The Contract Sum shall be increased or decreased by the difference in cost occasioned by such change and an appropriate Change Order shall be issued. However, no increase in the Contract Sum shall be allowed for such change unless the Contractor has acted promptly and responsively in submitting names as required.

5.2.4 The Contractor shall not change a Subcontractor, person or entity previously selected if the Owner or Architect makes reasonable objection to such change.

5.3 SUBCONTRACTUAL RELATIONS

5.3.1 By appropriate agreement, written where legally required for validity, the Contractor shall require each Subcontractor, to the extent of the Work to be performed by the Subcontractor, to be bound to the Contractor by terms of the Contract Documents, and to assume toward the Contractor all the obligations and responsibilities which the Contractor, by these Documents, assumes toward the Owner and Architect. Each subcontract agreement shall preserve and protect the rights of the Owner and Architect under the Contract Documents with respect to the Work to be performed by the Subcontractor so that subcontracting thereof will not prejudice such rights, and shall allow to the Subcontractor, unless specifically provided otherwise in the subcontract agreement, the benefit of all rights, remedies and redress against the Contractor that the Contractor, by the Contract Documents, has against the Owner. Where appropriate, the Contractor shall require each Subcontractor to enter into similar agreements with Sub-subcontractors. The Contractor shall make available to each proposed Subcontractor, prior to the execution of the subcontract agreement, copies of the Contract Documents to which the Subcontractor will be bound, and, upon written request of the Subcontractor, identify to the Subcontractor terms and conditions of the proposed subcontract agreement which may be at variance with the Contract Documents. Subcontractors shall similarly make copies of applicable portions of such documents available to their respective proposed Sub-subcontractors.

5.4 CONTINGENT ASSIGNMENT OF SUBCONTRACTS

5.4.1 Each subcontract agreement for a portion of the Work is assigned by the Contractor to the Owner provided that:

- **.1** assignment is effective only after termination of the Contract by the Owner for cause pursuant to Paragraph 14.2 and only for those subcontract agreements which the Owner accepts by notifying the Subcontractor in writing; and
- **.2** assignment is subject to the prior rights of the surety, if any, obligated under bond relating to the Contract.

5.4.2 If the Work has been suspended for more than 30 days, the Subcontractor's compensation shall be equitably adjusted.

ARTICLE 6

CONSTRUCTION BY OWNER OR BY SEPARATE CONTRACTORS

6.1 OWNER'S RIGHT TO PERFORM CONSTRUCTION AND TO AWARD SEPARATE CONTRACTS

6.1.1 The Owner reserves the right to perform construction or operations related to the Project with the Owner's own forces, and to award separate contracts in connection with other portions of the Project or other construction or operations on the site under Conditions of the Contract identical or substantially similar to these including those portions related to insurance and waiver of subrogation. If the Contractor claims that delay or additional cost is involved because of such action by the Owner, the Contractor shall make such Claim as provided elsewhere in the Contract Documents.

6.1.2 When separate contracts are awarded for different portions of the Project or other construction or operations on the site, the term "Contractor" in the Contract Documents in each case shall mean the Contractor who executes each separate Owner-Contractor Agreement.

6.1.3 The Owner shall provide for coordination of the activities of the Owner's own forces and of each separate contractor with the Work of the Contractor, who shall cooperate with them. The Contractor shall participate with other separate contractors and the Owner in reviewing their construction schedules when directed to do so. The Contractor shall make any revisions to the construction schedule and Contract Sum deemed necessary after a joint review and mutual agreement. The construction schedules shall then constitute the schedules to be used by the Contractor, separate contractors and the Owner until subsequently revised.

6.1.4 Unless otherwise provided in the Contract Documents, when the Owner performs construction or operations related to the Project with the Owner's own forces, the Owner shall be deemed to be subject to the same obligations and to have the same rights which apply to the Contractor under the Conditions of the Contract, including, without excluding others, those stated in Article 3, this Article 6 and Articles 10, 11 and 12.

6.2 MUTUAL RESPONSIBILITY

6.2.1 The Contractor shall afford the Owner and separate contractors reasonable opportunity for introduction and storage of their materials and equipment and performance of their activities and shall connect and coordinate the Contractor's construction and operations with theirs as required by the Contract Documents.

6.2.2 If part of the Contractor's Work depends for proper execution or results upon construction or operations by the Owner or a separate contractor, the Contractor shall, prior to proceeding with that portion of the Work, promptly report to the Architect apparent discrepancies or defects in such other construction that would render it unsuitable for such proper execution and results. Failure of the Contractor so to report shall constitute an acknowledgment that the Owner's or separate contractors' completed or partially completed construction is fit and proper to receive the Contractor's Work, except as to defects not then reasonably discoverable.

6.2.3 Costs caused by delays or by improperly timed activities or defective construction shall be borne by the party responsible therefor.

6.2.4 The Contractor shall promptly remedy damage wrongfully caused by the Contractor to completed or partially completed construction or to property of the Owner or separate contractors as provided in Subparagraph 10.2.5.

6.2.5 Claims and other disputes and matters in question between the Contractor and a separate contractor shall be subject to the provisions of Paragraph 4.3 provided the separate contractor has reciprocal obligations.

6.2.6 The Owner and each separate contractor shall have the same responsibilities for cutting and patching as are described for the Contractor in Paragraph 3.14.

6.3 OWNER'S RIGHT TO CLEAN UP

6.3.1 If a dispute arises among the Contractor, separate contractors and the Owner as to the responsibility under their respective contracts for maintaining the premises and surrounding area free from waste materials and rubbish as described in Paragraph 3.15, the Owner may clean up and allocate the cost among those responsible as the Architect determines to be just.

ARTICLE 7

CHANGES IN THE WORK

7.1 CHANGES

7.1.1 Changes in the Work may be accomplished after execution of the Contract, and without invalidating the Contract, by Change Order, Construction Change Directive or order for a minor change in the Work, subject to the limitations stated in this Article 7 and elsewhere in the Contract Documents.

7.1.2 A Change Order shall be based upon agreement among the Owner, Contractor and Architect; a Construction Change Directive requires agreement by the Owner and Architect and may or may not be agreed to by the Contractor; an order for a minor change in the Work may be issued by the Architect alone.

7.1.3 Changes in the Work shall be performed under applicable provisions of the Contract Documents, and the Contractor shall proceed promptly, unless otherwise provided in the Change Order, Construction Change Directive or order for a minor change in the Work.

7.1.4 If unit prices are stated in the Contract Documents or subsequently agreed upon, and if quantities originally contemplated are so changed in a proposed Change Order or Construction Change Directive that application of such unit prices to quantities of Work proposed will cause substantial inequity to the Owner or Contractor, the applicable unit prices shall be equitably adjusted.

7.2 CHANGE ORDERS

7.2.1 A Change Order is a written instrument prepared by the Architect and signed by the Owner, Contractor and Architect, stating their agreement upon all of the following:

.1 a change in the Work;

.2 the amount of the adjustment in the Contract Sum, if any; and

.3 the extent of the adjustment in the Contract Time, if any.

7.2.2 Methods used in determining adjustments to the Contract Sum may include those listed in Subparagraph 7.3.3.

7.3 CONSTRUCTION CHANGE DIRECTIVES

7.3.1 A Construction Change Directive is a written order prepared by the Architect and signed by the Owner and Architect, directing a change in the Work and stating a proposed basis for adjustment, if any, in the Contract Sum or Contract Time, or both. The Owner may by Construction Change Directive, without invalidating the Contract, order changes in the Work within the general scope of the Contract consisting of additions, deletions or other revisions, the Contract Sum and Contract Time being adjusted accordingly.

7.3.2 A Construction Change Directive shall be used in the absence of total agreement on the terms of a Change Order.

7.3.3 If the Construction Change Directive provides for an adjustment to the Contract Sum, the adjustment shall be based on one of the following methods:

.1 mutual acceptance of a lump sum properly itemized and supported by sufficient substantiating data to permit evaluation;

.2 unit prices stated in the Contract Documents or subsequently agreed upon;

.3 cost to be determined in a manner agreed upon by the parties and a mutually acceptable fixed or percentage fee; or

.4 as provided in Subparagraph 7.3.6.

7.3.4 Upon receipt of a Construction Change Directive, the Contractor shall promptly proceed with the change in the Work involved and advise the Architect of the Contractor's agreement or disagreement with the method, if any, provided in the Construction Change Directive for determining the proposed adjustment in the Contract Sum or Contract Time.

7.3.5 A Construction Change Directive signed by the Contractor indicates the agreement of the Contractor therewith, including adjustment in Contract Sum and Contract Time or the method for determining them. Such agreement shall be effective immediately and shall be recorded as a Change Order.

7.3.6 If the Contractor does not respond promptly or disagrees with the method for adjustment in the Contract Sum, the method and the adjustment shall be determined by the Architect on the basis of reasonable expenditures and savings of those performing the Work attributable to the change, including, in case of an increase in the Contract Sum, a reasonable allowance for overhead and profit. In such case, and also under Clause 7.3.3.3, the Contractor shall keep and present, in such form as the Architect may prescribe, an itemized accounting together with appropriate supporting data. Unless otherwise provided in the Contract Documents, costs for the purposes of this Subparagraph 7.3.6 shall be limited to the following:

.1 costs of labor, including social security, old age and unemployment insurance, fringe benefits required by agreement or custom, and workers' or workmen's compensation insurance;

.2 costs of materials, supplies and equipment, including cost of transportation, whether incorporated or consumed;

.3 rental costs of machinery and equipment, exclusive of hand tools, whether rented from the Contractor or others;

.4 costs of premiums for all bonds and insurance, permit fees, and sales, use or similar taxes related to the Work; and

.5 additional costs of supervision and field office personnel directly attributable to the change.

7.3.7 Pending final determination of cost to the Owner, amounts not in dispute may be included in Applications for Payment. The amount of credit to be allowed by the Contractor to the Owner for a deletion or change which results in a net decrease in the Contract Sum shall be actual net cost as confirmed by the Architect. When both additions and credits covering related Work or substitutions are involved in a change, the allowance for overhead and profit shall be figured on the basis of net increase, if any, with respect to that change.

7.3.8 If the Owner and Contractor do not agree with the adjustment in Contract Time or the method for determining it, the adjustment or the method shall be referred to the Architect for determination.

7.3.9 When the Owner and Contractor agree with the determination made by the Architect concerning the adjustments in the Contract Sum and Contract Time, or otherwise reach agreement upon the adjustments, such agreement shall be effective immediately and shall be recorded by preparation and execution of an appropriate Change Order.

7.4 MINOR CHANGES IN THE WORK

7.4.1 The Architect will have authority to order minor changes in the Work not involving adjustment in the Contract Sum or extension of the Contract Time and not inconsistent with the intent of the Contract Documents. Such changes shall be effected by written order and shall be binding on the Owner and Contractor. The Contractor shall carry out such written orders promptly.

ARTICLE 8

TIME

8.1 DEFINITIONS

8.1.1 Unless otherwise provided, Contract Time is the period of time, including authorized adjustments, allotted in the Contract Documents for Substantial Completion of the Work.

8.1.2 The date of commencement of the Work is the date established in the Agreement. The date shall not be postponed by the failure to act of the Contractor or of persons or entities for whom the Contractor is responsible.

8.1.3 The date of Substantial Completion is the date certified by the Architect in accordance with Paragraph 9.8.

8.1.4 The term "day" as used in the Contract Documents shall mean calendar day unless otherwise specifically defined.

8.2 PROGRESS AND COMPLETION

8.2.1 Time limits stated in the Contract Documents are of the essence of the Contract. By executing the Agreement the Contractor confirms that the Contract Time is a reasonable period for performing the Work.

8.2.2 The Contractor shall not knowingly, except by agreement or instruction of the Owner in writing, prematurely commence operations on the site or elsewhere prior to the effective date of insurance required by Article 11 to be furnished by the Contractor. The date of commencement of the Work shall not be changed by the effective date of such insurance. Unless the date of commencement is established by a notice to proceed given by the Owner, the Contractor shall notify the Owner in writing not less than five days or other agreed period before commencing the Work to permit the timely filing of mortgages, mechanic's liens and other security interests.

8.2.3 The Contractor shall proceed expeditiously with adequate forces and shall achieve Substantial Completion within the Contract Time.

8.3 DELAYS AND EXTENSIONS OF TIME

8.3.1 If the Contractor is delayed at any time in progress of the Work by an act or neglect of the Owner or Architect, or of an employee of either, or of a separate contractor employed by the Owner, or by changes ordered in the Work, or by labor disputes, fire, unusual delay in deliveries, unavoidable casualties or other causes beyond the Contractor's control, or by delay authorized by the Owner pending arbitration, or by other causes which the Architect determines may justify delay, then the Contract Time shall be extended by Change Order for such reasonable time as the Architect may determine.

8.3.2 Claims relating to time shall be made in accordance with applicable provisions of Paragraph 4.3.

8.3.3 This Paragraph 8.3 does not preclude recovery of damages for delay by either party under other provisions of the Contract Documents.

ARTICLE 9

PAYMENTS AND COMPLETION

9.1 CONTRACT SUM

9.1.1 The Contract Sum is stated in the Agreement and, including authorized adjustments, is the total amount payable by the Owner to the Contractor for performance of the Work under the Contract Documents.

9.2 SCHEDULE OF VALUES

9.2.1 Before the first Application for Payment, the Contractor shall submit to the Architect a schedule of values allocated to various portions of the Work, prepared in such form and supported by such data to substantiate its accuracy as the Architect may require. This schedule, unless objected to by the Architect, shall be used as a basis for reviewing the Contractor's Applications for Payment.

9.3 APPLICATIONS FOR PAYMENT

9.3.1 At least ten days before the date established for each progress payment, the Contractor shall submit to the Architect an itemized Application for Payment for operations completed in accordance with the schedule of values. Such application shall be notarized, if required, and supported by such data substantiating the Contractor's right to payment as the Owner or Architect may require, such as copies of requisitions from Subcontractors and material suppliers, and reflecting retainage if provided for elsewhere in the Contract Documents.

9.3.1.1 Such applications may include requests for payment on account of changes in the Work which have been properly authorized by Construction Change Directives but not yet included in Change Orders.

9.3.1.2 Such applications may not include requests for payment of amounts the Contractor does not intend to pay to a Subcontractor or material supplier because of a dispute or other reason.

9.3.2 Unless otherwise provided in the Contract Documents, payments shall be made on account of materials and equipment delivered and suitably stored at the site for subsequent incorporation in the Work. If approved in advance by the Owner, payment may similarly be made for materials and equipment suitably stored off the site at a location agreed upon in writing. Payment for materials and equipment stored on or off the site shall be conditioned upon compliance by the Contractor with procedures satisfactory to the Owner to establish the Owner's title to such materials and equipment or otherwise protect the Owner's interest, and shall include applicable insurance, storage and transportation to the site for such materials and equipment stored off the site.

9.3.3 The Contractor warrants that title to all Work covered by an Application for Payment will pass to the Owner no later than the time of payment. The Contractor further warrants that upon submittal of an Application for Payment all Work for which Certificates for Payment have been previously issued and payments received from the Owner shall, to the best of the Contractor's knowledge, information and belief, be free and clear of liens, claims, security interests or encumbrances in favor of the Contractor, Subcontractors, material suppliers, or other persons or entities making a claim by reason of having provided labor, materials and equipment relating to the Work.

9.4 CERTIFICATES FOR PAYMENT

9.4.1 The Architect will, within seven days after receipt of the Contractor's Application for Payment, either issue to the

Owner a Certificate for Payment, with a copy to the Contractor, for such amount as the Architect determines is properly due, or notify the Contractor and Owner in writing of the Architect's reasons for withholding certification in whole or in part as provided in Subparagraph 9.5.1.

9.4.2 The issuance of a Certificate for Payment will constitute a representation by the Architect to the Owner, based on the Architect's observations at the site and the data comprising the Application for Payment, that the Work has progressed to the point indicated and that, to the best of the Architect's knowledge, information and belief, quality of the Work is in accordance with the Contract Documents. The foregoing representations are subject to an evaluation of the Work for conformance with the Contract Documents upon Substantial Completion, to results of subsequent tests and inspections, to minor deviations from the Contract Documents correctable prior to completion and to specific qualifications expressed by the Architect. The issuance of a Certificate for Payment will further constitute a representation that the Contractor is entitled to payment in the amount certified. However, the issuance of a Certificate for Payment will not be a representation that the Architect has (1) made exhaustive or continuous on-site inspections to check the quality or quantity of the Work, (2) reviewed construction means, methods, techniques, sequences or procedures, (3) reviewed copies of requisitions received from Subcontractors and material suppliers and other data requested by the Owner to substantiate the Contractor's right to payment or (4) made examination to ascertain how or for what purpose the Contractor has used money previously paid on account of the Contract Sum.

9.5 DECISIONS TO WITHHOLD CERTIFICATION

9.5.1 The Architect may decide not to certify payment and may withhold a Certificate for Payment in whole or in part, to the extent reasonably necessary to protect the Owner, if in the Architect's opinion the representations to the Owner required by Subparagraph 9.4.2 cannot be made. If the Architect is unable to certify payment in the amount of the Application, the Architect will notify the Contractor and Owner as provided in Subparagraph 9.4.1. If the Contractor and Architect cannot agree on a revised amount, the Architect will promptly issue a Certificate for Payment for the amount for which the Architect is able to make such representations to the Owner. The Architect may also decide not to certify payment or, because of subsequently discovered evidence or subsequent observations, may nullify the whole or a part of a Certificate for Payment previously issued, to such extent as may be necessary in the Architect's opinion to protect the Owner from loss because of:

- **.1** defective Work not remedied;
- **.2** third party claims filed or reasonable evidence indicating probable filing of such claims;
- **.3** failure of the Contractor to make payments properly to Subcontractors or for labor, materials or equipment;
- **.4** reasonable evidence that the Work cannot be completed for the unpaid balance of the Contract Sum;
- **.5** damage to the Owner or another contractor;
- **.6** reasonable evidence that the Work will not be completed within the Contract Time, and that the unpaid balance would not be adequate to cover actual or liquidated damages for the anticipated delay; or
- **.7** persistent failure to carry out the Work in accordance with the Contract Documents.

9.5.2 When the above reasons for withholding certification are removed, certification will be made for amounts previously withheld.

9.6 PROGRESS PAYMENTS

9.6.1 After the Architect has issued a Certificate for Payment, the Owner shall make payment in the manner and within the time provided in the Contract Documents, and shall so notify the Architect.

9.6.2 The Contractor shall promptly pay each Subcontractor, upon receipt of payment from the Owner, out of the amount paid to the Contractor on account of such Subcontractor's portion of the Work, the amount to which said Subcontractor is entitled, reflecting percentages actually retained from payments to the Contractor on account of such Subcontractor's portion of the Work. The Contractor shall, by appropriate agreement with each Subcontractor, require each Subcontractor to make payments to Sub-subcontractors in similar manner.

9.6.3 The Architect will, on request, furnish to a Subcontractor, if practicable, information regarding percentages of completion or amounts applied for by the Contractor and action taken thereon by the Architect and Owner on account of portions of the Work done by such Subcontractor.

9.6.4 Neither the Owner nor Architect shall have an obligation to pay or to see to the payment of money to a Subcontractor except as may otherwise be required by law.

9.6.5 Payment to material suppliers shall be treated in a manner similar to that provided in Subparagraphs 9.6.2, 9.6.3 and 9.6.4.

9.6.6 A Certificate for Payment, a progress payment, or partial or entire use or occupancy of the Project by the Owner shall not constitute acceptance of Work not in accordance with the Contract Documents.

9.7 FAILURE OF PAYMENT

9.7.1 If the Architect does not issue a Certificate for Payment, through no fault of the Contractor, within seven days after receipt of the Contractor's Application for Payment, or if the Owner does not pay the Contractor within seven days after the date established in the Contract Documents the amount certified by the Architect or awarded by arbitration, then the Contractor may, upon seven additional days' written notice to the Owner and Architect, stop the Work until payment of the amount owing has been received. The Contract Time shall be extended appropriately and the Contract Sum shall be increased by the amount of the Contractor's reasonable costs of shut-down, delay and start-up, which shall be accomplished as provided in Article 7.

9.8 SUBSTANTIAL COMPLETION

9.8.1 Substantial Completion is the stage in the progress of the Work when the Work or designated portion thereof is sufficiently complete in accordance with the Contract Documents so the Owner can occupy or utilize the Work for its intended use.

9.8.2 When the Contractor considers that the Work, or a portion thereof which the Owner agrees to accept separately, is substantially complete, the Contractor shall prepare and submit to the Architect a comprehensive list of items to be completed or corrected. The Contractor shall proceed promptly to complete and correct items on the list. Failure to include an item on such list does not alter the responsibility of the Contractor to complete all Work in accordance with the Contract Documents. Upon receipt of the Contractor's list, the Architect will make an inspection to determine whether the Work or designated portion thereof is substantially complete. If the Architect's inspection discloses any item, whether or not included on the Contractor's list, which is not in accordance with the requirements of the Contract Documents, the Contractor shall, before issuance of the Certificate of Substantial Completion, complete or correct such item upon notification by the Architect. The Contractor shall then submit a request for another inspection by the Architect to determine Substantial Completion. When the Work or designated portion thereof is substantially complete, the Architect will prepare a Certificate of Substantial Completion which shall establish the date of Substantial Completion, shall establish responsibilities of the Owner and Contractor for security, maintenance, heat, utilities, damage to the Work and insurance, and shall fix the time within which the Contractor shall finish all items on the list accompanying the Certificate. Warranties required by the Contract Documents shall commence on the date of Substantial Completion of the Work or designated portion thereof unless otherwise provided in the Certificate of Substantial Completion. The Certificate of Substantial Completion shall be submitted to the Owner and Contractor for their written acceptance of responsibilities assigned to them in such Certificate.

9.8.3 Upon Substantial Completion of the Work or designated portion thereof and upon application by the Contractor and certification by the Architect, the Owner shall make payment, reflecting adjustment in retainage, if any, for such Work or portion thereof as provided in the Contract Documents.

9.9 PARTIAL OCCUPANCY OR USE

9.9.1 The Owner may occupy or use any completed or partially completed portion of the Work at any stage when such portion is designated by separate agreement with the Contractor, provided such occupancy or use is consented to by the insurer as required under Subparagraph 11.3.11 and authorized by public authorities having jurisdiction over the Work. Such partial occupancy or use may commence whether or not the portion is substantially complete, provided the Owner and Contractor have accepted in writing the responsibilities assigned to each of them for payments, retainage if any, security, maintenance, heat, utilities, damage to the Work and insurance, and have agreed in writing concerning the period for correction of the Work and commencement of warranties required by the Contract Documents. When the Contractor considers a portion substantially complete, the Contractor shall prepare and submit a list to the Architect as provided under Subparagraph 9.8.2. Consent of the Contractor to partial occupancy or use shall not be unreasonably withheld. The stage of the progress of the Work shall be determined by written agreement between the Owner and Contractor or, if no agreement is reached, by decision of the Architect.

9.9.2 Immediately prior to such partial occupancy or use, the Owner, Contractor and Architect shall jointly inspect the area to be occupied or portion of the Work to be used in order to determine and record the condition of the Work.

9.9.3 Unless otherwise agreed upon, partial occupancy or use of a portion or portions of the Work shall not constitute acceptance of Work not complying with the requirements of the Contract Documents.

9.10 FINAL COMPLETION AND FINAL PAYMENT

9.10.1 Upon receipt of written notice that the Work is ready for final inspection and acceptance and upon receipt of a final Application for Payment, the Architect will promptly make such inspection and, when the Architect finds the Work acceptable under the Contract Documents and the Contract fully performed, the Architect will promptly issue a final Certificate for Payment stating that to the best of the Architect's knowledge, information and belief, and on the basis of the Architect's observations and inspections, the Work has been completed in accordance with terms and conditions of the Contract Documents and that the entire balance found to be due the Contractor and noted in said final Certificate is due and payable. The Architect's final Certificate for Payment will constitute a further representation that conditions listed in Subparagraph 9.10.2 as precedent to the Contractor's being entitled to final payment have been fulfilled.

9.10.2 Neither final payment nor any remaining retained percentage shall become due until the Contractor submits to the Architect (1) an affidavit that payrolls, bills for materials and equipment, and other indebtedness connected with the Work for which the Owner or the Owner's property might be responsible or encumbered (less amounts withheld by Owner) have been paid or otherwise satisfied, (2) a certificate evidencing that insurance required by the Contract Documents to remain in force after final payment is currently in effect and will not be cancelled or allowed to expire until at least 30 days' prior written notice has been given to the Owner, (3) a written statement that the Contractor knows of no substantial reason that the insurance will not be renewable to cover the period required by the Contract Documents, (4) consent of surety, if any, to final payment and (5), if required by the Owner, other data establishing payment or satisfaction of obligations, such as receipts, releases and waivers of liens, claims, security interests or encumbrances arising out of the Contract, to the extent and in such form as may be designated by the Owner. If a Subcontractor refuses to furnish a release or waiver required by the Owner, the Contractor may furnish a bond satisfactory to the Owner to indemnify the Owner against such lien. If such lien remains unsatisfied after payments are made, the Contractor shall refund to the Owner all money that the Owner may be compelled to pay in discharging such lien, including all costs and reasonable attorneys' fees.

9.10.3 If, after Substantial Completion of the Work, final completion thereof is materially delayed through no fault of the Contractor or by issuance of Change Orders affecting final completion, and the Architect so confirms, the Owner shall, upon application by the Contractor and certification by the Architect, and without terminating the Contract, make payment of the balance due for that portion of the Work fully completed and accepted. If the remaining balance for Work not fully completed or corrected is less than retainage stipulated in the Contract Documents, and if bonds have been furnished, the written consent of surety to payment of the balance due for that portion of the Work fully completed and accepted shall be submitted by the Contractor to the Architect prior to certification of such payment. Such payment shall be made under terms and conditions governing final payment, except that it shall not constitute a waiver of claims. The making of final payment shall constitute a waiver of claims by the Owner as provided in Subparagraph 4.3.5.

9.10.4 Acceptance of final payment by the Contractor, a Subcontractor or material supplier shall constitute a waiver of claims by that payee except those previously made in writing and identified by that payee as unsettled at the time of final Application for Payment. Such waivers shall be in addition to the waiver described in Subparagraph 4.3.5.

ARTICLE 10

PROTECTION OF PERSONS AND PROPERTY

10.1 SAFETY PRECAUTIONS AND PROGRAMS

10.1.1 The Contractor shall be responsible for initiating, maintaining and supervising all safety precautions and programs in connection with the performance of the Contract.

10.1.2 In the event the Contractor encounters on the site material reasonably believed to be asbestos or polychlorinated biphenyl (PCB) which has not been rendered harmless, the Contractor shall immediately stop Work in the area affected and report the condition to the Owner and Architect in writing. The Work in the affected area shall not thereafter be resumed except by written agreement of the Owner and Contractor if in fact the material is asbestos or polychlorinated biphenyl (PCB) and has not been rendered harmless. The Work in the affected area shall be resumed in the absence of asbestos or polychlorinated biphenyl (PCB), or when it has been rendered harmless, by written agreement of the Owner and Contractor, or in accordance with final determination by the Architect on which arbitration has not been demanded, or by arbitration under Article 4.

10.1.3 The Contractor shall not be required pursuant to Article 7 to perform without consent any Work relating to asbestos or polychlorinated biphenyl (PCB).

10.1.4 To the fullest extent permitted by law, the Owner shall indemnify and hold harmless the Contractor, Architect, Architect's consultants and agents and employees of any of them from and against claims, damages, losses and expenses, including but not limited to attorneys' fees, arising out of or resulting from performance of the Work in the affected area if in fact the material is asbestos or polychlorinated biphenyl (PCB) and has not been rendered harmless, provided that such claim, damage, loss or expense is attributable to bodily injury, sickness, disease or death, or to injury to or destruction of tangible property (other than the Work itself) including loss of use resulting therefrom, but only to the extent caused in whole or in part by negligent acts or omissions of the Owner, anyone directly or indirectly employed by the Owner or anyone for whose acts the Owner may be liable, regardless of whether or not such claim, damage, loss or expense is caused in part by a party indemnified hereunder. Such obligation shall not be construed to negate, abridge, or reduce other rights or obligations of indemnity which would otherwise exist as to a party or person described in this Subparagraph 10.1.4.

10.2 SAFETY OF PERSONS AND PROPERTY

10.2.1 The Contractor shall take reasonable precautions for safety of, and shall provide reasonable protection to prevent damage, injury or loss to:

.1 employees on the Work and other persons who may be affected thereby;

.2 the Work and materials and equipment to be incorporated therein, whether in storage on or off the site, under care, custody or control of the Contractor or the Contractor's Subcontractors or Sub-subcontractors; and

.3 other property at the site or adjacent thereto, such as trees, shrubs, lawns, walks, pavements, roadways, structures and utilities not designated for removal, relocation or replacement in the course of construction.

10.2.2 The Contractor shall give notices and comply with applicable laws, ordinances, rules, regulations and lawful orders of public authorities bearing on safety of persons or property or their protection from damage, injury or loss.

10.2.3 The Contractor shall erect and maintain, as required by existing conditions and performance of the Contract, reasonable safeguards for safety and protection, including posting danger signs and other warnings against hazards, promulgating safety regulations and notifying owners and users of adjacent sites and utilities.

10.2.4 When use or storage of explosives or other hazardous materials or equipment or unusual methods are necessary for execution of the Work, the Contractor shall exercise utmost care and carry on such activities under supervision of properly qualified personnel.

10.2.5 The Contractor shall promptly remedy damage and loss (other than damage or loss insured under property insurance required by the Contract Documents) to property referred to in Clauses 10.2.1.2 and 10.2.1.3 caused in whole or in part by the Contractor, a Subcontractor, a Sub-subcontractor, or anyone directly or indirectly employed by any of them, or by anyone for whose acts they may be liable and for which the Contractor is responsible under Clauses 10.2.1.2 and 10.2.1.3, except damage or loss attributable to acts or omissions of the Owner or Architect or anyone directly or indirectly employed by either of them, or by anyone for whose acts either of them may be liable, and not attributable to the fault or negligence of the Contractor. The foregoing obligations of the Contractor are in addition to the Contractor's obligations under Paragraph 3.18.

10.2.6 The Contractor shall designate a responsible member of the Contractor's organization at the site whose duty shall be the prevention of accidents. This person shall be the Contractor's superintendent unless otherwise designated by the Contractor in writing to the Owner and Architect.

10.2.7 The Contractor shall not load or permit any part of the construction or site to be loaded so as to endanger its safety.

10.3 EMERGENCIES

10.3.1 In an emergency affecting safety of persons or property, the Contractor shall act, at the Contractor's discretion, to prevent threatened damage, injury or loss. Additional compensation or extension of time claimed by the Contractor on account of an emergency shall be determined as provided in Paragraph 4.3 and Article 7.

ARTICLE 11

INSURANCE AND BONDS

11.1 CONTRACTOR'S LIABILITY INSURANCE

11.1.1 The Contractor shall purchase from and maintain in a company or companies lawfully authorized to do business in the jurisdiction in which the Project is located such insurance as will protect the Contractor from claims set forth below which may arise out of or result from the Contractor's operations under the Contract and for which the Contractor may be legally liable, whether such operations be by the Contractor or by a Subcontractor or by anyone directly or indirectly employed by any of them, or by anyone for whose acts any of them may be liable:

.1 claims under workers' or workmen's compensation, disability benefit and other similar employee benefit acts which are applicable to the Work to be performed;

.2 claims for damages because of bodily injury, occupational sickness or disease, or death of the Contractor's employees;

.3 claims for damages because of bodily injury, sickness or disease, or death of any person other than the Contractor's employees;

.4 claims for damages insured by usual personal injury liability coverage which are sustained (1) by a person as a result of an offense directly or indirectly related to employment of such person by the Contractor, or (2) by another person;

.5 claims for damages, other than to the Work itself, because of injury to or destruction of tangible property, including loss of use resulting therefrom;

.6 claims for damages because of bodily injury, death of a person or property damage arising out of ownership, maintenance or use of a motor vehicle; and

.7 claims involving contractual liability insurance applicable to the Contractor's obligations under Paragraph 3.18.

11.1.2 The insurance required by Subparagraph 11.1.1 shall be written for not less than limits of liability specified in the Contract Documents or required by law, whichever coverage is greater. Coverages, whether written on an occurrence or claims-made basis, shall be maintained without interruption from date of commencement of the Work until date of final payment and termination of any coverage required to be maintained after final payment.

11.1.3 Certificates of Insurance acceptable to the Owner shall be filed with the Owner prior to commencement of the Work. These Certificates and the insurance policies required by this Paragraph 11.1 shall contain a provision that coverages afforded under the policies will not be cancelled or allowed to expire until at least 30 days' prior written notice has been given to the Owner. If any of the foregoing insurance coverages are required to remain in force after final payment and are reasonably available, an additional certificate evidencing continuation of such coverage shall be submitted with the final Application for Payment as required by Subparagraph 9.10.2. Information concerning reduction of coverage shall be furnished by the Contractor with reasonable promptness in accordance with the Contractor's information and belief.

11.2 OWNER'S LIABILITY INSURANCE

11.2.1 The Owner shall be responsible for purchasing and maintaining the Owner's usual liability insurance. Optionally, the Owner may purchase and maintain other insurance for self-protection against claims which may arise from operations under the Contract. The Contractor shall not be responsible for purchasing and maintaining this optional Owner's liability insurance unless specifically required by the Contract Documents.

11.3 PROPERTY INSURANCE

11.3.1 Unless otherwise provided, the Owner shall purchase and maintain, in a company or companies lawfully authorized to do business in the jurisdiction in which the Project is located, property insurance in the amount of the initial Contract Sum as well as subsequent modifications thereto for the entire Work at the site on a replacement cost basis without voluntary deductibles. Such property insurance shall be maintained, unless otherwise provided in the Contract Documents or otherwise agreed in writing by all persons and entities who are beneficiaries of such insurance, until final payment has been made as provided in Paragraph 9.10 or until no person or entity other than the Owner has an insurable interest in the property required by this Paragraph 11.3 to be covered, whichever is earlier. This insurance shall include interests of the Owner, the Contractor, Subcontractors and Sub-subcontractors in the Work.

11.3.1.1 Property insurance shall be on an all-risk policy form and shall insure against the perils of fire and extended coverage and physical loss or damage including, without duplication of coverage, theft, vandalism, malicious mischief, collapse, falsework, temporary buildings and debris removal including demolition occasioned by enforcement of any applicable legal requirements, and shall cover reasonable compensation for Architect's services and expenses required as a result of such insured loss. Coverage for other perils shall not be required unless otherwise provided in the Contract Documents.

11.3.1.2 If the Owner does not intend to purchase such property insurance required by the Contract and with all of the coverages in the amount described above, the Owner shall so inform the Contractor in writing prior to commencement of the Work. The Contractor may then effect insurance which will protect the interests of the Contractor, Subcontractors and Sub-subcontractors in the Work, and by appropriate Change Order the cost thereof shall be charged to the Owner. If the Contractor is damaged by the failure or neglect of the Owner to purchase or maintain insurance as described above, without so notifying the Contractor, then the Owner shall bear all reasonable costs properly attributable thereto.

11.3.1.3 If the property insurance requires minimum deductibles and such deductibles are identified in the Contract Documents, the Contractor shall pay costs not covered because of such deductibles. If the Owner or insurer increases the required minimum deductibles above the amounts so identified or if the Owner elects to purchase this insurance with voluntary deductible amounts, the Owner shall be responsible for payment of the additional costs not covered because of such increased or voluntary deductibles. If deductibles are not identified in the Contract Documents, the Owner shall pay costs not covered because of deductibles.

11.3.1.4 Unless otherwise provided in the Contract Documents, this property insurance shall cover portions of the Work stored off the site after written approval of the Owner at the value established in the approval, and also portions of the Work in transit.

11.3.2 Boiler and Machinery Insurance. The Owner shall purchase and maintain boiler and machinery insurance required by the Contract Documents or by law, which shall specifically cover such insured objects during installation and until final acceptance by the Owner; this insurance shall include interests of the Owner, Contractor, Subcontractors and Sub-subcontractors in the Work, and the Owner and Contractor shall be named insureds.

11.3.3 Loss of Use Insurance. The Owner, at the Owner's option, may purchase and maintain such insurance as will insure the Owner against loss of use of the Owner's property due to fire or other hazards, however caused. The Owner waives all rights of action against the Contractor for loss of use of the Owner's property, including consequential losses due to fire or other hazards however caused.

11.3.4 If the Contractor requests in writing that insurance for risks other than those described herein or for other special hazards be included in the property insurance policy, the Owner shall, if possible, include such insurance, and the cost thereof shall be charged to the Contractor by appropriate Change Order.

11.3.5 If during the Project construction period the Owner insures properties, real or personal or both, adjoining or adjacent to the site by property insurance under policies separate from those insuring the Project, or if after final payment property insurance is to be provided on the completed Project through a policy or policies other than those insuring the Project during the construction period, the Owner shall waive all rights in accordance with the terms of Subparagraph 11.3.7 for damages caused by fire or other perils covered by this separate property insurance. All separate policies shall provide this waiver of subrogation by endorsement or otherwise.

11.3.6 Before an exposure to loss may occur, the Owner shall file with the Contractor a copy of each policy that includes insurance coverages required by this Paragraph 11.3. Each policy shall contain all generally applicable conditions, definitions, exclusions and endorsements related to this Project. Each policy shall contain a provision that the policy will not be cancelled or allowed to expire until at least 30 days' prior written notice has been given to the Contractor.

11.3.7 Waivers of Subrogation. The Owner and Contractor waive all rights against (1) each other and any of their subcontractors, sub-subcontractors, agents and employees, each of the other, and (2) the Architect, Architect's consultants, separate contractors described in Article 6, if any, and any of their subcontractors, sub-subcontractors, agents and employees, for damages caused by fire or other perils to the extent covered by property insurance obtained pursuant to this Paragraph 11.3 or other property insurance applicable to the Work, except such rights as they have to proceeds of such insurance held by the Owner as fiduciary. The Owner or Contractor, as appropriate, shall require of the Architect, Architect's consultants, separate contractors described in Article 6, if any, and the subcontractors, sub-subcontractors, agents and employees of any of them, by appropriate agreements, written where legally required for validity, similar waivers each in favor of other parties enumerated herein. The policies shall provide such waivers of subrogation by endorsement or otherwise. A waiver of subrogation shall be effective as to a person or entity even though that person or entity would otherwise have a duty of indemnification, contractual or otherwise, did not pay the insurance premium directly or indirectly, and whether or not the person or entity had an insurable interest in the property damaged.

11.3.8 A loss insured under Owner's property insurance shall be adjusted by the Owner as fiduciary and made payable to the Owner as fiduciary for the insureds, as their interests may appear, subject to requirements of any applicable mortgagee clause and of Subparagraph 11.3.10. The Contractor shall pay Subcontractors their just shares of insurance proceeds received by the Contractor, and by appropriate agreements, written where legally required for validity, shall require Subcontractors to make payments to their Sub-subcontractors in similar manner.

11.3.9 If required in writing by a party in interest, the Owner as fiduciary shall, upon occurrence of an insured loss, give bond for proper performance of the Owner's duties. The cost of required bonds shall be charged against proceeds received as fiduciary. The Owner shall deposit in a separate account proceeds so received, which the Owner shall distribute in accordance with such agreement as the parties in interest may reach, or in accordance with an arbitration award in which case the procedure shall be as provided in Paragraph 4.5. If after such loss no other special agreement is made, replacement of damaged property shall be covered by appropriate Change Order.

11.3.10 The Owner as fiduciary shall have power to adjust and settle a loss with insurers unless one of the parties in interest shall object in writing within five days after occurrence of loss to the Owner's exercise of this power; if such objection be made, arbitrators shall be chosen as provided in Paragraph 4.5. The Owner as fiduciary shall, in that case, make settlement with insurers in accordance with directions of such arbitrators. If distribution of insurance proceeds by arbitration is required, the arbitrators will direct such distribution.

11.3.11 Partial occupancy or use in accordance with Paragraph 9.9 shall not commence until the insurance company or companies providing property insurance have consented to such partial occupancy or use by endorsement or otherwise. The Owner and the Contractor shall take reasonable steps to obtain consent of the insurance company or companies and shall, without mutual written consent, take no action with respect to partial occupancy or use that would cause cancellation, lapse or reduction of insurance.

11.4 PERFORMANCE BOND AND PAYMENT BOND

11.4.1 The Owner shall have the right to require the Contractor to furnish bonds covering faithful performance of the Contract and payment of obligations arising thereunder as stipulated in bidding requirements or specifically required in the Contract Documents on the date of execution of the Contract.

11.4.2 Upon the request of any person or entity appearing to be a potential beneficiary of bonds covering payment of obligations arising under the Contract, the Contractor shall promptly furnish a copy of the bonds or shall permit a copy to be made.

ARTICLE 12

UNCOVERING AND CORRECTION OF WORK

12.1 UNCOVERING OF WORK

12.1.1 If a portion of the Work is covered contrary to the Architect's request or to requirements specifically expressed in the Contract Documents, it must, if required in writing by the Architect, be uncovered for the Architect's observation and be replaced at the Contractor's expense without change in the Contract Time.

12.1.2 If a portion of the Work has been covered which the Architect has not specifically requested to observe prior to its being covered, the Architect may request to see such Work and it shall be uncovered by the Contractor. If such Work is in accordance with the Contract Documents, costs of uncovering and replacement shall, by appropriate Change Order, be charged to the Owner. If such Work is not in accordance with the Contract Documents, the Contractor shall pay such costs unless the condition was caused by the Owner or a separate contractor in which event the Owner shall be responsible for payment of such costs.

12.2 CORRECTION OF WORK

12.2.1 The Contractor shall promptly correct Work rejected by the Architect or failing to conform to the requirements of the Contract Documents, whether observed before or after Substantial Completion and whether or not fabricated, installed or completed. The Contractor shall bear costs of correcting such rejected Work, including additional testing and inspections and compensation for the Architect's services and expenses made necessary thereby.

12.2.2 If, within one year after the date of Substantial Completion of the Work or designated portion thereof, or after the date for commencement of warranties established under Subparagraph 9.9.1, or by terms of an applicable special warranty required by the Contract Documents, any of the Work is found to be not in accordance with the requirements of the Contract Documents, the Contractor shall correct it promptly after receipt of written notice from the Owner to do so unless the Owner has previously given the Contractor a written acceptance of such condition. This period of one year shall be extended with respect to portions of Work first performed after Substantial Completion by the period of time between Substantial Completion and the actual performance of the Work. This obligation under this Subparagraph 12.2.2 shall survive acceptance of the Work under the Contract and termination of the Contract. The Owner shall give such notice promptly after discovery of the condition.

12.2.3 The Contractor shall remove from the site portions of the Work which are not in accordance with the requirements of the Contract Documents and are neither corrected by the Contractor nor accepted by the Owner.

12.2.4 If the Contractor fails to correct nonconforming Work within a reasonable time, the Owner may correct it in accordance with Paragraph 2.4. If the Contractor does not proceed with correction of such nonconforming Work within a reasonable time fixed by written notice from the Architect, the Owner may remove it and store the salvable materials or equipment at the Contractor's expense. If the Contractor does not pay costs of such removal and storage within ten days after written notice, the Owner may upon ten additional days' written notice sell such materials and equipment at auction or at private sale and shall account for the proceeds thereof, after deducting costs and damages that should have been borne by the Contractor, including compensation for the Architect's services and expenses made necessary thereby. If such proceeds of sale do not cover costs which the Contractor should have borne, the Contract Sum shall be reduced by the deficiency. If payments then or thereafter due the Contractor are not sufficient to cover such amount, the Contractor shall pay the difference to the Owner.

12.2.5 The Contractor shall bear the cost of correcting destroyed or damaged construction, whether completed or partially completed, of the Owner or separate contractors caused by the Contractor's correction or removal of Work which is not in accordance with the requirements of the Contract Documents.

12.2.6 Nothing contained in this Paragraph 12.2 shall be construed to establish a period of limitation with respect to other obligations which the Contractor might have under the Contract Documents. Establishment of the time period of one year as described in Subparagraph 12.2.2 relates only to the specific obligation of the Contractor to correct the Work, and has no relationship to the time within which the obligation to comply with the Contract Documents may be sought to be enforced, nor to the time within which proceedings may be commenced to establish the Contractor's liability with respect to the Contractor's obligations other than specifically to correct the Work.

12.3 ACCEPTANCE OF NONCONFORMING WORK

12.3.1 If the Owner prefers to accept Work which is not in accordance with the requirements of the Contract Documents, the Owner may do so instead of requiring its removal and correction, in which case the Contract Sum will be reduced as appropriate and equitable. Such adjustment shall be effected whether or not final payment has been made.

ARTICLE 13

MISCELLANEOUS PROVISIONS

13.1 GOVERNING LAW

13.1.1 The Contract shall be governed by the law of the place where the Project is located.

13.2 SUCCESSORS AND ASSIGNS

13.2.1 The Owner and Contractor respectively bind themselves, their partners, successors, assigns and legal representatives to the other party hereto and to partners, successors, assigns and legal representatives of such other party in respect to covenants, agreements and obligations contained in the Contract Documents. Neither party to the Contract shall assign the Contract as a whole without written consent of the other. If either party attempts to make such an assignment without such consent, that party shall nevertheless remain legally responsible for all obligations under the Contract.

13.3 WRITTEN NOTICE

13.3.1 Written notice shall be deemed to have been duly served if delivered in person to the individual or a member of the firm or entity or to an officer of the corporation for which it was intended, or if delivered at or sent by registered or certified mail to the last business address known to the party giving notice.

13.4 RIGHTS AND REMEDIES

13.4.1 Duties and obligations imposed by the Contract Documents and rights and remedies available thereunder shall be in addition to and not a limitation of duties, obligations, rights and remedies otherwise imposed or available by law.

13.4.2 No action or failure to act by the Owner, Architect or Contractor shall constitute a waiver of a right or duty afforded them under the Contract, nor shall such action or failure to act constitute approval of or acquiescence in a breach thereunder, except as may be specifically agreed in writing.

13.5 TESTS AND INSPECTIONS

13.5.1 Tests, inspections and approvals of portions of the Work required by the Contract Documents or by laws, ordinances, rules, regulations or orders of public authorities having jurisdiction shall be made at an appropriate time. Unless otherwise provided, the Contractor shall make arrangements for such tests, inspections and approvals with an independent testing laboratory or entity acceptable to the Owner, or with the appropriate public authority, and shall bear all related costs of tests, inspections and approvals. The Contractor shall give the Architect timely notice of when and where tests and inspections are to be made so the Architect may observe such procedures. The Owner shall bear costs of tests, inspections or approvals which do not become requirements until after bids are received or negotiations concluded.

13.5.2 If the Architect, Owner or public authorities having jurisdiction determine that portions of the Work require additional testing, inspection or approval not included under Subparagraph 13.5.1, the Architect will, upon written authorization from the Owner, instruct the Contractor to make arrangements for such additional testing, inspection or approval by an entity acceptable to the Owner, and the Contractor shall give timely notice to the Architect of when and where tests and inspections are to be made so the Architect may observe such procedures.

The Owner shall bear such costs except as provided in Subparagraph 13.5.3.

13.5.3 If such procedures for testing, inspection or approval under Subparagraphs 13.5.1 and 13.5.2 reveal failure of the portions of the Work to comply with requirements established by the Contract Documents, the Contractor shall bear all costs made necessary by such failure including those of repeated procedures and compensation for the Architect's services and expenses.

13.5.4 Required certificates of testing, inspection or approval shall, unless otherwise required by the Contract Documents, be secured by the Contractor and promptly delivered to the Architect.

13.5.5 If the Architect is to observe tests, inspections or approvals required by the Contract Documents, the Architect will do so promptly and, where practicable, at the normal place of testing.

13.5.6 Tests or inspections conducted pursuant to the Contract Documents shall be made promptly to avoid unreasonable delay in the Work.

13.6 INTEREST

13.6.1 Payments due and unpaid under the Contract Documents shall bear interest from the date payment is due at such rate as the parties may agree upon in writing or, in the absence thereof, at the legal rate prevailing from time to time at the place where the Project is located.

13.7 COMMENCEMENT OF STATUTORY LIMITATION PERIOD

13.7.1 As between the Owner and Contractor:

.1 Before Substantial Completion. As to acts or failures to act occurring prior to the relevant date of Substantial Completion, any applicable statute of limitations shall commence to run and any alleged cause of action shall be deemed to have accrued in any and all events not later than such date of Substantial Completion;

.2 Between Substantial Completion and Final Certificate for Payment. As to acts or failures to act occurring subsequent to the relevant date of Substantial Completion and prior to issuance of the final Certificate for Payment, any applicable statute of limitations shall commence to run and any alleged cause of action shall be deemed to have accrued in any and all events not later than the date of issuance of the final Certificate for Payment; and

.3 After Final Certificate for Payment. As to acts or failures to act occurring after the relevant date of issuance of the final Certificate for Payment, any applicable statute of limitations shall commence to run and any alleged cause of action shall be deemed to have accrued in any and all events not later than the date of any act or failure to act by the Contractor pursuant to any warranty provided under Paragraph 3.5, the date of any correction of the Work or failure to correct the Work by the Contractor under Paragraph 12.2, or the date of actual commission of any other act or failure to perform any duty or obligation by the Contractor or Owner, whichever occurs last.

ARTICLE 14

TERMINATION OR SUSPENSION OF THE CONTRACT

14.1 TERMINATION BY THE CONTRACTOR

14.1.1 The Contractor may terminate the Contract if the Work is stopped for a period of 30 days through no act or fault of the Contractor or a Subcontractor, Sub-subcontractor or their agents or employees or any other persons performing portions of the Work under contract with the Contractor, for any of the following reasons:

.1 issuance of an order of a court or other public authority having jurisdiction;

.2 an act of government, such as a declaration of national emergency, making material unavailable;

.3 because the Architect has not issued a Certificate for Payment and has not notified the Contractor of the reason for withholding certification as provided in Subparagraph 9.4.1, or because the Owner has not made payment on a Certificate for Payment within the time stated in the Contract Documents;

.4 if repeated suspensions, delays or interruptions by the Owner as described in Paragraph 14.3 constitute in the aggregate more than 100 percent of the total number of days scheduled for completion, or 120 days in any 365-day period, whichever is less; or

.5 the Owner has failed to furnish to the Contractor promptly, upon the Contractor's request, reasonable evidence as required by Subparagraph 2.2.1.

14.1.2 If one of the above reasons exists, the Contractor may, upon seven additional days' written notice to the Owner and Architect, terminate the Contract and recover from the Owner payment for Work executed and for proven loss with respect to materials, equipment, tools, and construction equipment and machinery, including reasonable overhead, profit and damages.

14.1.3 If the Work is stopped for a period of 60 days through no act or fault of the Contractor or a Subcontractor or their agents or employees or any other persons performing portions of the Work under contract with the Contractor because the Owner has persistently failed to fulfill the Owner's obligations under the Contract Documents with respect to matters important to the progress of the Work, the Contractor may, upon seven additional days' written notice to the Owner and the Architect, terminate the Contract and recover from the Owner as provided in Subparagraph 14.1.2.

14.2 TERMINATION BY THE OWNER FOR CAUSE

14.2.1 The Owner may terminate the Contract if the Contractor:

.1 persistently or repeatedly refuses or fails to supply enough properly skilled workers or proper materials;

.2 fails to make payment to Subcontractors for materials or labor in accordance with the respective agreements between the Contractor and the Subcontractors;

.3 persistently disregards laws, ordinances, or rules, regulations or orders of a public authority having jurisdiction; or

.4 otherwise is guilty of substantial breach of a provision of the Contract Documents.

14.2.2 When any of the above reasons exist, the Owner, upon certification by the Architect that sufficient cause exists to justify such action, may without prejudice to any other rights or remedies of the Owner and after giving the Contractor and the Contractor's surety, if any, seven days' written notice, terminate employment of the Contractor and may, subject to any prior rights of the surety:

.1 take possession of the site and of all materials, equipment, tools, and construction equipment and machinery thereon owned by the Contractor;

.2 accept assignment of subcontracts pursuant to Paragraph 5.4; and

.3 finish the Work by whatever reasonable method the Owner may deem expedient.

14.2.3 When the Owner terminates the Contract for one of the reasons stated in Subparagraph 14.2.1, the Contractor shall not be entitled to receive further payment until the Work is finished.

14.2.4 If the unpaid balance of the Contract Sum exceeds costs of finishing the Work, including compensation for the Architect's services and expenses made necessary thereby, such excess shall be paid to the Contractor. If such costs exceed the unpaid balance, the Contractor shall pay the difference to the Owner. The amount to be paid to the Contractor or Owner, as the case may be, shall be certified by the Architect, upon application, and this obligation for payment shall survive termination of the Contract.

14.3 SUSPENSION BY THE OWNER FOR CONVENIENCE

14.3.1 The Owner may, without cause, order the Contractor in writing to suspend, delay or interrupt the Work in whole or in part for such period of time as the Owner may determine.

14.3.2 An adjustment shall be made for increases in the cost of performance of the Contract, including profit on the increased cost of performance, caused by suspension, delay or interruption. No adjustment shall be made to the extent:

.1 that performance is, was or would have been so suspended, delayed or interrupted by another cause for which the Contractor is responsible; or

.2 that an equitable adjustment is made or denied under another provision of this Contract.

14.3.3 Adjustments made in the cost of performance may have a mutually agreed fixed or percentage fee.

APPENDIX

Review of Some Quantitative Techniques for Risk Financing

The techniques of data analysis and decision making employed throughout the ARM curriculum, and therefore essential to the study of risk financing in ARM 56, were first presented in ARM 54. This Appendix summarizes these techniques for ARM 56 students who have not taken ARM 54 or who wish to refresh their recollection of these techniques. This Appendix is an integral part of the material assigned in ARM 56—knowledge of the techniques it reviews, or applications of these techniques, may be required on the ARM 56 national examination.

Many risk financing decisions—particularly those dealing with choices of risk financing techniques—require, first, forecasts of accidental losses and, second, projections of cash flows and rates of return that can be expected from commitments of resources to loss control. Therefore, this Appendix reviews techniques for forecasting losses and for evaluating investment alternatives.

FORECASTING ACCIDENTAL LOSSES

Sound risk financing relies on reasonably accurate forecasts of accidental losses and of resulting needs for cash. These forecasts may be made through a number of intuitive and quantitative techniques.

Need for Forecasting

Many business decisions and much executive thought often appear to be based on the false assumption that the future is perfectly predictable and static. Managers frequently make statements like "if we invest in this machine, it will raise our annual output by X units and lower our unit cost of production from $Y to $Z for each of the next ten years." Based on such statements, many managers then compare such a machine with others about which they often make equally confident statements.

If questioned closely and asked to be more precise in their thinking, many of these executives recognize the assumptions underlying such statements. They grant that the statement assumes that (1) the machine will be productive for ten years, no more and no less; (2) all other cost factors will remain unchanged, so that only the changes brought about by this machine need to be considered in deciding whether to purchase it; and (3) customers will continue to want the products related to this machine and will continue to pay the same price for those products, so that the per unit revenue from the machine will remain unchanged. In their defense, these executives may quite correctly claim that assumptions based on a known, unchanging world simplify their investment decisions.

Economists and other analysts of business decisions have labeled such assumptions *ceteris paribus,* Latin for "everything else remains unchanged" and can be predicted with absolute certainty. *Ceteris paribus* is a most useful assumption because it permits the conceptualization, as in Exhibit A-1, of an organization's costs and revenues under varying conditions. In Exhibit A-1, the downward sloping marginal revenue (MR) line in the upper portion of the diagram depicts the projected amount of *additional,* that is, marginal, revenue that in classical *ceteris paribus* economics is assumed a firm can earn by selling each additional unit of its product or service. The marginal cost (MC) line in this same portion of the exhibit indicates the presumed *additional* cost of producing each unit—again, a cost that in classical economics is generally assumed to be known with certainty. Marginal revenue is presumed to decline because, as consumers' desires for a product or service are more fully satisfied with greater output, they are willing to pay less for each additional, less needed unit. The shape of the MC line is determined by the facts that (1) the cost of the first item produced includes substantial start-up costs, (2) the marginal (additional) cost of each unit declines as efficiency increases until short-term capacity is reached, and (3) for still larger quantities, marginal cost rises in the short run as some existing productive resource (such as land and equipment or managerial skill) becomes overtaxed. This reduces operating efficiency (and raises the cost of each additional unit) as output increases even further.

Profit is the excess of revenue over cost. In this classical analysis, profit is maximized by increasing output until rising marginal cost equals falling marginal revenue. Below the maximum profit point, E in the upper portion of the exhibit, the marginal (additional) revenue generated by producing one more unit still exceeds the additional cost of that unit, indicating that profit can be increased by raising output. However, for additional output beyond level E, marginal cost exceeds marginal revenue, thus reducing profit. The same result is shown in the lower portion of Exhibit A-1, where the total revenue (TR) and total cost (TC) lines cumulate the per-unit marginal results in the upper portion of the diagram. The greatest distance between the total revenue and total cost curves in this lower diagram corresponds to the output level for point E in the upper portion of the diagram, where marginal cost equals marginal revenue.

If costs can be known with certainty, and if the world does not change, output level E maximizes profit for a profit-seeking organization. (For a nonprofit organization, the output level E allows the organization to achieve the greatest budget surplus or to generate the greatest output within a given budget.) Therefore, the total profit (TP) line in the lower portion of the exhibit, which shows the distance by which the TR line rises above the TC line, peaks at output level E. (Note that profit is negative at very low output, where total revenue does not yet balance high start-up costs, and in very high outputs, where excessive marginal costs swamp declining marginal revenues.)

In reality, however, the world is not static but dynamic. Change makes an organization's revenues and costs much less precisely predictable than the classical analysis suggests. Some changes, as in technology, consumer tastes, the costs of raw materials and other productive inputs, and government regulations, are external to an organization and may affect its revenues or costs favorably or unfavorably. Other internal factors also may have similar effects on revenues and costs. Some of these internal factors are the direct concern of risk management. The more obvious factors are the effects that accidental losses and the costs of recovering from them may have on the organization's revenues and costs. For example, an accident striking the organization or a key supplier may reduce the organization's revenues or increase its costs, thus cutting the organization's profitability. (Conversely, favorable events, which are not typically a concern of risk management, may increase the organization's profits beyond predicted levels by either increasing the organization's revenues or decreasing its costs.)

The economic possibilities that can occur in a changing world are graphed in Exhibit A-2, which is an adaptation of the upper portion of Exhibit A-1 dealing with marginal revenues and costs projected for various levels of output. In Exhibit A-2, the marginal revenue and marginal cost curves of Exhibit A-1 are shown as ranges of possible outcomes, not as single-value predictions, for any given output. These ranges, created by uncertainty and change, make decisions less precise and goal achievement less clearly defined.

The original marginal revenue and marginal cost curves from Ex-

Exhibit A-1
Profit Maximization with No Uncertainty and No Dynamic Change*

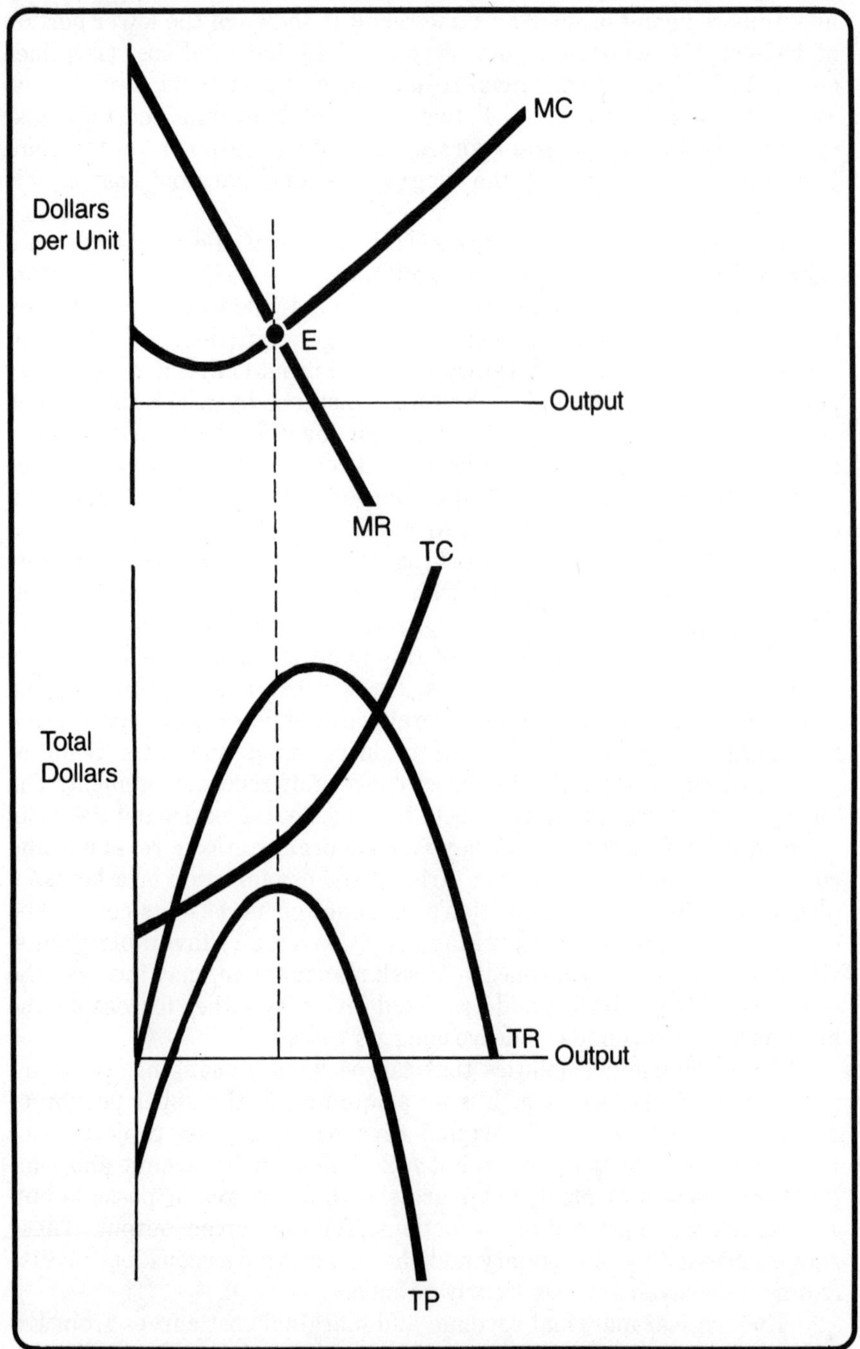

* Adapted with permission from Paul A. Samuelson, *Economics*, 11th ed. (NY: McGraw-Hill Book Co., 1980), p. 469.

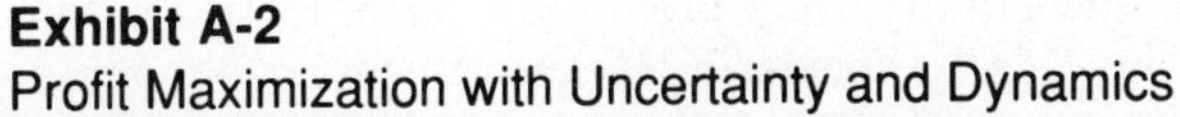

Exhibit A-2
Profit Maximization with Uncertainty and Dynamics

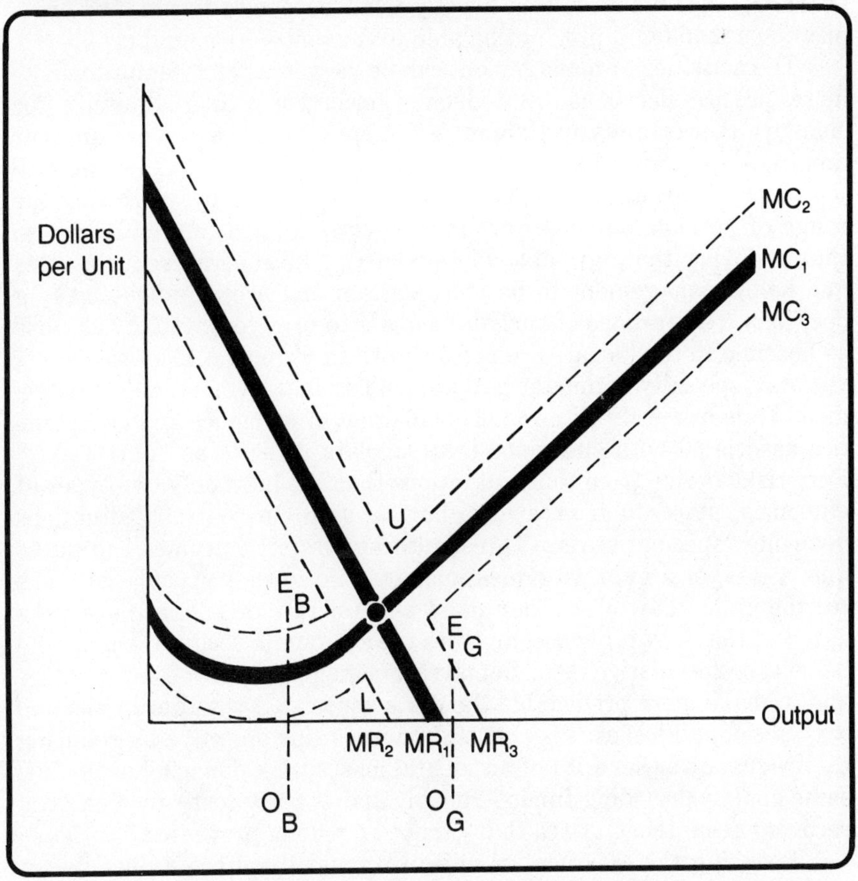

hibit A-1 are shown in Exhibit A-2 as the curves MR_1 and MC_1. Each is bordered by two additional MR or MC curves. Revenue and cost results less favorable than the single-value projections (MR_1 and MC_1) are shown as MR_2 and MC_2—lower revenues and higher costs than originally forecast. Results more favorable than those originally anticipated, higher revenues and lower costs, are portrayed by the MR_3 and MC_3 curves. Exhibit A-2 indicates that if favorable revenue results combined with favorable cost results at E_G, the organization can maximize profits by planning an output of O_G. If unfavorable revenues combine with unfavorable costs, then the organization can maximize profits by planning an output of O_B, which is shown on the horizontal output axis as significantly less than O_G, and revenue conditions. Because of changes and the managerial uncertainty they create, an organization's senior executives may not be able to decide in advance to plan for output of O_G or O_B. Not being certain exactly what output to target, the organization's managers may not be able to maximize its actual profits.

The activities of management can be viewed as an attempt to make more precise decisions by reducing uncertainty and adjusting for changes. (Uncertainty in Exhibit A-2 is approximately the rectangular area, UE_BLE_G, anywhere within which the ideal profit maximizing output level E may fall.) This rectangle can be reduced by narrowing the range of possible outcomes around the classical MR_1 and MC_1 curves, thus reducing the gap between O_B and O_G. In general, reducing this gap helps management to be more certain and precise about making decisions. The purpose of such decisions is to bring profitability as close as possible to the "ideal" (Point E) shown in Exhibit A-1.

As a specialty within the general field of management, risk management deals primarily with the particular set of dynamics and uncertainties associated with situations that scholars refer to as "pure risks." Pure risks derive from those situations that can have only two types of outcomes, status quo or a loss, but no gain. In contrast, situations involving "speculative risks" present three possible outcomes, the status quo, a loss, or a gain. Organizations are said to seek speculative risks for the gains they offer. They must also tolerate or endure pure risks as a cost that inevitably accompanies the attempt to secure the potential benefits of speculative risks. Sound risk management strives to minimize and to make more predictable the costs associated with pure risks and with accidental losses. Risk control pursues this objective by reducing the frequency or severity of accidental losses; risk financing seeks this same goal by providing funds—reliably and at a low cost—for financing recovery from those losses that cannot be wholly prevented.

Reaching this risk control objective must therefore reduce uncertainties about the occurrence and financing of recovery from accidental losses. This would narrow the ranges around the MR and MC curves in Exhibit A-2, bringing them closer to the ideal (Point E) shown in Exhibit A-1. Providing cost-effective, dependable risk control requires the best feasible predictions of (1) the frequency and severity of the losses from which the organization will need to finance recovery, and (2) the effects that alternative risk control measures will have on the present value of the organization's expected net cash flows.

Forecasting Techniques

Forecasting accidental losses or any other future event requires detecting past patterns and projecting them into the future. These patterns may be as simple as "no change." Studying the *Farmers' Almanac* suggests, more often than not, that tomorrow's weather can safely be presumed to be the same as today's. There also may be much truth in saying that this year's accidental losses for a particular organization will be about the same as last year's.

The pattern for the future may also be one of change. The advance of a cold front may signal more severe weather tomorrow. Plans to increase factory output may foretell a greater number of injuries to employees. Furthermore, if inflation is projected to continue, each of these employee injuries may be more costly next year. Even when the pattern is one of change, there are often important, constant elements: the frequency of work injuries may be predictably related to output levels, and the rate at which inflation increases the financial impact of a given injury may continue past inflationary trends. Thus, forecasting future losses by finding these patterns begins with deciding which of two basic patterns, "no change" or "change in a predictable way," applies. Under "no change" patterns, probability analysis is particularly appropriate for forecasting losses; under "change in a predictable way," regression analysis is the better choice.

Probability analysis is particularly effective when an organization has a substantial volume of data on past losses and fairly stable operations, which seem to suggest that patterns of past losses will continue in the future. In such a basically unchanging environment, past losses may be viewed as a sample of all possible losses that the organization could have suffered in the past and may suffer in the future. The larger this sample and the more stable the environment that has produced it, the more reliable the forecasts of future losses will be.

Like probability analysis, regression (or "trend") analysis looks for patterns in past losses and then projects these patterns into the future. Regression analysis looks for patterns of movement—changes in loss frequency or severity that may tend to move together with changes in some other variable (such as time production or employment) that is easier to forecast accurately than is loss experience.

Probability Analysis. For forecasting the frequency and severity of losses, probability analysis is appropriate where the basic forces presumed to cause losses are not expected to change. These forces include the nature of the organization's operations, the technology and personnel it employs, and its physical environment. (Changes in price levels are not relevant here because price changes alter only the "measuring stick" by which the financial severity of losses, not their physical severity or frequency, is measured.) Probability analysis begins with gathering as large a body of consistent historical loss data as possible. Presumably, data are drawn from a static "constant" probability distribution. These data will be used to estimate the parameters—principally the arithmetic mean and standard deviation—of the probability distribution that is presumed to persist in the future. (In contrast, the regression analysis to be discussed presumes a much more dynamic world with changing causes of losses.)

Probability is the relative frequency with which an event can be expected to occur in the long run in a stable environment. For example, given many tosses, a coin can be expected to come up "heads" as often as it comes up "tails." Given many rolls of one die from a pair of dice, a "4" can be expected to come up one-sixth of the time. According to one standard mortality table, slightly more than 2 percent of men who are sixty-two years old can be expected to die before reaching sixty-three.[1] Finally, of the many automobiles now on the road, insurance company statistics indicate that, in a recent year, 1 out of every 153 could be expected to be stolen within the year.[2]

Any probability can be expressed as a fraction. The probability of a "head" on a coin toss can be expressed as $\frac{1}{2}$, 50 percent, or 0.50. The probability of a "4" on one roll of one die can be expressed as $\frac{1}{6}$, $16\frac{2}{3}$ percent, or 0.167. Similarly, $\frac{1}{153}$, 0.654 percent, or 0.00654 are each proper ways of indicating the probability that a particular automobile would have been stolen during 1981. The probability of an event that is totally impossible is 0, the probability of an absolutely certain event is 1.0, and the probabilities of all events that are neither totally impossible nor absolutely certain are greater than 0 but less than 1.0.

Probabilities can be developed from theoretical considerations or from historical data. Probabilities associated with coin tosses or dice throws can be developed theoretically and are constant given the unchanging physical properties of devices like coins and dice. Probabilities associated with events such as the occurrence and frequency of car thefts must be developed from historical data, which, when considered together, will create a sample from which similar events may be predicted. While theoretical probabilities are always accurate, probabilities developed from historical data depend for their accuracy on sample size and representativeness. They are also subject to change as the data changes. Therefore, in order to maintain the accuracy of historically determined probabilities, the new data must be fed into the analysis as a "constant."

Characteristics of Probability Distributions. A probability distribution is a representation in a table or in a graph of all possible outcomes of a particular set of circumstances and of the probability of each possible outcome. Because every such distribution includes the probability of every possible outcome, which makes it certain that one and only one of these outcomes will occur, the sum of the probabilities in a complete probability distribution *must* be 1.0.

In addition to these definitional features, probability distributions are also described in terms of two other characteristics, central tendency and dispersion. The *central tendency* of a probability distribution is the single outcome within the distribution that, in some sense, is the "most representative" of all possible outcomes. The central tendency of a distribution may or may not correspond to the value directly beneath the hump of the distribution, depending on which measure of central tendency is used and on whether the distribution is "balanced" or symmetrical. The second characteristic, *dispersion,* describes the extent to which the distribution is spread out, rather than concentrated at a single outcome.

Central Tendency. Most probability distributions cluster around a particular value, which may or may not be in the exact center of the range of the distribution. This value often is used as the most representative outcome and, as stated, is referred to as central tendency. The three most widely accepted ways of identifying or measuring this most representative outcome are the *arithmetic mean,* the *median,* and the *mode.*

The arithmetic mean of a distribution is a more precise name for the common "average," which is the sum of the items in the distribution divided by the number of items. Calculating the arithmetic mean of a probability distribution is only slightly more complex: each outcome is multiplied by its respective probability, and the sum of these products is the mean of the distribution, or its "expected value." This procedure weights each value of the distribution by its probability, and the arithmetic mean (or expected value) of the distribution is this weighted average.

The second measure of central tendency is the median. The median of a series of numbers or of a probability distribution is the "value in the middle," that is, the value for which the number of lower observations or outcomes equals the number of higher observations. (When the number of observations or outcomes is an even number, the median is the arithmetic mean of the middle two.) The median of a probability distribution is the value for which the probability of higher outcomes is equal to the probability of lower outcomes. This value can be found by summing the cumulative probabilities in the distribution to find the outcome for which a cumulative probability of 50 percent is reached.

The third measure of central tendency is the mode. The mode of either a series of numbers or of a probability distribution is the single value that occurs most frequently. When a distribution has a single "hump" (or is unimodal), the mode is the value of the outcome directly beneath the peak of that "hump." For historical statistics on losses, no single precise dollar amount or exact number of annual losses may occur more frequently than any other specific quantity. However, if the losses are grouped, for example, into frequency classes such as 0 to 10, 11 to

20—or into severity classes like under $1,000, $1,001 to $2,000, and so on—then one of these classes will contain the greatest number of losses. This class, then, can properly be called the modal class of the frequency or loss severity distribution.

Dispersion (Variability). The second important characteristic of a probability distribution is its dispersion. This is the degree of variability around the mean or other essential tendency of the distribution. The less the dispersion of the distribution, the greater the likelihood that actual results will fall within a given range of that central tendency. Thus, less dispersion means less uncertainty in predicting that a result close to that central point will actually occur.

The most widely used measure of dispersion is the standard deviation. The standard deviation of a set of numbers is the square root of the average of the squared deviation of each number from the arithmetic mean of these numbers. It is a special kind of average, an average of deviations (or differences) between individuals, varied values, and the arithmetic mean of those values. The precise method for computing a standard deviation depends on whether the numbers whose standard deviation is sought are individual historical outcomes (such as the amounts of actual losses) or are, instead, values within a probability distribution (like the probability of a loss in the $5,001 to $10,000 class).

The following steps are used to find the standard deviation of a set of individual observations not involving probabilities:

1. Find the arithmetic mean of the observations (the sum of the observations divided by the number of observations).
2. Subtract the mean from each of the observations (with the result being positive for each observation larger than the mean and negative for each observation smaller than the mean).
3. Square each of the resulting differences (the rules of algebra making all resulting squares positive).
4. Find the sum of these squares.
5. Divide this sum by the number of observations minus one. (The theoretical justification for subtracting one is beyond the educational objectives of this course.)
6. Find the square root of the resulting quotient.

The following procedure is used to find the standard deviation for a probability distribution:

1. Find the expected value (arithmetic or mean) of the distribution.
2. Subtract this expected value from each outcome in the distribution.
3. Square each of the resulting differences.

4. Multiply each resulting square by the probability associated with the outcome for which the squared difference was computed in step 3.
5. Sum the resulting products.
6. Find the square root of the resulting sum.

The Normal Distribution—A Special Case. The normal distribution is a particular type of probability distribution that applies to a wide variety of physical phenomena involving variations around some central, average, or expected value. To illustrate, the useful lives of the belts that connect a series of machine tool lathes to their central power source are governed by a normal probability distribution. Each belt has a particular average or expected life before it will break, and the variability from belt to belt around this average is described by a normal probability distribution. Scheduling belt replacements often enough so that the probability of a belt breaking while in use is small requires knowing not only the arithmetic mean but also the standard deviation of the normal distribution of belt life.

In all normal distributions certain percentages of all outcomes fall within a given number of standard deviations above or below the mean of the distribution. As shown in Exhibit A-3, 34.13 percent of all outcomes fall within one standard deviation below the mean. By addition and because all normal distributions are symmetrical around this mean, 68.26 percent of all outcomes are within one standard deviation above or below the mean. The portion of a normal distribution that is between one and two standard deviations above the mean contains 13.59 percent of all outcomes, as does the portion between one and two standard deviations below the mean. Therefore, the area between the mean and two standard deviations above the mean contains 47.72 percent (34.13 + 13.59 percent) of all outcomes, and another 47.72 percent are two standard deviations or less below the mean. Consequently, 95.44 percent (twice 47.72 percent) of all outcomes are within two standard deviations above or below the mean.

Similarly, 2.15 percent of all outcomes are between two and three standard deviations above the mean, and another 2.15 percent are between two and three deviations below the mean. Thus, 49.87 percent (34.13 + 13.59 + 2.15 percent) of all outcomes are three standard deviations or less below the mean. The portion of the distribution between three standard deviations above the mean and three standard deviations below the mean contains 99.74 percent (twice 49.87 percent) of all outcomes. Only 0.26 percent (100 percent − 99.74 percent) of all outcomes lie beyond three standard deviations from the mean, and these are divided equally—0.13 percent above the mean and 0.13 percent below it.

To understand these relationships, recall the machine belts, each of

Exhibit A-3
The Normal Distribution — Percentages of Outcomes Within Specified Standard Deviations of the Mean

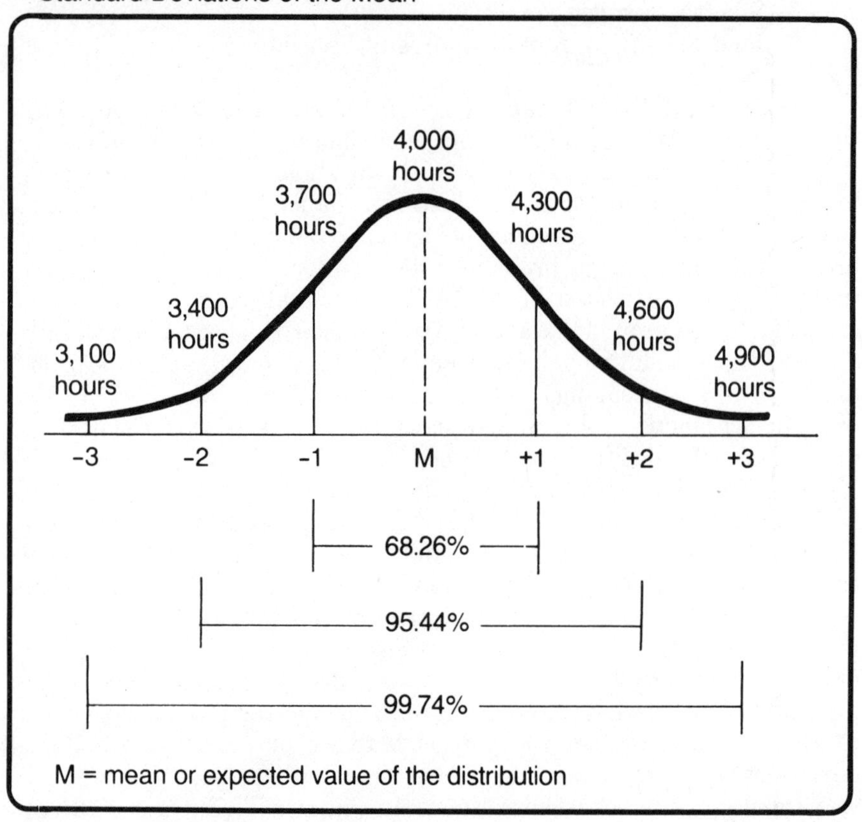

which has an expected arithmetic mean life of 4,000 hours with a standard deviation of 300 hours. If replacement of these belts is scheduled for their "expected life," after 4,000 hours of use, then there is a 50 percent chance that a belt will break before its scheduled replacement. However, if each belt is changed after only 3,700 hours of use (one standard deviation below the mean), then there is only a 15.87 percent (50 percent − 34.13 percent) chance that a belt will break before being changed. If this probability of breakage is still too high, then changing each belt after 3,400 hours of use (two standard deviations below the mean) reduces the probability of breakage to only 2.28 percent, the portion of any normal distribution that is more than two standard deviations below the mean. (This probability can be calculated as 50 percent minus the sum of 34.13 percent and 13.59 percent.) A more cautious practice would be to change belts routinely after only 3,100 hours (three standard deviations below the mean) so that the probability of a belt breaking before replacement would be only 0.13 percent, slightly more than one chance in 1,000.

Probability Calculations. Probability calculations are usually expressed in some generally useful symbols. The symbol p() means "probability of" the term in parentheses, so that p(A) means "the probability of A" occurring in a given time period, where A represents any specified event. Similarly, p(A+B) means "the probability of A and B" occurring in a given period. The symbol p(A or B) means the "probability that either A or B, or possibly both" will occur in a given period. This notation is flexible because any event or combination of events can be specified in the parentheses.

The symbol n appears frequently in probability distributions to designate the number of separate units from which a probability is developed or to which it is applied. The symbol m represents the number of these units that experience a particular event that is of interest. In a risk management context, n typically designates the number of exposures from which an empirical probability of loss is derived, and m indicates the number of exposures actually suffering loss. Thus, the general equation for the probability of a loss can be expressed as follows:

$$p(\text{loss}) = m/n$$

By algebraic manipulation, m—the expected number of losses—becomes the following:

$$m = \text{expected loss frequency} = np$$

The concept of a long-run expected value is so common in working with probabilities that the symbol E() is used to express "the expected number or value" of the event specified in the parentheses. For example, if n exposure units are subject to the probability, p, of loss annually, then the expected number of losses per year, E(L), can be expressed as:

$$E(L) = np$$

which can be read as "the expected annual number of losses equals the number of exposure units times the probability of loss to any one unit."

An important assumption in computing probabilities is that an event either occurs or does not occur—there are no other possibilities. These two alternatives are mutually exclusive; together they exhaust all possibilities. Therefore, the probability of any event, p(A), occurring and the probability of it not occurring, p(not A), add to one. For example, if the probability of loss to one unit in one year is 0.000950, then the probability that there will be no loss to that unit that year is 0.999050. In general,

$$p(A) + p(\text{not } A) = 1$$

and, by algebraic manipulation,

$$p(A) = 1 - p(\text{not } A)$$
$$p(\text{not } A) = 1 - p(A)$$

This basic notation is used in all probability analyses. Two applications most useful in risk management are computations of joint probabilities (the probability that two or more events will occur together at a given time) and of alternative probabilities (the probability that any one of two or more events will occur in a given time period). A joint probability is a probability that two or more events will happen within a given time. Before computing a joint probability, it is necessary to determine whether these events are independent. Two events, A and B, are independent if the occurrence or nonoccurrence of one does not affect the probability that the other will or will not occur. If A and B are independent, the probability of A is unchanged by the occurrence or nonoccurrence of B. Similarly, the probability of B is unchanged by the occurrence or nonoccurrence of A. For example, the probabilities that two buildings, widely distant from one another, will burn are independent of each other because a fire at one will not endanger the other. However, if the two buildings are close enough together that fire can spread from one to the other, their probabilities of loss from that fire are not independent. Specifically, each building alone may have a 3 percent chance of fire in a given year. But if the buildings are close together, a fire in one of them will raise the probability of fire in the other.

For independent events, the joint probability that all the events will occur in a given period is the product of their separate probabilities of occurring in that period. That is, if the two buildings just mentioned are distant, then the probability that both will burn in a year, p(2 fires), is equal to the probability of one, p(F1), times the probability of fire in the other, p(F2), as follows:

$$p(2\text{ fires}) = p(F1)p(F2)$$
$$p(2\text{fires}) = (0.03)(0.03) = 0.0009$$

For probabilities of dependent events—such as fires in both buildings if they are close together—the joint probability that both will burn is determined by multiplying the probability of fire in one building times the probability of fire in the second, given that there already is a fire in the first. This second probability, known as a conditional probability, can be expressed as P(F2 F1). If this conditional probability is 0.25, then, continuing with the same example, the probability of a fire in the first building followed by a fire in the second is determined by as follows:

$$p(F1 \text{ followed by } F2) =$$
$$p(F1)p(F\ F1) =$$
$$(0.03)(0.25) = 0.0075$$

Notice that this calculation is used to find the probability of a particular sequence of events, a fire in the first building followed by a fire in the second. It is not the probability of any other sequence of events, such as a fire in the second building spreading back to a fire in the first, nor does it include any allowance for the independent and simultaneous but not causal occurrence of both events. Thus, in dealing with joint probabilities of dependent events, it is crucial to specify the nature of the events, their sequence, and whether or not it was causal.

Along with joint probabilities of the combined occurrences of several events, risk management sometimes calls for the calculation of alternative probabilities of at least one (or more) of several events occurring in a given time period. Computing alternative probability requires knowing if the events are mutually exclusive. Two or more events are mutually exclusive if the occurrence of one makes the occurrence of any of the others impossible. For example, the occurrence of a fire loss and theft loss on the same day are not mutually exclusive events—both may happen on the same day. In contrast, the dollar amount an organization might suffer next year will be either (1) less than $5,000 or (2) $5,000 or more. These two categories of loss size are mutually exclusive.

For mutually exclusive events, the probability that either one will occur in a given time is the sum of their respective probabilities for occurring during that time. For example, assuming that a building cannot be destroyed both by fire and by flood in the same year and also that the probability of destruction by fire is 0.01 and by flood is 0.02, then the probability that the building will be destroyed by either flood or fire next year is 0.03. In general, for mutually exclusive events A and B, the alternative probability of one or the other occurring is the following:

$$p(A \text{ or } B) = p(A) + p(B)$$

When two or more events are not mutually exclusive, when more than one of them can occur in a given time period, care must be taken not to overstate the probability that at least one of them will occur. Such overstatement is common because of the mistaken "double accounting" of the joint probability of two or more of these alternative events. For events that are not mutually exclusive, the probability that at least one of them—and possibly both or all—will occur is the sum of their separate probabilities minus their joint probability.

The following example illustrates this concept. Assume that the probability of pilferage loss to goods in transit is 0.09 and the probability of a flood loss to these goods is 0.06 on a particular trip. It follows that the probability of loss by pilferage, water damage, *or both,* is the following:

$$\begin{aligned} \text{p(pilferage or water damage or both)} &= 0.009 + 0.06 - (0.09)(0.06) \\ &= 0.15 - 0.0054 \\ &= 0.1446 \end{aligned}$$

To compute the probability of pilferage or water damage, *but not both,* sum the probabilities of the two mutually exclusive ways that this result can occur. These are the probabilities of pilferage but no water damage and water damage but no pilferage. (Recall that the probability of an event not occurring equals one minus the probability of its occurring.) Computing these two probabilities and finding their sum yield the following:

$$\begin{aligned} \text{p(pilferage but no water damage)} &= (0.09)(1 - 0.06) \\ &= (0.09)(0.94) \\ &= 0.0846 \\ \text{p(water damage but no pilferage)} &= (0.06)(1 - 0.09) \\ &= (0.06)(0.91) \\ &= 0.0546 \end{aligned}$$

Therefore, p(pilferage or water damage but not both) = 0.0846 + 0.0546 = 0.1392. The probability of either kind of damage but not both is smaller than the probability of either kind of damage and possibly both because the first probability excludes the chance of a mutual occurrence.

Summary of Probability Analysis. If the world can be assumed to be stable then all past losses are only a sample of all possible losses, and that sample may or may not be representative. However, the greater the number of past losses, the larger the sample, and the more reliable the forecasts of future losses can be. The discussion about the basics of probability analysis has assumed such a stable world in which the causes of loss remain the same. In contrast, the explanation of how to forecast losses by regression assumes a more dynamic world.

Regression Analysis. Like probability analysis, regression analysis looks for patterns in past losses or other events and then projects these patterns into the future. Unlike probability analysis, however, regression looks for patterns of movement. For example, changes in loss frequency or severity may tend to move together with changes in some other variable (such as time measured in years or production in volumes of output), which is easier to forecast accurately than is loss experience. Regression analysis is also often called trend analysis, a name that reflects the fact that two or more trends—one more easily predictable than the other—tend to move together. Knowing one trend helps forecast the other.

Common sense trending can be done simply by charting some points on a graph and then connecting them with a straight or curved line that seems to fit. An example of such a trend line appears in Exhibit A-4. It shows the improving loss experience of a firm whose work injury rate has been declining (as shown by the solid portion of the trend line) and will presumably continue declining as suggested by the dashed portion of the line.

Regression analysis (technically, linear regression because only straight lines are calculated) involves computing the two determinants of a straight line that best "fits" the available data. The general equation for any straight line is the following:

$$Y = a + bX$$

where Y is the dependent variable, graphed vertically and to be predicted (such as loss frequency or severity), and X is the independent variable, graphed horizontally and used as a basis for forecasting the dependent variable. The value for a represents the point at which the straight regression trend line intersects the vertical Y axis; the value for b represents the slope of the line (the amount by which the line rises and falls for each unit change in the independent variable, X). The letter a or b may be either positive or negative. A positive b value indicates an increasing trend, and a negative b value indicates a decreasing trend. The independent variable, X, can be any factor (time, production, sales, number of trips, or personnel) that is quite readily known or predictable and that has some reasonable relationship with the dependent variable to be forecast.

Regression computations first involve gathering historical data on the joint movements of the independent and dependent variables, such as annual output, X, and annual number of losses, Y, as shown in columns (1) and (2) in the upper portion of Exhibit A-5. Second, the values shown in columns (3) and (4) in this exhibit are computed; third, the totals of these four columns are used to compute values for a and b using the following general equations:

$$a = \frac{(\text{Sum } y)(\text{Sum } x^2) - (\text{Sum } x)(\text{Sum } xy)}{n(\text{Sum } x^2) - (\text{Sum } x)^2}$$

$$b = \frac{n(\text{Sum } xy) - (\text{Sum } x)(\text{Sum } y)}{n(\text{Sum } x^2) - (\text{Sum } x)^2}$$

In these equations, n indicates the number of data points—four in this case—that is, the number of paired X and Y values. For clarity, these formulas also use the symbol Sum to mean the sum of the variable following the symbol. For example, Sum Y means the sum of the annual number of losses, nineteen in all. The resulting equation ($Y = 2.46 + 0.035X$) can be interpreted as the annual number of losses, and Y can

Exhibit A-4
Generalized Form of Hand-Drawn Linear Trend Line

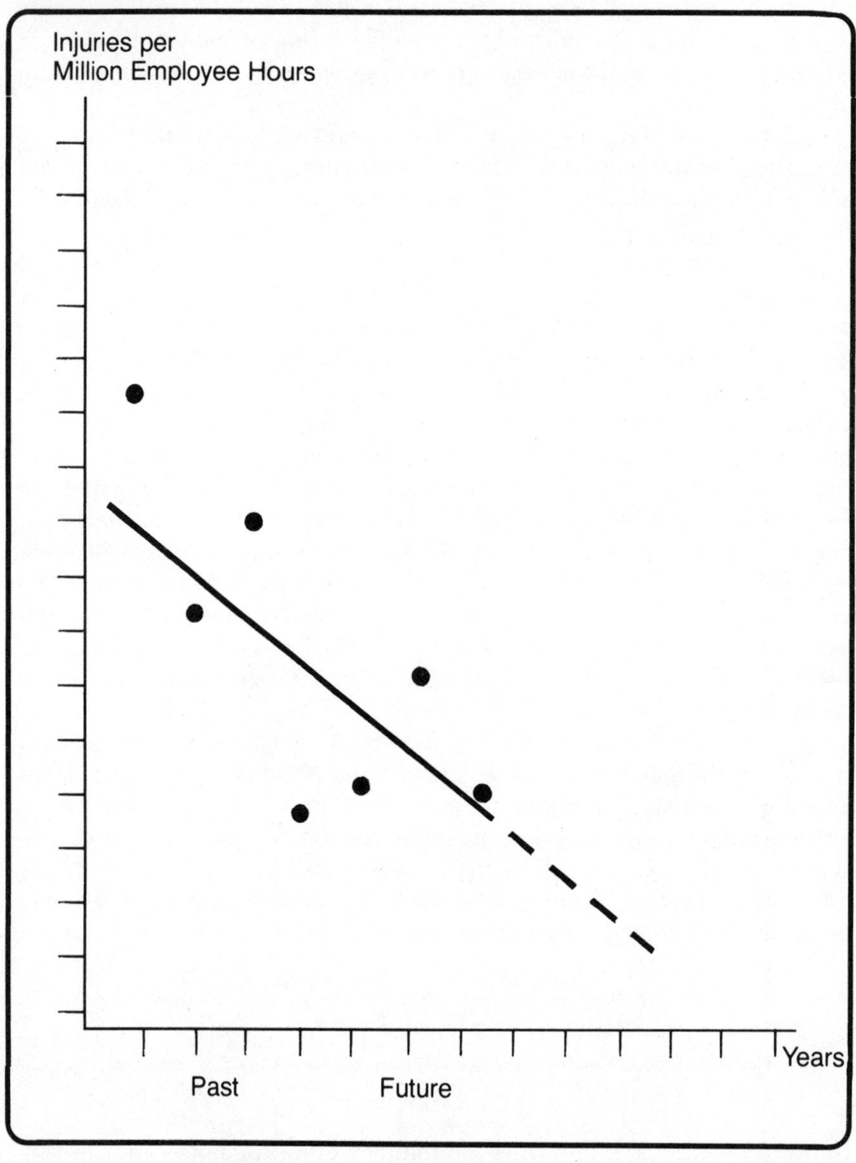

be expected to be 2.46 plus 0.035 times annual output (measured in some convenient unit such as hundreds of tons). For example, if the organization's output were 8,500 tons, the number of losses it would be reasonable to forecast would be the following:

$$
\begin{aligned}
Y &= 2.46 + 85(0.035) \\
&= 2.46 + 2.975 \\
&= 5.435 \text{ losses}
\end{aligned}
$$

Fractional losses being impossible (there may be five or six loss occurrences, but nothing in between), a reasonable forecast would be five losses in a year when the firm produced 85 units of output (each unit being 100 tons).

While arithmetically correct, these values may not be valid for very low or very high output. The use of mathematics must therefore be accompanied by common sense, for example, not extending a regression line too far beyond the limits of past occurrences.

EVALUATING INVESTMENT ALTERNATIVES

Cash enables an organization to obtain resources to fulfill its objectives. Cash—or more precisely, purchasing power, including credit—is a *necessary* means to *all* other ends. The net cash flow during any period measures an organization's ability to function effectively during that period and in the future. Therefore, in selecting uses for an organization's resources, senior management should give priority to commitments that promise the greatest net cash flow.

Concept of Present Value of Expected Annual After-Tax Net Cash Flow

An organization's net cash flow during any period is its cash receipts minus its cash disbursements for that period. If cash receipts exceed disbursements, net cash flow is positive; if disbursements exceed receipts, it is negative. Projecting how net cash flows are likely to be generated by alternative assets or activities provides an organization's management with a valid criterion for choosing where to invest to obtain the expected present value of the organization's future net cash flows.

In selecting an asset or activity, an organization must at least initially also take the loss exposures created by that asset or activity. How the organization chooses to cope with these loss exposures through any one or a combination of management techniques affects the cash flows from that asset or activity and thus also influences the net cash flow from the activity or asset. An organization maximizes its operating efficiency—expressed as profits for a profit-seeking organization and as

Exhibit A-5
Computation of Linear Regression Line

(1)	(2)	(3)	(4)
Output (x 100)	Annual Number of Losses		
(x)	(y)	(xy)	$(x)^2$
35	4	140	1,225
60	4	240	3,600
72	5	360	5,184
95	6	570	9,025
262	19	1,310	19,034

$$a = \frac{(19)\,(19{,}034) - (262)\,(1{,}310)}{4\,(19{,}034) - (262)} \qquad b = \frac{4\,(1{,}310) - (262)\,(19)}{4\,(19{,}034) - (262)}$$

$$= \frac{361{,}556 - 343{,}200}{76{,}136 - 68{,}644} \qquad = \frac{5{,}240 - 4{,}978}{76{,}136 - 68{,}644}$$

$$= \frac{18{,}426}{7{,}492} \qquad = \frac{562}{7{,}492}$$

$$= 2.46 \qquad = 0.035$$

budget surpluses or maximum output within a given budget for a non-profit organization—by selecting that combination of assets and activities that, when coupled with the most cost-effective combination of risk management techniques, maximizes the expected present value of the organization's future net cash flow. Applying this decision rule in selecting risk control techniques requires an understanding of (1) expected net cash flows, (2) present value of net cash flows, and (3) annual after-tax net cash flows.

Expected Net Cash Flows. An expected value is the arithmetic mean or average of a series of numbers or of a probability distribution. Several probability distributions are implicit in the projection of the future net cash flows from an organization's business activities. These may include probabilities of consumer demand and resulting revenues, of cash expenses, and of dividend and other distributions to stockholders and/or other owners. The organization's actual net cash flow for a future period is the joint outcome of the events covered by these probability distributions. Risk management introduces comparable probability distributions for the combined effects of (1) accidental losses and (2) the risk management techniques for managing them. Traditional managerial finance has largely ignored risk management concerns.

The best single estimate of the outcome of each of these probability distributions is the arithmetic mean of that distribution; therefore, the net cash flow generated by the arithmetic mean outcomes of the probability distribution is referred to as the "expected net cash flow." There is no assurance that the expected net cash flow will actually materialize in the next accounting period, but this expected value is the single best estimate for any one future period. Therefore, in the long run, the best decisions, the ones that have the greatest chance of being accurate, are based on these expected values.

Present Value of Net Cash Flow. Some assets or activities require cash expenditures and generate cash receipts all in a single accounting period. For example, a food processing firm is likely to buy raw materials or merchandise inventory to process and sell much of this inventory in the same accounting period. For such operations, cash inflows and outflows tend to match period for period, and there is little concern for what is known as the "time value of money." However, other assets or activities are likely to entail current cash expenditures (as well as future expenditures) that can be expected to generate cash receipts only in the future. When cash receipts and expenditures are spread over several accounting periods, these cash flows must be "discounted" for their distance into the future. This discounting reduces all future cash inflows and outflows to "present values," thereby reflecting the "time value of money." A dollar presently available, or "in hand," has a greater time value than does a dollar to be received in the future because the dollar in hand can be invested to start earning money now. In contrast, a dollar to be received in the future cannot be invested to generate earnings until that future date. The greater the rate of return a dollar in hand can earn, the greater is its value relative to a future dollar, and the lesser is the value of the future dollar relative to the present dollar. Conversely, the longer it will be until a future dollar is received, the less is its present value when compared with the value of a dollar in hand. It follows that the present value of a dollar varies inversely with the interest rate the dollar could earn if currently in hand and when in the future the dollar is to be received.

To properly evaluate a business proposal, as for an investment, in terms of the present value of the cash inflows and outflows that can be expected from that proposal, it is important to know how to compute the present value of (1) a present payment, (2) a single future payment, (3) a series of equal future payments, and (4) a series of unequal future payments.

The present value of a *present payment* (the value of a current receipt or disbursement) is the face amount of that payment; no discounting is required. The present value of a *single future payment* can be found by referring to a "present value table" as shown in Exhibit A-6. This type of table indicates the amount that must be invested today at a given interest rate for a given number of years to generate $1 as a single payment at the end of that number of years. Similarly, a table such as Exhibit A-7 accumulates the individual present values from Exhibit A-6 to give the present value of a series of *equal future payments.* This present value is the sum that must be invested today at a given annual interest rate to generate $1 at the end of each of the next specified number of years, when the initial investment and the interest earned will have been exhausted. The present value of a series of *unequal future payments* can be found by multiplying the face amount of each future payment by the appropriate present value factor from Exhibit A-6 and then summing the present values of these individual payments to find the present value of the entire stream.

Annual After-Tax Net Cash Flow. In and of itself, the net cash flow from an investment made in any year or other given period is equal to the cash inflows or revenues it produces minus the cash outflows or expenses it requires during that period.

However, net cash flow is subject to one complication, income taxes. Like other cash outlays, income taxes must be deducted from cash revenues in computing net cash flows. The peculiarity of income taxes arises from the fact that they are computed as a percentage of *taxable income,* not as a percentage of net cash inflows. Therefore, in computing the cash outflow for income taxes, noncash revenue and expense items must be considered to arrive at taxable income. For risk management purposes, noncash revenues such as an increase in accounts receivable are not germane. However, an important noncash expense, the accrual of depreciation on assets whose useful life extends beyond one annual accounting period, is most pertinent.

In this text and the ARM program, straight-line depreciation is used to compute this noncash depreciation expense unless otherwise specified. Salvage value is assumed to be zero unless otherwise specified. Thus, for example, if the initial investment in an asset with a seven-year useful life is $35,000, the annual depreciation expense is $5,000. While not a cash outflow, depreciation should be added to other expenses when computing taxable income. Also in this text and the ARM program, income taxes are assumed (for ease of calculation) to be 50 percent of taxable income unless otherwise specified.

Exhibit A-8 illustrates the general procedure for calculating annual after-tax net cash flows—actually, the *differential,* or changed, net cash flows. In this case, an organization buys the $35,000 machine with the seven-year expected useful life as mentioned. Assume that purchasing this machine is expected to add $12,000 a year to the organization's revenue, $500 to its annual maintenance expenses, and $100 to its insurance costs. Under these assumptions, the differential after-tax net cash flow (NCF) as a result of investing in the machine can be expected to be $8,200, as shown at the bottom of the exhibit.

A simple case of how risk management decisions can affect net cash flows is the possibility that improved maintenance for this machine, costing an additional $25 per year, would qualify the machine for a reduced insurance rate, cutting annual insurance expenses by $40. Such an additional maintenance expenditure would raise the before-tax NCF on the machine by $15 to $11,415, and the after-tax NCF accordingly.

Evaluation of Net Cash Flows

When funds invested in one accounting period generate cash revenues in one or more future periods, four factors are involved in evaluating the net cash flows from that investment:

- The amount of the initial investment
- The annual rate of return, expressed as a percentage of the initial investment
- The estimated useful life of the proposal, the number of years (or other periods) for which it will produce cash flows
- The differential annual after-tax net cash flows associated with the proposal

Exhibit A-6
Present Value of $1 Received at the End of Period

Years Hence	1%	2%	4%	6%	8%	10%	12%	14%	15%	16%
1	0.990	0.980	0.962	0.943	0.926	0.909	0.893	0.877	0.870	0.862
2	0.980	0.961	0.925	0.890	0.857	0.826	0.797	0.769	0.756	0.743
3	0.971	0.942	0.889	0.840	0.794	0.751	0.712	0.675	0.658	0.641
4	0.961	0.924	0.855	0.792	0.735	0.683	0.636	0.592	0.572	0.552
5	0.951	0.906	0.822	0.747	0.681	0.621	0.567	0.519	0.497	0.476
6	0.942	0.888	0.790	0.705	0.630	0.564	0.507	0.456	0.432	0.410
7	0.933	0.871	0.760	0.665	0.583	0.513	0.452	0.400	0.376	0.354
8	0.923	0.853	0.731	0.627	0.540	0.467	0.404	0.351	0.327	0.305
9	0.914	0.837	0.703	0.592	0.500	0.424	0.361	0.308	0.284	0.263
10	0.905	0.820	0.676	0.558	0.463	0.386	0.322	0.270	0.247	0.227
11	0.896	0.804	0.650	0.527	0.429	0.350	0.287	0.237	0.215	0.195
12	0.887	0.788	0.625	0.497	0.397	0.319	0.257	0.208	0.187	0.168
13	0.879	0.773	0.601	0.469	0.368	0.290	0.229	0.182	0.163	0.145
14	0.870	0.758	0.577	0.442	0.340	0.263	0.205	0.160	0.141	0.125
15	0.861	0.743	0.555	0.417	0.315	0.239	0.183	0.140	0.123	0.108
16	0.853	0.728	0.534	0.394	0.292	0.218	0.163	0.123	0.107	0.093
17	0.844	0.714	0.513	0.371	0.270	0.198	0.146	0.108	0.093	0.080
18	0.836	0.700	0.494	0.350	0.250	0.180	0.130	0.095	0.081	0.069
19	0.828	0.686	0.475	0.331	0.232	0.164	0.116	0.083	0.070	0.060
20	0.820	0.673	0.456	0.312	0.215	0.149	0.104	0.073	0.061	0.051
21	0.811	0.660	0.439	0.294	0.199	0.135	0.093	0.064	0.053	0.044
22	0.803	0.647	0.422	0.278	0.184	0.123	0.083	0.056	0.046	0.038
23	0.795	0.634	0.406	0.262	0.170	0.112	0.074	0.049	0.040	0.033
24	0.788	0.622	0.390	0.247	0.158	0.102	0.066	0.043	0.035	0.028
25	0.780	0.610	0.375	0.233	0.146	0.092	0.059	0.038	0.030	0.024
26	0.772	0.598	0.361	0.220	0.135	0.084	0.053	0.033	0.026	0.021
27	0.764	0.586	0.347	0.207	0.125	0.076	0.047	0.029	0.023	0.018
28	0.757	0.574	0.333	0.196	0.116	0.069	0.042	0.026	0.020	0.016
29	0.749	0.563	0.321	0.185	0.107	0.063	0.037	0.022	0.017	0.014
30	0.742	0.552	0.308	0.174	0.099	0.057	0.033	0.020	0.015	0.012
40	0.672	0.453	0.208	0.097	0.046	0.022	0.011	0.005	0.004	0.003
50	0.608	0.372	0.141	0.054	0.021	0.009	0.003	0.001	0.001	0.001

18%	20%	22%	24%	25%	26%	28%	30%	35%	40%	45%	50%
0.847	0.833	0.820	0.806	0.800	0.794	0.781	0.769	0.741	0.714	0.690	0.667
0.718	0.694	0.672	0.650	0.640	0.630	0.610	0.592	0.549	0.510	0.476	0.444
0.609	0.579	0.551	0.524	0.512	0.500	0.477	0.455	0.406	0.364	0.328	0.296
0.516	0.482	0.451	0.423	0.410	0.397	0.373	0.350	0.301	0.260	0.226	0.198
0.437	0.402	0.370	0.341	0.328	0.315	0.291	0.269	0.223	0.186	0.156	0.132
0.370	0.335	0.303	0.275	0.262	0.250	0.227	0.207	0.165	0.133	0.108	0.088
0.314	0.279	0.249	0.222	0.210	0.198	0.178	0.159	0.122	0.095	0.074	0.059
0.266	0.233	0.204	0.179	0.168	0.157	0.139	0.123	0.091	0.068	0.051	0.039
0.225	0.194	0.167	0.144	0.134	0.125	0.108	0.094	0.067	0.048	0.035	0.026
0.191	0.162	0.137	0.116	0.107	0.099	0.085	0.073	0.050	0.035	0.024	0.017
0.162	0.135	0.112	0.094	0.086	0.079	0.066	0.056	0.037	0.025	0.017	0.012
0.137	0.112	0.092	0.076	0.069	0.062	0.052	0.043	0.027	0.018	0.012	0.008
0.116	0.093	0.075	0.061	0.055	0.050	0.040	0.033	0.020	0.013	0.008	0.005
0.099	0.078	0.062	0.049	0.044	0.039	0.032	0.025	0.015	0.009	0.006	0.003
0.084	0.065	0.051	0.040	0.035	0.031	0.025	0.020	0.011	0.006	0.004	0.002
0.071	0.054	0.042	0.032	0.028	0.025	0.019	0.015	0.008	0.005	0.003	0.002
0.060	0.045	0.034	0.026	0.023	0.020	0.015	0.012	0.006	0.003	0.002	0.001
0.051	0.038	0.028	0.021	0.018	0.016	0.012	0.009	0.005	0.002	0.001	0.001
0.043	0.031	0.023	0.017	0.014	0.012	0.009	0.007	0.003	0.002	0.001	
0.037	0.026	0.019	0.014	0.012	0.010	0.007	0.005	0.002	0.001	0.001	
0.031	0.022	0.015	0.011	0.009	0.008	0.006	0.004	0.002	0.001		
0.026	0.018	0.013	0.009	0.007	0.006	0.004	0.003	0.001	0.001		
0.022	0.015	0.010	0.007	0.006	0.005	0.003	0.002	0.001			
0.019	0.013	0.008	0.006	0.005	0.004	0.003	0.002	0.001			
0.016	0.010	0.007	0.005	0.004	0.003	0.002	0.001	0.001			
0.014	0.009	0.006	0.004	0.003	0.002	0.002	0.001				
0.011	0.007	0.005	0.003	0.002	0.002	0.001	0.001				
0.010	0.006	0.004	0.002	0.002	0.002	0.001	0.001				
0.008	0.005	0.003	0.002	0.002	0.001	0.001	0.001				
0.007	0.004	0.003	0.002	0.001	0.001	0.001					
0.001	0.001										

Exhibit A-7

Present Value of $1 Received Annually at the End of Each Period for N Periods

Years (N)	1%	2%	4%	6%	8%	10%	12%	14%	15%	16%
1	0.990	0.980	0.962	0.943	0.926	0.909	0.893	0.877	0.870	0.862
2	1.970	1.942	1.886	1.833	1.783	1.736	1.690	1.647	1.626	1.605
3	2.941	2.884	2.775	2.673	2.577	2.487	2.402	2.322	2.283	2.246
4	3.902	3.808	3.630	3.465	3.312	3.170	3.037	2.914	2.855	2.798
5	4.853	4.713	4.452	4.212	3.993	3.791	3.605	3.433	3.352	3.274
6	5.795	5.601	5.242	4.917	4.623	4.355	4.111	3.889	3.784	3.685
7	6.728	6.472	6.002	5.582	5.206	4.868	4.564	4.288	4.160	4.039
8	7.652	7.325	6.733	6.210	5.747	5.335	4.968	4.639	4.487	4.344
9	8.566	8.162	7.435	6.802	6.247	5.759	5.328	4.946	4.772	4.607
10	9.471	8.983	8.111	7.360	6.710	6.145	5.650	5.216	5.019	4.833
11	10.368	9.787	8.760	7.887	7.139	6.495	5.988	5.453	5.234	5.029
12	11.255	10.575	9.385	8.384	7.536	6.814	6.194	5.660	5.421	5.197
13	12.134	11.343	9.986	8.853	7.904	7.103	6.424	5.842	5.583	5.342
14	13.004	12.106	10.563	9.295	8.244	7.367	6.628	6.002	5.724	5.468
15	13.865	12.849	11.118	9.712	8.559	7.606	6.811	6.142	5.847	5.575
16	14.718	13.578	11.652	10.106	8.851	7.824	6.974	6.265	5.954	5.669
17	15.562	14.292	12.166	10.477	9.122	8.022	7.120	6.373	6.047	5.749
18	16.398	14.992	12.659	10.828	9.372	8.201	7.250	6.467	6.128	5.818
19	17.226	15.678	13.134	11.158	9.604	8.365	7.366	6.550	6.198	5.877
20	18.046	16.351	13.590	11.470	9.818	8.514	7.469	6.623	6.259	5.929
21	18.857	17.011	14.029	11.764	10.017	8.649	7.562	6.687	6.312	5.973
22	19.660	17.658	14.451	12.042	10.201	8.772	7.645	6.743	6.359	6.011
23	20.456	18.292	14.857	12.303	10.371	8.883	7.718	6.792	6.390	6.044
24	21.243	18.914	15.247	12.550	10.529	8.985	7.784	6.835	6.434	6.073
25	22.023	19.523	15.622	12.783	10.675	9.077	7.843	6.873	6.464	6.097
26	22.795	20.121	15.983	13.003	10.810	9.161	7.896	6.906	6.491	6.118
27	23.560	20.707	16.330	13.211	10.935	9.237	7.943	6.935	6.514	6.136
28	24.316	21.281	16.663	13.406	11.051	9.307	7.984	6.961	6.534	6.152
29	25.066	21.844	16.984	13.591	11.158	9.370	8.022	6.983	6.551	6.166
30	25.808	22.396	17.292	13.765	11.258	9.427	8.055	7.003	6.566	6.177
40	32.835	27.355	19.793	15.046	11.925	9.779	8.244	7.105	6.642	6.234
50	39.196	31.424	21.482	15.762	12.234	9.915	8.304	7.133	6.661	6.246

18%	20%	22%	24%	25%	26%	28%	30%	35%	40%	45%	50%
0.847	0.833	0.820	0.806	0.800	0.794	0.781	0.769	0.741	0.714	0.690	0.667
1.566	1.528	1.492	1.457	1.440	1.424	1.392	1.361	1.289	1.224	1.165	1.111
2.174	2.106	2.042	1.981	1.952	1.923	1.868	1.816	1.696	1.589	1.493	1.407
2.690	2.589	2.494	2.404	2.362	2.320	2.241	2.166	1.997	1.849	1.720	1.605
3.127	2.991	2.864	2.745	2.689	2.635	2.532	2.436	2.220	2.035	1.876	1.737
3.498	3.326	3.167	3.020	2.951	2.885	2.759	2.643	2.385	2.168	1.983	1.824
3.812	3.605	3.416	3.242	3.161	3.083	2.937	2.802	2.508	2.263	2.057	1.883
4.078	3.837	3.619	3.421	3.329	3.241	3.076	2.925	2.598	2.331	2.108	1.922
4.303	4.031	3.786	3.566	3.463	3.366	3.184	3.019	2.665	2.379	2.144	1.948
4.494	4.192	3.923	3.682	3.571	3.465	3.269	3.092	2.715	2.414	2.168	1.965
4.656	4.327	4.035	3.776	3.656	3.544	3.335	3.147	2.752	2.438	2.185	1.977
4.793	4.439	4.127	3.851	3.725	3.606	3.387	3.190	2.779	2.456	2.196	1.985
4.910	4.533	4.203	3.912	3.780	3.656	3.427	3.223	2.799	2.468	2.204	1.990
5.008	4.611	4.265	3.962	3.824	3.695	3.459	3.249	2.814	2.477	2.210	1.993
5.092	4.675	4.315	4.001	3.859	3.726	3.483	3.268	2.825	2.484	2.214	1.995
5.162	4.730	4.357	4.003	3.887	3.751	3.503	3.283	2.834	2.489	2.216	1.997
5.222	4.775	4.391	4.059	3.910	3.771	3.518	3.295	2.840	2.492	2.218	1.998
5.273	4.812	4.419	4.080	3.928	3.786	3.529	3.304	2.844	2.494	2.219	1.999
5.316	4.844	4.442	4.097	3.942	3.799	3.539	3.311	2.848	2.496	2.220	1.999
5.353	4.870	4.460	4.110	3.954	3.808	3.546	3.316	2.850	2.497	2.221	1.999
5.384	4.891	4.476	4.121	3.963	3.816	3.551	3.320	2.852	2.498	2.221	2.000
5.410	4.909	4.488	4.130	3.970	3.822	3.556	3.323	2.853	2.498	2.222	2.000
5.432	4.925	4.499	4.137	3.976	3.827	3.559	3.325	2.854	2.499	2.222	2.000
5.451	4.937	4.507	4.143	3.981	3.831	3.562	3.327	2.855	2.499	2.222	2.000
5.467	4.948	4.514	4.147	3.985	3.834	3.564	3.329	2.856	2.499	2.222	2.000
5.480	4.956	4.520	4.151	3.988	3.837	3.566	3.330	2.856	2.500	2.222	2.000
5.492	4.964	4.524	4.154	3.990	3.839	3.567	3.331	2.856	2.500	2.222	2.000
5.502	4.970	4.528	4.157	3.992	3.840	3.568	3.331	2.857	2.500	2.222	2.000
5.510	4.975	4.531	4.159	3.994	3.841	3.569	3.332	2.857	2.500	2.222	2.000
5.517	4.979	4.534	4.160	3.995	3.842	3.569	3.332	2.857	2.500	2.222	2.000
5.548	4.997	4.544	4.166	3.999	3.846	3.571	3.333	2.857	2.500	2.222	2.000
5.554	4.999	4.545	4.167	4.000	3.846	3.571	3.333	2.857	2.500	2.222	2.000

Any projected set of net cash flows can be evaluated by either of two methods, the net present value method of the time-adjusted rate of return method. The lower portion of Exhibit A-8 demonstrates both methods for evaluating a proposal that involves a $35,000 acquisition. The estimated useful life of the investment is seven years, and it is expected to generate additional annual after-tax net cash inflows of $8,200.

Net Present Value Method. The net present value method can be used only when there is a predetermined minimum acceptable rate of return, here presumed to be 14 percent after taxes. Typically, this minimum rate will be given to, not established by, a risk management professional. This person will use the rate to evaluate the cash inflows and outflows from any proposed investment, including a proposed risk financing technique.

Any proposed investment whose projected cash inflows have a present value greater than the present value of the required outflows is acceptable by this criterion. In Exhibit A-8, for instance, the additional annual net cash inflows are a constant $8,200 each year, and the only required cash outflow is the $35,000 initial cost of the investment. The first step in using the net present value method is to calculate the net present value of the additional annual after-tax net cash flows.

Exhibit A-7 indicates that the present value of $1 received annually at the end of each year for the next seven years at 14 percent interest compounded annually corresponds to a value of 4.288. Multiplying this present value factor by $8,200 yields the present value of the differential net cash inflows, $35,161.60. In other words, $35,161.60 is the amount that would have to be invested today at 14 percent interest compounded annually to receive $8,200 at the end of each year for the next seven years. The last $8,200 would leave the fund with the zero balance. The net present value of the proposed investment is the present value of the differential net cash inflows minus the present value of the investment, $35,000. Therefore, the net present value of this proposed investment is $161.60, which is derived by subtracting the required $35,000 initial investment from the $35,161.60 present value of the investment's future cash inflows. This positive result shows that the proposed investment will generate at least the minimum acceptable 14 percent rate of return.

Time-Adjusted Rate of Return Method. Exhibit A-8 also illustrates the same result using the time-adjusted rate of return method. The cost of the investment is $35,000; it is expected to generate after-tax net cash flows of $8,200 a year for seven years. Therefore, $35,000 can be considered the present value of $8,200 to be received annually at the end of each of the next seven years at some yet unknown time-adjusted rate of return. To find this rate, divide $35,000 by $8,200, yield-

Exhibit A-8
Calculation of Differential Annual After-Tax Net Cash Flow

Differential cash revenues		$12,000
Less: Differential cash expenses (except income taxes):		
Maintenance expense	$ 500	
Insurance expense	100	600
Before-tax NCF:		$11,400
Less: Differential income taxes:		
Before-tax NCF	$11,400	
Less differential depreciation expense ($35,000/7 years)	5,000	
Taxable income	$ 6,400	
Income taxes (50%)		3,200
After-tax NCF:		$ 8,200

Evaluation of Differential Annual NCF

Factors:
Initial investment — $35,000
Useful life — 7 years
Differential annual after-tax NCF — $8,200
Minimum acceptable rate of return —14% annually.

Evaluation by the Net Present Value Method:

Present value of differential NCF ($8,200 x 4.288)	$35,161.60
Less: Present value of initial investment	35,000.00
Net present value	$ 161.60

Evaluation by the Time-Adjusted Rate of Return Method:

$$\frac{\text{Initial investment}}{\text{Differential NCF}} = \frac{\$35,000}{\$\ 8,200} = 4.268 = \text{present value factor}$$

Interpolation to Find the Exact Time-Adjusted Rate of Return (r):

	Rate of Return	Present Value Factors	Present Value Factors
	15%	4.288	4.288
	r		4.268
	15%	4.160	
Differences:	1%	0.128	0.020

r = 14% + ([0.020/0.128] x 1%)
= 14% + 0.16%
= 14.16%

ing a present value factor of 4.268 for the investment. Therefore, $4,268 is the present value of $1 to be received annually at the end of each of the next seven years at the yet undetermined time-adjusted rate of return. To determine this rate, look in the seven-year row in Exhibit A-7 for the present value factor that comes closest to 4.268. The factor of 4.268 lies between 4.288 for a 14 percent rate of return and 4.160 for a 15 percent return over a seven-year period. Therefore, the time-adjusted rate of return for this investment is between 14 and 15 percent compounded annually.

Finding a more precise time-adjusted rate of return for this investment requires an interpolation process as is illustrated at the bottom of Exhibit A-8. The total difference between the present value factors for 14 percent and 15 percent returns is 0.128 (4.288 − 4.160). The difference between the present value factor for a 14 percent return and the present value factor for this asset is 0.020 (4.288 − 4.268). Since lower present value factors are associated with higher rates of return for any given number of years, the asset has a time-adjusted rate of return that is higher than 14 percent. It is higher by an amount equal to 0.020/0.128 of 1 percent. (The 1 percentage point is the difference between the rates of return for the two columns in Exhibit A-7 used for this interpolation.) Because 0.020/0.128 of 1 percent is approximately 0.16 percent, the time-adjusted rate of return on this asset is approximately 14.16 percent (14 percent + 0.16 percent), which is more than the minimum acceptable rate of return of 14 percent. Therefore, again the investment should be made.

Tax Considerations. After-tax, not before-tax, net cash flows determine an organization's command over productive resources. Because an organization cannot use for its own purpose the cash it must pay as taxes, taxes reduce usable cash inflows. Therefore, for organizations subject to taxes of any kind, cash outflows to pay taxes reduce net cash flows available to purchase productive resources for the present and the future.

One of the reasons risk financing decisions for public entities may differ from those of private profit-seeking organizations is that public organizations are generally not subject to federal or state income or excise taxes. Therefore, computations of expected after-tax net cash flows tend to be simpler for these public organizations than for profit-seeking private enterprises. Furthermore, such organizations do not distinguish between before-tax and after-tax net cash flows, making depreciation an irrelevant expense for any tax purposes. For a public organization that does not pay taxes, the after-tax net cash flow is equal to the before-tax (and the before-depreciation) net cash flow. For example, in Exhibit A-8, the after-tax NCF for a taxable organization is $8,200; for a tax-exempt organization, the equivalent figure is the before-tax NCF of $11,400, shown near the top of the exhibit.

Summary of Cash Flow Analysis

To enhance its operating efficiency, every profit-seeking and nonprofit public or private organization needs to make the best possible use of its cash, the resource through which it purchases all of its other productive resources. Using cash most effectively requires maximizing the expected present value of the organization's future annual after-tax net cash flows. The choice by an organization of a particular risk management alternative affects its net cash flows. Therefore, to the extent feasible, an organization should select those risk management, particularly risk financing, alternatives that contribute most to the expected present value of its annual after-tax net cash flows. However, organizations often have other objectives besides maximizing operating efficiency; moreover, legal requirements, owners' and senior management's tolerance for uncertainty, and simple shortages of resources may keep an organization from achieving an ideal level of operating efficiency. Nonetheless, the accurate evaluation of expected present values and net cash flows will move an organization to a better level of operating efficiency, thus improving its means of achieving its fundamental mission.

Appendix Notes

1. Gathering historical data involves not only data on the frequency and severity of losses but also on the circumstances (physical conditions, levels of output, or state of the economy, for example) that logically may be related to the frequency or severity of these losses. This requires compiling data that is complete, consistently expressed, relevant to risk management (especially with respect to valuation of losses), and organized to facilitate the analysis.
2. For the most current available information, see the latest annual issue of *MVMA Motor Vehicle Facts and Figures* (Detroit, MI: Motor Vehicle Manufacturers Association).

Index

A

B

C

D

E

F

J

L

M

N

O

Q

R

S

T

U

W